THE
New World
Reader

THE
New World
Reader

Thinking and Writing
about the Global Community

Fourth Edition

Gilbert H. Muller

The City University of New York
LaGuardia College

WADSWORTH
CENGAGE Learning·

Australia · Brazil · Japan · Korea · Mexico · Singapore · Spain · United Kingdom · United States

WADSWORTH
CENGAGE Learning·

The New World Reader: Thinking and Writing about the Global Community, Fourth Edition
Gilbert H. Muller

Publisher: Monica Eckman
Acquiring Sponsoring Editor: Kate Derrick
Development Editor: Larry Goldberg
Assistant Editor: Danielle Warchol
Editorial Assistant: Marjorie Cross
Media Editor: Janine Tangney
Executive Marketing Manager: Stacey Purviance
Marketing Manager: Lydia LeStar
Senior Marketing Communications Manager: Linda Yip
Rights Acquisitions Specialist: Alexandra Ricciardi
Art and Design Direction, Production Management, and Composition: Cenveo Publisher Services
Manufacturing Planner: Betsy Donaghey
Cover Image: Corbis.com

For product information and technology assistance, contact us at **Cengage Learning Customer & Sales Support, 1-800-354-9706**

For permission to use material from this text or product, submit all requests online at **www.cengage.com/permissions**.

Further permissions questions can be emailed to **permissionrequest@cengage.com**.

Library of Congress Control Number: 2012943887

ISBN 13: 978-1-133-31032-7

ISBN 10: 1-133-31032X

Wadsworth
20 Channel Center Street
Boston, MA 02210
USA

Cengage Learning is a leading provider of customized learning solutions with office locations around the globe, including Singapore, the United Kingdom, Australia, Mexico, Brazil and Japan. Locate your local office at **international.cengage.com/region**

Cengage Learning products are represented in Canada by Nelson Education, Ltd.

For your course and learning solutions, visit **www.cengage.com**.

Purchase any of our products at your local college store or at our preferred online store **www.cengagebrain.com**.

Instructors: Please visit **login.cengage.com** and log in to access instructor-specific resources.

Printed in the United States of America
1 2 3 4 5 6 7 16 15 14 13 12

For Sadie Rain and Vivian Dalia
Global Girls

Brief Contents

Contents

3 | America and the World: How Do Others Perceive Us?   63

11 | The Fate of the Earth: Can We Preserve the Global Environment?   344

Rhetorical Contents

Narration

Description

Illustration

Comparison and Contrast

Definition

Classification

Process Analysis

Causal Analysis

Argument and Persuasion

Culture or Conflict?
Images of Globalization

Is Beauty Universal? Global Body Images

PREFACE

We live in a world of transformations, affecting almost every aspect of what we do. For better or worse, we are being propelled into a global order that no one fully understands, but which is making its effects felt upon all of us.

—Anthony Giddens

Now in its fourth edition, *The New World Reader* presents provocative essays about contemporary global issues and challenges. The book provides students with the resources needed to think and write in ways that foster varieties of global understanding and citizenship. In an era marked by conflicts on many continents and ongoing clashes across civilizations, students need to interrogate their relationship to their home nation—whether they are from the United States or elsewhere—and also their personal place in the world. Do they agree, for example, with the controversial novelist Salman Rushdie's contention that the West has met the "Rest"? The writers in this text deal with this question as well as those global issues that increasingly shape our lives. Superlative writers from a variety of backgrounds and perspectives reveal in this new edition of *The New World Reader* that globalization is *the* big story, the most pressing issue of our times.

Students using *The New World Reader* will find interconnected chapters and selections dealing with such strategic global questions as the changing demographics of the United States, the impact of terrorism on individuals as well as entire populations, the nature of globalization, the clash of cultures and civilizations, the changing roles of women and men in the global arena, the ways in which first-world nations can successfully address global poverty and disease, and the state of the global environment. Challenged by such well-known contemporary thinkers and writers as Richard Rodriguez, Edwidge Danticat, Peter Singer, Amy Tan, Bharati Mukherjee, and Kofi Annan, today's students will be encouraged to come to grips with a world that is now subject to complex and often mystifying transformations.

This book demonstrates that critical thinking about our new global century begins when students consider unfamiliar perspectives and arguments, when they are open to new global ideas and perceptions. Put differently, *The New World Reader* encourages intercultural and transnational inquiry. As such, the design of the anthology encourages students to ask not only who they are in this society but also who they are in the world. Many of the diversity themes that teachers of college writing find especially productive and stimulating—gender and sexuality, race and ethnicity, class and cultural orientation—lend themselves to these issues of local and global perception. The selections in the text present a tapestry of diversity in both a local and a global light, moving from personalized encounters with cultures to analytical and argumentative treatment of topics. Students are provided the opportunity to move across cultures and continents, interrogating and assessing authors' insights into our evolving transnational society.

The writers in *The New World Reader* present keen emotional and intellectual insights into our new global era. Most of the essays are relatively brief and provocative and serve as models for the types of personal, analytical, and argumentative papers that college composition teachers ask their students to write. The vast majority of these essays were written after September 11, 2001, and many are recent, dealing with such emerging issues as the "Arab Spring," climate change, and natural disasters. Drawn from a wide variety of authorial backgrounds and sources, and offering diverse angles of opinion and perspectives, the readings in this text lend themselves to thoughtful responses, class debate, small-group discussion, and online research. Some of the longer essays—for example, Jamaica Kincaid on the nature of colonialism and Lisa Miller on how to raise a "global kid"—orient students to those forms of discourse that they will encounter in humanities and social science courses. With introductions to chapters and writers, previewing questions, a three-part apparatus following each essay, two four-color photo essays, three appendices offering guidelines on conducting research in the global era and defining rhetorical and global terms, and extensive Web resources, *The New World Reader* can serve as the core text in composition courses.

Features

Lively Selections in Chapters That Challenge Our Understanding of Ourselves and Others

The New World Reader presents sixty-nine essays in eleven interrelated chapters. The first chapter introduces students to the challenges of thinking, reading, and writing about their place in the new global era. Ten subsequent chapters, each consisting of essays that move from personal and op-ed pieces to more complex selections, focus on key aspects of our increasingly globalized culture, presenting ideas and themes that radiate through the text.

- **Chapter 1. Thinking, Reading, and Writing about the New Global Era.** This concise introductory chapter offers guidelines for students as they think, read, and write about key issues in twenty-first century America and the world. Clear thinking about the "new world order" involves knowledge of both what has gone before and what lies ahead, as well as mastery of the analytical and cognitive skills at the heart of the reading and writing processes. Three brief essays permit students to practice their critical thinking, reading, and writing skills: Nicholas D. Kristof on contrasting approaches to education in the United States and China, Susan Bordo on the globalization of eating disorders, and Chrystia Freeland on the rise of the super-rich.

- **Chapter 2. New American Mosaic: Are We Becoming a Universal Nation?** Presenting compelling insights into the new American demographics, Bharati Mukherjee, Richard Rodriguez, and others examine the ways in which both native and "fourth wave" patterns of acculturation are changing the face of the American nation while fostering a greater appreciation of other cultures. The chapter introduces students to the idea that globalization is not only "out there" but also "here"—a phenomenon that might very well be embodied (as Dwight N. Hopkins suggests in an essay) in President Barack Obama.

- **Chapter 3. America and the World: How Do Others Perceive Us?** Suggested by teachers who used earlier editions of *The New World Reader*, this chapter explores the implications (and reverberations) of America's increasingly interventionist position on the global stage. Such essays as Mehdi Hasan's "Why I Could Never Hate America" and Fareed Zakaria's "A New Middle East" explore shifting global attitudes toward the idea of America.

- **Chapter 4. Speaking in Tongues: Does Language Unify or Divide?** Presenting essays by Amy Tan, Isabel Allende, and other provocative writers, this chapter explores the varied ways in which language forms identity and cultural relationships in our increasingly polyglot world.

- **Chapter 5. Global Relationships: Are Sex and Gender Roles Changing?** Across the globe, the perception of gender and the larger struggle for human rights vary in the amount of change they are undergoing. Joseph Contreras offers a revealing appreciation of his sexual orientation and changing family values in Latin America and elsewhere, and Mike Ceaser opens a "dark window" on human trafficking. The last essay, by Barbara Ehrenreich and Annette Fuentes, "Life on the Global Assembly Line," is a contemporary classic, detailing the exploitation of women in factories overseas.

- **Chapter 6. The Challenge of Globalization: What Are the Consequences?** The debate over globalization, whether framed in economic, political, environmental, or cultural terms, serves increasingly to define our lives in the twenty-first century. Essays by Thomas L. Friedman, Lisa Miller, Jared Diamond, and others argue the benefits and dangers of globalization.

- **Chapter 7. Culture Wars: Whose Culture Is It, Anyway?** This chapter examines the impact of popular American culture on the nation and on the world. From American-style shopping malls in developing nations to the broadcast of American sitcoms in Islamic nations, the new American landscape has had a global impact. Among writers offering critical appraisals of the contemporary culture wars are Henry Louis Gates Jr., Amy Chua, and Jamaica Kincaid.

- **Chapter 8. The Clash of Civilizations: Is Conflict Avoidable?** Building on the issues raised in the first seven chapters, this unit offers a critical examination of the clash-of-civilizations debate. Essays by such prominent global analysts as Amartya Sen and Samuel P. Huntington alert students to the fact that today's global conflicts do not spring spontaneously from September 11, 2001, but rather have deep historical and political antecedents.

- **Chapter 9. The Age of Terror: What Is the Just Response?** In the fourth edition of *The New World Reader*, this chapter has been revised to take at once a broader and deeper view of the causes and consequences of international terror. Suzanne Berne offers what has already become a contemporary classic on her response to the World Trade Center disaster, while Nobel Prize winner Shirin Ebadi recounts the moment when she discovered that forces in Iran were planning to assassinate her.

- **Chapter 10. Global Aid: Can We Reduce Disease and Poverty?** Suggested by reviewers and inspired by recent hopeful developments in the global struggle for economic justice, this chapter describes the many ways in which people worldwide are working to raise the living standards of their fellow citizens. Frontline reporting by Jeffrey Sachs in Africa, Edwidge Danticat in Haiti, and Anuradha Mittal in India, among other perspectives, captures the monumental responses by ordinary citizens and workers to natural disasters.

- **Chapter 11. The Fate of the Earth: Can We Preserve the Global Environment?** From global warming to weapons of mass destruction, the Earth's ecology faces major challenges. Essays by Rachel Carson, Al Gore, Jane Goodall, Bill McKibben, and others offer insights into how we might save the environment—and the world—for future generations.

Three Distinctive Appendices

- **Appendix A. Conducting Research in the New Global Era.** This unit provides students with cutting-edge, practical information on the kinds of research skills they are expected to acquire during their college careers. The appendix stresses the new world of information technology that increasingly guides research and offers extensive guidelines on locating and evaluating print and online sources.

- **Appendix B. Glossary of Rhetorical Terms.** Concise definitions of dozens of key rhetorical terms provide a handy reference for students.

- **Appendix C. Glossary of Globalization Terms.** This appendix makes the vocabulary of globalization, drawn from political science, history, economics, and other disciplines, accessible to students.

A Second Table of Contents by Rhetorical Mode

This rhetorical table of contents adds flexibility for teachers who prefer to organize their syllabus around such traditional forms as narration and description, comparison and contrast, process and causal analysis, and argumentation and persuasion.

Consistent Editorial Apparatus with a Sequenced Approach to Exercises

The New World Reader provides brief introductions to all chapters, highlighting the central issues raised by the writers in each section. All readings contain substantial author headnotes followed by a prereading question. Following each essay, three carefully sequenced sets totaling ten questions provide students with the opportunity to respond to the form and content of the text in ways that promote reading, writing, discussion, group work, and Internet exploration.

- **Before Reading.** One question asks students to think about their current understanding or interpretation of an event or a condition.

- **Thinking about the Essay.** Five questions build on the student's ability to comprehend how the writer's ideas develop through essential rhetorical and stylistic techniques.

- **Responding in Writing.** Three writing activities reflect and expand the questions in the first section, offering opportunities for students to write personal, analytical, and argumentative responses to the text.

- **Networking.** Two questions encourage small-group and Internet work. One question promotes collaborative learning. The other question provides practice in the use of Internet and library sources to conduct deeper exploration and research into issues raised by the author.

Exciting Visual Materials

Students today need to read and analyze visual as well as written texts. *The New World Reader* integrates photographs, artwork, cartoons, graphs, and maps into the chapters. The fourth edition includes a popular four-color insert devoted to examining the question of "Culture or Conflict?" as well as a four-color insert on standards of global beauty. These illustrations add a visual dimension to aid students' comprehension of the issues raised by written texts. All visual materials offer questions for informed response and analysis.

Instructor's Resource Manual

The New World Reader 4E Online Instructor's Resource Manual provides an abundance of materials to give instructors maximum flexibility in planning and customizing their courses. This manual helps instructors prepare for class more quickly and effectively with such resources as discussion suggestions and suggested answers for questions on the text readings. The IRM can be found on the password-protected instructor's Companion Website.

Companion Website

This complimentary-access Companion Website contains an extensive library of interactive exercises and animations that cover grammar, mechanics, and punctuation. It also includes a complete library of student papers and a section on avoiding plagiarism.

NEW to this Edition

For the fourth edition of *The New World Reader*, we have strengthened the emphasis on contemporary global issues by offering essays on very recent topics and trends. Students and teachers will be able to ponder the emergence of Barack Obama as a new type of American president; examine climate change from competing perspectives; explore the "Arab Spring"; consider the impact of social media on international affairs; and interrogate the causes underlying the surge in worldwide human trafficking. Such current issues, integrated into the book's well-received and flexible pattern of organization, enhance the book's appeal.

- **Twenty-nine New Selections.** Provocative and compelling essays include work by such well-known authors, commentators, and public advocates and intellectuals as Richard Rodriguez, Fareed Zakaria, Elie Wiesel, David Sedaris, Al Gore, and Edwidge Danticat.

- **Exciting New Authors.** To introduce students to emerging writers with fresh ideas and perspectives—and also to established professionals who might not be well-known—we present Ellis Cose on the changing demographics of the United States; Ted Gup on the Asian-American superiority complex; Elaine Sciolino on the controversy over wearing the veil in France; Randa Faroohar on the rise of the global woman as a force in economics; and other compelling new authors.

- **Fresh Visuals for Critical Thinking and Response.** Drawn from a wide range of modes including photographs, advertisements, and cartoons, these new images (including two color inserts) offer students and teachers the opportunity to investigate stylistic and thematic links across print and visual dimensions.

- **An Updated and Expanded Research Section (Appendix A).** Fresh citations conform to the seventh edition of the *MLA Handbook for Writers of Research Papers*. Also new to this edition is an annotated essay on the

WikiLeaks scandal and celebrity culture by the well-known educator and feminist scholar, Laura Kipnis.

Acknowledgments

This book is the result of very special relationships—and considerable seren-dipity—among friends, collaborators, reviewers, and supporters. I was first alerted to the possibility of developing a global reader by my good friend and former colleague John Chaffee, an acclaimed author and specialist in critical thinking and philosophy. To John I offer my gratitude for his faith in an old friend.

I learned long ago that any college text is only as good as the editorial staff developing it, and here there are several special people who saved me much grief, improved the book, and prevented me from sounding at times like a turgid academician. First and foremost, I want to especially acknowl-edge Kathy Sands-Boehmer, the senior development editor for this book. Kathy, with the indispensible help of my day-to-day development editor Larry Goldberg, juggled countless electronic transmissions, assembled the text with amazing intelligence and unfailing good humor, and kept the train running on time. Thanks also go to Lyn Uhl, my publisher, and Kate Der-rick, my sponsoring editor, who have supported *The New World Reader* from the start. I am grateful to Anne Talvacchio, the project manager, for her careful attention to detail. I am also grateful to Alexandra Ricciardi and Jennifer Wagner for their fine work in tracking down permissions.

I would like to thank my friend and agent, John Wright, who negotiated the contract for this book. Finally, I am grateful to my wife, Laleh Mostafavi-Muller, a specialist in international relations and the Middle East, who offered support and advice as the design for this book evolved.

Several reviewers wrote detailed appraisals of the manuscript, recommen-dations for changes and improvements, and praise and cautionary advice, and their collective wisdom informs this book. Thanks go to the following reviewers for the fourth edition:

Heather Akers, *University of Alabama Tuscaloosa*
Pat Artz, *Bellevue University*
Daniel Bergen, *Marquette University*
Elaine Bobrove, *Camden County College*
Roxana Cazan, *Indiana University Bloomington*
Julia Chavez, *Saint Martin's University*
Violet Dutcher, *Eastern Mennonite University*
Marti Eads, *Eastern Mennonite University*
Tyler Farrell, *Marquette University*
Kathleen Fitzpatrick, *Daniel Webster College*
Jeannine Fontaine, *Duquesne University*
Donna Rae Foran, *Marquette University*

Eric Hyman, *Fayetteville State University*
Deborah Kanter, *Hudson County Community College*
Katherine Kapitan, *Buena Vista University*
Maria Keaton, *Marquette University*
Therese Novotny, *Marquette University*
David Pryor, *University of the Incarnate Word*
Sorina Riddle, *Pfeiffer University*
Hale Savard, *Golden West College*
Shelina Shariff, *Baruch College*
Ghanashyam Sharma, *University of Louisville*
Grace Urbanski, *Marquette University*
Usha Wadhwani, *Hudson County Community College*

We continue to be grateful for the insights of reviewers whose suggestions helped in the development of previous editions of *The New World Reader:*

Cathryn Amdahl, *Harrisburg Area Community College*
Maryam Barrie, *Washtenaw Community College*
James Borton, *University of South Carolina, Sumter*
Sandra L. Clark, *University of Wyoming*
Debra L. Cumberland, *Winona State University*
John Dailey, *New Jersey City University*
Stephen F. Evans, *University of Kansas*
Eileen Ferretti, *Kingsborough Community College*
Len Gougeon, *University of Scranton*
Tim Gustafson, *University of Minnesota*
Jeff Henderson, *Kalamazoo Valley Community College*
William K. Lawrence, *George Mason University*
Anna Maheshwari, *Schoolcraft College*
Steven Mayers, *City College of San Francisco*
Dr. Nancy Nanney, *Chair, Humanities Division, West Virginia
    University at Parkersburg*
Pearlie Peters, *Rider University*
Avantika Rohatgi, *San Jose State University*
Gail Samis, *Salisbury University English Department*
Renee Schlueter, *Kirkwood Community College*
Henry Schwarz, *Georgetown University*
Karl Shaddox, *University of Alabama, Huntsville*
Micheline M. Soong, *Hawaii Pacific University*
Anne Meade Stockdell-Giesler, Ph.D., *University of Tampa*
Randall J. VanderMey, *Westmont College*
William Vaughn, *Central Missouri State University*
Mark Wiley, *California State University, Long Beach*
Rosemary Winslow, *Catholic University of America*
Julie Yen, *California State University, Sacramento*

~Gilbert H. Muller

Thinking, Reading, and Writing about the New Global Era

Global forces are shaping societies, nations, and international systems as never before. Evolving trends—among them the spread of worldwide communications networks, the "clash of civilizations," **terrorism** in many regions and most continents, environmental challenges, and transnational population shifts—suggest that the last century, the "American century" as *Time* magazine's Henry Luce called it, is over and we have entered a new era. In a world where much seems increasingly interconnected, it is no longer sufficient to think locally. Instead, we need to reflect critically on new global realities, assessing the ways in which other peoples, belief systems, traditions, and cultures impact our lives. In the twenty-first century, our well-being and arguably our very survival will depend on our ability to harness the forces unleashed by the dynamics of the new global era.

Regardless of what we choose to call this emerging era—the post-9/11 world, the new world order, the post–Cold War period, the age of **globalization**, the information or digital age—we exist today in a global landscape characterized by rapid transformations. To comprehend these transformations, we should not confuse, as the historian Francis Fukuyama reminds us, our national needs with our universal ones. We must also consider what writer and *New York Times* syndicated columnist Thomas Friedman terms the "super-story." For Friedman (who asserts in one of his books that the world is "flat"), the super-story involves all the trends of globalization, including world trade, the formation of transnational economic and political alignments, the spread of **information technology,** and even new dating and marriage patterns, that affect national and transnational behavior. Writers like Fukuyama and Friedman offer insights into global challenges and the arguments surrounding them. To meet these challenges, we must recognize that we are connected to one another both in the

An Azad University student uses an Internet café in Tehran, Iran. Access to the Internet is still highly restricted in some countries and by some cultures.

Thinking about the Image

1. Closely examine all of the details of this photograph. (For example, what is on the table next to this woman's elbow?) In what ways does this photograph reinforce standard images in the American media of Muslim women? In what ways is the photograph surprising?

2. Do you agree that access to the Internet provides a kind of empowerment? Why or why not?

3. In her essay "When Afghanistan Was at Peace," Margaret Atwood notes of her book *The Handmaid's Tale* (partly inspired by her travels in Afghanistan) that "there is freedom to and freedom from. But how much of the first should you have to give up in order to assure the second?" How might the woman in this photograph respond?

4. Do a search for Islamic Azad University. Visit this website and compare it to that of your own college. What are the similarities between your schools and how they present themselves? How are they different?

United States and to people around the world. No longer isolated by two oceans and seemingly immune to the world's turmoil, we suddenly have to reexamine and reargue our complex fate.

In order to comprehend our complex fate and prepare for life in the twenty-first century, we will explore in this book some of the key ways we perceive and interact with our new world. In our flattened world, as Thomas Friedman terms it, where everything seems close and immediate—where cell phones, cable, and the Internet connect us instantaneously to a polyglot universe of people and events—we will try to establish parameters for what it means to exist in this global era. Family, community, state, and nation no longer suffice in the construction of our new identity, for today we are citizens of the world. As such, we have to find ways to manage change, negotiate transnational borders, understand diverse viewpoints, and defuse major **conflicts** if we are to survive and prosper in the new global era.

Critical Thinking

Are you ready for the brave new world of the twenty-first century, the new global era? Do you know enough about *globalization*—the interplay of cultures, societies, economies, and political systems—that is changing your world? Assuredly, you will study this new era in various courses, prepare for careers in it, sit next to people from around the world in your classes, and perhaps even marry into it. The three thousand people from around the world who died in the World Trade Center disaster were working, collaborating, and living in this new world. Among the dead were civilians and citizens from sixty-two countries, including 250 Indians, 200 Pakistanis, 200 Britons, and 23 Japanese. Sadly, there were other individuals—those who perpetrated this event—who felt threatened by the new international order represented by the 9/11 victims.

Your success in college hinges in part on your ability to make choices based on knowledge, experience, and careful reflection about the new world order. You will have to think critically about the global contexts that influence you and your nation. *Critical thinking* is clear thinking: it is a type of mental practice in which you respond to issues logically and, for the purposes of this course, deal with texts and the meanings they generate among class members. Often you will have to *rethink* your opinions, beliefs, and attitudes, and this, too, is a hallmark of critical thinking—the willingness to discard weak ideas or biased opinions for more mature or simply more logical intellectual opinions. For example, how do you define a *terrorist*? Why would Americans define a terrorist as anyone who takes the lives of innocent civilians, while others around the world view such individuals not as terrorists but as freedom fighters or defenders of the faith? Such questions do not admit easy or facile responses. They require deep and complex thought, for we live in a complex world.

To work effectively with the readings in this text, which deal with varieties of global experience, you need to develop a repertoire of critical thinking skills. In all likelihood, you have come to college possessing many of these skills. But it is important to refine, strengthen, and expand these skills to achieve a degree of authority over any given body of knowledge. How, then, do you think critically about—in other words, study and interpret—any given text? How do you look closely at the ideas of writers and evaluate them? How do you respond critically in writing? Having a repertoire of critical thinking skills creates the foundation for being a critical reader and writer.

Every writer in this textbook had a project much like the projects that you will develop: to articulate clearly and convincingly a key idea or nucleus of related ideas about an aspect of human experience—whether in the United States or elsewhere. They developed their ideas by using the repertoire of critical thinking skills—which for our purposes we can associate with key rhetorical strategies. **Rhetoric** is the art of writing or speaking, often to convince an audience about a particular issue. **Rhetorical strategies** are the key patterns that writers employ in this effort to clarify ideas and opinions. We divide these patterns into three major groups: *narration* and *description; exposition* (consisting of definition, comparison and contrast, illustration, process analysis, causal analysis, and classification); and *argument* and *persuasion*. These are not just the classic patterns of rhetoric but also powerful ways of thinking about and understanding our world.

Research demonstrates that different people think most effectively in different ways, or **cognitive styles.** You might like to argue; however, hopefully you argue not in the style of *Crossfire* or *Hardball*, where viewpoints often are reduced simplistically to positions on the political "right" or "left," but rather with reasonableness and respect. Or you might be great at telling a story to make a point. Or perhaps you have a talent for analyzing global events. All writing reflects one or more of those cognitive styles that we see reflected in narration and description, exposition, and argumentation. You can gain control over your reading and writing practices by selecting from among these major rhetorical strategies or thinking styles.

Narration and Description

Narration can be briefly described as telling a story, and **description** as the use of vivid **sensory detail**—sight, sound, smell, taste, touch—to convey either a specific or an overall impression. Although narration and description are not always treated in studies of reasoning, the truth of the matter is that it is foolish not to consider these strategies as aspects of the thinking process. The study of narration and description reveals that this type of thinking can produce authority in college writing.

Some composition theorists actually believe that narration and description, relying as they do on the creation of a personal **voice**—your personal response—is the gateway to successful student writing. For example, where were you during a recent national or global crisis? How did you feel? What was your response? How did you get through the day and the aftermath? If you were answering these questions in an essay, you would need to employ a special kind of thinking and reflection, one in which you get in touch with your feelings and find vivid ways to express and make sense of them. It would be useless to say that you are not engaged in reasoning because you would employ narration and description—perhaps even insert **visual texts** downloaded from the Web—to arrive at your personal form of truth about the event. In all likelihood, you would also state or imply a **thesis** (a main idea) and even other generalizations about the event that go beyond pure narration or description; in fact, the vast majority of essays, while they might reflect one or two dominant rhetorical patterns or styles of organizational thought, tend to reveal mixed patterns or approaches to the writing process.

Exposition

Exposition is a relatively broad term that defines a type of writing in which you explain or convey information about a subject. Expository writing is the form of writing that in all likelihood you will be required to produce in college courses. In an expository essay, you set forth facts and ideas—in other words, detailed explanations—to support a thesis, or main idea. As a form of critical thinking, expository writing provides a way of clarifying many of the cultural, political, and economic forces that mold global events today.

To produce effective expository essays, you need to develop skill and fluency in the use of several key rhetorical strategies, among them *definition, comparison* and *contrast, illustration, causal analysis, process analysis,* and *classification.* The use of any one or several of the patterns will dictate your approach to a given topic or problem, and the effective application of these strategies will help to create an authoritative voice, for the readers of your expository essay will see that you are using these rhetorical patterns to think consistently about a body of information and present it coherently. Once again, you employ specific reasoning abilities to make sense of your world.

When you consider the international events that increasingly shape both local and personal life—indeed, that are shaping your identity—it is clear that you must think critically about the best way to approach these events. The way you are able to reason about events, the perspectives you may develop on a particular problem, will inform your understanding of the subject and your ability to convey this understanding in writing.

Think about a term that already has been introduced and that you will encounter in numerous essays in this collection—*globalization.* This is one of the many terms that you will have to look at closely as you come to an understanding of the global forces shaping lives, identities, **cultures,** and civilizations in the twenty-first century. How might you unravel the significance of this word, gain authority over it, explore its relevance to various texts that you will read, and ultimately express your understanding of it in writing?

To start, *definition* of a complex term like *globalization* might be in order. (Definitions for many of the key terms relating to globalization appear in Appendix C.) As a way of thinking about a subject, **definition** is a statement about what a word or phrase means. It is always useful to be able to state this meaning in one or two sentences, as we have already done earlier in this chapter—"the interplay of cultures, societies, economies, and political systems" in the world today. But entire books have been and are being written about globalization, for it is a complex and controversial subject. We call these longer explanations **extended definitions**, which typically rely on other rhetorical strategies to expand the field of understanding. Finally, you might very well have a highly personal understanding of a term like *globalization*. Perhaps you have witnessed or read about workers in overseas factories producing Nikes for a few cents a day and consequently have mixed feelings about the Nikes you are wearing today. In this instance, globalization has a special meaning for you, and we term this special meaning a **stipulative definition** because it is colored highly by your experience. Remember, as with all discussions of rhetorical strategies, you are developing and polishing critical thinking skills. With definition, you are taking abstract ideas and making them comprehensible and concrete.

A second way to approach globalization would be through comparative thinking. **Comparison** and **contrast** is a cognitive process wherein you consider the similarities and differences of things. Imagine that your instructor asks you to write an essay entitled "Two Ways of Looking at Globalization." The title itself suggests that you have to employ a comparative method to explain and analyze this phenomenon. You would need a thesis to unify this comparative approach, and three or four key points of comparison and/or contrast to support it. The purpose of comparison and contrast is usually to state a preference for one thing over the other or to judge which one is superior. For example, if you maintain that globalization is about inclusion, while those opposing globalization define it as a new form of colonialism or exploitation, you are evaluating and judging two positions.

Any approach to a subject requires a thoughtful and accurate use of **illustration**—that is, the use of examples to support an idea. Illustration, which we also call **exemplification**, enables you to make abstract ideas concrete. Normally, several examples or one key extended example serves to illustrate your main and minor ideas about a subject. If, for example, you want to demonstrate that globalization is a trend that will foster understanding among nations and peoples, you would have to provide facts, statistics, examples, details drawn from personal experience, testimonials, and expert opinions to support your position. Illustration is the bedrock of virtually all ways of thinking, reading, and writing about a topic. Whether telling a story, explaining a topic, or arguing a point (which we deal with in the next section), illustration provides the evidence required to produce a powerful text. Illustration teaches the value of using the information of others—typically the texts of others—in order to build a structure for your own paper.

Causal analysis and *process analysis* are two other forms of intellectual practice that can shape your critical approaches to topics. **Causal analysis,** sometimes called **cause-and-effect analysis**, answers the basic human question *Why?* It deals with a chain of happenings and the predictable consequences of these happenings. Like all the forms of thinking presented in this introductory section, causal analysis parallels our everyday thinking patterns. When we ask why terrorists attacked some city or tourist destination, why so many people in the **Third World** oppose globalization, or why the Internet can foster international cooperation, we are looking for causes or conditions and examining consequences and results (or effects). **Process analysis,** on the other hand, answers the question *How?* It takes things apart in order to understand how they operate or function. Many varieties of process analysis deal with "how-to" subjects involving steps in a correct sequence— for example, how to prepare fajitas. But process analysis is also central to the treatment of broad global trends. How did globalization come about? How do we combat overpopulation of the planet? How do we prevent global warming? Process analysis can help explain the subtle and complex nature of relationships existing within a chain of events.

The last major form of exposition is **classification,** in which information is divided into categories or groups for the purpose of clarifying relationships among them. Some experts would term classification a "higher-order" reasoning skill. In actuality, classification again resembles a great deal of everyday thinking: we classify friends, teachers, types of music, types of cuisine, and so forth. Classification is a way of taking a large body of information and breaking it down (dividing it) into categories for better understanding. It relies on analytical ability—critical thinking that explores parts within a whole. For example, if you were to write an essay entitled "Approaches to Globalization," you could establish three categories— political, economic, and cultural—to divide your subject into coherent parts. The secret to using classification effectively is to avoid the temptation to have your categories overlap excessively. (Did you notice that classification was used to organize this section on exposition?)

Writers skilled in exposition are smart and credible. They write with authority because they can think clearly in a variety of modes. With exposition you make critical thinking choices, selecting those rhetorical strategies that provide the best degree of understanding for your readers, your audience.

Argument and Persuasion

Argument is a special type of reasoning. It appears in texts—written, spoken, or visual—that express a debatable **point of view**. Stated more rigorously, argument is a process of reasoning in which the truth of some main **proposition** (or claim) is shown to be true (that is, based on the truth of other minor propositions or premises). Closely allied to argument is **persuasion,** in which you invite an audience through rational, emotional, and ethical appeals to adopt your viewpoint or embark on a course of action. Aristotle in his *Rhetoric* spoke of the appeals as *logos, ethos*, and *pathos*—reason, beliefs, and emotion working together to guide an audience to a proper understanding or judgment of an issue. Argument—the rational component in persuasion—enables you to think responsibly about global issues and present your viewpoints about them in convincing fashion.

The dividing line between various forms of exposition and argumentation is a fine one. Where does a *thesis* leave off and a *claim* (the main argumentative point) begin? Some experts would say that "everything's an argument," and in the arena of global affairs this seems to be true. Issues of religion, race, class, gender, and culture are woven into the very fabric of both our local and global lives, and all of these issues trigger vigorous positions and responses. And the international environment is such that conflict and change seemingly provoke argumentative viewpoints and positions.

The distinctive feature of argumentative thinking is that you give reasons in support of a **claim** or **major proposition**. The claim is what you are trying to prove in an argument. The **reasons**, also called **minor propositions**, offer proof for the major claim. And you support each minor proposition with **evidence**—those various types of illustration mentioned in the previous section as well as logical explanations or abstract thinking used to buttress your basic reasons. If you don't "have the facts"—let's say about global inequality, the Kyoto Protocol on Climate Change, or the worldwide reach of McDonald's—you will not be able to stake a claim and defend it vigorously.

The British philosopher Steven Toulmin emphasizes that underpinning any argument or claim is a **warrant,** which he defines as an assumption, belief, or principle that is taken for granted. The warrant validates the link between the claim and the support. It might be stated or unstated. Many practices of nations, beliefs of citizens, and policies of political groups rest on such warrants. For example, if you assume that the United States is now the world's only **superpower**—a warrant—you can use this principle to claim that the United States should use its power to intervene in rogue states. Or if you believe that people have the right to free themselves from oppression—a warrant at the heart of the Declaration of Independence—you might use this warrant to claim that oppressed citizens have the right to start revolutions to break their chains.

Consider the warrants concerning the war on terrorism embedded in the following paragraph, written by Harold Hongju Koh, a former assistant secretary of state in the administration of President Bill Clinton and a professor of international law at Yale University:

> Our enemies in this war are out to destroy our society precisely because it is open, tolerant, pluralistic and democratic. In its place, they seek to promote one that is closed, vengeful, repressive and absolutist. To secure genuine victory, we must make sure that they fail, not just in their assault on our safety but also in their challenge to our most fundamental values.
>
> —"Preserving American Values"

Here the writer predicates his claim about the need to achieve victory over our "enemies" on an entire catalog of "fundamental values" that in essence are warrants—that is, principles and beliefs. Also notice the way in which he employs the comparative method to structure his argument in this brief but revealing paragraph.

By their explosive or contentious nature, many global subjects and international issues call for argumentative responses. Your topic might be global warming, the Patriot Act, immigration along the United States–Mexico border, outsourcing of jobs, or the possibility of peace between Israel and the Palestinians. In such instances, your opinions and beliefs will require you to recognize that other people, nations, and cultures might approach the argument from entirely different perspectives. Thus, one unique challenge when developing arguments on international topics requires you to cross cultural boundaries, understand the attitudes and assumptions held by people outside your country, and contend with diverting opinions in a global context.

Stated differently, arguments on global topics require you to recognize competing global perspectives. In all likelihood, your argumentative paper will be grounded in a Western tradition based in part on rationalism, Judeo-Christian values, and various systems of freedom and individual rights. (It will be based as well on classic Greek and Roman principles of argument.) But warrants inherent in the Western tradition do not necessarily make your claim universal. Consider that newspapers around the world use almost two dozen euphemisms for *terrorist*, including *attacker, bomber, commando, criminal, extremist, fighter, guerrilla, hostage-taker, insurgent, militant, radical, rebel,* and *separatist.* (On the website www.newssafety.com, Reuters' Nidal al-Mughrabi offers advice on this matter to fellow reporters in Gaza: "Never use the word terrorist or terrorism describing Palestinian gunmen and militants; people consider them heroes of the conflict.") How you define and interpret a word can determine the method and purpose of an argument.

Not everyone experiences the world or argues global issues from your system of opinions and beliefs. Fortunately, the Internet and the World

Source: Harold Hongju Koh, "Preserving American Values," from *The Age of Terror: America and the World after September 11* by Strobe Talbott and Nayan Chanda (New York: Basic Books, 2002), p. 169.

Wide Web, various translation engines that open international newspaper sites to research, broadcast and visual clips, and even international discussion groups offer you ways to interact globally with other writers, their texts, and their arguments. By searching globally for non-U.S. viewpoints and contending with them, you will be able to write distinctive argumentative papers that go beyond mainstream propositions.

Before launching arguments over "homeland security," the pros and cons of globalization, the Arab-Israeli conflict, the rise of interracial and intercultural dating, or any other global or transnational subject, you once again have an obligation to think clearly and critically about these matters. Argumentation provides a logical way to present a viewpoint, deal fairly with opposing viewpoints, and hopefully arrive at a consensus. The psychologist Carl Rogers offers a new way of looking at argumentation when he suggests that both the communicator presenting an argument and the audience are participants in a dialogue—much like psychotherapy—in which they try to arrive at knowledge, understanding, and truth. At its best, argument results in intelligent **discourse**, a meeting of the minds, and even a strengthening of civic values.

Thinking about an Essay

China: The Educated Giant

NICHOLAS D. KRISTOF

Nicholas D. Kristof is a reporter and columnist for *The New York Times*. He was born in Chicago, Illinois, in 1959 and received a B.A. degree from Harvard University (1981) and a law degree from Oxford University (1983). He also has a diploma in Arabic language from the American University in Cairo. He writes: "Since my student days, when I began to travel with a backpack around Africa and Asia, I have had a fascination with foreign lands, cultures, and languages." Kristof and his wife, Sheryl WuDunn, who is also a *New York Times* reporter, won the Pulitzer Prize for their coverage of the Tiananmen Square massacre in 1989. Based in Asia for many years, Kristof and WuDunn have used their experiences there to write *China Awakes* (1994), *The Japanese Economy at the Millennium* (1999), and *Thunder from the East: Portrait of a Rising Asia* (2000). In the following essay, which appeared in the *Saturday Evening Post* in 2007, Kristof makes a provocative claim about the relative merits of the Chinese and American educational systems.

With China's trade surplus with the United States soaring, the tendency in the U.S. will be to react with tariffs and other barriers. But instead we should take a page from the Chinese book and respond by boosting education.   1

One reason China is likely to overcome the U.S. as the world's most important country in this century is that China puts more effort into building human capital than we do.   2

The area in south Guangdong Province is my wife's ancestral hometown. Sheryl's grandparents left villages here because they thought they could find better opportunities for their children in "Meiguo"—"Beautiful Country," as the U.S. is called in Chinese. And they did. At Sheryl's family reunions, you feel inadequate without a doctorate.   3

But that educational gap between China and America is shrinking rapidly. I visited several elementary and middle schools accompanied by two of my children. And in general, the level of math taught even in peasant schools is similar to that in my kids' own excellent schools in the New York area.   4

My kids' school system doesn't offer foreign languages until the seventh grade. These Chinese peasants begin English studies in either first grade or third grade, depending on the school.   5

Frankly, my daughter got tired of being dragged around schools and having teachers look patronizingly at her schoolbooks and say, "Oh, we do that two grades younger."   6

There are, I think, four reasons why Chinese students do so well.   7

First, Chinese students are hungry for education and advancement and work harder. In contrast, U.S. children average 900 hours a year in class and 1,023 in front of a television.   8

Here in Sheryl's ancestral village, the students show up at school at about 6:30 a.m. to get extra tutoring before classes start at 7:30. They go home for a lunch break at 11:20 and then are back at school from 2:00 p.m. until 5:00. They do homework every night and weekend, and an hour or two of homework each day during their eight-week summer vacation.   9

The second reason is [that] China has an enormous cultural respect for education, part of its Confucian legacy, so governments and families alike pour resources into education. Teachers are respected and compensated far better, financially and emotionally, in China than in America.   10

Recently, I wrote about the boomtown of Dongguan, which had no 11 colleges when I first visited it 20 years ago. The town devotes 21 percent of its budget to education, and it now has four universities. An astonishing 58 percent of the residents age 18 to 22 are enrolled in a university.

A third reason is that Chinese believe that those who get the best 12 grades are the hardest workers. In contrast, Americans say in polls that the best students are the ones who are innately the smartest. The upshot is that Chinese kids never have an excuse for mediocrity.

Chinese education has its own problems, including bribes and fees to 13 get into good schools, huge classes of 50 or 60 students, second-rate equipment and lousy universities. But the progress in the last quarter-century is breathtaking.

It's also encouraging that so many Chinese will shake their heads 14 over this column and say it really isn't so. They will complain that Chinese schools teach rote memorization but not creativity or love of learning. That kind of debate is good for the schools and has already led to improvements in English instruction, so that urban Chinese students can communicate better in English [than] Japanese or South Koreans.

After I visited Sheryl's ancestral village, I posted a video of it on the 15 Web. Soon I was astonished to see an exciting posting on my blog from a woman who used to live in that village.

Litao Mai, probably one of my distant in-laws, grew up in a house 16 she could see on my video. Her parents had only a third-grade education, but she became the first person in the village to go to college. She now works for Merrill Lynch in New York and describes herself as "a little peasant girl" transformed into "a capitalist on Wall Street."

That is the magic of education, and there are 1.3 billion more behind 17 Ms. Mai.

So let's not respond to China's surpluses by putting up trade barriers. 18 Rather, let's do as we did after the Soviet Union's launch of Sputnik in 1957: raise our own education standards to meet the competition.

Questions for Critical Thinking

1. What is *your* opinion of China as an emerging world power? What assumptions and attitudes do you bring to the subject? How open are you to an essay entitled "China: The Educated Giant"? Why would such a topic invite—almost demand—careful critical thinking? What assumptions do you think Kristof makes about his readers?

2. Why does Kristof refer to his family in this essay? Do you agree or disagree with the effectiveness of this strategy? Answer these questions in groups of three or four class members.

3. Where does Kristof use narration and description to organize part of the essay? What is the effect?

4. Kristof employs numerous expository strategies in this essay. Locate and identify them, explaining what they contribute to the substance and the organization of the essay.

5. Does Kristof construct an argument in this essay or is he simply reporting an educational or cultural development? How do you know?

Reading Critically

Most of the essays in this book were written within the last ten years, but the ideas in them run through the history of cultures and civilizations. Consequently, we have to "read" the contemporary ideas contained in these selections through lenses that scan centuries and continents. We have to read critically—analyzing, interpreting, and reassessing new and old ideas in the light of our own experience. When, for example, a writer accuses the United States of **imperialism**, we need to understand the history of this phenomenon as well as interrogate its relevance to the American experience. Is the United States the new imperial power? Are we facing the same conflicts and contradictions that imperial powers through the ages have confronted? To read actively is to be able to think critically about ideas in texts that have deep roots in world history.

As you read the selections in this book, you will discover that careful, critical reading about global issues can complement the talent you already have as a member of the generation that has grown up during the **information age.** Some say that college students have so much trouble with written texts because their culture privileges new forms of technology—call it visual or computer literacy—over older forms of print like the essays you find in this collection. But just as you probably think critically about information acquired through electronic and visual media, you can readily acquire an ability to read written texts critically and to respond to them in discussion and writing. One of the paradoxes of our era is that although we are spending more and more time in front of our computers, we also are buying more books and magazines.

Our most respected thinkers still use the written word to convey their ideas about the issues of our day. They might post these texts on the Web in various forms ranging from online magazines to blogs, but the reality is that these texts appear before us as products of the print universe. Only print can fully convey the intricacy of ideas writers have about our contemporary lives. Speech cannot rival the power of the printed word, as our propensity for tuning out the "talking heads" on television demonstrates.

Moreover, with speech we rarely have the opportunity to go back and evaluate what has been said; with written texts, we can assess the presentation of ideas. As a reader, therefore, you have an obligation to deal seriously with the ideas presented by the writers (many of them famous) in this book and to respond critically and coherently to them. You need to learn strategies that will permit you to read texts in this manner.

There are various ways in which readers can respond to any given text. You, a reader, bring varieties of personal experience—and indeed your personality—to a written text. Your social and cultural background also affects your response to texts. In short, there are several ways to respond critically to both written and visual communication.

You bring numerous personal experiences to the reading of any given text. After all, you have attitudes and opinions, likes and dislikes—a unique range of experience. You construct meaning through these personal experiences, which are rooted in your cultural background and community. If, for example, you read an essay on Islam (there are several in this book) and are Muslim yourself, you probably have personal experience of the text that might or might not be shared by other members of the class.

Along with personal experience, you also *think* about a text in special ways. Cognitive psychologists assert that when you were very young, you probably could not always distinguish fantasy from reality (which is why young children respond so powerfully to fairy tales and cartoons). When you were older—say in junior high school—you were able to seek one true meaning in a text. Then, as in your high school years, you developed an ability to consider multiple meanings and interpretations. The critical intelligence that you bring to a college environment is one that must reason, hypothesize, argue, classify, define, and predict as you contend with any given text that deals with complex global issues.

Of course, the text itself is also important: you cannot center all of its meaning on your personal experience. In fact, some teachers will tell you to eliminate personal experience, moralizing, and impressionistic opinion from your writing and focus on the intrinsic meaning of the text. Thus, you become a hunter of the "truth" of a text, which reveals itself in the language, style, and structure of the work. Fortunately, there are rhetorical strategies and **conventions** that govern texts (many introduced in this book) that will help you to discover these formal truths.

The college classroom—especially the English classroom—is the place where you wrestle with the truths of a text. In this environment, you are not an isolated reader but part of a community of readers. This community or society of readers reflects the diverse features of gender, race and ethnicity, class, education, religion, politics, region, and nation. As a member of this group, you want to share insights with others for the purpose of understanding or consensus (if there is an argument framing the text and discussion). You do not surrender your personal impressions of a text as much as you become a member of what the critic Stanley Fish calls the "interpretive community." In this book, every essay contains an exercise designed to strengthen your reading and writing skills within smaller interpretative or collaborative communities.

Finally, the act of reading critically leads you into the deepest regions of culture and the forces that reveal and inform our experience of the world. Cultural theorists contend that deeply held worldviews and ideologies— for instance, **capitalism** and **socialism**, or Islam and Christianity—are the bedrock of any social configuration. Various institutions, power structures, cultural conventions, gender roles, and "fields of discourse" like medicine and law dictate the ways we respond to a text. As you read the essays in the next chapter, "New American Mosaic," from a cultural perspective, you will have to assess the way your viewpoint on **immigration** has been formed by these deep structures of culture. Through such analysis, you can avoid biased, nationalistic, and religiously intolerant ways of thinking about a text, engaging instead in critical thought and sound, reflective argument.

When reading argumentative essays in a global context, you should consider these critical questions:

- What is the purpose of the text? What claim or main idea does the writer want to develop?
- What is the writer's background? Was the writer born in the United States or overseas?
- Who is the writer's audience? Does the writer demonstrate an awareness that U.S. and non-U.S. readers might respond differently to the content and method of the text?
- Does the writer consider the values, assumptions, and experiences of readers from other cultures?
- Does the writer treat opposing viewpoints or perspectives, especially if they come from non-U.S. sources, accurately and fairly?
- What reasons or minor propositions support the writer's claim?
- How accurate and representative is the writer's supporting evidence? Does the writer rely solely on evidence from U.S. sources, or does credible evidence from reliable global sources also appear?
- Is the shape of the writer's argument logically convincing?

Steps to Reading Critically

With a basic understanding of how ways of reading influence your approach to a text, you can now follow steps that will enable you to read critically. You should treat any "system" for critical reading flexibly, but with the conviction that it is important to extract and evaluate the meanings that professional writers want to convey to their audience. Here are guidelines for effective critical reading.

1. *Start with the conviction that critical reading, like critical thinking, requires active reading.* It is not like passively watching television. Instead, critical reading involves intellectual engagement with the text. Consequently, read with a pen or pencil in hand, underlining or circling key words, phrases, and sentences, asking questions in the margins, and making observations—a process called **annotation**. These annotations will serve as guidelines for a second reading and additional responses in writing.

2. *Pause from time to time to reflect on what you are reading.* What is the writer's main idea? What are his or her basic methods (recall the rhetorical strategies) for developing ideas? What **tone**, or voice, does the writer convey, and why? What is the writer's **purpose**? Is it to argue an issue, explain, analyze, or what? What varieties of illustration or evidence does the writer provide?

3. *Employ your critical thinking skills to interrogate the text.* Use some of the **reader response theories** to explore its deepest meanings. For example, test the text against your personal experience or against certain cultural preconceptions. Think critically about the writer's argument, if there is one, and whether it withstands the test of logic and the conventions of argumentation.

4. *Consider the implied **audience** for the text.* How does the writer address you as part of this audience? Do you actually feel that you are part of this primary audience, a secondary reader, or largely forgotten or excluded? If you feel excluded, what features of the essay have caused you to be removed from this community of readers? How might you make yourself a part of this "universe of discourse" nevertheless?

5. *Write a **précis**, or **summary**, of the essay.* These "shorthand" techniques will help you to focus your thoughts and prepare for class discussions and subsequent writing assignments.

These five steps for critical reading should suggest that critical reading, much like critical thinking and critical writing, involves rereading. If you follow these guidelines, you will be able to enter the classroom community of readers with knowledge and authority and be prepared for productive class discussion.

Reading Visual Texts

You have to read visual texts—advertisements, tables and graphs, cartoons, artwork, photographs, and illustrations—with the same care you bring to the critical reading of written texts. Indeed, "visuals" seem like the new mother of our information age, for we are bombarded with images that invite, sometimes demand, our response. Whether dealing with spam on our computers, contending with that ubiquitous beer commercial on television, responding to a photograph of the latest disaster in a newspaper account, or trying to decipher what a graph on the federal deficit *really* means, we know that visual texts are constructions designed to influence us in carefully contrived ways.

We must, therefore, attempt to be critical readers of visual texts so that the powerful images of our culture and civilization do not seduce or overwhelm us without proper evaluation. Visual texts, after all, tend to be instruments of persuasion. A **symbol** like the American eagle, the Islamic crescent, or the red star of China can trigger powerful personal and collective responses. Similarly, political advertisements and commercials often manipulate visual texts to persuade voters to act for a candidate or against (as with negative ads) an opposing candidate. To bring this discussion to the local level, log on to your campus website. What forms of visual text do you encounter that enhance the written text? Look especially for images that suggest that your campus is culturally and globally diverse.

To read visual texts with the same critical authority you bring to scrutinizing written texts, you should consider the following questions:

- In what culture or context did the image originate? Who is the author? What is the source?
- What implicit messages are conveyed by the images and symbols?
- How is the visual designed or organized, and what is the effect of this arrangement?
- What is the purpose of the visual? What does the visual want the viewer to believe?
- What evidence is provided, and how can it be verified?
- What is the relationship of the visual to the printed text?

Visual images complement and at times overwhelm print or even make printed text unnecessary. Whether appearing on T-shirts, in ads in the glossiest fashion magazines, or marching across a computer screen, visual images usher us into a world of meaning. And we need to apply the same critical perspective to this visual universe that we do to its print counterpart.

Reading an Essay Critically

The Globalization of Eating Disorders

SUSAN BORDO | Susan Bordo was born in 1947 in Newark, New Jersey. She attended Carleton University (B.A., 1972) and the State University of New York at Stony Brook (Ph.D., 1982). A well-known feminist scholar, Bordo is the Singletary Chair in the Humanities and a professor of

English and Women's Studies at the University of Kentucky. In this selection, written as a preface to the tenth anniversary edition of her Pulitzer Prize–nominated book *Unbearable Weight: Feminism, Western Culture, and the Body* (2003), Bordo offers an overview of a new kind of epidemic, fueled by Western media images, that is affecting cultures around the world.

The young girl stands in front of the mirror. Never fat to begin with, 1
she's been on a no-fat diet for a couple of weeks and has reached her goal weight: 115 lb., at 5'4"—exactly what she should weigh, according to her doctor's chart. But in her eyes she still looks dumpy. She can't shake her mind free of the "Lady Marmelade" video from Moulin Rouge. Christina Aguilera, Pink, L'il Kim, and Mya, each one perfect in her own way: every curve smooth and sleek, lean-sexy, nothing to spare. Self-hatred and shame start to burn in the girl, and envy tears at her stomach, enough to make her sick. She'll never look like them, no matter how much weight she loses. Look at that stomach of hers, see how it sticks out? Those thighs—they actually jiggle. Her butt is monstrous. She's fat, gross, a dough girl.

As you read the imaginary scenario above, whom did you picture 2
standing in front of the mirror? If your images of girls with eating and body image problems have been shaped by *People* magazine and Lifetime movies, she's probably white, North American, and economically secure. A child whose parents have never had to worry about putting food on the family table. A girl with money to spare for fashion magazines and trendy clothing, probably college-bound. If you're familiar with the classic psychological literature on eating disorders, you may also have read that she's an extreme "perfectionist" with a hyper-demanding mother, and that she suffers from "body-image distortion syndrome" and other severe perceptual and cognitive problems that "normal" girls don't share. You probably don't picture her as black, Asian, or Latina.

Read the description again, but this time imagine twenty-something 3
Tenisha Williamson standing in front of the mirror. Tenisha is black, suffers from anorexia, and feels like a traitor to her race. "From an African-American standpoint," she writes, "we as a people are encouraged to embrace our big, voluptuous bodies. This makes me feel terrible because I don't want a big, voluptuous body! I don't ever want to be fat—ever, and I don't ever want to gain weight. I would rather die from starvation

Susan Bordo, "The Globalization of Eating Disorders" from *Unbearable Weight: Feminism, Western Culture, and the Body*, 2003. Reprinted by permission of the author.

than gain a single pound."[1] Tenisha is no longer an anomaly. Eating and body image problems are now not only crossing racial and class lines, but gender lines. They have also become a global phenomenon.

Fiji is a striking example. Because of their remote location, the Fiji   4
islands did not have access to television until 1995, when a single station was introduced. It broadcasts programs from the United States, Great Britain, and Australia. Until that time, Fiji had no reported cases of eating disorders, and a study conducted by anthropologist Anne Becker showed that most Fijian girls and women, no matter how large, were comfortable with their bodies. In 1998, just three years after the station began broadcasting, 11 percent of girls reported vomiting to control weight, and 62 percent of the girls surveyed reported dieting during the previous months.[2]

Becker was surprised by the change; she had thought that Fijian cul-   5
tural traditions, which celebrate eating and favor voluptuous bodies, would "withstand" the influence of media images. Becker hadn't yet understood that we live in an empire of images, and that there are no protective borders.

In Central Africa, for example, traditional cultures still celebrate vo-   6
luptuous women. In some regions, brides are sent to fattening farms, to be plumped and massaged into shape for their wedding night. In a country plagued by AIDS, the skinny body has meant—as it used to among Italian, Jewish, and black Americans—poverty, sickness, death. "An African girl must have hips," says dress designer Frank Osodi. "We have hips. We have bums. We like flesh in Africa." For years, Nigeria sent its local version of beautiful to the Miss World competition. The contestants did very poorly. Then a savvy entrepreneur went against local ideals and entered Agbani Darego, a light-skinned, hyper-skinny beauty. (He got his inspiration from M-Net, the South African network seen across Africa on satellite television, which broadcasts mostly American movies and television shows.) Agbani Darego won the Miss World Pageant, the first Black African to do so. Now, Nigerian teenagers fast and exercise, trying to become "lepa"—a popular slang phrase for the thin "it" girls that are all the rage. Said one: "People have realized that slim is beautiful."[3]

How can mere images be so powerful? For one thing, they are   7
never "just pictures," as the fashion magazines continually maintain

---

1. From the Colours of Ana website (http://coloursofana.com//ss8.asp). [This and subsequent notes in the selection are the author's.]
2. Reported in Nancy Snyderma, *The Girl in the Mirror* (New York: Hyperion, 2002), p. 84.
3. Norimitsu Onishi, "Globalization of Beauty Makes Slimness Trendy," *The New York Times*, Oct. 3, 2002.

(disingenuously) in their own defense. They speak to young people not just about how to be beautiful but also about how to become what the dominant culture admires, values, rewards. They tell them how to be cool, "get it together," overcome their shame. To girls who have been abused they may offer a fantasy of control and invulnerability, immunity from pain and hurt. For racial and ethnic groups whose bodies have been deemed "foreign," earthy, and primitive, and considered unattractive by Anglo-Saxon norms, they may cast the lure of being accepted as "normal" by the dominant culture.

In today's world, it is through images—much more than parents,   8
teachers, or clergy—that we are taught how to be. And it is images, too, that teach us how to see, that educate our vision in what's a defect and what is normal, that give us the models against which our own bodies and the bodies of others are measured. Perceptual pedagogy: "How to Interpret Your Body 101." It's become a global requirement.

I was intrigued, for example, when my articles on eating disorders   9
began to be translated, over the past few years, into Japanese and Chinese. Among the members of audiences at my talks, Asian women had been among the most insistent that eating and body image weren't problems for their people, and indeed, my initial research showed that eating disorders were virtually unknown in Asia. But when, this year, a Korean translation of *Unbearable Weight* was published, I felt I needed to revisit the situation. I discovered multiple reports on dramatic increases in eating disorders in China, South Korea, and Japan. "As many Asian countries become Westernized and infused with the Western aesthetic of a tall, thin, lean body, a virtual tsunami of eating disorders has swamped Asian countries," writes Eunice Park in *Asian Week* magazine. Older people can still remember when it was very different. In China, for example, where revolutionary ideals once condemned any focus on appearance and there have been several disastrous famines, "little fatty" was a term of endearment for children. Now, with fast food on every corner, childhood obesity is on the rise and the cultural meaning of fat and thin has changed. "When I was young," says Li Xiaojing, who manages a fitness center in Beijing, "people admired and were even jealous of fat people since they thought they had a better life. . . . But now, most of us see a fat person and think 'He looks awful.' "[4]

Clearly, body insecurity can be exported, imported, and marketed—   10
just like any other profitable commodity. In this respect, what's happened

4. Reported in Elizabeth Rosenthal, "Beijing Journal: China's Chic Waistline: Convex to Concave," *The New York Times*, Dec. 9, 1999.

with men and boys is illustrative. Ten years ago men tended, if anything, to see themselves as better looking than they (perhaps) actually were. And then (as I chronicle in detail in my book *The Male Body*) the menswear manufacturers, the diet industries, and the plastic surgeons "discovered" the male body. And now, young guys are looking in their mirrors, finding themselves soft and ill defined, no matter how muscular they are. Now they are developing the eating and body image disorders that we once thought only girls had. Now they are abusing steroids, measuring their own muscularity against the oiled and perfected images of professional athletes, body-builders, and *Men's Health* models. Now the industries in body-enhancement—cosmetic surgeons, manufacturers of anti-aging creams, spas and salons—are making huge bucks off men, too.

What is to be done? I have no easy answers. But I do know that we   11 need to acknowledge, finally and decisively, that we are dealing here with a cultural problem. If eating disorders were biochemical, as some claim, how can we account for their gradual "spread" across race, gender, and nationality? And with mass media culture increasingly providing the dominant "public education" in our children's lives—and those of children around the globe—how can we blame families? Families matter, of course, and so do racial and ethnic traditions. But families exist in cultural time and space—and so do racial groups. In the empire of images, no one lives in a bubble of self-generated "dysfunction" or permanent immunity. The sooner we recognize that—and start paying attention to the culture around us and what it is teaching our children—the sooner we can begin developing some strategies for change.

Reading and Responding to an Essay

1. After reading Bordo's essay, reread and annotate it. Underline or circle key words, phrases, and sentences. Ask questions and make observations in the margins. Next to the title, write a phrase or sentence explaining what you think the title means.

2. In class groups of three or four, discuss your personal responses to this essay. Share with group members your experience of the text and why you respond to it the way you do. Would you say that your ideal image of physical beauty is based on personal or shared values? Do you know people whose ideas of beauty contrast with your own? Do you think of this difference as a matter of opinion, cultural difference, or simply personal taste?

3. Bordo claims, "In today's world, it is through images—much more than parents, teachers, or clergy—that we are taught to be." How essential is this premise to the writer's claim? What kinds of evidence does she use to support the claim?

4. Examine the language, style, and structure of the essay. Do you find the writer's style to be engaging or accessible? Why or why not? Why does she repeat words and phrases (termed *anaphora* in rhetoric)? Where does she employ description, illustration, comparison, and the basis of case studies followed by general diagnosis—basically a problem–solution method of essay development?

5. Explain the ways in which you could interpret this essay from psychological, cultural, and social perspectives.

Writing in Response to Reading

The distinguished writers in this book, many of them recipients of major awards such as the Nobel and Pulitzer Prizes, are professionals. When dealing typically with local and world events—especially with the relationship of a liberal and open society like the United States to the world community—they employ a broad range of stylistic and rhetorical skills to construct meaning. They write for numerous reasons or purposes, although an argumentative edge appears in many of the essays. All engage in strategic thinking and rethinking as they tackle the promises and prospects of our new global era.

It is useful at the outset of a course in college writing to think like a professional writer or at least a professional writer in the making. With each essay you write, imagine that you are trying to produce "publishable prose." Indeed, you will have the opportunity to write letters to the editor, post papers on the Web, pool and present research findings with other classmates, and engage in many tasks that assume the character of the professional writer who composes for a specific audience and for a specific purpose. At the least, by treating yourself as a writer capable of producing publishable prose, you will impress your instructor with your seriousness and aspirations.

Many of the issues and momentous events treated by the writers in this book demand no less than a "professional" response based on your ability to deal critically in writing with the strategic questions the essays raise. Indeed, critical thinking and writing about our common global condition is one measure of a pluralistic and tolerant society. By thinking and rethinking, writing and rewriting about your world, you contribute to the creation of open democratic discourse.

How, then, do you write about the new global era and its many challenges, or about any other topic for that matter? Globalization has changed the way people think about themselves and their relation to the world. Even ideas have become global; communication of these ideas now can span the world in milliseconds. As a writer in this brave new world of globalization, you need to apply in writing that repertoire of critical thinking skills mentioned at the outset of this chapter to make sense of contemporary life on this planet.

To start, you must have a basic understanding of the world of global interrelationships that characterizes life in the twenty-first century. The noted historian Paul Kennedy defines globalization as "the ever-growing integration of economies and societies because of new communications, newer trade and investment patterns, the transmissions of cultural images and messages, and the erosion of local and traditional ways of life in the face of powerful economic forces from abroad." Kennedy, as we might expect from a historian, is quick to note that this new world of globalization did not spring immediately from the ashes of 9/11 but can be detected in different guises in the rise and fall of great civilizations. For example, what the British Empire once termed "progress," we now call globalization. Today, the United States is the Great Power—its financial, cultural, military, and high tech capacities unrivaled by other nations. Whether its Great Power status—its overarching control of the forces of globalization—will create new forms of "progress" for peoples and nations around the world is the central debate underlying the chapters in this book.

Writers like Paul Kennedy are "professional" in the sense that they know their subject. They are informed. But their informed essays do not result from some divinely inspired moment of creativity. When professional writers sit down to tackle an issue of importance, they know that beyond the knowledge they bring to the subject, they will have to consider various perspectives on the subject and even experiment with various methods of composition. Everyone composes differently, but it is fair to say that a good essay is the result of planning, writing, and revision, and such an essay reflects some of the key thinking strategies outlined in the first part of this chapter. There is a common consensus among professionals, including teachers of writing, that a **composing process**, consisting of *prewriting, drafting*, and *revision*, is the best way to approach the creation of a successful essay.

Prewriting

Prewriting is that preliminary stage in the composing process in which you map out mentally and in writing your overall approach to the subject. Prewriting in the context of this book begins when you read critically and respond to an essay. Perhaps you annotate the essay, summarize it mentally, or take notes on paper or the computer. Or maybe you take notes during class discussion. Next, you size up the nature of the writing project appearing in the exercises at the end of the essay or provided by the instructor. At this early stage, it is clear that already you are thinking, responding, and writing critically about the project at hand.

Composing processes are unique to each writer, but there are certain areas of the prewriting process that are necessary for you to consider:

- *Who is your audience?* A college writing assignment means that your primary audience will be your professor, who knows the "print code" and anticipates well-organized and grammatically correct prose. But there are secondary audiences to consider as well, and you might have to adjust your level of discourse to them. If you are working collaboratively, you have members of the group to satisfy. If you exchange papers with another class member for evaluation, this also creates a new audience. Or perhaps you will need to create an electronic portfolio of your best work as a graduation requirement; here the people who assess the quality of the portfolio become judges of your work.
- *What is your purpose?* Is your purpose to tell a story, describe, inform, argue, evaluate, or combine any number of these basic goals? Knowing your purpose in advance of actually drafting the essay will permit you to control the scope, method, and tone of the composition.
- *What is your thesis or claim?* Every paper requires a controlling idea or **assertion**. Think about and write down, either in shorthand or as a complete sentence, the main idea or claim that you plan to center your paper on.
- *How will you design your essay?* Planning or outlining your paper in advance of actually writing it can facilitate the writing process. Complete outlines, sketch outlines, sequenced notes, and visual diagrams can all serve as aids once the actual drafting begins.
- *How can you generate preliminary content?* Notes can be valuable. **Brainstorming**, in which you write without stop for a certain amount of time, can also activate the creative process. Joining online discussion groups or working collaboratively in the classroom also can result in raw content and ideas for development.

Prewriting provides both content and a plan of operation before moving to the next stage in the composing process.

Drafting

Once you have attended to the preliminary, or prewriting, stage in the composing process, you can move to the second stage, which is the actual **drafting** of the paper. Applying an Aristotelian formula, be certain to have a beginning, middle, and end. Your introduction—ideally one opening paragraph—should center the topic, be sufficiently compelling to engage your reader, and contain a thesis or claim. The body of the essay should offer a series of paragraphs supporting your main idea or central assertion. The conclusion should wrap things up in an emphatic or convincing way.

Here is a checklist for drafting an essay:

- Does your title illuminate the topic and capture the reader's interest?
- Does your opening paragraph "hook" the reader? Does it establish and limit the topic? Does it contain a thesis or claim?
- Do all body paragraphs support the thesis? Is there a main idea (called a **topic sentence**) controlling each paragraph? Are all paragraphs well developed? Do they contain sufficient examples or evidence?
- Does the body hold together? Is there a logical sequence to the paragraphs? In other words, is the body of the essay **unified** and **coherent**, with **transitions** flowing from sentence to sentence and paragraph to paragraph?
- Have you selected the best critical thinking strategies to develop the paper and meet the expectations set out in your introduction?
- Is your conclusion strong and effective?
- Think of drafting as the creation of a well-constructed plot. This plot does not begin, develop, and end haphazardly, but rather in a carefully considered sequence. Your draft should reveal those strategies and elements of the composing process that produce an interesting and logically constructed plot.

Revision

There are professional writers who rarely, if ever, revise their work, and there are others who spend forever getting every word and sentence just right. Yet most professional writers do some amount of **revision**, either on their own initiative or in response to other experts, normally editors and reviewers. As the American poet Archibald MacLeish observed, the composing process consists of the "endless discipline of writing and rewriting and rewriting."

Think of the essay that in all likelihood you have put up on your computer screen not as a polished or final product but as a rough draft. Use the grammar and spell-checker features of your software program to clean up this draft, remembering that this software is not infallible and sometimes is even misleading. Then revise your essay, creating a second draft, with the following questions serving as guidelines:

- Is the essay long enough to satisfy the demands of the assignment?
- Is the topic suitable for the assignment?
- Is there a clear thesis or claim?
- Is the purpose or intention of the essay clear?
- Is the essay organized sensibly? Are the best rhetorical patterns used to facilitate reader interest and comprehension?
- Are all sentences grammatically correct and sufficiently varied in structure?

- Is there sufficient evidence, and is all information derived from other sources properly attributed?
- Does the manuscript conform to acceptable guidelines for submitting written work?

Successful writing blends form and content to communicate effectively with an audience. The guidelines offered in this section tap your ability to think and write critically about the global issues raised in this book. To be a global citizen, you must become aware of others, make sense of the world, and evaluate varieties of experience. To be a global writer, you have to translate your understanding of these global relationships into well-ordered and perceptive prose.

Writing in Response to an Essay

The Rich Are Different from You and Me

CHRYSTIA FREELAND

> Chrystia Freeland, who is of Ukrainian extraction, was born in Peace River, Canada, in 1968. She graduated from Harvard University and attended St. Anthony's College Oxford as a Rhodes Scholar. Freeland has been a correspondent and editor for several publications including Toronto's *The Globe and Mail* and the *Financial Times*, where she was Moscow bureau chief. Based on her overseas experience, she wrote *Sale of the Century: Russia's Wild Ride from Communism to Capitalism* (2000). Today she is the editor of Thomson Reuters Digital. In this article from the July/August 2011 issue of *The Atlantic Monthly*, Freeland argues that the expanding differences between the super-wealthy and the rest of the world population is a dangerous global trend.

The rich are always with us, as we learned from the Bette Davis film   1
of that name, released in the teeth of the Great Depression. The most memorable part of that movie was its title—but that terrific phrase turns out not to be entirely true. In every society, some people are richer than others, but across time and geography, the gap between the rich and the rest has varied widely.

The reality today is that the rich—especially the very, very rich—are   2
vaulting ahead of everyone else. Between 2002 and 2007, 65 percent of
all income growth in the U.S. went to the richest 1 percent of the population. That lopsided distribution means that today, half of the national
income goes to the richest 10 percent. In 2007, the top 1 percent controlled 34.6 percent of the wealth—significantly more than the bottom
90 percent, who controlled just 26.9 percent.

That is a huge shift from the post-war decades, whose golden glow   3
may have arisen largely from the era's relative income equality. During
the Second World War, and in the four decades that followed, the top
10 percent took home just a third of the national income. The last time
the gap between the people on top and everyone else was as large as it is
today was during the Roaring '20s.

The rise of today's super-rich is a global phenomenon. It is particu-   4
larly marked in the United States, but it is also happening in other developed economies like the United Kingdom and Canada. Income inequality
is also increasing in most of the go-go emerging-market economies, and
is now as high in Communist China as it is in the U.S.

These global super-rich work and play together. They jet between the   5
Four Seasons in Shanghai and the Four Seasons in New York to do business; descend on Davos, Switzerland, to network; and travel to St. Bart's
to vacation. Many are global nomads with a fistful of passports and several far-flung homes. They have more in common with one another than
with the folks in the hinterland back home, and increasingly, they are
forming a nation unto themselves.

This international plutocracy is emerging at a moment when global-   6
ization and the technology revolution are hollowing out the middle class
in most Western industrialized nations. Many of today's super-rich
started out in the middle and make most of their money through work,
not inheritance. Ninety-five years ago, the richest 1 percent of Americans
received only 20 percent of their income from paid work; in 2004, that
income proportion had tripled, to 60 percent.

These meritocrats are the winners in a winner-take-all world. Among   7
the big political questions of our age are whether they will notice that
everyone else is falling behind, and whether they will decide it is in their
interests to do something about that.

Responding in Writing

1. As a prewriting strategy, brainstorm about this article for five minutes. Try
   to capture your impressions of the essay as you respond to the ideas and
   elements in it.

2. Working in groups of four, list everything that you know about the super-rich and the rest of the global population. Try to generate ideas not just about the United States but also about at least three other nations or geographic areas. Select one member of your group to present your findings to the class.

3. "Professional" writing is partly the result of an author's mastery of the subject and the expertise he or she brings to it. A writer's ethos may consist of a wide range of qualities: moral authority, sincerity, humility, humor, **satire**, and seriousness of purpose. Consider your response to the voice you hear in this essay. How would you characterize Freeland's tone or voice? Where do you find instances of this voice, and how would you characterize it?

4. Write an analysis of this essay. What evidence suggests that Freeland has a target audience in mind, and who might this audience be? What is Freeland's claim or argument? What tone does she use to advance her claim? How does she present this argument, in terms of an introduction, body, and conclusion, and how persuasive do you find it to be? What is the nature of her evidence? What ideas about the United States and global economics and culture does she want the audience to gain from a critical reading of the text?

5. Go online and find out more about the super-rich and the rest of the global population. Write a report on your findings and summarize it in an oral presentation to the class.

New American Mosaic: Are We Becoming a Universal Nation?

Martin Luther King Jr. believed in the need for what he termed a "world house," a commitment to a society of global inclusion. "We are all caught up in an inescapable web of mutuality, tied in a single garment of destiny," he declared. Indeed, there are interconnected forces governing our world, and American demographic trends reflect the transnational movement of peoples on today's planet. Accelerating this transformation has been the recent arrival of tens of millions of immigrants to the United States. Instead of repeating earlier immigration patterns in which peoples arrived from Europe, these new immigrants travel here from all parts of the globe: Asia, Africa, the Caribbean, Central and South America. Today, new immigrants are changing the traditional notion of what it means to be "American." Arguably, because of the strikingly diverse nature of its citizenry, the United States is in the process of becoming a universal nation.

The writers in this chapter reflect in their own ethnic and racial origins the broad mosaic—some prefer to call it a kaleidoscope—that characterizes life in the United States today. Consider the historical magnitude of this national transformation. North America once belonged to native tribes, and the legacy of slavery, which began in 1621 when a Dutch man-of-war ship brought the first Africans to the Jamestown colony, also served to diversify the nation in ways that we continue to grapple with today. But from colonial times to 1965, the United States drew its population largely from Europe. First came the English, Scots-Irish, Germans, and French. The second great wave that began in the 1870s and continued up to World War I brought tens of millions of immigrants from southern and eastern Europe. For centuries, immigrants from non-European parts of the world were systematically excluded, with restrictive quotas preserving certain assumptions about the racial and ethnic character of the nation. For example, in

Thinking about the Image

1. Are the people portrayed in this cartoon stereotypes? How can you tell? Do you find the stereotypes offensive, or do they help the cartoons make sense? Can you think of any comedians or hip-hop artists who use stereotypes in a way that points out an uncomfortable truth?

2. This cartoon uses **irony** to make its point. What specifically is ironic about this cartoon?

3. What political situation or issue is Steve Kelley, the cartoonist, responding to in this cartoon? What is his opinion? Does he make his point effectively?

her haunting memoir *China Men*, the acclaimed writer Maxine Hong Kingston devotes an entire chapter to listing the dozens of immigration statutes designed to exclude people from China from America's shores.

The Immigration Act of 1965 abolished all such quotas and opened the United States—for the first time in the nation's history—to the world's population. Now everyone presumably had a fair opportunity to achieve the American Dream, whatever this ambiguous term might mean. And arrive they did—from Mexico, Vietnam, India, Nigeria, Cuba, the Philippines, Iran, and China—all seeking a place in the new global nation. Of course, this contemporary collision and intersection of peoples, races, and cultures is not only an American phenomenon; many countries in Europe are dealing with similar patterns. But nowhere is this new global reality more apparent than in the United States. In certain states—California, for example—and in many major American cities, "minorities" have become majorities. According to the most recent census data, by 2056 the "average" American will be as likely to trace his or her origins to the Hispanic world, Asia, or the Pacific islands as to Europe. These demographic changes are often reflected on college campuses, with students from scores of national backgrounds speaking dozens of languages sharing classes together.

The story of American civilization is still unfinished, but the authors in this chapter suggest certain directions it will take. They write about conflicts and challenges posed by the new American Dream, which is ostensibly open to, if not necessarily desired by, all the peoples of the world. They wrestle with America's complex fate. They ask collectively: How can America continue to be a beacon for peoples from around the planet seeking work, safety, security, freedom, and the right to freely practice and preserve their own customs and beliefs? They ask: Can America be—should it be—the model for a universal nation?

Red, Brown, and Blue

ELLIS COSE

Ellis Cose was born in Chicago in 1951 and grew up in one of the city's high-rise public housing projects. He attended the University of Illinois Chicago (B.A., 1972) and George Washington University (M.A., 1974) before embarking on a distinguished career as a writer, columnist, reporter, and editor. Cose has worked for several major publications including the *Detroit Free Press*, *New York Daily News*, *Time*, and *Newsweek*. He is also the author of many well-received and best-selling books. Several works explore the personal and political lives of black Americans, among them *The Rage of a Political Class* (1994), *The Envy of the World* (2002), and *The End of Anger* (2011). Cose appears frequently on television shows and radio programs. In this 2010 essay from *Newsweek*, Cose examines the racial transformation taking place in American society.

Before Reading

If, as most demographers predict, blacks, Latinos, and Asian-Americans will be a majority in the United States by 2050, what social, political, and economic consequences would you predict?

W ould America be so different if blacks, Latinos, and people of Asian   1
descent collectively became the new majority? It's not an idle question. According to the most recent U.S. Census projections, that's precisely where the United States is likely headed—by 2050 or thereabouts. It's important to distinguish this from concerns around the decennial Census scheduled for this year. Communities of color have a history of being undercounted, so advocates are mobilizing to make sure the new count is as accurate as possible. Those numbers, after all, confer power—via allocation of federal dollars and reapportionment of political representation. The Census projections have no power at all. And, truth be told, the future they imagine is unlikely to ever come to pass. For while the projections say much about our current racial assumptions, they are a poor measure for what lies ahead.

In America's early days, it was virtually impossible to conceive of a   2
citizen as being other than white. The first U.S. naturalization act made whiteness a condition of gaining citizenship. So courts heard case after case from would-be white people who appeared to be something else. In 1922, a Japanese national who had lived in the United States for 20 years told the Supreme Court that most Japanese hailed from Caucasian "root stocks." The high court disagreed. Next year, a high-caste Hindu claimed he too was white. The justices found him no more persuasive.

This was during a time when even Europeans were divided into lesser and   3
better grades of white. Italians, Eastern Europeans, and Jews were, in many quarters, deemed to be of altogether different (and inferior) stock. Such ideas, though preposterous, defined debate and shaped immigration laws.

In an essay titled "How Did Jews Become White Folks?" anthropolo-   4
gist Karen Brodkin Sacks asks: "Did Jews and other Euroethnics become white because they became middle class? Or did being incorporated in an expanded version of whiteness open up the economic doors to middle-class status?" Both tendencies, she concluded, were at work. But her larger point is that nothing about race is static.

That's even more obvious today. A few generations back, racially   5
mixed couples were an anomaly. But between the 1990 and 2000 census, the percentage of racially intermarried couples nearly doubled. More significantly, when Gallup's pollsters surveyed Americans' attitudes toward interracial relationships in 2005, the majority were accepting. Ninety-five percent of Americans under 30 approved, compared to roughly

Culture or Conflict?
Images of Globalization

This portfolio of images from around the world presents a visual paradox: Is global culture a happy consumer wonderland where the fries are always crisp and the music always loud? Or has globalization simply packaged and marketed a bland, simplified version of the basics of culture, such as food and fashion, to an increasingly busy and distracted global population?

For millennia, trade between nation-states has introduced and shared aspects of culture, but the electronic telecommunication that is available now between countries has enabled instant blending of customs and has caused regional cultures and languages to fight to keep their own traditions vibrant. French-speaking Quebecois agitate for independence from the rest of English-speaking Canada. The ecotourism movement struggles to maintain the integrity of fragile cultures and environments, even as it imports Western tourists with their cash, cameras, and expectations for plumbing. The slow-food movement, which originated in Italy, calls on communities to nurture biodiversity and sustainable agriculture through renewed appreciation of their culinary heritage.

As you examine the following images, be especially attentive to the irony that lies in the details. *Irony* is a quality of being unexpected, incongruous, or out of place, juxtapositions that make something as common as a bottle of soda seem suddenly, entirely strange. That strangeness leads to a realization that there is more to the image than meets the eye; the nomad's tent topped by a satellite dish or the camel carrying an expensive mountain bicycle can be perceived either as a widening of opportunities and experiences or a flattening out of cultural vitality.

Many readings in this book describe the clashing of cultures and civilizations. Can consumer culture, based on these images, foster cooperation rather than clashes? After all, in a 1996 op-ed piece in *The New York Times*, foreign correspondent Thomas Friedman argued that no two countries that both have a McDonald's have ever fought a war against each other. What do you think?

1

© AP Photo/Enric Marti

Coca-Cola in Egypt. An Egyptian girl drinks from a bottle of Coca-Cola in a shop in downtown Cairo, Egypt. After an Internet rumor that the Coca-Cola logo, if looked at upside-down or in a mirror, reads "No Mohammed, No Mecca" in Arabic, a top religious authority in Egypt studied the label and finally declared that "there is no defamation to the religion of Islam from near or far."

Considering the Image

1. Why would Coca-Cola be a target for such a rumor? Can you think of other examples in which consumer goods were boycotted as the symbols of a larger culture, value system, or belief?

2. What, to your eye, is particularly revealing or compelling about this image? What does the photographer want you to see? Does this image support or contradict images that you see in the media about women in the Middle East?

Big Bird in Shanghai. More than 90 percent of the households in the twelve major cities of the People's Republic of China have television sets. One of the favorite programs, reaching 120 million Chinese viewers, is *Sesame Street*. Here, Big Bird, known as *Zhima Jie,* appears on Shanghai television.

Considering the Image

1. How did the photographer capture a specific mood in this picture? What is the expression on the children's faces? Why does Big Bird loom over them? Do you think that there are universal values that make *Sesame Street* popular not just in China but throughout the world? Justify and explain your response.

2. Do you think the photographer wants to make a statement about ''cultural imperialism'' or the impact of globalization on national cultures, or simply capture a specific moment and scene? Explain your response. Why might globalization, which involves in part the transnational movement of media across cultures, be a force for democracy in China and elsewhere?

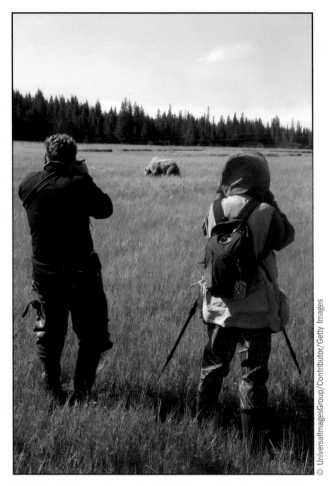

"Shooting" Bear. Two ecotourists photograph a bear in Alaska.

© UniversalImagesGroup/Contributor/Getty Images

Considering the Image

1. Do you think that the photographer was thinking about the act of hunting when setting up this shot? Explain your response.

2. Whose perspective do you assume as you view this photograph: the hikers', the bear's, the photographer's? How might all three perspectives be reflected in the overall image?

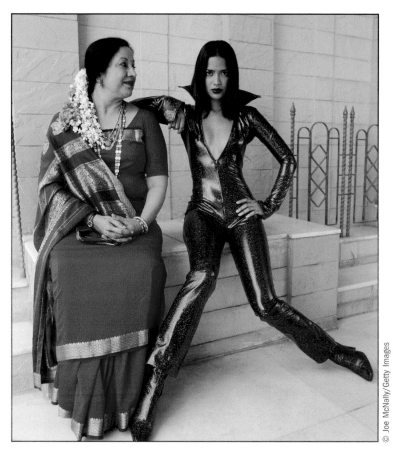

Sophisticated Ladies.   Nakshatra Reddy is a biochemist who is married to a prosperous businessman in Mumbai (formerly Bombay). Her daughter, Meghana, dressed in a PVC suit of her own design, is a model and former host on a local music channel.

Considering the Image

1. How does the photographer stage or set up this scene? How does the photographer emphasize certain cultural contrasts between mother and daughter, and what is the purpose? Why is it important for viewers to know that mother and daughter represent a wealthy Indian family rather than a middle-class or poor one?

2. The daughter in this family represents a familiar Western type. How would you describe her? What are her sources of imitation? Do you think that the daughter has succumbed to the lure of Western popular culture, or might she be making a statement about her global identity? Explain your response.

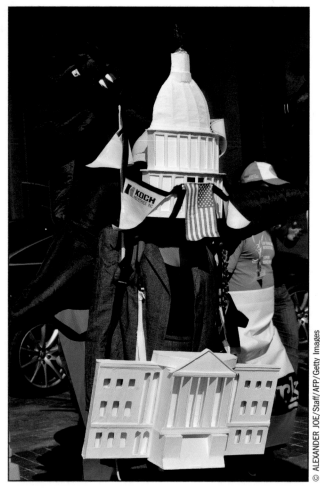

© ALEXANDER JOE/Staff/AFP/Getty Images

Globalization Protest.   Greenpeace activists and supporters protest outside the Global Business Day conference in Durban, South Africa, on December 5, 2011.

Considering the Image

1. What details stand out in this photograph? Do the elements seem cluttered to you? How many details can you identify? What ultimately is the dominant impression?

2. Does the photographer want to make a statement about globalization or simply capture a specific moment without editorializing about it? Justify your response.

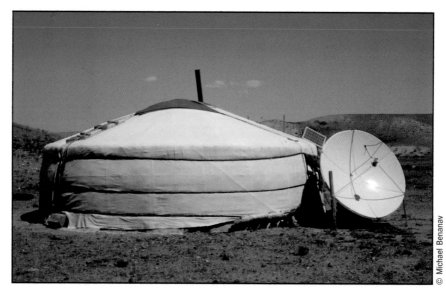

Modern Conveniences.   The *ger* is the traditional, portable home of the nomadic people of Mongolia. A cone-shaped structure of felt stretched over a timber frame, with an opening in the top or a pipe to vent smoke from the stove, the *ger* is a symbol both of freedom and of hospitality. Many residents of Mongolia's capital, Ulaan Baatar, still live in traditional *gers*, and in keeping with their nomadic routes, any visitor is warmly greeted and offered shelter and food, as well as many modern conveniences. Here, a *ger* is outfitted with a satellite dish.

Considering the Image

1. This photo suggests not so much a clash of cultures as a fusion of ancient ways and modern technology. Why might a nomadic culture, like that of rural Mongolia, value the latest in communications technology?

2. Many writers define the so-called electronic gap or digital divide as one of the great challenges—and opportunities—for the twenty-first century. What does this image suggest to you about the digital divide? Granted, we do not know from this photograph if that satellite dish is being used to watch CNN or MTV; should that even matter? Why or why not?

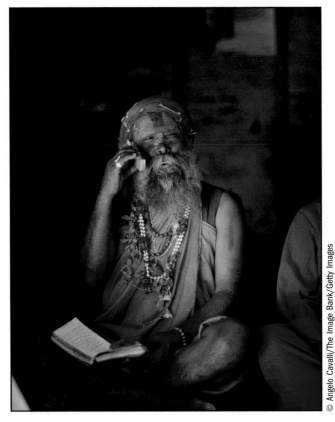

Mixing Cultures. Sadhu (Hindu ascetic) uses a mobile phone in the Pashupatinath (Hindu temple) in Kathmandu, Nepal, 2005.

Considering the Image

1. What impression do you think this photograph conveys? What sensory images and elements, such as sight and colors, stand out? How do these elements highlight the impact of Western popular culture on traditional Indian culture? How is the photograph composed so as to illustrate the blending (or conflict) of cultures?

2. What point do you think the photographer is attempting to make? Does the photographer advance a thesis or claim about the clash of civilizations, or the viability of old cultural practices in an age of globalization? Justify your response.

45 percent of those over 64. Indeed, the majority of younger people claimed to have dated a person of a different race or ethnic background.

Census Bureau demographers are highly skilled. But there is no way 6 they can program projections to capture the complexity of Americans' shifting attitudes. To their credit, they have tried. The 2000 Census, for instance, allowed Americans a wider range of options than did the 1990 Census. Racial categories were increased from five to six. For the first time Americans were allowed to claim more than one racial identity, and American Indians and Alaska natives were allowed to name their tribes. But there was no attempt to measure Americans' increasing propensity to propagate with partners of other races. As Census demographer Fred Hollmann told me, "We did not feel we had enough information from history to make an assumption on that particular issue."

By the same token, there is not enough information to say how 7 quickly other groups will go the route of the Italians and Jews and become more white than not. What is certain is that young people—whether choosing mates, categorizing people, or simply hanging out—are less likely than their elders to erect rigid racial walls. We also know that it's only a matter of time before DNA testing persuades many "whites" that they are much more mixed than they ever imagined.

So what does that mean for the future America? At the very least, it 8 means two things: that whites are not in danger of becoming a minority in the foreseeable future because the white category (or its equivalent) will likely expand to encompass many we now consider to be minorities. But more important, race is not going to be quite as big a deal as it is now; in the America of tomorrow—whatever people decide to call themselves—race will not be synonymous with destiny. That's a future worth embracing.

Thinking about the Essay

1. What connotations does the title of this essay raise for you? What subtle **allusion** is Cose making here, and what is the writer's purpose?

2. Consider the writer's introductory paragraph. Why is it so dense with information? Does the writer establish his claim in this introduction? Why or why not?

3. Summarize Cose's argument. How does he state the problem? What evidence does he provide? Does he offer a solution? Justify your response by referring to the text.

4. Where does Cose employ comparison and contrast? How does the comparative method reinforce Cose's claim?

5. Identify those places in the essay where the writer poses a question. What is the effect? Does the writer answer these questions or not? Explain.

Responding in Writing

6. Cose writes that young people "are less likely than their elders to erect rigid racial walls" (paragraph 7). Write an essay in which you agree or disagree with this statement, offering your own reasons and support for the position you take.

7. Write an essay entitled "The New Majority" in which you discuss the same demographic patterns that Cose raises in his article.

8. In considering the demographic changes already occurring in the United States, are you optimistic or pessimistic about the nation's future? Respond to this question in a personal essay.

Networking

9. In small groups, discuss the issues raised by Cose's essay and whether or not you think his approach is fair and balanced. Offer a summary of your discussion to the class.

10. Access the U.S. Census Bureau's website, and examine the most recent data on race and ethnicity. What do these data suggest about future demographic trends? Write a brief summary of your findings.

American Dreamer

BHARATI MUKHERJEE

Bharati Mukherjee was born in Calcutta, India, in 1940. She attended the universities of Calcutta and Baroda, where she received a master's degree in English and ancient English culture. In 1961 she came to the United States to attend the Writer's Workshop at the University of Iowa, receiving a Ph.D. degree in English and comparative literature. Mukherjee became an American citizen in 1988; she is married to the writer Clark Blaise, with whom she has published two books, *Days and Nights in Calcutta* and *The Sorrow of the Terror*. Mukherjee's books of fiction include *The Middleman and Other Stories*, which won the 1988 National Book Critics Circle Award for fiction; *Jasmine* (1989); *The Holder of the World* (1993); and *The Tree Bride* (2004). She is currently professor of English at the University of California at Berkeley. In the following essay, which was published in 1993 in *Mother Jones*, Mukherjee displays both narrative power and keen analytical strength in rejecting any hyphenated status as an American.

Before Reading

Mukherjee, writing in 1993, hyphenates such words as African-American and Asian-American. As a matter of style, why don't we use hyphenated race compounds today? Why do these terms even exist?

The United States exists as a sovereign nation. "America," in contrast, exists as a myth of democracy and equal opportunity to live by, or as an ideal goal to reach. 1

I am a naturalized U.S. citizen, which means that, unlike native-born citizens, I had to prove to the U.S. government that I merited citizenship. What I didn't have to disclose was that I desired "America," which to me is the stage for the drama of self-transformation. 2

I was born in Calcutta and first came to the United States—to Iowa City, to be precise—on a summer evening in 1961. I flew into a small airport surrounded by cornfields and pastures, ready to carry out the two commands my father had written out for me the night before I left Calcutta: Spend two years studying creative writing at the Iowa Writers' Workshop, then come back home and marry the bridegroom he selected for me from our caste and class. 3

In traditional Hindu families like ours, men provided and women were provided for. My father was a patriarch and I a pliant daughter. The neighborhood I'd grown up in was homogeneously Hindu, Bengali-speaking, and middle-class. I didn't expect myself to ever disobey or disappoint my father by setting my own goals and taking charge of my future. 4

When I landed in Iowa 35 years ago, I found myself in a society in which almost everyone was Christian, white, and moderately well-off. In the women's dormitory I lived in my first year, apart from six international graduate students (all of us were from Asia and considered "exotic"), the only non-Christian was Jewish, and the only nonwhite an African-American from Georgia. I didn't anticipate then, that over the next 35 years, the Iowa population would become so diverse that it would have 6,931 children from non-English-speaking homes registered as students in its schools, nor that Iowans would be in the grip of a cultural crisis in which resentment against immigrants, particularly refugees from Vietnam, Sudan, and Bosnia, as well as unskilled Spanish-speaking workers, would become politicized enough to cause the Immigration and Naturalization Service to open an "enforcement" office in Cedar Rapids in October for the tracking and deporting of undocumented aliens. 5

In Calcutta in the '50s, I heard no talk of "identity crisis"—communal   6
or individual. The concept itself—of a person not knowing who he or she
is—was unimaginable in our hierarchical, classification-obsessed society.
One's identity was fixed, derived from religion, caste, patrimony, and
mother tongue. A Hindu Indian's last name announced his or her forefathers' caste and place of origin. A Mukherjee could *only* be a Brahmin
from Bengal. Hindu tradition forbade intercaste, interlanguage, interethnic
marriages. Bengali tradition even discouraged emigration: To remove oneself from Bengal was to dilute true culture.

Until the age of 8, I lived in a house crowded with 40 or 50 relatives.   7
My identity was viscerally connected with ancestral soil and genealogy. I
was who I was because I was Dr. Sudhir Lal Mukherjee's daughter,
because I was a Hindu Brahmin, because I was Bengali-speaking, and
because my *desh*—the Bengali word for homeland—was an East Bengal
village called Faridpur.

The University of Iowa classroom was my first experience of coedu-   8
cation. And after not too long, I fell in love with a fellow student named
Clark Blaise, an American of Canadian origin, and impulsively married
him during a lunch break in a lawyer's office above a coffee shop.

That act cut me off forever from the rules and ways of upper-middle-   9
class life in Bengal, and hurled me into a New World life of scary
improvisations and heady explorations. Until my lunch-break wedding, I
had seen myself as an Indian foreign student who intended to return to
India to live. The five-minute ceremony in the lawyer's office suddenly
changed me into a transient with conflicting loyalties to two very different cultures.

The first 10 years into marriage, years spent mostly in my husband's   10
native Canada, I thought of myself as an expatriate Bengali permanently
stranded in North America because of destiny or desire. My first novel, *The
Tiger's Daughter*, embodies the loneliness I felt but could not acknowledge,
even to myself, as I negotiated the no man's land between the country of my
past and the continent of my present. Shaped by memory, textured with nostalgia for a class and culture I had abandoned, this novel quite naturally
became an expression of the expatriate consciousness.

It took me a decade of painful introspection to put nostalgia in per-   11
spective and to make the transition from expatriate to immigrant. After
a 14-year stay in Canada, I forced my husband and our two sons to
relocate to the United States. But the transition from foreign student to
U.S. citizen, from detached onlooker to committed immigrant, has not
been easy.

culture

The years in Canada were particularly harsh. Canada is a country   12
that officially, and proudly, resists cultural fusion. For all its rhetoric
about a cultural "mosaic," Canada refuses to renovate its national self-
image to include its changing complexion. It is a New World country
with Old World concepts of a fixed, exclusivist national identity. Canadian official rhetoric designated me as one of the "visible minority"
who, even though I spoke the Canadian languages of English and
French, was straining "the absorptive capacity" of Canada. Canadians
of color were routinely treated as "not real" Canadians. One example:
In 1985 a terrorist bomb, planted in an Air-India jet on Canadian soil,
blew up after leaving Montreal, killing 329 passengers, most of whom
were Canadians of Indian origin. The prime minister of Canada at the
time, Brian Mulroney, phoned the prime minister of India to offer Canada's condolences for India's loss.

Those years of race-related harassments in Canada politicized me and   13
deepened my love of the ideals embedded in the American Bill of Rights.
I don't forget that the architects of the Constitution and the Bill of
Rights were white males and slaveholders. But through their declaration,
they provided us with the enthusiasm for human rights, and the initial
framework from which other empowerments could be conceived and
enfranchised communities expanded.

I am a naturalized U.S. citizen and I take my American citizenship   14
very seriously. I am not an economic refugee, nor am I a seeker of political asylum. I am a voluntary immigrant. I became a citizen by choice,
not by simple accident of birth. important.

Yet these days, questions such as who is an American and what is   15
American culture are being posed with belligerence, and being answered
with violence. Scapegoating of immigrants has once again become the
politicians' easy remedy for all that ails the nation. Hate speeches fill
auditoriums for demagogues willing to profit from stirring up racial ani-
mosity. An April Gallup poll indicated that half of Americans would like
to bar almost all legal immigration for the next five years.

The United States, like every sovereign nation, has a right to formu-   16
late its immigration policies. But in this decade of continual, large-scale
diasporas, it is imperative that we come to some agreement about who
"we" are, and what our goals are for the nation, now that our community includes people of many races, ethnicities, languages, and religions.

The debate about American culture and American identity has to   17
date been monopolized largely by Eurocentrists and ethnocentrists whose
rhetoric has been flamboyantly divisive, pitting a phantom "us" against

a demonized "them." All countries view themselves by their ideals. Indians idealize the cultural continuum, the inherent value system of India, and are properly incensed when foreigners see nothing but poverty, intolerance, strife, and injustice. *ethical*

[Americans see themselves as the embodiments of liberty, openness,   18
and individualism, even as the world judges them for drugs, crime, violence, bigotry, militarism, and homelessness.] I was in Singapore in 1994 when the American teenager Michael Fay was sentenced to caning for having spray-painted some cars. While I saw Fay's actions as those of an individual, and his sentence as too harsh, the overwhelming local sentiment was that vandalism was an "American" crime, and that flogging Fay would deter Singapore youths from becoming "Americanized." Conversely, in 1994, in Tavares, Florida, the Lake County School Board announced its policy (since overturned) requiring middle school teachers to instruct their students that American culture, by which the board meant European-American culture, is inherently "superior to other foreign or historic cultures." The policy's misguided implication was that culture in the United States has not been affected by the American Indian, African-American, Latin-American, and Asian-American segments of the population. The sinister implication was that our national identity is so fragile that it can absorb diverse and immigrant cultures only by recontextualizing them as deficient.

Our nation is unique in human history in that the founding idea of   19
"America" was in opposition to the tenet that a nation is a collection of like-looking, like-speaking, like-worshipping people. The primary criterion for nationhood in Europe is homogeneity of culture, race, and religion—which has contributed to blood-soaked balkanization in the former Yugoslavia and the former Soviet Union.

America's pioneering European ancestors gave up the easy homoge-   20
neity of their native countries for a new version of Utopia. [Now, in the 1990s, we have the exciting chance to follow that tradition and assist in the making of a new American culture that differs from both the enforced assimilation of a "melting pot" and the Canadian model of a multicultural "mosaic."] *setting*

The multicultural mosaic implies a contiguity of fixed, self-sufficient,   21
utterly distinct cultures. Multiculturalism, as it has been practiced in the United States in the past 10 years, implies the existence of a central culture, ringed by peripheral cultures. The fallout of official multiculturalism is the establishment of one culture as the norm and the rest as aberrations. At the same time, the multiculturalist emphasis on race- and

ethnicity-based group identity leads to a lack of respect for individual differences within each group, and to vilification of those individuals who place the good of the nation above the interests of their particular racial or ethnic communities.

We must be alert to the dangers of an "us" vs. "them" mentality. In 22 California, this mentality is manifesting itself as increased violence between minority, ethnic communities. The attack on Korean-American merchants in South Central Los Angeles in the wake of the Rodney King beating trial is only one recent example of the tragic side effects of this mentality. On the national level, the politicization of ethnic identities has encouraged the scapegoating of legal immigrants, who are blamed for economic and social problems brought about by flawed domestic and foreign policies.

We need to discourage the retention of cultural memory if the aim of 23 that retention is cultural balkanization. We must think of American culture and nationhood as a constantly reforming, transmogrifying "we."

In this age of diasporas, one's biological identity may not be one's only 24 identity. Erosions and accretions come with the act of emigration. The experience of cutting myself off from a biological homeland and settling in an adopted homeland that is not always welcoming to its dark-complexioned citizens has tested me as a person, and made me the writer I am today.

I choose to describe myself on my own terms as an American, rather 25 than as an Asian-American. Why is it that hyphenation is imposed only on non-white Americans? Rejecting hyphenation is my refusal to categorize the cultural landscape into a center and its peripheries; it is to demand that the American nation deliver the promises of its dream and its Constitution to all its citizens equally.

My rejection of hyphenation has been misrepresented as race treachery 26 by some India-born academics on U.S. campuses who have appointed themselves guardians of the "purity" of ethnic cultures. Many of them, though they reside permanently in the United States and participate in its economy, consistently denounce American ideals and institutions. They direct their rage at me because, by becoming a U.S. citizen and exercising my voting rights, I have invested in the present and not the past; because I have committed myself to help shape the future of my adopted homeland; and because I celebrate racial and cultural mongrelization.

What excites me is that as a nation we have not only the chance to 27 retain those values we treasure from our original cultures but also the chance to acknowledge that the outer forms of those values are likely to change. Among Indian immigrants, I see a great deal of guilt about the inability to hang on to what they commonly term "pure culture."

Parents express rage or despair at their U.S.-born children's forgetting of, or indifference to, some aspects of Indian culture. Of those parents I would ask: What is it we have lost if our children are acculturating into the culture in which we are living? Is it so terrible that our children are discovering or are inventing homelands for themselves?

Some first-generation Indo-Americans, embittered by racism and by 28 unofficial "glass ceilings," construct a phantom identity, more-Indian-than-Indians-in-India, as a defense against marginalization. I ask: Why don't you get actively involved in fighting discrimination? Make your voice heard. Choose the forum most appropriate for you. If you are a citizen, let your vote count. Reinvest your energy and resources into revitalizing your city's disadvantaged residents and neighborhoods. Know your constitutional rights, and when they are violated, use the agencies of redress the Constitution makes available to you. Expect change, and when it comes, deal with it!

As a writer, my literary agenda begins by acknowledging that Amer- 29 ica has transformed me. It does not end until I show that I (along with the hundreds of thousands of immigrants like me) am minute-by-minute transforming America. The transformation is a two-way process: It affects both the individual and the national-cultural identity.

Others who write stories of migration often talk of arrival at a new 30 place as a loss, the loss of communal memory and the erosion of an original culture. I want to talk of arrival as a gain. *ethical*

Thinking about the Essay

1. What is the significance of the title? How is Mukherjee a dreamer? Why does the idea of America inspire dreams? What impact does the American Dream have on one's identity? For example, Mukherjee says in paragraph 7 that she had a clear sense of identity when she was in India. How has this sense of identity changed now that she is an American?

2. What is Mukherjee's purpose in writing this essay? Does she want to tell a story, analyze an issue, argue a position? Remember that this article appeared in *Mother Jones*, a progressive or left-of-center magazine. What does her primary audience tell you about her intentions?

3. Why does Mukherjee divide her essay into four parts? What are the relationships among these sections? Why has she used this pattern of organization? Where does she employ comparison and contrast and definition to achieve coherence among these parts?

4. Mukherjee refers to Eurocentrics and ethnocentrics. What do these terms mean to you? Discuss your understanding of these terms with other members of the class.

Responding in Writing

5. Write a summary of Mukherjee's essay, capturing as many of her major ideas as possible in no more than 300 words.

6. Write your own essay titled "American Dreamer," referring specifically to the dreams that immigrants—perhaps even you or members of your family—have had about coming to this country.

7. Mukherjee asserts, "We must be alert to the dangers of an 'us' vs. 'them' mentality (paragraph 23)." Write an argumentative essay responding to this statement, referring to other assertions by Mukherjee to amplify your own position.

Networking

8. In small groups, develop a summary of Mukherjee's essay. Next, compose a list of outstanding questions you still might have about her essay. For example, has she overlooked or diminished the importance of a specific topic, or has she personalized the subject too much? Finally, collaborate on a letter to the author in which you lay out your concerns.

9. Download from a search engine all the information that you can find about Bharati Mukherjee. Then compose a brief analytical profile of the author in which you highlight her career and the impact that living in several cultures has had on her work. Use "American Dreamer" as a foundation for this presentation, and be certain to provide citations for your Web research. (For information on citing online sources, see Appendix A: Conducting Research in the New Global Era.)

Why Diversity Matters

Lee C. Bollinger

Lee C. Bollinger is an acclaimed First Amendment scholar and university administrator. Born in Santa Rosa, California, in 1946 and raised there and in Bend, Oregon, Bollinger attended the University of Oregon (B.S., 1968) and subsequently received his law degree from Columbia University Law School (1971). As president of two distinguished universities—Michigan and then Columbia—Bollinger has been in the front lines in the debate over college diversity and affirmative action. Bollinger's support for an open, pluralistic educational culture and society is inherent in his scholarship, notably *The Tolerant Society: Freedom of Speech and Extremist Speech in America* (1968) and *Images of a Free*

Press (1991). In the following essay from the June 1, 2007, issue of *The Chronicle of Higher Education*, Bollinger claims that we cannot understand America—or the world—without being exposed to a full spectrum of peoples and beliefs.

Before Reading

Do you think that affirmative action is still relevant to college life today, or have we moved into what some call a "post-racial" environment that makes affirmative action unnecessary? Explain.

During this frantic admissions season, it is easy for our applicants to think that the most important moment in their college career is when they rip open the mail to find out where they got in and where they didn't. But we in higher education understand that the admissions process has less to do with rewarding each student's past performance—although high performance is clearly essential—than it does with building a community of diverse learners who will thrive together and teach one another.

When it comes to creating the kinds of diversity we sorely need in this country, however, disturbing trends and setbacks are making it difficult for many public schools and universities to succeed. The reality is that as much as we may want to believe that racial prejudice is a relic of history, conscience and experience tell us better.

Even now, the Supreme Court is considering two public-school cases out of Washington and Kentucky that would subvert the resounding principle that *Brown v. Board of Education* established 53 years ago on May 17, 1954, that "separate is inherently unequal." If successful, both cases would ban local districts from developing voluntary desegregation programs that seek to maintain racial balance in our schools and counteract the worst resegregation crisis we have faced since the early days of the civil-rights movement.

According to the 2000 census, only 14 percent of white students attend multiracial schools, while nearly 40 percent of both black and Latino students attend intensely segregated schools where 90 percent to 100 percent are from minority groups. Further, almost half of all black and Latino students attend schools where three-quarters or more

Lee C. Bollinger, "Why Diversity Matters," *The Chronicle of Higher Education*, Washington: June 1, 2007, Vol. 53, Iss. 39, pg. B20. © 2007 Lee C. Bollinger. Reprinted by permission of the author.

students are poor, compared with only 5 percent of white students; in extremely poor schools, 80 percent of the students are black and Latino.

Beyond elementary and secondary schools, higher education continues to face its own challenges, including statewide bans on affirmative action. Recent news reports have noted how hard some of our leading public universities are working to revise recruitment and admissions policies to comply with those bans without jeopardizing the diversity of the students who attend their campuses. What's important, however, is why those universities are trying so hard to maximize diversity—even though no law requires it, and in several states affirmative action is explicitly forbidden.

I have been deeply involved in two U.S. Supreme Court cases—*Gratz v. Bollinger* and *Grutter v. Bollinger* (2003)—that ultimately upheld the constitutionality of affirmative-action policies at public universities. Let me suggest why, having vindicated the legality of affirmative action, higher education must not lose the practical and political battles to maintain racially, ethnically, and socioeconomically diverse student bodies.

Universities understand that to remain competitive, their most important obligation is to determine—and then deliver—what future graduates will need to know about their world and how to gain that knowledge. While the last century witnessed a new demand for specialized research, prizing the expert's vertical mastery of a single field, the emerging global reality calls for new specialists who can synthesize a diversity of fields and draw quick connections among them. In reordering our sense of the earth's interdependence, that global reality also cries out for a new age of exploration, with students displaying the daring, curiosity, and mettle to discover and learn entirely new areas of knowledge.

The experience of arriving on a campus to live and study with classmates from a diverse range of backgrounds is essential to students' training for this new world, nurturing in them an instinct to reach out instead of clinging to the comforts of what seems natural or familiar. We know that connecting with people very—or even slightly—different from ourselves stimulates the imagination; and when we learn to see the world through a multiplicity of eyes, we only make ourselves more nimble in mastering—and integrating—the diverse fields of knowledge awaiting us.

Affirmative-action programs help achieve that larger goal. And the universities that create and carry them out do so not only because overcoming longstanding obstacles to people of color and women in higher education is the right thing to do, but also because policies that encourage a comprehensive diversity help universities achieve their mission. Specifically, they are indispensable in training future leaders how to lead all of society, and by attracting a diverse cadre of students and faculty, they increase our universities' chances of filling in gaps in our knowledge with research and teaching on a wider—and often uncovered—array of subjects.

At the same time, such policies foster a greater spirit of community 10 on campuses as well as between universities and the cities and town they call home. The days of the gated university are past, and affirmative action is crucial to making our universities welcoming places for community members to visit, take classes, and inspire their children to dream.

Opponents of affirmative action forget that broader purpose in their 11 demand for what they see as a "pure" admissions meritocracy based on how students perform in high school and on standardized tests. But it is far less important to reward past performance—and impossible to isolate a candidate's objective talent from the contextual realities shaping that performance—than to make the best judgment about which applicants can contribute to help form the strongest class that will study and live together. For graduate schools and employment recruiters, that potential is the only "merit" that matters because in an increasingly global world, it is impossible to compete without already knowing how to imagine, understand, and collaborate with a diverse and fluid set of colleagues, partners, customers, and government leaders.

By abolishing all public affirmative-action programs, voters in Cali- 12 fornia and Michigan (and other states if affirmative-action opponents are successful) have not only toppled a ladder of equal opportunity in higher education that so many of us fought to build and the Supreme Court upheld in 2003. They will almost assuredly make their great public universities less diverse—and have, in fact, done so in California, where the impact has become clear—and therefore less attractive options to potential students and, ultimately, less valuable contributors to our globalized society.

As the president of a private university, I am glad that independent 13 institutions retain the autonomy to support diversity efforts that make our graduates more competitive candidates for employers and graduate schools, as well as better informed citizens in our democracy and the world. But as an alumnus of one public university and a former president of another, I worry about a future in which one of America's great success stories slides backward from the mission of providing generations of young Americans with access to an affordable higher education.

From the establishment of the land-grant colleges in the 1860s to the 14 GI Bill after World War II to the Higher Education Act of 1965, our public universities have advanced the notion that in educating college students for the world they will inhabit, it is necessary to bring people together from diverse parts of society and to educate them in that context. Far from being optional or merely enriching, it is the very essence of what we mean by a liberal or humanistic education.

It is also vital for establishing a cohesive, truly national society—one 15 in which rising generations learn to overcome the biases they absorb as children while also appreciating the unique talents their colleagues bring to any equation. Only education can get us there.

As Thurgood Marshall knew so well: "The legal system can open 16 doors and sometimes even knock down walls. But it cannot build bridges. . . . We will only attain freedom if we learn to appreciate what is different and muster the courage to discover what is fundamentally the same." Cutting affirmative action short now only betrays that history of social progress. And, in the process, it threatens the core value of academically renowned public universities at a time when many Americans list rising tuition costs as one of their gravest economic concerns.

All of this leads to the conclusion that diversity—one of the great 17 strengths of American education—is under siege today. At the elementary- and secondary-school levels, resegregation is making it exceedingly difficult for minority students to get the resources that inspire rising generations to apply to and then attend college. At the same time, the elimination of affirmative action programs at our public universities is keeping admissions officials from lifting those same students up to offset the structural inequalities they had to face in getting there.

As we honor the parents, students, lawyers, and nine justices who 18 spoke with one voice in *Brown* on that May day 53 years ago, we would all do well to remember that when it comes to responsible diversity programs—those that help our public schools and our great public universities fulfill their historic roles as avenues of economic and cultural mobility—what is wise is also what is just.

Thinking about the Essay

1. What is Bollinger's **claim** and where does he state it? On what **warrant** does Bollinger base his claim? Discuss why you agree or disagree with his claim and the warrant underpinning it.

2. Where and why does Bollinger use emotional and ethical appeals in his approach to his primary audience? At what points does he stress his authority in addressing this audience?

3. What minor propositions does Bollinger use to buttress his claim?

4. What forms of evidence does Bollinger use to support his argument?

5. How does Bollinger refute the arguments of those opposed to affirmative action? Do you find his strategy to be effective? Justify your response.

Responding in Writing

6. Summarize the main points of reasoning that inform Bollinger's claim, and then discuss the extent to which you find his argument reasonable and convincing.

7. Bollinger asserts that students must be educated for twenty-first century realities. Write an essay in which you explore the relevance of diversity and affirmative action to this challenge.

8. Write a response to Bollinger explaining why (or why not) you agree with his premise, and how his essay reflects life and conditions on your college campus.

Networking

9. Form small groups and debate the merits of diversity and affirmative action in higher education. Select one member of the group to join a class forum presenting the results of your debate.

10. Go online and read about the decision of the Supreme Court in the two public-school cases that Bollinger alludes to in paragraph 3. How do these decisions relate to Bollinger's conclusion that diversity is under siege today?

Who Is a Whiz Kid?

TED GUP

Ted Gup has had a varied and distinguished career as a freelance writer, investigative reporter, attorney, editor, and college professor. He was born in Lima, Ohio, in 1950; attended Trinity College (Ireland); graduated from Brandeis University; and received his law degree from Case Western Reserve University, where he taught for many years. Gup has contributed articles to numerous newspapers and magazines including *National Geographic*, *The Washington Post*, *The New York Times*, *Newsweek*, and *The Wall Street Journal*. His award-winning books are *The Book of Honor* (2001), *Nation of Secrets* (2007), and *A Secret Gift* (2010). Gup currently is professor and chair of the journalism department of Emerson College in Boston. In this essay from the popular journal *Newsweek*, Gup examines the dangers inherent in stereotyping Asian-American students.

Before Reading

Do you think that you can stereotype students based on their racial, ethnic, or social background? Why or why not? What problems might you raise in stereotyping such students? Have you ever been stereotyped by teachers, peers, or others—or have you engaged in stereotyping?

Shortly after joining a national magazine some years ago as a writer, 1 I found myself watching in horror as the week's cover story was prepared. The story was about "Asian-American whiz kids," and it featured a series of six student portraits, each face radiating with an intellectual brilliance. Being new to the enterprise, I was at first tentative in my criticism, cautioning that such a story was inherently biased and fueled racial and ethnic stereotypes. My criticism was dismissed. "This is something good we are saying about them," one top editor remarked. I reduced my criticism to writing. "What," I asked, "would be the response if the cover were about 'Jewish whiz kids'? Would anyone really dare to produce such an obviously offensive story?" My memo was ignored. Not long after, the cover appeared on the nation's newsstands, and the criticism began to fly. The editors were taken aback.

As a former Fulbright Scholar to China I have long taken a strong in- 2 terest in the portrayal of Asian-Americans. But my interest went well beyond the academic. Even as the cover was being prepared, I was waiting to adopt my first son from Korea. His name was to be David. He was five months old when he arrived. This did not stop even some otherwise sophisticated friends from volunteering that he would no doubt be a good student. Probably a mathematician, they opined, with a tone that uncomfortably straddled jest and prediction. I tried to take it all with good humor, this idea that a five-month-old who could not yet sit up, speak a word or control his bowels was already destined for academic greatness. Even his major seemed foreordained.

Many Asian-Americans seem to walk an uneasy line between taking 3 pride in their remarkable achievements and needing to shake off stereotypes. The jokes abound. There is the apocryphal parent who asks, "Where is the other point?" when his or her child scores a 99 on a test. Another familiar refrain has the young Asian-American student enumerating his or her hobbies: "studying, studying and more studying."

Several months after David arrived he and I entered a small mom- 4 and-pop convenience store in our neighborhood. The owners were Korean. I noticed that the husband, standing behind the cash register, was eyeing my son. "Is he Korean?" he asked. "Yes," I nodded. He reached out for him and took him into his arms. "He'll be good in math," declared the man. "My God," I muttered. Not him, too!

It was preposterous. It was funny. And it was unnerving. Embedded   5
in such elevated expectations were real threats to my son. Suppose, I wondered, he should turn out to be only a mediocre student, or, worse yet, not a student at all. I resented the stereotypes and saw them for what they were, the other side of the coin of racism. It is easy to delude one's self into thinking it harmless to offer racial compliments, but that is an inherent contradiction in terms. Such sweeping descriptives, be they negative or positive, deny the one thing most precious to all peoples— individuality. These stereotypes are pernicious for two reasons. First, such attributes are relative and tend to pit one race against another. Witness the seething enmity in many inner cities between Korean store owners and their African-American patrons. Stereotypes that hint at superiority in one race implicitly suggest inferiority in another. They are ultimately divisive, and in their most virulent form, even deadly. Who can forget the costs of the Aryan myth?

Such stereotypes also place a crushing burden on Asian-Americans.   6
Few would deny that disproportionate numbers of Asian surnames appear each year among the winners of the Westinghouse Science prizes or in the ranks of National Merit Scholars. But it might be a reflection of parental influences, personal commitment and cultural predilections, not genetic predisposition. A decade ago, as a Fulbright Lecturer in Beijing, I saw firsthand the staggering hours my Chinese students devoted to their studies. Were my students in the United States to invest similar time in their books I would have every reason to expect similar results.

I have often been told that Koreans are the "Jews of Asia," a refer-   7
ence to both their reported skills in business and their inherent intelligence. As a Jew, I cannot help but wince at such descriptions. I remember being one of the very few of my faith in a Midwest boarding school. There were many presumptions weighing on me, most of them grounded in my religion. My own classroom performance almost single handedly disabused my teachers of the myth that Jews were academically gifted. I barely made it through. Whether it was a lack of intelligence or simple rebellion against expectation, I do not know. I do know that more than once the fact that I was Jewish was raised as evidence that I could and should be doing better. Expectations based on race, be they raised or lowered, are no less galling.

David is now in the first grade. He is already taking math with the   8
second graders and asking me about square roots and percentiles.

I think back to the Korean merchant who took him in his arms and pronounced him a math whiz. Was he right? Do Asian-Americans have it easier, endowed with some special strand of DNA? The answer is a resounding no. Especially in our house. My son David has learning disabilities to overcome and what progress he has made is individual in the purest and most heroic sense. No one can or should take that away from him, suggesting that he is just another wunderkind belonging to a favored race.

A year after my first son arrived, we adopted his brother from Korea.   9
His name is Matthew. Let it be known that Matthew couldn't care less about math. He's a bug man. Slugs and earthworms. I suspect he will never be featured on any cover stories about Asian-American whiz kids, but I will continue to resist anything and anyone who attempts to dictate either his interests or his abilities based on race or place of birth. Bugs are fine by me and should be more than fine by him.

Thinking about the Essay

1. How does the writer's introductory paragraph set the stage for the development of his claim or argument?

2. Why does Gup inject himself into this essay, frequently employing an ''I'' or first-person point of view? What is his purpose? Do you find this strategy to be effective or not? Justify your response.

3. What supporting points does the writer make in support of his claim? Where do they appear?

4. Where does the writer use comparison and contrast to bolster his argument?

5. Do you find the closing paragraph to be effective? Why or why not?

Responding in Writing

6. Write a personal account of your contact with students from different races, ethnicities, and cultural backgrounds. Explain how you have managed to avoid stereotyping such students, how you were stereotyped, or how you stereotyped a certain group.

7. Argue for or against the proposition that Asian-American students actually are superior to other groups of students. Be certain to support your claim with evidence.

8. Compose a classification essay that describes and analyzes various types of students who typically populate college campuses.

Networking

9. In small groups, discuss the harmful nature of stereotypes in labeling students but also in the broader society. Appoint one member of the group to take notes and a second member to make a summary to the class.

10. Locate at least three blogs that deal with Asian-American students or students of any other ethnic or racial group. Monitor these blogs for a week, and then write a précis about your findings.

Beyond Black and White: The Hawaiian President

DWIGHT N. HOPKINS

Dwight N. Hopkins, who was born in Richmond, Virginia, in 1953, is a professor of theology at the University of Chicago. He holds degrees from Harvard University (B.A., 1976), Union Theological Seminary (M.Div., 1984), and the University of Cape Town (Ph.D., 2000). Much of Hopkins's work deals with the intersection of race and religion in the modern world. Among his books are *Shoes That Fit Our Feet: Sources for a Constructive Black Theology* (1993), *Heart and Head: Black Theology—Past, Present, and Future* (2002), *Being Human: Race, Culture, and Religion* (2005), and *Walk Together Children: Black and Womanist Theologies, Church and Theological Education* (2010). In this essay, which appeared in the February 10, 2009, issue of *The Christian Century*, Hopkins offers a provocative assessment of Barack Obama as a new type of American.

Before Reading

Do you think that Americans will ever transcend their preoccupation with race? Why or why not?

Since the November presidential election, friends, colleagues and casual acquaintances throughout the United States and across the world have written me and claimed Barack Obama as the son of their state, race, country or region. Of course, countless black Americans have celebrated the fact that "in our lifetime, one of us is in the White House."

How is it possible that Hawaii claims Obama as its own; Indonesia   2
and parts of Asia perceive him as reflective of their experiences; Kenya cries in ecstasy to have a blood relative on 1600 Pennsylvania Avenue; all of Africa embraces him as a close kin of that continent; Kansans believe his roots sink deep within their soil; and black Americans, without much critical self-reflection, relish the idea that the 44th president is black like them?

The fact that Obama is perceived as belonging in a variety of ways   3
to such disparate groups points up at least one persistent and absurd concept in race relations in America: the one-drop rule.

Coming out of slavery and segregation, the one-drop rule was one of   4
the most egregious dimensions of white supremacy. When Africans arrived in the New World in chains, all of their children were called black and thus were enslaved, even if one biological parent was white. If it was determined that a person who looked white had any African or black ancestors, that white person was reclassified as black. A drop of black blood in one's genealogy could instantly transform a white citizen into a black slave.

Long after slavery the one-drop rule persisted in racial classification,   5
and oddly enough, was eventually accepted by black Americans. This led to all manner of absurdities. Walter White, a pioneering leader of the NAACP, was so white-looking that he once attended a high-society function where some of the whites present wondered why he had brought his "black" wife. The irony was that White was, according to the one-drop rule, black, and his so-called black wife was actually white.

The one-drop-of-black-blood rule is unique to the U.S. It presupposes   6
a black-white paradigm. On one extreme are "white" people, on the other, "black" people. Lost in these absolutes is the kaleidoscope of Asian Americans, Caribbean Americans, African Americans, Pacific Islander Americans, Latino-Hispanic Americans, Middle Eastern Americans, European Americans, American Indians and all the complexities of identity that make us unique human beings.

What race is Obama? Shortly after the election, the venerable John   7
Lewis, a member of Congress from Georgia, stated that no black person who had come out of segregation and the civil rights movement could have been elected the first black president. And in fact Obama did not. Obama redefines what it means to be black. His ancestors did not come from the glorious West African empires of centuries ago. To my knowledge, he has no biological connection to those empires' encounter with

the European slave trade. His family history does not flow from de jure and de facto segregation. During the civil rights struggle, the black power movement and reparation efforts, he was living in Asia and the Pacific Islands. He has never lived in the (segregated or nonsegregated) southern U.S. In his major speeches, he has not mentioned two heroic icons of black manhood—Martin Luther King Jr. and Malcolm X. He was not born into nor did he grow up in a black church. He did not assemble black preachers and civil rights stalwarts together and from that base launch his presidential campaign.

Obama is Hawaiian. He is familiar with flip-flops, surfing, snorkel- 8 ing, Aloha Spirit and 'Ohana family values. Before he lived in Chicago's segregated black community, his social reality was Asia and the Pacific more than the southern U.S. Born in Hawaii in 1961, he grew up along-side Japanese Hawaiians, Chinese Hawaiians, Filipino Hawaiians, Pacific Island Hawaiians, Native Hawaiians and white Hawaiians. The black-white paradigm of the mainland did not dominate his reality. In fact, whites were and still are a minority in Hawaii, and except for the occasional vacationer and military personnel, blacks were and are a rarity.

Obama spent ages six to ten in Indonesia, going to school and speak- 9 ing Indonesian. His Indonesian stepfather gave him an ape as a pet. This pet was not caged but lived in their backyard.

Obama was nurtured in a white environment. His Kansan white 10 mother (not from the South) reared him with the help of his white grandparents. (All accounts indicate that no black men or women, boys or girls ever lived in his home until he married and had his own children.) To illustrate how different his upbringing was from that of most black Americans, who call their grandmothers Big Mama, Ma Dear or Grandma, Obama's intimate name for his white grandmother was Toot—the Hawaiian endearment for grandmother.

Obama has never identified himself as an Afrocentric person or a 11 pan-Africanist. Yet he is more African than the overwhelming majority of black Americans. There need be no genetic test to find out what West African "tribe" his ancestors came from centuries ago. His ancestry is from Kenya, a country in East Africa from which the enslaved rarely came. His father voluntarily came to the U.S. as a student in 1959. Before that, he was a goat herder in Kenya. President Obama has visited the exact location where his father and other ancestors were born. He understands the "tribal" language, politics, economics, religions, foods, songs, indigenous names, folktales, clothing, dances, illnesses, personalities and gravesites. When he pours libations (spilling liquids on the ground in memory of the dead), he is not talking about unknown Africans lost in the slave trade. Like Africans born on the continent, he can pour libations to his specific blood family members and directly on family gravesites. Some of those burial grounds ate still next to family compounds in Kenya. Obama doesn't have to change his English "slave master's" name to an African one; his name is already African.

Growing up, Obama was certainly aware of the mainland's obsession 12 with race. Witness the Afro hairstyle he adopted at Punahou, one of the most elite private schools in the U.S., and his idolizing of NBA star Julius "Dr. J" Erving. But it wasn't until he was 22 and came to the heavily segregated South Side of Chicago that, for the first time in a sustained manner, he engaged the particularities (and some might say the peculiarities) of traditional black-white race relations, including the one-drop rule.

Segregated Chicago offered Obama three things: a black family 13 through marriage, a black community through grass roots organizing and a black church through baptism.

While black Americans may not be quite right in their declaration that 14 Obama is only "one of us," the 44th president does symbolize a change in the U.S. If not going so far as to redefine race in America, Obama might expand what race means. Perhaps he will help the millions of Americans with black and white parents, black and Asian parents and black and Latino/Hispanic parents integrate the various tuggings of their identities–identities that have been too often forced into narrow racial options.

Like all American citizens, this Hawaiian, Polynesian, Indonesian, 15 Asian, white, Kenyan and black human being is caught up in the narrative of the black-white paradigm, a structure still rooted in the absurdity of the one-drop-of-black-blood rule. Yes, he is black. But no one can understand him deeply who does not appreciate the rainbow racial mixtures of his Hawaiian origins.

Thinking about the Essay

1. How does Hopkins's title reveal his purpose? What is his claim, and where does he state it?

2. Why does Hopkins begin in a personal mode? Which paragraphs constitute his introduction, and how does he use this introduction to structure the body of the essay?

3. Hopkins is writing for a specialized group of readers. Why would these readers be especially interested in his essay? Would a more general audience be equally absorbed by this article? Why or why not?

4. How successful do you think Hopkins is in explaining the paradox of race in America and how Barack Obama transcends conventional notions of black and white? Justify your assessment by referring to specific passages and **motifs** in the essay.

5. In part, this essay is about the limitations of racial categorization, but Hopkins is also interested in the causal connections that have perpetuated such classification throughout American history. Where in the essay does Hopkins analyze the reasons why Americans are so preoccupied with race and the effects of this obsession?

Responding in Writing

6. Hopkins argues that the election of Barack Obama to the presidency in 2008 is a watershed in the history of America's history of racial classification. In an argumentative essay, agree or disagree with the writer's claim.

7. In an **analytical essay**, explore the reasons why you think Americans have been so preoccupied with race. Do you think that today's younger Americans are moving beyond racial classification? Justify your response with compelling reasons.

8. Hopkins claims that Barack Obama is a "Hawaiian President." Explain why you agree or disagree with this notion.

Networking

9. Form two groups and debate the proposition that the election of Barack Obama to the presidency means that Americans have finally transcended the politics of race.

10. Go online and find out more about Barack Obama's life in Hawaii. Then construct your own profile of Obama based on this information.

Deportation Order

RANDA JARRAR

Randa Jarrar was born in Chicago in 1978. Of Egyptian and Jordanian heritage, she grew up in Kuwait and Egypt. At the age of thirteen, she moved back to the United States. She is an award-winning writer and translator living in Austin, Texas. Her first novel is *A Map of Home*. In this essay from a 2010 issue of *The Progressive*, Jarrar recounts a family crisis rooted in the complexities of U.S. immigration policy.

Randa Jarrar, "Deportation Order" from *The Progressive*, March 2010. Used by permission of *The Progressive*.

Before Reading

Should the children of documented or undocumented families residing in the United States be deported for any legal infraction? Why or why not?

Just after New Year's of 2005, my younger brother, Raed, then a 1
senior at the University of Maryland, came home to D.C. after visiting
our parents in Kuwait. The security people at Dulles Airport detained
and questioned him for hours, then told him he was a deportable alien.
He had two weeks to surrender to authorities. Once he did, he was sent
to a jail in Virginia.

A few days after his imprisonment, I got an e-mail from his lawyer 2
that he needed contact lens solution. I rushed out and bought it, sent it
off with his prisoner ID number on the envelope, went home, and spent
the rest of the day in bed.

Unlike my brother, I was born in the U.S., and never had to work 3
for my little blue passport. My Egyptian/Jordanian family did; they all
took tests and held little flags and swore to do or not do things—all but
my brother, who was too flaky at eighteen to fill out the proper forms
or take buses to the right offices. He was left behind in our family's
Becoming American journey. In 2001, he was living with students who
sold pot. When they got busted, he went to jail for five days, and did a
few dozen hours of community service. And he was being deported four
years later because that had been "a crime of moral turpitude."

My brother called me collect, and I got up the courage to ask him 4
what the jail in Virginia looked like.

"They let us congregate for religious reasons inside a small strip. They 5
seal it off with yellow tape. You can pray or talk inside the yellow line."

A few days later, my father called me in a panic. 6

"Your brother is turning into a fundie," he said. 7

"Don't be ridiculous." 8

"He told mom he is writing a sermon for this Friday's prayers." 9

I pictured my brother reading a sermon in the small space, his hand 10
resting on the yellow tape on the floor.

"That's so sweet," I said. 11

"It is not sweet; it is crazy. Please stop him. He will come out of that 12
jail a fanatic!"

"That'll never happen," I said. "Don't you know him at all? He is 13
just finding a way to cope." I couldn't tell my father that my brother
liked liquor and women too much to become religious.

In order to get the government to reverse the deportation, we hired a 14
psychologist to determine the level of hardship my brother's absence

would cause us. By the time the therapist called me, the lawyer had written me an e-mail saying I was the only sane person in my family.

His final court date was March 22. I met my parents in a hotel in the same building as the courthouse. At dinner the night before the hearing, my father couldn't figure out how to work the pepper shaker. He kept trying to find the magic way, and, finally, I reached over and twisted the top. "It's simple," he said, shocked. He always thinks things are much harder than they actually are. 15

After dinner, we took the elevator up to our rooms. "I'm sick," my father said. "The therapist gave me my file today. I need help." 16

I'd been waiting to hear those words all my life. 17

My mother, who has always hated therapists because she thinks all people talk about in therapy is what a terrible person she is, interrupted. "I passed the test. The doctor said I was severely depressed. I wanted him to think so! I wanted to prove the hardship!" She smiled and danced around the hotel room. 18

The morning of the hearing, we all sat in the waiting area with other families. The rows of white plastic chairs faced a wall. It felt like we were all on a plane, being deported. Inside the courtroom, my brother was on a monitor, defending his moral fiber. An hour passed. "Maybe the judge will just let him out after this," I said. 19

"That is wishful thinking," my father said, closing his eyes. Everything had to be like that pepper shaker. 20

Less than fifteen minutes later, the judge stopped the hearing. "I've heard enough," he said, leafing through dozens of family photos. 21

He released my brother and reversed the deportation order. 22

But it wasn't over. I had to map the jail, print out the directions, and sit in the car with my parents as they screamed at each other all the way from D.C., through traffic, across Virginia. 23

Four hours after we set out, we reached the jail. We parked outside the entrance and waited. My brother's silhouette appeared against the electric fence. Soon we were embracing him. His hair was shaved close. In the car, he told us stories of the men he'd been living with. 24

As we approached College Park, my father grew impatient with the printed map and the unfamiliar roads. He ignored my brother's directions, and soon we were going the wrong way up a highway road. After all we'd done, my father jeopardized our lives out of impatience. Or maybe he was determined that he wouldn't let the government do the destruction for him. In any case, by the time we reached my brother's apartment, we were all anxious to leave the small prison of the rental 25 car. We stood awkwardly around Raed's coffee table, reluctant to admit that we got along a lot easier in crisis. A few minutes passed, and we shuffled our feet and said goodbye. My brother waved to us from the doorway, as though we'd just spent the last few hours visiting, and were now heading home.

When my brother was four, he broke into a parked Cadillac in our 26 apartment building's parking lot. He and his best friend hung out in the big American car's velvety seats and pretended to drive, their short legs dangling high above the floor. A neighbor saw them and brought my brother home. My father yelled all that night. Then, he stood up, knowing what he had to do. He would take my brother to the police; he would put him in jail. To teach him a lesson. He would.

"Get ready," he told my brother. 27

I watched as my brother went to the front door, bent down, and 28 silently, without the smallest murmur of resistance, strapped on his small, leather shoes.

Then he straightened up, looked down the hallway, and waited. 29

Inside the courtroom, my brother was on a monitor, defending his 30 moral fiber.

Thinking about the Essay

1. How does the writer characterize various members of her family? What tone does she take in describing her mother, father, and brother? What causal connections do you detect between their behavior and the deportation order that Raed receives?

2. What elements of narration does Jarrar utilize in order to create a dramatic plot?

3. Would you say that Jarrar's main purpose is simply to tell a tale about her family, or does she have a broader purpose in mind? Might she be advancing an argument? Why or why not?

4. Many of the writer's paragraphs are very brief one-sentence units. What is your response to this strategy? Does this technique aid or damage the overall coherence and unity of the essay? Explain.

5. The last five paragraphs constitute Jarrar's conclusion. How does this end unit reinforce the issues raised in the body of her essay?

Responding in Writing

6. Argue for or against the proposition that anyone violating immigration policy should be eligible for deportation.

7. Compose an argumentative essay in which you support or oppose a "dream act" that provides a pathway to citizenship for undocumented immigrants.

8. Should the children of undocumented immigrants be eligible for in-state college tuition? Respond to this question in an argumentative essay.

Networking

9. Exchange your essay based on this reading with another class member. Then peer critique your partner's paper, focusing on the relative effectiveness of the argument.

10. Go online to find out more about deportation policies in the United States. Based on your findings, write a brief action report in which you advocate changes in specific policies.

The "Great Wall of America"

RICHARD RODRIGUEZ

Richard Rodriguez was born in San Francisco, California, in 1944. The son of Mexican immigrants, he moved during childhood to Sacramento, the capital of California. After high school, Rodriguez attended the University of California Berkeley and Columbia University, receiving degrees from these institutions. He achieved immediate success with his first book, *Hunger of Memory: The Education of Richard Rodriguez* (1982), a sensitive and revealing memoir of his childhood. His other books include *Days of Obligation: My Argument with My Mexican Father* (1992) and *Brown: The Last Discovery of America* (2002). Rodriguez contributes essays to many publications including *Time, American Scholar,* and *Mother Jones.* He also appears on National Public Radio and *PBS NewsHour.* In this essay, published in the *Los Angeles Times* in 2010, Rodriguez criticizes from a broad global perspective the utility of walls that separate nations and peoples.

Before Reading

The U.S.-Mexico border is almost 2,000 miles long. Can walls and other barriers prevent the passage of people back and forth across this border? Should they? Justify your response.

B etween cynicism and hypocrisy lies the 2,000-mile U.S.-Mexico border. 1
America is raising a wall in the desert to separate Mexican drug exporters from American drug consumers, to separate Latin American peasants
who will work for low wages from the Americans who would hire them.

The Great Wall of America, straddling less than half the length of the 2
border, descends into canyons and across the desert floor. For the Mexican, it represents a high hurdle. For the American, it is an attempt to
stop the Roadrunner's progress with an Acme Border Sealing Kit.

In some places the wall is made of tennis-court-style cyclone fencing 3
or dark mesh of the sort used for barbeque grills in public parks. In
other places the wall is a palisade of 20-foot-tall bars that make a cage
of both sides. The most emphatic segments are constructed of graffiti-
ready slabs of steel.

On the Mexican side, if you stand with your back to the wall, you 4
will see the poorest neighborhoods, built right up to the line. These
frayed, weedy streets have become the killing fields in an international
drug war; they are more daunting than the dangers of climbing the wall.

The traditional Mexican accommodation to moral failure—the bribed 5
policeman—has degenerated to lawlessness in places such as Juarez and
Tijuana, where police kill federal soldiers who kill police who kill drug
gangsters who kill other gangsters of the sort who did kill, apparently
with impunity, at least 15 teenagers celebrating a soccer victory. Punch
911 and you get the devil.

On the American side, if you stand with your back to the wall, you 6
will see distance, as the United States recedes from the border. There is a
shopping mall with big-box stores half a mile away. There is a highway
that eventually leads to suburban streets laid out in uniform blocks, and
cul-de-sacs where Mexican gardeners are the only ambulatory human life.

The suburban grid belies America's disorder. Grandma's knockoff 7
Louis Vuitton handbag is so full of meds it sounds like a snake rattle.
Grandma shares a secret addiction with her drug-addled dude of a grand-
son, whose dad prowls the Home Depot parking lot in his Japanese
pickup, looking to hire a couple of Mexicans to clear out some dry scrub.

From a distant height, America's wall might seem a wonderful stunt, 8
like Christo and Jeanne-Claude's "Running Fence" of 1976—a 24-mile-
long curtain that ran over the Northern California foothills to the sea.
Before it was dismantled, "Running Fence" rippled and swelled with
breezes off the Pacific.

David Tomb, an artist known for his studio portrait paintings, has 9
for several years been hiking the Southwestern borderlands, drawing the

birds of the region. Tomb tells me he has noticed how often the American wall interferes with the movement of the many animals that inhabit the desert and canyons—wolves, coyotes, mountain lions, even snakes. His bird subjects are able to fly over the wall, as are butterflies, as are Piper Cub cocaine consignments.

In the remotest regions of northern Mexico, the terrain is so treacher-   10 ous that nature itself forms the wall against America. Desperation moves migrants to attempt ever-more-treacherous terrain to achieve U.S. soil.

In recession America 2010, the lament most often heard is that the   11 middle class is losing its grip on the American dream. (We have redefined the American dream as the ability of a succeeding generation to earn more than its preceding generation.)

On patriotism-for-profit talk radio and television, the illegal immi-   12 grant is, by definition, criminal. She comes to steal the American dream. But in my understanding, the dream belongs to the desperation of the poor and always has. The goddess of liberty in New York harbor still advertises for the tired and the poor, the wretched refuse. I tell you, there is an unlucky man in the Sonoran Desert today who will die for a chance to pluck dead chickens in Georgia or change diapers in a rest home in Nevada.

Great empires expand beyond their own borders. Empires in decline   13 build walls.

As it stands, the Great Wall of America is a fraction of the length of   14 the Great Wall of China. China's dragon-spined ramparts, once a wonder of isolation, are now a draw for tourists, even while China trespasses its own borders to forge the Chinese century. The dragon flies to Africa and to Latin America. While American soldiers die in Afghanistan, the Chinese venture to Kabul to negotiate mineral rights.

The nearer precedent to the American Wall may be Israel's wall in   15 the West Bank. More than 400 miles long, the Israeli "barrier"—in some places a fence, in others a concrete mass nearly twice the height of the Berlin Wall—was constructed, according to Israeli officials, to deter terrorists. After Sept. 11, the fear one heard in America was that agents of violence from the Middle East might easily disguise themselves as Latin American peasants and trespass into our midst.

What more obvious reason is there for a wall than protection? Any   16 nation should police those who come and go across its borders. But in the United States, as in Israel, the wall has created a new anxiety. Once the wall is in place, anxiety about the coming outsider changes to an anxiety about who belongs within.

The question that has lately been debated in the Knesset is bluntly 17
stated: Who is a Jew? In Israel, the answer to the question concerns religion and citizenship. But it entails further practical considerations. Israel
has decided to rid itself of 400 children of illegal foreign workers (some
of whom built the West Bank wall), children who were born in Israel,
speak Hebrew as their mother tongue and know no other country.

The question that has lately been taken up by U.S. senators is bluntly 18
stated: Who is an American? Republicans have proposed excising the
part of the 14th Amendment that guarantees citizenship to anyone born
on U.S. soil. GOP Sen. Lindsey Graham of South Carolina refers to foreign women who come to this country to "drop" their babies. Graham
chooses **diction** that describes inhuman beasts of burden.

I cannot guess whether this new nativism—though it overrules 19
nativity—is serious business or merely a play for reelection. The irony
remains: The land of the free that the wall was built to protect—the literal
"homeland," soil so infused with sacred legend it was deemed by the mak-
ers of the Constitution more important than blood in determining citizenship—is threatened from within. And the wall that is supposed to proscribe
the beginning of America becomes the place where America ends.

Thinking about the Essay

1. What expectations does Rodriguez have of his audience? Who might this
   audience be, and where is it situated? What tone or voice does Rodriguez
   use to address these readers? Is he objective, ironic, sympathetic, critical,
   or what? Justify your response by citing the text.

2. What is the significance of the title? Why does Rodriguez put most of the
   title in quotes?

3. What is Rodriguez's argument, and where does he state it most clearly? What
   elements of the argument does he highlight or employ to justify his claim?

4. How does the concept of the "great wall" function as a symbol? How does
   this symbol serve to deepen the meaning and also unify the essay? What
   other symbols can you detect?

5. Why does Rodriguez use allusions in the essay? Identify these allusions
   and explain how they contribute to the argument.

Responding in Writing

6. Write a complete analysis of Rodriguez's argumentative technique in his
   essay. Evaluate the success he achieves (or lack of it) in convincing the
   audience of his claim.

7. Write an argumentative essay for or against the proposition that a wall separating the United States and Mexico is required to prevent undocumented immigration.

8. Argue for or against the notion, advanced by Rodriguez, that historically, walls and other barriers have never been successful in separating nations and peoples.

Networking

9. Divide the class into two groups, and then debate the proposition that strong fences make good neighbors. Relate this proposition to the current debate over immigration.

10. Conduct online research into one barrier mentioned by Rodriguez in his essay: the wall and other impediments separating Israel and Palestine. Consult at least three links in this research. Summarize your findings in a précis that you present to the class.

America and the World: How Do Others Perceive Us?

One of the key elements supporting the idea of America is a belief in freedom, democracy, and human rights—what we often term American exceptionalism. This ideal, as we saw in the previous chapter, has been a motivating impulse in all waves of immigration, especially for the flood of peoples from around the world who have found their way to the United States since 1965, transforming the nation into a global village. But does the rest of the world believe that the United States is truly a "city upon a hill" as President Ronald Reagan (borrowing a phrase from one of the nation's first immigrants, Governor John Winthrop of Massachusetts Bay Colony) declared? Are we truly a beacon of democratic promise for other nations? Do we promote democracy and human rights everywhere? Or are we "ugly Americans" constantly meddling in the affairs of other nations? What ideals and values—especially when projected by American foreign policy or even American tourists abroad—do we actually represent?

Today the conflicts inherent in the "war on terror" and "clash of civilizations"—framed by a suspicion of American-style capitalism, democracy, and imperialism—fuel a widespread belief that the world's reigning superpower acts out of self-interest rather than altruism. For many, the United States is not a bastion of democracy but a destructive element—a Great Satan in the minds of some. That we led the wars of the last century against the totalitarian forces of Nazism, fascism, and communism apparently has become a historic footnote. That we provide international aid today to developing nations and victims of natural disasters, that we share information and technology openly, and that we promote democracy at great human and material cost all seem lost in a maelstrom of anti-Americanism. In a world of

Chinese customers buy snacks from a store decorated with ads for an American soft drink company in Beijing, China.

Thinking about the Image

1. What is your response to this image? Is it positive or negative? Explain your response.

2. Identify and analyze the elements in this photograph that contribute to the dominant impression or overall effect. What point of view, if any, does the photographer want to convey?

3. Why is this image divided into three parts? What relationships do you detect among the units? What is the dominant impression?

4. Research the Pepsi Cola Corporation in China and its impact on local culture. Write a summary of your findings.

predators, the United States appears to many as the most insatiable enemy. Yet with the election of Barack Obama to the presidency in 2008, there emerged a degree of hope for a revival of American exceptionalism around the world.

The truth, of course, is that the image America projects to the world has always been a function of what others have projected onto it. As the world's superpower, the United States faces today the option of not only inspiring ideals of democracy and freedom in the rest of the world but of trying to remake nations and regions—as in the case of Iraq and the broader Middle East—according to those ideals. The problem is that the very *idea* of America is symbolically saturated with conflicting aspirations and associations. The ideals that America would transmit to the world will inevitably clash with rival ideals that have been projected from afar. If, for example, we are guardians of the free world, then what forces are we guarding the world *against*? How can the United States unilaterally pursue debatable policies and still maintain moral authority on the world stage? What ideals, beyond self-interest, would justify intervention in the affairs of other nations? For instance, recent administrations have promoted democracy in the Middle East; but many in the area view Washington's actions as an amoral attempt to control the region, destroy traditional societies, and guarantee access to oil.

Of course, not everyone hates the United States or is cynical about its role in the world. The Islamic Republic of Iran might denounce America as the Great Satan (and England as the Lesser Satan), but Iranians love Americans in particular and the West in general. Again, the truth lies in the beholder and the ways in which we construct national mythologies for ourselves. Some might engage in a frenzy of anti-Americanism and even want to harm the United States for what they perceive America does to the rest of the world; but many others around the world, especially in moments of crisis, are thankful for American food during famine, tents and medical supplies after earthquakes and tsunamis, the promotion of human rights, and even military intervention (as in Libya) to prevent genocide. The global village does admire America's political and economic freedoms, along with its wealth, culture, and technology, even as it might be appalled by certain foreign policy doctrines and behavior on the world stage.

The essays in this chapter deal with America's complex relationship with the rest of the world and with the psychological factors behind both current anti-American and pro-American attitudes. The wars in Afghanistan and Iraq and the repercussions of the "Arab Spring" have affected the image of America in ways that we are only beginning to understand. ("As the savagery of the images coming out of Iraq demonstrate all too well," writes Sasha Abramsky in an essay appearing in this chapter, "we live in a world where image is if not everything, at least crucial.") The famous film footage of the cavalry charge up San Juan Hill that made Theodore Roosevelt's reputation during the Spanish-American War was, as we now know, a staged reenactment filmed after the real charge took place. Today, more than a hundred years after Roosevelt's charge, it is no easy task to alter the perception of America as an aggressive imperialist power; but it is still possible, after the fact, to examine and learn from the images, actions, and mythologies that are at its source.

Why I Could Never Hate America

MEHDI HASAN | Mehdi Hasan graduated from Christ Church College, Oxford in 2000 with a degree in Philosophy, Politics, and Economics. He began his career as a journalist by answering phones, conducting research, and serving in several progressively important positions at newspapers and television studios in London. Today, Hasan is senior editor for politics at the *New Statesman*. He has also contributed articles to the *Evening Standard*, *Daily Mail*, and *The New York Times*, while appearing on a variety of television news shows. In this posting from his blog at the *New Statesman*, Mehdi recounts a difficult personal episode at Bush Intercontinental Airport in Houston that tests his faith in the American experience.

Before Reading

Have you ever had a problem while boarding a flight or coming off one at an American airport? In a more general sense, what is your experience of security policies at airports, bus terminals, or train stations? Why might the conflicts that overseas travelers experience in the United States contribute to a sense of anti-Americanism?

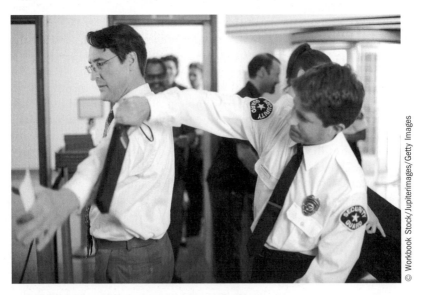

A security officer searches a businessman at the airport.

Mehdi Hasan, "Why I Could Never Hate America" (*New Statesman*, March 22, 2010. Reprinted with permission by *New Statesman*.

"Any jokes or inappropriate remarks may result in your arrest," says a robotic voice over the Tannoy at Bush Intercontinental Airport in Houston, as I join the silent procession of bleary-eyed passengers disembarking from the plane after a ten-hour transatlantic flight. Welcome, as they say, to the United States.

I'm in Texas on holiday, making the annual pilgrimage to see my in-laws. I married an American in 2003, and each time we return to her homeland I'm reminded of the *New Yorker* journalist Hendrik Hertzberg's description of the "brutal fuck-you that greets foreigners arriving in the United States," and his call to U.S. immigration officials to stop making "preventive war" on innocent tourists. "It might make us more friends."

But making friends isn't high on the agenda at Bush Intercontinental. This is my ninth trip to Houston since 2000, and it doesn't get any easier. I attributed a rare smooth entry in March last year to the change in administration, from bellicose Bush to benign Barack. My mistake.

"What is the purpose of your trip?" asks a morose airport official, thumbing through my passport and refusing to look me in the eye. The badge on his arm says "U.S. Customs and Border Patrol," part of the department of homeland security. Perhaps I don't look happy enough to be here on holiday. Moments later, I'm deposited in a homeland security "holding lounge." "Why am I here?" I ask the nearest uniformed officer. "Random check," he grunts. Random? I'm sitting in a room filled exclusively with black, Hispanic and Asian passengers.

Name and shame

Nor is it my first time in this "lounge." A few years ago I spent several hours here, detained because my surname matched that of a wanted insurgent inside Iraq. Yes, "Hasan"—the Middle Eastern equivalent of "Smith" or "Jones." Incidentally, I note an addition to the waiting room in the form of a giant map of Afghanistan and Pakistan. Iraq is so 2003.

Why does my detention matter? Isn't my inconvenience far less important than U.S. airport security? Of course, but as the former secretary of state Colin Powell remarked in 2007: "We are taking too much counsel of our fears . . . Let's make sure people come to Disney World and not throw them up against the wall in Orlando simply because they have a Muslim name . . . Let's show the world a face of openness and what a democratic system can do."

Time and again we have been told that the "war on terror" is at its core a struggle for hearts and minds. Not so on U.S. borders, where foreigners are met, in Hertzberg's words, with "delays, ugliness, sullen contempt and near chaos while being treated alternately as cattle or potential terrorists." Despite Hollywood's best efforts, millions of people across the world no longer consider the U.S. to be "the land of the free and the home of the brave" (to quote the national anthem), the "shining city upon a hill" (Ronald Reagan), or the "indispensable nation" (Madeleine Albright).

Indeed, anti-Americanism is rife. Some argue it has a long and   8
shameful history, pre-dating even the founding of the United States in 1776. In the mid-18th century, the French naturalist the Comte de Buffon—together with Voltaire and the Dutch philosopher Cornelius de Pauw, among others—condemned the "degeneracy" of the inhabitants of the Americas. But as the British historian Tony Judt points out, anti-Americanism today is not confined to smug intellectuals—European or otherwise. Most foreigners are untroubled by the cultural dominance of the U.S., and many even aspire to the so-called American way of life. "Most of them don't despise America, and they certainly don't hate Americans," Judt writes. "What upsets them is U.S. foreign policy. . . ."

There is evidence to support this. During the eight years of the Bush   9
administration, with its lawless and bloody wars, positive opinion of the U.S. declined in most European countries. A Pew Global Attitudes Project poll showed how, between 2000 and 2006, "favourable opinions" of the U.S. dropped from 83 percent to 56 percent in the UK, from 62 percent to 39 percent in France and from 78 percent to 37 percent in Germany. In the Middle East, Zogby International found that negative attitudes towards the U.S. jumped between 2002 and 2004, from 76 percent to 98 percent in Egypt, from 61 percent to 88 percent in Morocco and from 87 percent to 94 percent in Saudi Arabia—and these are allies of Uncle Sam. Respondents in most of these countries said they objected, above all, to U.S. foreign policies that they considered unjust.

Love, actually

In *Destiny Disrupted: a History of the World Through Islamic Eyes*, the   10
Afghan-American writer Tamim Ansary shows how the Middle Eastern view of the U.S. in the early 20th century was much more positive than negative. Wilsonian idealism was seductive to Arabs living under colonial rule but craving self-determination. It was, Ansary argues, only after the CIA-funded coup against the secular, democratically elected prime minister of Iran, Muhammed Mossadeq, that anger and disillusionment with the U.S. spread across the region.

Noam Chomsky, bête noire of the right, has long argued that the 11 notion of anti-Americanism itself seeks to excuse the crimes of U.S. elites and "identify state policy with the society, the people, the culture." It is an important point. I condemn the actions of the U.S. government in Iraq, Afghanistan and Yemen, without attacking my American friends in Houston, LA or New York.

"I am willing to love all mankind," Samuel Johnson said, "except an 12 American." I cannot agree. I may be considered anti-American, in that I abhor many U.S. foreign policies, but the person I love most happens to be an American. America is not the American government. Nor is it the U.S. border patrol.

Thinking about the Essay

1. What is Hasan's claim, and where does he state it? How does he support his argument?

2. How does the writer establish a specific tone and mood in the opening paragraph?

3. Do you think that Hasan engages in **refutation** in this essay? Why or why not?

4. Hasan divides his essay into brief sections. Explain whether or not you think this strategy detracts from the unity of the selection.

5. What allusions do you find in this essay? List these references, identify each one, and then explain the writer's purpose in presenting them.

Responding in Writing

6. Write an analysis of the argumentative style, structure, and tone that Hasan employs in this essay.

7. Argue for or against the proposition that anti-Americanism is an improper or overblown reaction to current U.S. foreign policy.

8. Basing your essay on the statement by Noam Chomsky in paragraph 11, write a paper in which you offer a strategy whereby one can be critical of certain American foreign policy initiatives but at the same time maintain a pro-American perspective.

Networking

9. In small groups, debate the proposition that anti-American attitudes ignore or undermine the efforts of the American government and American people to do good around the world. Present the outcome of this debate to the class.

10. Locate Hasan's blog on the Internet, and provide a profile based on your reading of at least three of his postings.

Avatar: Politics Made Easy—Too Easy

SAM GINDIN

Sam Gindin was born in Siberia, grew up in Canada and attended the University of Manitoba, and pursued graduate studies at the University of Wisconsin at Madison. For much of his working life, Gindin was associated with the Canadian Auto Workers union, serving as a research director and assistant to the president. Since his retirement in 2000, Gindin has been the Visiting Packer Chair in Social Science at York University in Toronto. Gindin's writing focuses on organized labor in Canada and the United States and on global capitalism. In addition to articles for magazines and social science journals, Gindin has written a history, *The Canadian Auto Workers* (1995). In this essay from the March/April 2010 issue of *Canadian Dimension*, Gindin compares the events depicted in the film *Avatar* with several U.S. wars.

Before Reading

How do you explain the popularity of science fiction films and especially *Avatar* (if you have seen it)? Might one possibility be that such films encourage us to speculate on the state of American civilization and global civilization—on this planet and elsewhere?

A good portion of the Left, coming to a James Cameron 3-D flick   1
with relatively low political expectations, emerged excited about the politics of *Avatar*. That the film is a gross over-simplification is readily acknowledged, but its enthusiasts insist that the film contributes to a popular delegitimization of American imperialism. The bad guys are a resource-hungry corporation backed by the U.S. army, and the film has you cheering against the Americans and for the environmentally friendly natives (the Navi). And a marine—a paraplegic no less—makes the moral choice to switch sides and join the opposition. What more could one ask for in a film that will soon be the largest grossing film of all time, not just in the U.S. but also abroad?

Sam Gindin, "Avatar: Politics Made Easy—Too Easy" (*Canadian Dimension*, March/April 2010). Used by permission of *Canadian Dimension*.

Canadian director James Cameron poses in front of an *Avatar* movie poster before a promotion.

I don't think the film's political problems lie in its over-simplifications, 2 but in the easy and ultimately apolitical sympathies it evokes. Let's start with the ending. The Navi are overseeing the defeated American soldiers shuffling into their inter-planetary ships to return to earth. How can this obvious link to the Vietcong victory in Vietnam not be progressive? The question, however, isn't being critical of the American role in Vietnam; that hardly seems all that radical (especially with Vietnam now comfortably integrated into the capitalist fold). The issue rather is whether or not the film's sentiments translate into our identifying with the resistance in Iraq, Afghanistan, or Palestine. And the answer clearly is that they don't because those masked and shadowy fighters ambushing convoys in deserts or setting off bombs in devastated cities can't match the innocent nobility of the sleek Navi living in their utopian green world.

Moreover, imperialism is only bad in the film when it involves a direct 3 military assault. The tension only emerges when the Americans (including the decent liberal scientists) can't co-opt the natives in other ways; when education, health, and market relations (selling their precious resources) don't get the job done. Everyday imperialism, the imposition of capitalism without massive carpet-bombing, is apparently OK.

In fact, if the film's anti-colonialism resonates, it's not in terms of the 4 wars in the Middle East but with the destruction of Native society in the

Americas. Yet for all the sympathies for Native people wanting to retain their land, history is rewritten so the actual tragedy and ongoing native struggles are replaced—and belittled. What we get is a feel-good fantasy of their defeating American power. They can tame and fly prehistoric birds, and their link to nature brings other prehistoric animals to join the battle on their side. Above all, the paraplegic American marine comes to lead them (incidentally winning the heart of the chief's daughter Pocahontas and gains legs so along with what actually happened to Native people, we don't have to think too much about paraplegics either).

Yes, there is a progressive message lurking here, and it's nice to see   5
Natives routing the U.S. army. But what does this vicarious pleasure really mean? What does it teach or inspire? Does the film really delegitimize the U.S. army, or just the John Wayne stereotype? When the marine asks "What do we have to offer them other than light beer?" is it challenging our consumerist culture or is this $500 million dollar film a much more substantive affirmation of that culture?

Is the film anti-capitalist, as suggested by its critique of the one cor-   6
poration in the film, or only anti-capitalism's bad apples? And if the only alternatives are capitalism or going back to nature (the movie offers no other option), doesn't that really guarantee that most people will only become jaded and cynical with capitalism—or even enjoy watching films critical of particular capitalist values—but never really move to a collective attempt to transform it?

Thinking about the Essay

1. What assumptions does Gindin make about his audience for this essay? (Consider that he is writing for an alternative or progressive Canadian magazine.) How does the writer make the essay interesting for secondary readers who might be interested in film but not the argument he seems to be making about American foreign policy?

2. What is Gindin's claim? Does he state this claim in one place or develop it slowly? Explain.

3. What evidence does the writer provide to support his claim?

4. Where does Gindin pose questions in this essay? What is his purpose, and what is the effect of this strategy?

5. Film critics tend to both explain the movie and evaluate it. Does Gindin offer sufficient explanation—especially for someone who might not have seen *Avatar*? And what is his evaluation? Does he think that the film is good, bad, great, or what? How do you know?

Responding in Writing

6. Write a response to Gindin's assertion that *Avatar* fails to illuminate the deep issues raised by imperialism and capitalism—that films like *Avatar* are nothing but "feel-good" fantasies.

7. Argue for or against the proposition that a reviewer or critic should have an ideological or political position when evaluating a film.

8. Write an essay about a specific film genre—science fiction, Westerns, horror films, crime films—and how this genre illuminates the role of the United States in global affairs or the way others perceive American society. Include references to at least three films to support your claim or thesis.

Networking

9. In small discussion groups, discuss what each participant knows about *Avatar*. Then discuss the film in terms of American values and the role of the United States as an "imperial" power. Judge the effectiveness of Gindin's argument, and then report your conclusions to the class.

10. Gindin's essay was one of several on *Avatar* that appeared in *Canadian Dimension*. There were also numerous online postings in response to this debate over *Avatar*. Go online to read these articles and postings, and then write a summary based on your findings.

A New Middle East

Fareed Zakaria

Fareed Zakaria is a writer, political scientist, and magazine and television news commentator. He was born and raised in Bombay, India, the son of politically progressive parents who were also practicing Muslims. Zakaria emigrated to the United States to attend Yale University and subsequently Harvard University, where he received a Ph.D. in political science. He is the author of *From Wealth to Power: The Unusual Origins of America's World Role* (1998), *The Future of Freedom: Illiberal Democracy at Home and Abroad* (2004), and *The Post-American World* (2008). Zakaria writes an opinion column for *Time* and appears frequently as a commentator and anchor on television news shows. In the following essay, which appeared in a 2011 issue of *Time*, Zakaria places current U.S. relations in the Middle East against a broad historical backdrop.

Before Reading

Has the United States always had the best interests of Middle Eastern nations in mind when conducting its foreign policy, or has it based its policies on self-interest? Explain.

E ver since the end of the Cold War, the U.S. has been the dominant   1
and unrivaled power in the Middle East. That situation is changing, not because another great power is entering the region but because the Arabs are becoming more independent, unlikely to ally themselves submissively to any outside patron. Egypt's decision to establish relations with Iran and Hamas is one part of this trend. Washington cannot change it, nor should it try. This is the new, democratic Arab world.

If you look at the region today, there have been two (mostly) peace-   2
ful revolutions in Tunisia and Egypt, an insurgency against Muammar Gaddafi's reign in Libya, a continuing revolt in Yemen and now a series of protests in Syria. Beyond those major demonstrations, there have been protests of a kind in almost every other Arab country. And there is every

© KHALED DESOUKI/AFP/Getty Images

Riot police guard a group of demonstrators showing their support for policemen Awad Ismail Suleiman and Mahmud Salah Amin, outside a court in the Mediterranean city of Alexandria on July 27, 2010, during the policemen's trial on charges of using excessive force and killing 28-year-old Khaled Said.

reason to believe that the forces unleashed in the region will continue to roil it for months or even years.

For centuries, the Arabs have been dominated by outside powers. By the 16th century, Mongols and Persians had been replaced by the Ottoman Empire, which ruled Arabia for 400 years. As Ottoman power began to wane, first the French and then the British entered the Middle East, and in 1919, after the collapse of the Ottoman Empire, they carved up the region, creating countries with the stroke of a pen and establishing local chieftains as the monarchs of these new states.

As Europe's empires themselves collapsed after World War II, the two superpowers took their place, choosing client states to support and secure. When the Cold War ended, Arab states that had supported the U.S. prospered. Those that had not, found themselves out in the cold; they either got new sponsors (Syria moved on to Iran) or tried to make their peace with the U.S. (which explains Libya's renunciation of its nuclear weapons). In any event, the U.S. became the dominant power, and most countries accommodated themselves to its priorities.

But over the past 10 years, the U.S. has lost the willingness and the capacity to maintain this quasi-imperial stance. It lost its will because it realized—under Presidents George W. Bush and Barack Obama—that its unqualified support of Arab dictators had spawned an extremist terrorist movement that was at its core anti-American. U.S. support for Arab regimes became more tentative and qualified. But Washington, exhausted by two wars, the financial crisis and a deep recession, also lost its capacity to act. As a result, indigenous forces in the Arab world—fueled by demographics, technology and a youth movement—began stirring. These forces, now unleashed, will not suddenly disappear.

There are some places in the Arab world that are so small and so rich that they might remain largely unchanged. But beyond the handful of oil sheikdoms, every society in the region is feeling the forces of change. Even in places where repression seems to have worked up to now, it is unlikely to work forever. Take Bahrain, whose government shut down protests in the country but at a huge cost. It has exacerbated a Shi'ite–Sunni divide, and it has effectively become a quasi-protectorate of the Saudi monarchy. That does not presage long-term stability for the country.

Whatever the outcome in Syria, Libya and Yemen, it's safe to say that five years from now, these places will look very different. The one experiment with genuine pre-emptive reform appears to be in Morocco, where the King has proposed effectively ceding a great many of his powers to an elected Prime Minister. If that succeeds, it will be a powerful model, and there will be pressure for the Gulf monarchies and Jordan to follow suit.

What does this mean for the U.S.? Zbigniew Brzezinski pointed   8
out to me that if you go back to 1975, the U.S. was closely allied with all four major states in the region—Iran, Egypt, Turkey and Saudi Arabia. Today every one of those relationships is troubled. But that is a sign of the strange nature of the U.S.'s regional dominance. We were allied with regimes—like those of the Shah of Iran, Egypt's dictators and the Turkish military—that could not last as the winds of modernity swept by.

Now Washington will have to make alliances with a more modern,   9
democratic, populist Middle East but one where its ties will be more real and more stable. Just as it moved its support from South Korean and Taiwanese dictators to democrats, from Pinochet and Marcos to the democratic forces in Chile and the Philippines, it will now have to find a way to shift support from the princes of the Arab world to the people. It is a difficult journey but a vital one.

Thinking about the Essay

1. Consider Zakaria's purpose in writing this essay. Does he want to argue a position, educate readers, persuade his audience to accept a basic premise or opinion, or some combination of these? Explain.

2. How does Zakaria link his introductory and concluding paragraphs? What is the effect, and how does his claim emerge from this linkage?

3. How does Zakaria organize his essay in terms of an introduction, body, and conclusion?

4. What types of evidence and comparative information does Zakaria provide to support his claim?

5. Explain the overall tone that Zakaria established in this essay, pointing to specific sentences that illuminate the writer's position.

Responding in Writing

6. Using Zakaria's essay as a springboard, write an essay with the title "A New Middle East" in which you address the issue of the role of the United States in promoting what we now call the Arab Spring.

7. Write a comparative essay focusing on the relationship between the United States and one of the nations mentioned by Zakaria in his article.

8. In an argumentative essay, respond to the proposition that the United States can no longer afford to support dictatorships and tyrannies around the world.

Networking

9. With one other class member, subject Zakaria's essay to close analysis and evaluation. Provide a summary and response to class members.

10. Conduct online research to find out more about Zakaria's opinions. Read at least three of the writer's opinion pieces that he wrote for *Newsweek* and *Time* magazines in the past five years. Then write an argumentative essay in which you broadly agree or disagree with Zakaria's opinions about the role of the United States in global affairs.

The America I Love

ELIE WIESEL | Elie Wiesel was awarded the Nobel Peace Prize in 1986. Born in Romania in 1928, he was sent at the age of fifteen to a Nazi concentration camp along with his mother, father, and sister. Only Wiesel survived. He was liberated by American forces at Buchenwald in 1945. Wiesel's first book, *Night* (1960), recounted his experience at Buchenwald; he has written more than forty books since then and has become a major voice in the campaign for global peace and security. Wiesel became a U.S. citizen in 1963. In the following essay, published in *Parade* magazine in 2004, Wiesel takes issue with critics of American foreign policy.

Before Reading

Do you think that the positive role of the United States in foreign affairs often is unappreciated by peoples and nations that benefit from our aid? Why or why not?

The day I received American citizenship was a turning point in my   1
life. I had ceased to be stateless. Until then, unprotected by any government and unwanted by any society, the Jew in me was overcome by a feeling of pride mixed with gratitude.

From that day on, I felt privileged to belong to a country which, for   2
two centuries, has stood as a living symbol of all that is charitable and

decent to victims of injustice everywhere—a country in which every person is entitled to dream of happiness, peace and liberty; where those who have are taught to give back.

Grandiloquent words used for public oratory? Even now, as America is in the midst of puzzling uncertainty and understandable introspection because of tragic events in Iraq, these words reflect my personal belief. For I cannot forget another day that remains alive in my memory: April 11, 1945.   3

That day I encountered the first American soldiers in the Buchenwald concentration camp. I remember them well. Bewildered, disbelieving, they walked around the place, hell on earth, where our destiny had been played out. They looked at us, just liberated, and did not know what to do or say. Survivors snatched from the dark throes of death, we were empty of all hope—too weak, too emaciated to hug them or even speak to them. Like lost children, the American soldiers wept and wept with rage and sadness. And we received their tears as if they were heartrending offerings from a wounded and generous humanity.   4

Ever since that encounter, I cannot repress my emotion before the flag and the uniform—anything that represents American heroism in battle. That is especially true on July Fourth. I reread the Declaration of Independence, a document sanctified by the passion of a nation's thirst for justice and sovereignty, forever admiring both its moral content and majestic intonation. Opposition to oppression in all its forms, defense of all human liberties, celebration of what is right in social intercourse: All this and much more is in that text, which today has special meaning.   5

Granted, U.S. history has gone through severe trials, of which anti-black racism was the most scandalous and depressing. I happened to witness it in the late Fifties, as I traveled through the South. What did I feel? Shame. Yes, shame for being white. What made it worse was the realization that, at that time, racism was the law, thus making the law itself immoral and unjust.   6

Still, my generation was lucky to see the downfall of prejudice in many of its forms. True, it took much pain and protest for that law to be changed, but it was. Today, while fanatically stubborn racists are still around, some of them vocal, racism as such has vanished from the American scene. That is true of anti-Semitism too. Jew-haters still exist here and there, but organized anti-Semitism does not—unlike in Europe, where it has been growing with disturbing speed.   7

As a great power, America has always seemed concerned with other people's welfare, especially in Europe. Twice in the 20th century, it saved the "Old World" from dictatorship and tyranny.   8

America understands that a nation is great not because its economy   9
is flourishing or its army invincible but because its ideals are loftier.
Hence America's desire to help those who have lost their freedom to
conquer it again. America's credo might read as follows: For an individual, as for a nation, to be free is an admirable duty—but to help others
become free is even more admirable.

Some skeptics may object: But what about Vietnam? And Cambodia?   10
And the support some administrations gave to corrupt regimes in Africa
or the Middle East? And the occupation of Iraq? Did we go wrong—and
if so, where?

And what are we to make of the despicable, abominable "interroga-   11
tion methods" used on Iraqi prisoners of war by a few soldiers (but even
a few are too many) in Iraqi military prisons?

Well, one could say that no nation is composed of saints alone. None   12
is sheltered from mistakes or misdeeds. All have their Cain and Abel. It
takes vision and courage to undergo serious soul-searching and to favor
moral conscience over political expediency. And America, in extreme situations, is endowed with both. America is always ready to learn from its
mishaps. Self-criticism remains its second nature.

Not surprising, some Europeans do not share such views. In extreme   13
left-wing political and intellectual circles, suspicion and distrust toward
America is the order of the day. They deride America's motives for its
military interventions, particularly in Iraq. They say: It's just money. As
if America went to war only to please the oil-rich capitalists.

They are wrong. America went to war to liberate a population too   14
long subjected to terror and death.

We see in newspapers and magazines and on television screens the mass   15
graves and torture chambers imposed by Saddam Hussein and his accompli-
ces. One cannot but feel grateful to the young Americans who leave their families, some to lose their lives, in order to bring to Iraq the first rays of hope—
without which no people can imagine the happiness of welcoming freedom.

Hope is a key word in the vocabulary of men and women like myself   16
and so many others who discovered in America the strength to overcome
cynicism and despair. Remember the legendary Pandora's box? It is filled
with implacable, terrifying curses. But underneath, at the very bottom,
there is hope. Now as before, now more than ever, it is waiting for us.

Thinking about the Essay

1. Where does Wiesel make his claim? Why doesn't he place it in his introductory paragraph?

2. Consider that the writer published this essay in the July Fourth edition of a popular magazine. How does Wiesel adjust his tone to a broad readership and to the occasion? Do you find his tone to be effective? Justify your response with reference to the text.

3. From the start of this essay, Wiesel fashions a specific mood. How would you describe the emotional impact he attempts to project? Why, for example, does he mention the day he became an American citizen; the Declaration of Independence; and April 11, 1945? Does he combine emotional appeals with logical ones? Why or why not?

4. Explain the writer's use of cause-and-effect analysis to structure his essay.

5. Do you find Wiesel's conclusion to be effective? Why or why not?

Responding in Writing

6. Wiesel asserts that "Americans are taught to give back." Write a paper defending or criticizing this proposition. Provide at least three reasons in support of your position.

7. Do you think that citizens can criticize their country while at the same time remaining loyal and patriotic? Respond to this question in an argumentative essay.

8. Compose an extended definition of patriotism, using Wiesel's ideas as a point of departure.

Networking

9. As a class, debate the proposition that Wiesel is being too patriotic in his "love" of America. (We call this excessive patriotism jingoism.)

10. Conduct online research on a debatable, ambiguous, or regrettable aspect of recent U.S. policy—for instance, the invasion of Iraq, "enhanced" interrogation, resistance to climate change, and so forth. Then write an argumentative essay explaining why this action was justified or unjustified and what this says about the America you love.

Americans Are Tuning Out the World

ALKMAN GRANITSAS

Alkman Granitsas is an American-born journalist who has reported on global issues in Asia and Europe for more than ten years. He has been a staff writer for the *Asian Wall Street Journal* and has contributed articles to *Business Week*, the *Far Eastern Economic Review*, and numerous other journals. Granitsas is currently based in Athens, where he is writing a book on the Balkans. In the following essay, from the November 24, 2005, issue of the online journal *Yale Global,* Granitsas warns against the consequences of a trend toward cultural and political isolationism in the United States.

Before Reading

Do you believe that America is "a shining city on the hill"? Why or why not?

For all the talk about a global village, there are actually two communities in the world today: Americans and everyone else. The average Frenchman, Brazilian, or Pakistani is becoming more attuned to the American way of life, but Americans themselves are increasingly tuning out the rest of the globe. At a time when U.S. power, benefiting from globalization, is unchallenged in the world, a disinterested electorate could be a recipe for trouble.

Foreigners have long bemoaned the "isolationist" attitude of Americans—safely protected by two oceans and their tabula rasa history. But over the last several decades, that isolation has deepened. Americans now pay less attention to international affairs, and read less foreign news than at any time in the last two generations. Relative to the global boom in international travel, tourism, and business, fewer Americans go overseas or study a foreign language at university. The truth is that Americans are becoming relatively less—not more—engaged with the world in general.

A few facts. Since the early 1970s, the American public has paid less and less attention to foreign affairs. According to Gallup polls from presidential election years 1948 through 1972, Americans used to rank foreign affairs as the most important issue facing the nation. Since then, however, with the single exception of the 2004 elections, the economy has been ranked first.

Over the same period, the percentage of American university students studying a foreign language has steadily declined. According to a report funded by the U.S. Department of Education, in 1965, more than 16 percent of all American university students studied a foreign language. Now only 8.6 percent do.

It has long been known that fewer Americans have passports, and travel less, than their counterparts in other developed economies. And while a record 21 percent of all Americans now have passports and are traveling more, the number going overseas in the past 20 years—not just to neighboring Canada and Mexico—has grown at a slower rate than the number of overseas visitors to America or the growth in international tourism in general. And indeed, during the late 1980s and early 1990s, the number of Americans even applying for a passport declined in several years.

American media coverage of foreign affairs has also been diminish-   6
ing. For example, according to a 2004 Columbia University survey, the presence of foreign news stories in American newspapers has been dropping since the late 1980s. In 1987, overseas news accounted for about 27 percent of front page stories in American newspapers—about the same as a decade earlier. By 2003, foreign news accounted for just 21 percent of front page stories, while coverage of domestic affairs more than doubled over the same period. On television, both the number of American network news bureaus overseas and the amount of air-time spent on foreign news fell by half in the 1990s.

Why are Americans progressively tuning out the rest of the world?   7
The reason is twofold. But both confirm the cherished belief of most Americans: that their country is a "shining city on the hill." And the rest of the world has relatively little to offer.

Consider first, that for the past 45 years, Americans have witnessed a   8
massive immigration boom. Since 1960, more than 20 million immigrants have come to the United States—the greatest influx of newcomers in the last hundred years, surpassing even the wave of immigrants that arrived in the first three decades of the 20th century. Two-thirds of these newcomers—more than 15 million—have come in just the past 25 years.

That they should come bears out the myth that America is a melting   9
pot of peoples. Indeed, the iconic images of the first Plymouth Rock Pilgrims and the Ellis Island immigrants of the early 1900s are at the very center of American popular mythology. More recently, news footage of Mexican-Americans rushing the fences on the southern borders shows that America attracts all comers. And every single American—from the mid-western blue collar worker to the pedigreed New England blue-blood—knows their forebears came from someplace else. Chances are they've met or know someone—the Bangladeshi working at the 7-Eleven, the Chinese scientist on TV, the Somali cab driver at the airport—who has come even more recently.

With the whole world apparently trying to get to America, the aver-   10
age American can only ask: why look to the rest of the world? After all,

why would everyone try to come here if there was anything worthwhile over there? It is telling that according to a 2002 National Geographic survey, 30 percent of Americans believed the population of America to be between 1 and 2 billion people. For most Americans, it must seem like everyone is rushing the fences these days.

The second reason is that for much of the last two decades most (but   11 not all) Americans have seen their economic well-being grow relative to the rest of the world. Through much of the 1990s, American consumer confidence and real disposable income have risen at their fastest levels since the relatively golden age of U.S. economic growth of the 1960s. These have been matched by perceptions of increased wealth from a stock market rally that, with interruptions, lasted from the early 1980s until three years ago.

Why should that matter? Because since the days of ancient Rome, it   12 is an axiom of political science that economic well-being dulls the appetite of citizens to participate in civil affairs. It is something that de Tocqueville observed more than a hundred years ago.

"There is, indeed, a most dangerous passage in the history of a dem-   13 ocratic people," de Tocqueville observed. "When the taste for physical gratifications among them has grown more rapidly than their education and their experience of free institutions . . . the discharge of political duties appears to them to be a troublesome impediment which diverts them from their occupations and business."

Long before 9/11, the Asian tsunami, SARS, the bird flu, and the rela-   14 tively weaker dollar, Americans were already growing less interested in the rest of the world. Since then, they have found even more reasons to tune out.

The implications, however, are disturbing. Because of America's pre-   15 eminent position in world affairs—and its role in "globalization," its foreign policy matters more than any other country on earth. But can America shape a responsible foreign policy with such an uninformed electorate? The world may be turning into a "global village," but the average American has moved to the suburbs.

Thinking about the Essay

1. What is Granitsas's claim and where does he state it? Do you detect any warrant underpinning his claim? Explain.

2. How does Granitsas connect perceptions about immigration to the United States to the isolationist attitude of the average American?

3. Where does the essay shift from factual support of a claim to the causal analysis and attribution of psychological motives?

4. Why does Granitsas quote Alexis de Tocqueville at length (paragraph 13)? Who was de Tocqueville, and what does quoting him add to the argument of the essay?

5. Where in the essay does the author provide answers immediately following the question he has posed? Are there rhetorical questions anywhere in the essay? Why are these questions left unanswered, and what function do they serve in the essay?

Responding in Writing

6. In a brief essay, critique the "axiom" that economic well-being dulls the appetite of citizens to participate in civil affairs. Can you think of exceptions to this rule?

7. Write down your response to the popular view that Americans have a "tabula rasa history." Why would non-Americans view American history in this way?

8. Make a list of the factual indicators Granitsas mentions in the essay as measures of the engagement of the American public. What are the diagnostic limitations of each indicator? Analyze these indicators in an essay.

Networking

9. Do you rank foreign affairs as the most important issue facing the United States? Poll members of your class and, in a class discussion, attempt to explain the majority opinion.

10. Compare the coverage of one foreign affairs issue over the course of a week in two online journals, one published in the United States and one published in a foreign country (the French *Le Monde*, for example, or the British *Guardian*).

Waking Up from the American Dream

SASHA ABRAMSKY

Sasha Abramsky is a freelance journalist and author who writes on politics and culture. He was born in England and studied politics, philosophy, and economics at Balliol College, Oxford, and moved to New York in 1993 to study journalism at Columbia University. His first book, *Hard Time Blues: How Politics Built a Prison Nation* (2002), examines the American prison system. Abramsky's most recent book, *Inside Obama's Brain*, was published in 2009. Abramsky is currently a Senior Fellow at the New York City–based Demos

Foundation. In the following essay, published in the July 23, 2004, issue of *The Chronicle of Higher Education*, Abramsky asks why foreign sympathy for America, inspired by faith in the American Dream, has dissipated at the turn of the new century.

Before Reading

Do you feel that the recent crisis of confidence in the United States among other nations also reflects a global loss of confidence in the ideal of the American Dream?

© Michael S. Yamashita/Documentary/Corbis

A public display of anti-American sentiment in Tehran.

Sasha Abramsky, "Waking Up from the American Dream," from *The Chronicle of Higher Education*, 7/23/04. Sasha Abramsky is a Senior Fellow at the Demos Institute and author of *Inside Obama's Brain* (Penguin Portfolio, 2009), and is also the founder of the website www.thevoicesofpoverty.org and is working on a book on poverty in America. Reprinted by permission of the author.

L ast year I visited London and stumbled upon an essay in a Sunday   1
paper written by Margaret Drabble, one of Britain's pre-eminent
ladies of letters. "My anti-Americanism has become almost uncontrol-
lable," she wrote. "It has possessed me, like a disease. It rises up in my
throat like acid reflux, that fashionable American sickness. I now loathe
the United States and what it has done to Iraq and the rest of the help-
less world."

The essay continued in the same rather bilious vein for about a thou-   2
sand words, and as I read it, two things struck me: The first was how
appalled I was by Drabble's crassly oversimplistic analysis of what
America was all about, of who its people were, and of what its culture
valued; the second was a sense somewhat akin to fear as I thought
through the implications of the venom attached to the words of this gentle scribe of the English bourgeoisie. After all, if someone whose country
and class have so clearly benefited economically from the protections
provided by American military and political ties reacts so passionately to
the omnipresence of the United States, what must an angry, impoverished young man in a failing third world state feel?

I grew up in London in the 1970s and 1980s, in a country that was   3
struggling to craft a postcolonial identity for itself, a country that was,
in many ways, still reeling from the collapse of power it suffered in the
post–World War II years. Not surprisingly, there was a strong anti-
American flavor to much of the politics, the humor, the cultural chitchat
of the period; after all, America had dramatically usurped Britannia on
the world stage, and who among us doesn't harbor some resentments at
being shunted onto the sidelines by a new superstar?

Today, however, when I talk with friends and relatives in London,   4
when I visit Europe, the anti-Americanism is more than just sardonic
asides, rueful Monty Python–style jibes, and haughty intimations of superiority. Today something much more visceral is in the air. I go to my
old home and I get the distinct impression that, as Drabble put it, people
really *loathe* America somewhere deep, deep in their gut.

A Pew Research Center Global Attitudes Project survey recently   5
found that even in Britain, America's staunchest ally, more than 6 out of
10 people polled believed the United States paid little or no attention to
that country's interests. About 80 percent of French and German
respondents stated that, because of the war in Iraq, they had less confidence in the trustworthiness of America. In the Muslim countries surveyed, large majorities believed the war on terror to be about
establishing U.S. world domination.

Indeed, in many countries—in the Arab world and in regions, such as   6
Western Europe, closely tied into American economic and military structures—popular opinion about both America the country and Americans
as individuals has taken a serious hit. Just weeks ago, 27 of America's
top retired diplomats and military commanders warned in a public statement, "Never in the 2¼ centuries of our history has the United States
been so isolated among the nations, so broadly feared and distrusted."

If true, that suggests that, while to all appearances America's allies   7
continue to craft policies in line with the wishes of Washington, underneath the surface a new dynamic may well be emerging, one not too dissimilar to the Soviet Union's relations with its reluctant satellite states in
Eastern Europe during the cold war. America's friends may be quiescent
in public, deeply reluctant to toe the line in private. Drabble mentioned
the Iraq war as her primary *casus belli* with the United States. The statement from the bipartisan group calling itself Diplomats and Military
Commanders for Change focused on the Bush administration's recent
foreign policy. But to me it seems that something else is also going on.

In many ways, the Iraq war is merely a pretext for a deeper discon-   8
tent with how America has seemed to fashion a new global society, a
new economic, military, and political order in the decade and a half
since the end of the cold war. America may only be riding the crest of a
wave of modernization that, in all likelihood, would have emerged without its guiding hand. But add to the mix a discontent with the vast
wealth and power that America has amassed in the past century and a
deep sense of unease with the ways in which a secular, market-driven
world divvies up wealth and influence among people and nations, and
you have all the ingredients for a nasty backlash against America.

I'm not talking merely about the anti-globalism of dispossessed Third   9
World peasants, the fears of the loss of cultural sovereignty experienced
by societies older and more traditional than the United States, the anger
at a perceived American arrogance that we've recently been reading so
much about. I'm talking about something that is rooted deeper in the
psyches of other nations. I guess I mean a feeling of being marginalized
by history; of being peripheral to the human saga; of being footnotes for
tomorrow's historians rather than main characters. In short, a growing
anxiety brought on by having another country and culture dictating
one's place in the society of nations.

In the years since I stood on my rooftop in Brooklyn watching the   10
World Trade Center towers burn so apocalyptically, I have spent at least
a part of every day wrestling with a host of existential questions. I can't

help it—almost obsessively I churn thoughts over and over in my head, trying to understand the psychological contours of this cruel new world. The questions largely boil down to the following: Where has the world's faith in America gone? Where is the American Dream headed?

What is happening to that intangible force that helped shape our modern world, that invisible symbiotic relationship between the good will of foreigners and the successful functioning of the American "way of life," that willingness by strangers to let us serve as the repository for their dreams, their hopes, their visions of a better future? In the same way that the scale of our national debt is made possible only because other countries are willing to buy treasury bonds and, in effect, lend us their savings, so it seems to me the American Dream has been largely facilitated by the willingness of other peoples to lend us their expectations for the future. Without that willingness, the Dream is a bubble primed to burst. It hasn't burst yet—witness the huge numbers who still migrate to America in search of the good life—but I worry that it is leaking seriously.   11

Few countries and cultures have risen to global prominence as quickly as America did in the years after the Civil War. Perhaps the last time there was such an extraordinary accumulation of geopolitical, military, and economic influence in so few decades was 800 years ago, with the rise of the Mongol khanates. Fewer still have so definitively laid claim to an era, while that era was still unfolding, as we did—and as the world acknowledged—during the 20th century, "the American Century."   12

While the old powers of Europe tore themselves apart during World War I, the United States entered the war late and fought the fight on other people's home terrain. While whole societies were destroyed during World War II, America's political and economic system flourished, its cities thrived, and its entertainment industries soared. In other words, as America rose to global pre-eminence during the bloody first half of the 20th century, it projected outward an aura of invulnerability, a vision of "normalcy" redolent with consumer temptations and glamorous cultural spectacles. In an exhibit at the museum on Ellis Island a few years back, I remember seeing a copy of a letter written by a young Polish migrant in New York to his family back home. Urging them to join him, he wrote that the ordinary person on the streets of America lived a life far more comfortable than aristocrats in Poland could possibly dream of.   13

In a way America, during the American Century, thus served as a safety valve, allowing the world's poor to dream of a better place   14 somewhere else; to visualize a place neither bound by the constraints of old nor held hostage to the messianic visions of revolutionary Marxist or Fascist movements so powerful in so many other parts of the globe.

Throughout the cold war, even as America spent unprecedented 15 amounts on military hardware, enough was left over to nurture the mass-consumption culture, to build up an infrastructure of vast proportions. And despite the war in Vietnam, despite the dirty wars that ravaged Latin America in the 1980s, despite America's nefarious role in promoting coups and dictatorships in a slew of countries-cum-cold-war-pawns around the globe, somehow much of the world preserved a rosy-hued vision of America that could have been culled straight from the marketing rooms of Madison Avenue.

Now something is changing. Having dealt with history largely on its 16 own terms, largely with the ability to deflect the worst of the chaos to arenas outside our borders (as imperial Britain did in the century following the defeat of Napoleon in 1815, through to the disastrous events leading up to World War I in 1914), America has attracted a concentrated fury and vengeful ire of disastrous proportions. The willingness to forgive, embodied in so much of the world's embrace of the American Dream, is being replaced by a rather vicious craving to see America—which, under the Bush administration, has increasingly defined its greatness by way of military triumphs—humbled. Moreover, no great power has served as a magnet for such a maelstrom of hate in an era as saturated with media images, as susceptible to instantaneous opinion-shaping coverage of events occurring anywhere in the world.

I guess the question that gnaws at my consciousness could be 17 rephrased as: How does one give an encore to a bravura performance? It's either an anticlimax or, worse, a dismal failure—with the audience heading out the doors halfway through, talking not of the brilliance of the earlier music, but of the tawdriness of the last few bars. If the 20th century was the American Century, its best hopes largely embodied by something akin to the American Dream, what kind of follow-up can the 21st century bring?

In the immediate aftermath of September 11, an outpouring of genu- 18 ine, if temporary, solidarity from countries and peoples across the globe swathed America in an aura of magnificent victimhood. We, the most powerful country on earth, had been blindsided by a ruthless, ingenious, and barbaric enemy, two of our greatest cities violated. We demanded the world's tears, and, overwhelmingly, we received them. They were, we felt, no less than our due, no more than our merit. In the days after the trade center collapsed, even the Parisian daily *Le Monde*, not known for its pro-Yankee sentimentality, informed its readers, in an echo of John F. Kennedy's famous "Ich bin ein Berliner" speech, that "we are all Americans now."

Perhaps inevitably, however, that sympathy has now largely dissi- 19 pated. Powerful countries under attack fight back—ruthlessly, brutally, with all the economic, political, diplomatic, and military resources at their disposal. They always have; like as not, they always will. In so doing, perhaps they cannot but step on the sensibilities of smaller, less powerful dare I say it, less *imperial* nations and peoples. And as Britain, the country in which I grew up, discovered so painfully during the early years of World War II, sometimes the mighty end up standing largely alone, bulwarks against history's periodic tidal waves. In that fight, even if they emerge successful, they ultimately emerge also tarnished and somewhat humbled, their power and drive and confidence at least partly evaporated on the battlefield.

In the post–September 11 world, even leaving aside Iraq and all the 20 distortions, half-truths, and lies used to justify the invasion, even leaving aside the cataclysmic impact of the Abu Ghraib prison photographs, I believe America would have attracted significant wrath simply in doing what had to be done in routing out the Taliban in Afghanistan, in reorienting its foreign policy to try and tackle international terror networks and breeding grounds. That is why I come back time and again in my mind to the tactical brilliance of Al Qaeda's September 11 attacks: If America hadn't responded, a green light would have been turned on, one that signaled that the country was too decadent to defend its vital interests. Yet in responding, the response itself was almost guaranteed to spotlight an empire bullying allies and enemies alike into cooperation and subordination and, thus, to focus an inchoate rage against the world's lone standing super-power. Damned if we did, damned if we didn't.

Which brings me back to the American Dream. In the past even as 21 our power grew, much of the world saw us, rightly or wrongly, as a moral beacon, as a country somehow largely outside the bloody, gory, oft-tyrannical history that carved its swath across so much of the world during the American Century. Indeed, in many ways, even as cultural elites in once-glorious Old World nations sneered at upstart, crass, consumerist America, the masses in those nations idealized America as some sort of Promised Land, as a place of freedoms and economic possibilities simply unheard of in many parts of the globe. In many ways, the

American Dream of the last 100-some years has been more something dreamed by foreigners from afar, especially those who experienced fascism or Stalinism, than lived as a universal reality on the ground in the United States.

Things look simpler from a distance than they do on the ground. In the past foreigners might have idealized America as a place whose streets were paved if not with gold, at least with alloys seeded with rare and precious metals, even while those who lived here knew it was a gigantic, complicated, multifaceted, continental country with a vast patchwork of cultures and creeds coexisting side by messy side. Today, I fear, foreigners slumber with dreamy American smiles on their sleeping faces no more; that intangible faith in the pastel-colored hue and soft contours of the Dream risks being shattered, replaced instead by an equally simplistic dislike of all things and peoples American. 22

Paradoxically these days it is the political elites—the leaders and policy analysts and defense experts—who try to hold in place alliances built up in the post–World War II years as the *pax Americana* spread its wings, while the populaces shy away from an America perceived to be dominated by corporations, military musclemen, and empire-builders-in-the-name-of-democracy; increasingly they sympathize with the unnuanced critiques of the Margaret Drabbles of the world. The Pew survey, for example, found that sizable majorities in countries such as Jordan, Morocco, Turkey, Germany, and France believed the war on terror to be largely about the United States wanting to control Middle Eastern oil supplies. 23

In other words, the *perception*—never universally held, but held by enough people to help shape our global image—is changing. Once our image abroad was of an exceptional country accruing all the power of empire without the psychology of empire; now it is being replaced by something more historically normal—that of a great power determined to preserve and expand its might, for its own selfish interests and not much else. An exhibit in New York's Whitney Museum last year, titled "The American Effect," presented the works of 50 artists from around the world who portrayed an America intent on world dominance through military adventurism and gross consumption habits. In the run-up to the war in Iraq, Mikhail Gorbachev lambasted an America he now viewed as operating in a manner "far from real world leadership." Nelson Mandela talked of the United States as a country that "has committed unspeakable atrocities in the world." 24

Maybe the American Dream always was little more than marketing 25
hype (the author Jeffrey Decker writes in *Made in America* that the term
itself was conjured up in 1931 by a populist historian named James
Truslow Adams, perhaps as an antidote to the harsh realities of Depres-
sion-era America). But as the savagery of the images coming out of Iraq
demonstrate all too well, we live in a world where image is if not everything, at least crucial. Perhaps I'm wrong and the American Dream will
continue to sweeten the sleep of those living overseas for another century. I certainly hope, very much, that I'm wrong—for a world denuded
of the Dream, however far from complex reality that Dream might have
been, would be impoverished indeed. But I worry that that encore I mentioned earlier won't be nearly as breathtaking or as splendid as the original performance that shaped the first American century.

Thinking about the Essay

1. Why does Abramsky wait until paragraph 3 to inform the reader that he grew up in London? What effect does this strategic withholding of information have upon you as a reader?

2. List some of the illustrations that Abramsky invokes as ''barometers'' of public sentiment.

3. According to Abramsky, why is it important for the future of America that foreigners continue to idealize the country and believe in some concept of an American Dream?

4. How does Abramsky characterize American power as being the result of a symbiotic relationship or exchange with the rest of the world?

5. The concluding sentence picks up an extended **metaphor** (or conceit) that was introduced earlier in the essay. How effective is this metaphor as a structuring device?

Responding in Writing

6. Do you feel that the Iraq war is merely a pretext for a deeper discontent with America? In a brief essay, speculate on the nature of the discontent underlying one critique of the Iraq war that you have heard expressed.

7. Reread the no-win scenario outlined in paragraph 20. Do you agree with Abramksy's statement that America ''would have attracted significant wrath simply in doing what had to be done''? Defend your opinion in an argumentative essay.

8. Have you ever felt ''marginalized by history'' as a result of your place of birth, time of birth, or other factors beyond your control? Write an essay explaining some of the factors that would contribute to that feeling.

Networking

9. In groups of three or four, list some key features of the American Dream, and share these lists with the class. Is there a concept of the American Dream common to everyone in the class?

10. Go online and view (or read about) some of the works that were on display in The American Effect exhibit at New York's Whitney Museum. Do you detect a ''party line'' in the way these artists view America? Are there perceptions of America that Abramsky might consider ''nuanced''?

4

Speaking in Tongues: Does Language Unify or Divide Us?

The diverse voices in the previous chapters reflect some of the numerous ethnic and racial aspects of the new American mosaic—as well as global perceptions of American exceptionalism. Part of this mosaic is the variety of languages we hear on American streets and college campuses. Of course, you have been taught to speak and write the same language—that standard variety of English that places you in the college classroom today. Knowing the standard English "code" provides you with a powerful tool, offering pragmatic and liberating ways to gain control over your world.

However, other languages might compete for your attention at home or in your community. Powerful constituencies—politicians and advertisers among them—exploit this fact. For example, some Anglo politicians try to speak Spanish to Latino crowds (often to the amusement of native Spanish speakers). Other constituencies, threatened by our multilingual world, try to enact "English-only" laws in various states. Moreover, governments often use language—for example, words like "patriotism" or "Islamic fascism"—to advance political goals. Language can unify or divide a community or nation, but basically it remains a mark of your identity. To know a language or languages permits you to navigate your community, culture, and even global society.

Imagine, for example, what it would be like if you were illiterate. For one thing, you wouldn't be in college. You might not be able to read a menu or fill out a job application. You might not be interested in voting because you cannot read the names of the candidates. Illiteracy in reality is common around the world—and far more common in the United States than you might think.

We have vivid reminders of both the cost of illiteracy and also the power of literacy in film and literature. In the film *Driving Miss Daisy*, the character played by Morgan Freeman goes through most of his life

© AP Photo/Robert Mecca

The neighborhood of Elmhurst, Queens, in New York City, is one of the most ethnically and linguistically diverse places in the world. At Elmhurst's Newtown High School alone, students come from more than 100 countries and at least 39 languages are spoken. In this photograph, local schoolchildren take part in the neighborhood's annual International Day Festival on May 27, 1999.

Thinking about the Image

1. Recall a class photograph from your childhood. Was your school as diverse as this group of schoolchildren, or not? What are the advantages of being exposed to so many nationalities and languages at such a young age? What are the disadvantages?

2. News photographers often shoot many images of the same event, sometimes even multiple rolls of film, and then decide with their editors which unique image best captures the spirit of the event. Why do you think this photo was selected?

3. Are there parades for various ethnic or social groups in your community? How are those events covered in the local news media?

4. Would this parade have achieved its purpose, or appealed to its audience, as effectively if the marchers were adults instead of children? Why or why not? Would the message (or purpose) have been different? In what way?

pretending to read the daily newspaper. When Daisy (played by Jessica Tandy) teaches him to read, his world—and his comprehension of it—expands. Or consider one of the memorable sequences in *The Autobiography of Malcolm X*. Malcolm teaches himself to read and write when he is in prison. He starts at the beginning of the dictionary and works his way to the end. Going into prison as Richard Little, he comes out as Malcolm X, his identity reconstructed not only by the acquisition of a new system of belief—Islam—but also by a newly acquired literacy. In his writing and in his recovered life, Malcolm X harnessed the power of language to transform himself and his understanding of the world.

Think of language, then, as a radical weapon. Language permits you to share experiences and emotions, process information, analyze situations and events, defend a position, advocate a cause, and make decisions. Language contributes to the growth of the self. Language is the bedrock of our academic, social, and professional lives. Language is a liberating force—but some writers in this chapter remind us that language can also be culturally and politically divisive.

The idea that language is the key to our identity and our perception of the world is not new. Early Greek and Roman philosophers believed that you could not be a good thinker or writer unless you were a good person. Assuming that you are a good person, you possess a repertoire of mental skills that you can bring to bear on various situations and dimensions of your life. You can draw inferences, interpret conditions, understand causal relationships, develop arguments, make intelligent choices, and so forth. But have you ever found yourself in a situation where you know what you mean but not how to say it? Or think of how difficult it must be for people acquiring a second language; they know what they mean in their primary language but cannot express it in their new one. The essays in this chapter deal with precisely this situation.

The writers in this chapter illuminate the power and paradox of language. They link language, culture, politics, and identity. They use language with skill, intelligence, and emotion. They work with the problems and contradictions of language, seeking answers to the question, "Who am I, and where do my words—my languages—fit into the American as well as the world mosaic?"

Tweet Like an Egyptian

KEVIN CLARKE | Kevin Clarke is a writer living in New York City. He contributes articles on religion, culture, and politics to uscatholic.org and maintains a blog at this site. Clarke also is an associate editor at the publication *America: The National Catholic Weekly*. In this article from the April 2011 issue of *U.S. Catholic*, Clarke examines the impact of social networking on recent upheavals and revolutions in the Arab world.

Before Reading

What is your response to the assertion that the "Arab Spring" would not have been possible without various forms of social networking and new ways of communicating with people demanding political change?

In the early days of the World Wide Web, HTML wizards maintained the googly-eyed optimism of people who thought they were changing the world. Here was a civically electrifying form of communication that would obliterate time and space and the distance between people. Agonizing over our 2,400 baud TCP connections, and sharing strategies over regional bulletin board systems, there was a brief shining moment of giddy joy in the very new and unironic enthusiasm for the very bold.   1

Then the retailers and the marketers and the pornographers arrived. In the space of just a few months the Internet transformed from the electronic marketplace of new ideas and experiences into, well, just the same old marketplace of crud nobody really needed.   2

But since January in the Arab world that early promise of revolution and real change that drove the first Internet reasserted itself. It was not just that the protesters for human freedom, civil rights, economic justice, and the end of soul-crushing oligarchy in Egypt and elsewhere used the latest social networking technologies of the Internet to organize themselves and outmaneuver the entrenched authority in their respective societies. It was not just that they used the Internet to get their message out to the rest of the world and to inspire likeminded protests in other nations.   3

The young people who took to the streets in Egypt and Tunisia were not demanding a freedom they could only imagine, they were demanding the freedom they had already experienced in their virtual lives, a freedom they wanted to translate into their actual daily lives. On the Internet they had already learned what it looked and felt like to inhabit a society where opinions were welcome and thoughts could be freely expressed, an alternative reality that encouraged the limitlessness of imagination and the life-affirming energy of human freedom.   4

But the Internet did even more. It empowered them with the information they needed to question and challenge authority in their nonvirtual societies.   5

Wikileaks has endured white-hot criticism for its purported irrespon-   6
sibility in releasing U.S. classified documents and diplomatic cables that
capture what U.S. officials really think about conditions and political
characters around the world. The data dump orchestrated by Wikileaks,
a new kind of communication outlet that could only have been brought
to life via the infrastructure, capability, and spirit of the Internet, has
been condemned as a threat to the lives of confidential sources and to diplomacy as we know it. So far, however, what it has mostly proved to
be is a regime-shattering tool of information sharing.

Most people in Tunisia endured a begrudging awareness of the larce-   7
nous leadership of the Ben Ali regime. But something about seeing the
depth of that larceny and civic indifference spelled out in a U.S. State
Department cable was the electronic straw that broke the camel's back
and propelled people into the streets.

No one knows where this new era of Internet-generated people   8
power may ultimately lead. In chaos there is both opportunity and danger. It's still possible that the energy for change and thirst for freedom
on the Arab streets today could be subverted. Revolutions have been co-
opted before. But it is at least as likely that the Internet will continue to
be a viaduct of energy and information that empowers and enlightens
rather than degrades and distracts. It maintains its potential to be a force
that makes real the spiritual connectedness of all people.

Maybe it will be a force strong enough to rouse the democratic   9
impulses of the people in a nation which, though materially better off
than many other states, maintains levels of income and resource inequity
and poverty that rival any demoralized society in the developing world.
If you're wondering what state I'm talking about, get online and explore
a little bit.

Thinking about the Essay

1. What is Clarke's claim in this essay? Does he state this claim or imply it? Explain your response.

2. How do the title and opening paragraph grasp and hold the reader's interest?

3. This essay appeared in a journal affiliated with the Catholic Church. What can we assume about the writer's audience and the values of the writer and his readership? How are these values reflected in the essay?

4. What examples does Clarke use to support his claim?

5. Clarke's closing paragraphs attempt to prompt his audience to action. How does he develop this persuasive technique?

Responding in Writing

6. Do you agree or disagree with the claim that social networking empowers people around the world with the information they need "to question and challenge authorities in their nonvirtual societies" (paragraph 5)? Write an argumentative essay in response to this question.

7. The writer presents several examples to support his claim. Do you find these examples to be sufficient, effective, and persuasive? Justify your response in an analytical essay.

8. Clarke discusses WikiLeaks in paragraph 6. Find out more about WikiLeaks, and then write an argument either in favor of or opposed to the release of classified documents.

Networking

9. Work in small groups of four or five. Pool your knowledge about the impact of the Internet and social networking on global political change. After discussing this topic as a group, report to the class on your findings, using specific evidence to support your conclusions.

10. Go online with another student and—as Clarke recommends—"explore a little bit." In your exploration, research the impact of Twitter on one specific protest movement. Take notes on your findings, and report them to the class.

Leave Your Name at the Border

MANUEL MUNOZ

Manuel Munoz, who was born in 1972 in Dinuba, California, has written two well-received collections of short fiction, *Zigzagger* (2003) and *The Faith Healer of Olive Avenue* (2007), inspired by his childhood in the San Joaquin Valley. The son of farm workers in California's Central Valley, Munoz was the first person in his family to go to college, receiving a B.A. from Harvard University and an M.F.A. from Cornell University. Munoz is the recipient of a National Endowment for the Arts fellowship in fiction, the Whiting Writers' Award, a New York Foundation for the Arts Fellowship, and a 2009 O. Henry Prize for a short story. Munoz contributes stories and essays to periodicals including the *Boston Review*, *Edinburgh Review*, and *The New York Times*. In this article from the August 1, 2007, issue of *The New York Times*, Munoz discusses

the problems and power of code-switching as he pon-
ders the ways in which various constituencies perceive
him—and his name.

Before Reading

Do you have an immigrant name, a mainstream or assimilated name, or something in between? Is your name "white" or "not white"? What do you think your
name—first or last—tells others about who you are and where you are from?

A t the Fresno airport, as I made my way to the gate, I heard a name   1
over the intercom. The way the name was pronounced by the gate
agent made me want to see what she looked like. That is, I wanted to
see whether she was Mexican. Around Fresno, identity politics rarely
deepen into exacting terms, so to say "Mexican" means, essentially, "not
white." The slivered self-identifications Chicano, Hispanic, Mexican-
American and Latino are not part of everyday life in the Valley. You're
either Mexican or you're not. If someone wants to know if you were
born in Mexico, they'll ask. Then you're From Over There—de allá.
And leave it at that.

The gate agent, it turned out, was Mexican. Well-coiffed, in her 30s,   2
she wore foundation that was several shades lighter than the rest of her
skin. It was the kind of makeup job I've learned to silently identify at
the mall when I'm with my mother, who will say nothing about it until
we're back in the car. Then she'll point to the darkness of her own skin,
wondering aloud why women try to camouflage who they are.

I watched the Mexican gate agent busy herself at the counter, profes-   3
sional and studied. Once again, she picked up the microphone and, with
authority, announced the name of the missing customer: "Eugenio Reyes,
please come to the front desk."

You can probably guess how she said it. Her Anglicized pronuncia-   4
tion wouldn't be unusual in a place like California's Central Valley. I
didn't have a Mexican name there either: I was an instruction guide.

When people ask me where I'm from, I say Fresno because I don't   5
expect them to know little Dinuba. Fresno is a booming city of nearly
500,000 these days, with a diversity—white, Mexican, African-American,
Armenian, Hmong and Middle Eastern people are all well represented—
that shouldn't surprise anyone. It's in the small towns like Dinuba that
surround Fresno that the awareness of cultural difference is stripped

down to the interactions between the only two groups that tend to live there: whites and Mexicans. When you hear a Mexican name spoken in these towns, regardless of the speaker's background, it's no wonder that there's an "English way of pronouncing it."

I was born in 1972, part of a generation that learned both English 6 and Spanish. Many of my cousins and siblings are bilingual, serving as translators for those in the family whose English is barely functional. Others have no way of following the Spanish banter at family gatherings. You can tell who falls into which group: Estella, Eric, Delia, Dubina, Melanie. It's intriguing to watch "American" names begin to dominate among my nieces and nephews and second cousins, as well as with the children of my hometown friends. I am not surprised to meet 5-year-old Brandon or Kaitlyn. Hardly anyone questions the incongruity of matching these names with last names like Trujillo or Zepeda. The English-only way of life partly explains the quiet erasure of cultural difference that assimilation has attempted to accomplish. A name like Kaitlyn Zepeda doesn't completely obscure her ethnicity, but the half-step of her name, as a gesture, is almost understandable.

Spanish was and still is viewed with suspicion: Always the language 7 of the vilified illegal immigrant, it segregated schoolchildren into English-only and bilingual programs; it defined you, above all else, as part of a lower class. Learning English, though, brought its own complications. It was simultaneously the language of the white population and a path toward the richer, expansive identity of "American." But it took getting out of the Valley for me to understand that "white" and "American" were two very different things.

Something as simple as saying our names "in English" was our 8 unwittingly complicit gesture of trying to blend in. Pronouncing Mexican names correctly was never encouraged. Names like Daniel, Olivia and Marco slipped right into the mutability of the English language. I remember a school ceremony at which the mathematics teacher, a white man, announced the names of Mexican students correctly and caused some confusion, if not embarrassment. Years later we recognized that he spoke in deference to our Spanish-speaking parents in the audience, caring teacher that he was.

These were difficult names for a non-Spanish speaker: Araceli, 9 Nadira, Luis (a beautiful name when you glide the u and the i as you're supposed to). We had been accustomed to having our birth names altered for convenience. Concepción was Connie. Ramón was Raymond. My cousin Esperanza was Hope—but her name was pronounced

"Hopie" because any Spanish speaker would automatically pronounce the e at the end.

Ours, then, were names that stood as barriers to a complete embrace   10
of an American identity, simply because their pronunciations required a slip into Spanish, the otherness that assimilation was supposed to erase. What to do with names like Amado, Lucio or Élida? There are no English "equivalents," no answer when white teachers asked, "What does your name mean?" when what they really wanted to know was "What's the English one?" So what you heard was a name butchered beyond recognition, a pronunciation that pointed the finger at the Spanish language as the source of clunky sound and ugly rhythm.

My stepfather, from Ojos de Agua, Mexico, jokes when I ask him   11
about the names of Mexicans born here. He deliberately stumbles over pronunciations, imitating our elders who have difficulty with Bradley and Madelyn. "Ashley Sánchez. ¿Tú crees?" He wonders aloud what has happened to the "nombres del rancho"—traditional Mexican names that are hardly given anymore to children born in the States: Heraclio, Madaleno, Otilia, Dominga. My stepfather's experience with the Anglicization of his name—Antonio to Tony—ties into something bigger than learning English. For him, the erasure of his name was about deference and subservience. Becoming Tony gave him a measure of access as he struggled to learn English and get more fieldwork.

This isn't to say that my stepfather welcomed the change, only that   12
he could not put up much resistance. Not changing put him at risk of being passed over for work. English was a world of power and decisions, of smooth, uninterrupted negotiation. Clear communication meant you could go unsupervised. Every gesture made toward convincing an employer that English was on its way to being mastered had the potential to make a season of fieldwork profitable. It's curious that many of us growing up in Dinuba adhered to the same rules. Although as children of farm workers we worked in the fields at an early age, we'd also had the opportunity to stay in one town long enough to finish school. Most of us had learned English early and splintered off into a dual existence of English at school, Spanish at home. But instead of recognizing the need for fluency in both languages, we turned it into a peculiar kind of battle. English was for public display. Spanish was for privacy—and privacy quickly turned to shame. The corrosive effect of assimilation is the displacement of one culture over another, the inability to sustain more than one way of being. It isn't a code word for racial and ethnic acculturation only. It applies to needing to belong, of seeing from the

outside and wondering how to get in and then, once inside, realizing there are always those still on the fringe.

When I went to college on the East Coast, I was confronted for the first 13 time by people who said my name correctly without prompting; if they stumbled, there was a quick apology and an honest plea to help with the pronunciation. But introducing myself was painful: already shy, I avoided meeting people because I didn't want to say my name, felt burdened by my own history. I knew that my small-town upbringing and its limitations on Spanish would not have been tolerated by any of the students of color who had grown up in large cities, in places where the sheer force of their native languages made them dominant in their neighborhoods. It didn't take long for me to assert the power of code-switching in public, the transferring of words from one language to another, regardless of who might be listening. I was learning that the English language composed new meanings when its constrictions were ignored, crossed over or crossed out. Language is all about manipulation, or not listening to the rules.

When I come back to Dinuba, I have a hard time hearing my name 14 said incorrectly, but I have an even harder time beginning a conversation with others about why the pronunciation of our names matters. Leaving a small town requires an embrace of a larger point of view, but a town like Dinuba remains forever embedded in an either/or way of life. My stepfather still answers to Tony and, as the United States–born children grow older, their Anglicized names begin to signify who does and who does not "belong"—who was born here and who is de allá.

My name is Manuel. To this day, most people cannot say it correctly, 15 the way it was intended to be said. But I can live with that because I love the alliteration of my full name. It wasn't the name my mother, Esmeralda, was going to give me. At the last minute, my father named me after an uncle I would never meet. My name was to have been Ricardo. Growing up in Dinuba, I'm certain I would have become Ricky or even Richard, and the journey toward the discovery of the English language's extraordinary power in even the most ordinary of circumstances would probably have gone unlearned.

I count on a collective sense of cultural loss to once again swing the 16 names back to our native language. The Mexican gate agent announced Eugenio Reyes, but I never got a chance to see who appeared. I pictured an older man, cowboy hat in hand, but I made the assumption on his name alone, the clash of privileges I imagined between someone de allá and a Mexican woman with a good job in the United States. Would she speak to him in Spanish? Or would she raise her voice to him as if he were hard of hearing?

But who was I to imagine this man being from anywhere, based on   17
his name alone? At a place of arrivals and departures, it sank into me
that the currency of our names is a stroke of luck: because mine was not
an easy name, it forced me to consider how language would rule me if I
allowed it. Yet I discovered that only by leaving. My stepfather must live
in the Valley, a place that does not allow that choice, every day. And
Eugenio Reyes—I do not know if he was coming or going.

Thinking about the Essay

1. Why do you think that Munoz begins his essay—and ends it as well—at the Fresno, California, airport? On what and whom does he focus, and how does this focus serve to illuminate his broader analysis?

2. What is Munoz's thesis, and where does he state it? How does the "corrosive effect of assimilation" inform this thesis?

3. Munoz organizes this essay around a series of contrasts. What is the primary contrast? What are additional contrasts that inform this comparative structure?

4. Why does Munoz introduce so many names in this essay—sometimes lists of names, as in paragraphs 6 and 9? Do you find these names to be a distraction, or do they reinforce the writer's thesis? Explain.

5. Explain the ways in which Munoz merges narrative, personal experience, analysis, and perhaps even argument in this essay. What does his strategy tell you about mixing modes or patterns when writing an essay?

Responding in Writing

6. Write a **personal essay** about your own name, combining narrative, descriptive, and expository techniques.

7. Write an analytical paper on what Munoz terms "the power of code-switching in public" (paragraph 13).

8. Argue for or against the proposition that assimilation can have a corrosive effect.

Networking

9. In groups of three or four, develop a list of all the names—and variants of names—that Munoz introduces in his essay. Discuss the relevance of these names to Munoz's argument. Appoint one member of the group to present your evaluation.

10. Go online and find out more about "code-switching." Provide a critique of your research in a brief paper.

Mother Tongue

AMY TAN

Amy Tan was born in San Francisco, California, in 1952, only two and a half years after her parents emigrated from China to the United States. She was educated at San Jose State University and the University of California at Berkeley and then worked as a reporter and technical writer. Tan is best known as a novelist whose fiction focuses on the conflict in culture between Chinese parents and their Americanized children. Her first novel, *The Joy Luck Club* (1989), was highly popular and adapted by Hollywood as a feature film. Tan's other novels are *The Kitchen God's Wife* (1991), *The Hundred Secret Senses* (1995), *The Bonesetter's Daughter* (2001), and *Saving Fish from Drowning* (2006). Tan published a nonfiction work, *The Opposite of Fate: A Book of Musings*, in 2003. Tan's complicated relationship with her mother, Daisy, who died of Alzheimer's disease in 1999 at the age of eighty-three, is central to much of her fiction. In this essay, published in 1990 in *The Threepenny Review*, Tan, who has a master's degree in linguistics, invokes her mother in exploring the "Englishes" that immigrants employ as they navigate American culture.

Before Reading

How many "Englishes" do you speak, and what types of English do you speak in various situations? Is the English you speak in the classroom the same as you speak in your home or dormitory?

I am not a scholar of English or literature. I cannot give you much   1
more than personal opinions on the English language and its variations in this country or others.

I am a writer. And by that definition, I am someone who has always   2
loved language. I am fascinated by language in daily life. I spend a great deal of my time thinking about the power of language—the way it can evoke an emotion, a visual image, a complex idea, or a simple truth. Language is the tool of my trade. And I use them all—all the Englishes I grew up with.

Recently, I was made keenly aware of the different Englishes I do   3
use. I was giving a talk to a large group of people, the same talk I had
already given to half a dozen other groups. The nature of the talk was
about my writing, my life, and my book, *The Joy Luck Club*. The talk
was going along well enough, until I remembered one major difference
that made the whole talk sound wrong. My mother was in the room.
And it was perhaps the first time she had heard me give a lengthy
speech, using the kind of English I have never used with her. I was saying things like, "The intersection of memory upon imagination" and
"There is an aspect of my fiction that relates to thus-and-thus"—a
speech filled with carefully wrought grammatical phrases, burdened, it
suddenly seemed to me, with nominalized forms, past perfect tenses, con-
ditional phrases, all the forms of standard English that I had learned in
school and through books, the forms of English I did not use at home
with my mother.

Just last week, I was walking down the street with my mother, and I   4
again found myself conscious of the English I was using, the English I do
use with her. We were talking about the price of new and used furniture
and I heard myself saying this: "Not waste money that way." My husband was with us as well, and he didn't notice any switch in my English.
And then I realized why. It's because over the twenty years we've been
together I've often used that same kind of English with him, and sometimes he even uses it with me. It has become our language of intimacy, a
different sort of English that relates to family talk, the language I grew
up with.

So you'll have some idea of what this family talk I heard sounds like,   5
I'll quote what my mother said during a recent conversation which I vid-
eotaped and then transcribed. During this conversation, my mother was
talking about a political gangster in Shanghai who had the same last
name as her family's, Du, and how the gangster in his early years
wanted to be adopted by her family, which was rich by comparison.
Later, the gangster became more powerful, far richer than my mother's
family, and one day showed up at my mother's wedding to pay his
respects. Here's what she said in part:

"Du Yusong having business like fruit stand. Like off the street kind.   6
He is Du like Du Zong—but not Tsung-ming Island people. The local
people call putong, the river east side, he belong to that side local people. That man want to ask Du Zong father take him in like become own
family. Du Zong father wasn't look down on him, but didn't take seriously, until that man big like become a mafia. Now important person,

very hard to inviting him. Chinese way, came only to show respect, don't stay for dinner. Respect for making big celebration, he shows up. Mean gives lots of respect. Chinese custom. Chinese social life that way. If too important won't have to stay too long. He come to my wedding. I didn't see, I heard it. I gone to boy's side, they have YMCA dinner. Chinese age I was nineteen."

You should know that my mother's expressive command of English   7 belies how much she actually understands. She reads the *Forbes* report, listens to *Wall Street Week*, converses daily with her stockbroker, and reads all of Shirley MacLaine's books with ease—all kinds of things I can't begin to understand. Yet some of my friends tell me they understand 50 percent of what my mother says. Some say they understand 80 to 90 percent. Some say they understand none of it, as if she were speaking pure Chinese. But to me, my mother's English is perfectly clear, perfectly natural. It's my mother tongue. Her language, as I hear it, is vivid, direct, full of observation and imagery. That was the language that helped shape the way I saw things, expressed things, made sense of the world.

Lately, I've been giving more thought to the kind of English my   8 mother speaks. Like others, I have described it to people as "broken" or "fractured" English. But I wince when I say that. It has always bothered me that I can think of no way to describe it other than "broken," as if it were damaged and needed to be fixed, as if it lacked a certain wholeness and soundness. I've heard other terms used, "limited English," for example. But they seem just as bad, as if everything is limited, including people's perceptions of the limited English speaker.

I know this for a fact, because when I was growing up, my mother's   9 "limited" English limited *my* perception of her. I was ashamed of her English. I believed that her English reflected the quality of what she had to say. That is, because she expressed them imperfectly her thoughts were imperfect. And I had plenty of empirical evidence to support me: the fact that people in department stores, at banks, and at restaurants did not take her seriously, did not give her good service, pretended not to understand her, or even acted as if they did not hear her.

My mother has long realized the limitations of her English as well.   10 When I was fifteen, she used to have me call people on the phone to pretend I was she. In this guise, I was forced to ask for information or even to complain and yell at people who had been rude to her. One time it was a call to her stockbroker in New York. She had cashed out her small portfolio and it just so happened we were going to go to New

York the next week, our very first trip outside California. I had to get on the phone and say in an adolescent voice that was not very convincing, "This is Mrs. Tan."

And my mother was standing in the back whispering loudly, "Why   11
he don't send me check, already two weeks late. So mad he lie to me, losing me money."

And then I said in perfect English, "Yes, I'm getting rather concerned.   12
You had agreed to send the check two weeks ago, but it hasn't arrived."

Then she began to talk more loudly. "What he want, I come to New   13
York tell him front of his boss, you cheating me?" And I was trying to calm her down, make her be quiet, while telling the stockbroker, "I can't tolerate any more excuses. If I don't receive the check immediately, I am going to have to speak to your manager when I'm in New York next week." And sure enough, the following week there we were in front of this astonished stockbroker, and I was sitting there red-faced and quiet, and my mother, the real Mrs. Tan, was shouting at his boss in her impeccable broken English.

We used a similar routine just five days ago, for a situation that was   14
far less humorous. My mother had gone to the hospital for an appointment, to find out about a benign brain tumor a CAT scan had revealed a month ago. She said she had spoken very good English, her best English, no mistakes. Still, she said, the hospital did not apologize when they said they had lost the CAT scan and she had come for nothing. She said they did not seem to have any sympathy when she told them she was anxious to know the exact diagnosis, since her husband and son had both died of brain tumors. She said they would not give her any more information until the next time and she would have to make another appointment for that. So she said she would not leave until the doctor called her daughter. She wouldn't budge. And when the doctor finally called her daughter, me, who spoke in perfect English—lo and behold—we had assurances the CAT scan would be found, promises that a conference call on Monday would be held, and apologies for any suffering my mother had gone through for a most regrettable mistake.

I think my mother's English almost had an effect on limiting my pos-   15
sibilities in life as well. Sociologists and linguists probably will tell you that a person's developing language skills are more influenced by peers. But I do think that the language spoken in the family, especially in immigrant families which are more insular, plays a large role in shaping the language of the child. And I believe that it affected my results on achievement tests, IQ tests, and the SAT. While my English skills were

never judged as poor, compared to math, English could not be considered my strong suit. In grade school I did moderately well, getting perhaps B's, sometimes B-pluses, in English and scoring perhaps in the sixtieth or seventieth percentile on achievement tests. But those scores were not good enough to override the opinion that my true abilities lay in math and science, because in those areas I achieved A's and scored in the ninetieth percentile or higher.

This was understandable. Math is precise; there is only one correct 16 answer. Whereas, for me at least, the answers on English tests were always a judgment call, a matter of opinion and personal experience. Those tests were constructed around items like fill-in-the-blank sentence completion, such as, "Even though Tom was, Mary thought he was." And the correct answer always seemed to be the most bland combinations of thoughts, for example, "Even though Tom was shy, Mary thought he was charming," with the grammatical structure "even though" limiting the correct answer to some sort of semantic opposites, so you wouldn't get answers like, "Even though Tom was foolish, Mary thought he was ridiculous." Well, according to my mother, there were very few limitations as to what Tom could have been and what Mary might have thought of him. So I never did well on tests like that.

The same was true with word analogies, pairs of words in which you 17 were supposed to find some sort of logical, semantic relationship—for example, "*Sunset* is to *nightfall* as _____ is to _____." And here you would be presented with a list of four possible pairs, one of which showed the same kind of relationship: *red* is to *stoplight, bus* is to *arrival, chills* is to *fever, yawn* is to *boring.* Well, I could never think that way. I knew what the tests were asking, but I could not block out of my mind the images already created by the first pair, "*sunset* is to *nightfall*"—and I would see a burst of colors against a darkening sky, the moon rising, the lowering of a curtain of stars. And all the other pairs of words—red, bus, stoplight, boring—just threw up a mass of confusing images, making it impossible for me to sort out something as logical as saying: "A sunset precedes nightfall" is the same as "a chill precedes a fever." The only way I would have gotten that answer right would have been to imagine an associative situation, for example, my being disobedient and staying out past sunset, catching a chill at night, which turns into feverish pneumonia as punishment, which indeed did happen to me.

I have been thinking about all this lately, about my mother's English, 18 about achievement tests. Because lately I've been asked, as a writer, why there are not more Asian Americans represented in American literature.

Why are there few Asian Americans enrolled in creative writing programs? Why do so many Chinese students go into engineering? Well,
these are broad sociological questions I can't begin to answer. But I have
noticed in surveys—in fact, just last week—that Asian students, as a
whole, always do significantly better on math achievement tests than in
English. And this makes me think that there are other Asian-American
students whose English spoken in the home might also be described as
"broken" or "limited." And perhaps they also have teachers who are
steering them away from writing and into math and science, which is
what happened to me.

Fortunately, I happen to be rebellious in nature and enjoy the chal-   19
lenge of disproving assumptions made about me. I became an English
major my first year in college, after being enrolled as pre-med. I started
writing non-fiction as a freelancer the week after I was told by my former boss that writing was my worst skill and I should hone my talents
toward account management.

But it wasn't until 1985 that I finally began to write fiction. And at   20
first I wrote using what I thought to be wittily crafted sentences, sentences that would finally prove I had mastery over the English language.
Here's an example from the first draft of a story that later made its way
into *The Joy Luck Club*, but without this line: "That was my mental
quandary in its nascent state." A terrible line, which I can barely
pronounce.

Fortunately, for reasons I won't get into today, I later decided I   21
should envision a reader for the stories I would write. And the reader I
decided upon was my mother, because these were stories about mothers.
So with this reader in mind—and in fact she did read my early drafts—I
began to write stories using all the Englishes I grew up with: the English
I spoke to my mother, which for lack of a better term might be described
as "simple"; the English she used with me, which for lack of a better
term might be described as "broken"; my translation of her Chinese,
which could certainly be described as "watered down"; and what I imagined to be her translation of her Chinese if she could speak in perfect
English, her internal language, and for that I sought to preserve the
essence, but neither an English nor a Chinese structure. I wanted to capture what language ability tests can never reveal: her intent, her passion,
her imagery, the rhythms of her speech and the nature of her thoughts.

Apart from what any critic had to say about my writing, I knew I   22
had succeeded where it counted when my mother finished reading my
book and gave me her verdict: "So easy to read."

Thinking about the Essay

1. Explain the multiple meanings of Tan's title and how they illuminate the essay. What are the four ways Tan says language can work?

2. What is Tan's thesis, and where does it appear? How do we know her point of view about other "Englishes"? Does she state it directly or indirectly, and where?

3. How do narration and description interact in this essay? How does Tan describe her mother? What is the importance of dialogue?

4. What is Tan's viewpoint about language? Does she state that language should always be "simple"? Why or why not? To the extent that Tan's mother is an intended audience for her essay, is her language simple? Explain your answer by specific reference to her words and sentences. Finally, why does Tan's mother find her daughter's writing easy to understand?

5. How and where does Tan use humor in this essay? Where does Tan employ amusing anecdotes? What is her purpose in presenting these anecdotes, and how do they influence the essay's overall tone?

Responding in Writing

6. Tan suggests that the way we use language reflects the way we see the world. Write an essay based on this observation. Feel free to present an analytical paper or a narrative and descriptive essay, or to blend these patterns as does Tan.

7. Should all Americans speak and write the same language? Answer this question in an argumentative essay.

8. Tan writes about the "shame" she once experienced because of her mother's speech (paragraph 9). Write an essay about the dangers of linking personality or behavior to language. Can this linkage be used to promote racist, sexist, or other discriminatory ideas?

Networking

9. With two other class members, draw up a list of all the "Englishes" you have encountered. For example, how do your parents speak? What about relatives? Friends? Classmates? Personalities on television? Share your list with the class.

10. Conduct Internet or library research on the role of stereotyping by language in American radio and/or film. You might want to look into the popularity of the Charlie Chan series or Amos and Andy, or focus on a particular film that stereotypes a group. Present your information in an analytical and evaluative essay.

Mute in an English-Only World

CHANG-RAE LEE

Chang-rae Lee was born in 1965 in Seoul, South Korea. He and his family emigrated to the United States in 1968. Lee attended public schools in New Rochelle, New York; graduated from Yale University (B.A., 1987); and received an M.F.A. degree from the University of Oregon (1993). His first novel, *Native Speaker* (1995), won several prizes, including the Ernest Hemingway Foundation/PEN Award for First Fiction. He has also written *A Gesture Life* (1999) and *Aloft* (2004), and he has published fiction and nonfiction in many magazines, including *The New Yorker* and *Time*. Lee has taught in the creative writing programs at the University of Oregon and Hunter College; today he is part of the Humanities Council and creative writing program at Princeton University. In the following essay, which appeared on the **op-ed** page of *The New York Times* in 1996, Lee remembers his mother's efforts to learn English, using literary memoir to comment on recent laws passed by certain towns in New Jersey requiring English on all commercial signs.

Before Reading

Should all commercial signs have English written on them, in addition to any other language? What about menus in ethnic restaurants?

When I read of the troubles in Palisades Park, N.J., over the prolif- 1
eration of Korean-language signs along its main commercial strip, I unexpectedly sympathized with the frustrations, resentments and fears of the longtime residents. They clearly felt alienated and even unwelcome in a vital part of their community. The town, like seven others in New Jersey, has passed laws requiring that half of any commercial sign in a foreign language be in English.

Now I certainly would never tolerate any exclusionary ideas about 2
who could rightfully settle and belong in the town. But having been raised in a Korean immigrant family, I saw every day the exacting price and power of language, especially with my mother, who was an outsider in an English-only world.

In the first years we lived in America, my mother could speak only   3
the most basic English, and she often encountered great difficulty whenever she went out.

We lived in New Rochelle, N.Y., in the early '70s, and most of the   4
local businesses were run by the descendants of immigrants who, generations ago, had come to the suburbs from New York City. Proudly dot-
ting Main Street and North Avenue were Italian pastry and cheese
shops, Jewish tailors and cleaners and Polish and German butchers and
bakers. If my mother's marketing couldn't wait until the weekend, when
my father had free time, she would often hold off until I came home
from school to buy the groceries.

Though I was only 6 or 7 years old, she insisted that I go out shop-   5
ping with her and my younger sister. I mostly loathed the task, partly
because it meant I couldn't spend the afternoon playing catch with my
friends but also because I knew our errands would inevitably lead to an
awkward scene, and that I would have to speak up to help my mother.

I was just learning the language myself, but I was a quick study, as chil-   6
dren are with new tongues. I had spent kindergarten in almost complete
silence, hearing only the high nasality of my teacher and comprehending little
but the cranky wails and cries of my classmates. But soon, seemingly mere
months later, I had already become a terrible ham and mimic, and I would
crack up my father with impressions of teachers, his friends and even himself.
My mother scolded me for aping his speech, and the one time I attempted to
make light of hers I rated a roundhouse smack on my bottom.

For her, the English language was not very funny. It usually meant   7
trouble and a good dose of shame, and sometimes real hurt. Although she
had a good reading knowledge of the language from university classes in
South Korea, she had never practiced actual conversation. So in America,
she used English flashcards and phrase books and watched television with
us kids. And she faithfully carried a pocket workbook illustrated with
stick-figure people and compound sentences to be filled in.

But none of it seemed to do her much good. Staying mostly at home   8
to care for us, she didn't have many chances to try out sundry words
and phrases. When she did, say, at the window of the post office, her
readied speech would stall, freeze, sometimes altogether collapse.

One day was unusually harrowing. We ventured downtown in the   9
new Ford Country Squire my father had bought her, an enormous station wagon that seemed as long—and deft—as an ocean liner. We were
shopping for a special meal for guests visiting that weekend, and my
mother had heard that a particular butcher carried fresh oxtails—which
she needed for a traditional soup.

We'd never been inside the shop, but my mother would pause before 10 its window, which was always lined with whole hams, crown roasts and ropes of plump handmade sausages. She greatly esteemed the bounty with her eyes, and my sister and I did also, but despite our desirous cries she'd turn us away and instead buy the packaged links at the Finast supermarket, where she felt comfortable looking them over and could easily spot the price. And, of course, not have to talk.

But that day she was resolved. The butcher store was crowded, and 11 as we stepped inside the door jingled a welcome. No one seemed to notice. We waited for some time, and people who entered after us were now being served. Finally, an old woman nudged my mother and waved a little ticket, which we hadn't taken. We patiently waited again, until one of the beefy men behind the glass display hollered our number.

My mother pulled us forward and began searching the cases, but the 12 oxtails were nowhere to be found. The man, his big arms crossed, sharply said, "Come on, lady, whaddya want?" This unnerved her, and she somehow blurted the Korean word for oxtail, soggori.

The butcher looked as if my mother had put something sour in his 13 mouth, and he glanced back at the lighted board and called the next number.

Before I knew it, she had rushed us outside and back in the wagon, 14 which she had double-parked because of the crowd. She was furious, almost vibrating with fear and grief, and I could see she was about to cry.

She wanted to go back inside, but now the driver of the car we were 15 blocking wanted to pull out. She was shooing us away. My mother, who had just earned her driver's license, started furiously working the pedals. But in her haste she must have flooded the engine, for it wouldn't turn over. The driver started honking and then another car began honking as well, and soon it seemed the entire street was shrieking at us.

In the following years, my mother grew steadily more comfortable 16 with English. In Korean, she could be fiery, stern, deeply funny and ironic; in English, just slightly less so. If she was never quite fluent, she gained enough confidence to make herself clearly known to anyone, and particularly to me.

Five years ago, she died of cancer, and some months after we buried 17 her I found myself in the driveway of my father's house, washing her sedan. I liked taking care of her things; it made me feel close to her. While I was cleaning out the glove compartment, I found her pocket English workbook, the one with the silly illustrations. I hadn't seen it in nearly 20 years. The yellowed pages were brittle and dog-eared. She had fashioned a plain-paper wrapping for it, and I wondered whether she meant to protect the book or hide it.

I don't doubt that she would have appreciated doing the family shop- 18 ping on the new Broad Avenue of Palisades Park. But I like to think, too, that she would have understood those who now complain about the Korean-only signs.

I wonder what these same people would have done if they had seen 19 my mother studying her English workbook—or lost in a store. Would they have nodded gently at her? Would they have lent a kind word?

Thinking about the Essay

1. What is the author's purpose? Is he trying to paint a picture of his mother, describe an aspect of the immigrant experience, convey a thesis, argue a point, or what? Explain your response.

2. What is unusual about Lee's introduction? How does his position on the issue raised defy your expectations?

3. Lee offers stories within stories. How are they ordered? Which tale receives greatest development, and why?

4. Lee uses *colloquial language* in this essay. Identify some examples. What is the effect?

5. What is the dominant impression that you have of Lee's mother? How does he bring her to life?

Responding in Writing

6. Construct a profile of the writer. What do we learn about Lee? What are his values? What is his attitude toward English? How does this son of immigrant parents establish himself as an authority? How does he surprise us with his perspective on language?

7. In a personal essay, tell of a time when you were embarrassed either by the language of someone close to you or by your own use of language in a social or business situation.

8. Both Amy Tan and Chang-rae Lee focus on their mothers' handling of their second language—English. Write a comparative essay in which you explain the similarities and differences in the authors' approaches to their subject.

Networking

9. With two other class members, discuss the emotional appeal of Lee's essay. Look especially at his conclusion. Share your responses with the class.

10. Write an e-mail to your instructor, suggesting two additional questions you would ask about Lee's essay if you were teaching it.

The Power of Words in Wartime

ROBIN TOLMACH LAKOFF

> Robin Tolmach Lakoff was born in Brooklyn, New
> York, in 1942 and educated at Radcliffe College (B.A.,
> 1964), Indiana University (M.A., 1965), and Harvard
> University (Ph.D., 1967). An influential linguist who
> serves on the faculty at the University of California at
> Berkeley, Lakoff has written several studies focusing on
> the influence of language on social attitudes—especially
> attitudes toward women and "others." Among her
> most important works are *Language and Women's
> Place* (1975), *Talking Power: The Politics of Language
> in Our Lives* (1990), and *The Language of War*
> (2000). The following essay appeared in *The New York
> Times* on May 18, 2004.

Before Reading

What does "stereotyping" mean? What is the relationship between stereotyping and such words in wartime as "terrorist," "jihadist," "invader," and "infidel"?

An American soldier refers to an Iraqi prisoner as "it." A general 1
speaks not of "Iraqi fighters" but of "the enemy." A weapons manufacturer doesn't talk about people but about "targets."

Bullets and bombs are not the only tools of war. Words, too, play 2
their part.

Human beings are social animals, genetically hard-wired to feel compassion toward others. Under normal conditions, most people find it 3
very difficult to kill.

But in war, military recruits must be persuaded that killing other people is not only acceptable but even honorable. 4

The language of war is intended to bring about that change, and not only 5
for soldiers in the field. In wartime, language must be created to enable combatants and noncombatants alike to see the other side as killable, to overcome the innate queasiness over the taking of human life. Soldiers, and those who remain at home, learn to call their enemies by names that make them seem not quite human—inferior, contemptible and not like "us."

The specific words change from culture to culture and war to war.   6
The names need not be obviously demeaning. Just the fact that we can
name them gives us a sense of superiority and control. If, in addition, we
give them nicknames, we can see them as smaller, weaker and child-
like—not worth taking seriously as fully human.

The Greeks and Romans referred to everyone else as "barbarians"—   7
etymologically those who only babble, only go "bar-bar." During the
American Revolution, the British called the colonists "Yankees," a term with
a history that is still in dispute. While the British intended it disparagingly, the
Americans, in perhaps the first historical instance of reclamation, made the
word their own and gave it a positive spin, turning the derisive song "Yankee
Doodle" into our first, if unofficial, national anthem.

In World War I, the British gave the Germans the nickname   8
"Jerries," from the first syllable of German. In World War II, Americans
referred to the Japanese as "Japs."

The names may refer to real or imagined cultural and physical differ-   9
ences that emphasize the ridiculous or the repugnant. So in various wars,
the British called the French "Frogs." Germans have been called
"Krauts," a reference to weird and smelly food. The Vietnamese were
called "slopes" and "slants." The Koreans were referred to simply as
"gooks."

The war in Iraq has added new examples. Some American soldiers   10
refer to the Iraqis as "hadjis," used in a derogatory way, apparently
unaware that the word, which comes from the Arabic term for a pilgrimage to Mecca, is used as a term of respect for older Muslim men.

The Austrian ethologist Konrad Lorenz suggested that the more   11
clearly we see other members of our own species as individuals, the
harder we find it to kill them.

So some terms of war are collective nouns, encouraging us to see the   12
enemy as an undifferentiated mass, rather than as individuals capable of
suffering. Crusaders called their enemy "the Saracen," and in World
War I, the British called Germans "the Hun."

American soldiers are trained to call those they are fighting against   13
"the enemy." It is easier to kill an enemy than an Iraqi.

The word "enemy" itself provides the facelessness of a collective   14
noun. Its non-specificity also has a fear-inducing connotation; enemy
means simply "those we are fighting," without reference to their identity.

The terrors and uncertainties of war make learning this kind of lan-   15
guage especially compelling for soldiers on the front. But civilians back
home also need to believe that what their country is doing is just and

necessary, and that the killing they are supporting is in some way different from the killing in civilian life that is rightly punished by the criminal justice system. The use of the language developed for military purposes by civilians reassures them that war is not murder.

The linguistic habits that soldiers must absorb in order to fight make   16
atrocities like those at Abu Ghraib virtually inevitable. The same language that creates a psychological chasm between "us" and "them" and enables American troops to kill in battle, makes enemy soldiers fit subjects for torture and humiliation. The reasoning is: They are not really human, so they will not feel the pain.

Once language draws that line, all kinds of mistreatment become   17
imaginable, and then justifiable. To make the abuses at Abu Ghraib unthinkable, we would have to abolish war itself.

Thinking about the Essay

1. Lakoff wrote this essay as an op-ed article for a newspaper. What aspects of style, thesis placement, paragraph organization, length, and tone does she employ to satisfy the demands of an op-ed contribution?

2. What is Lakoff's purpose in this essay? Does she want to inform readers about language, analyze words in wartime, argue about the Iraq war, or what?

3. Lakoff organizes her essay around causes and effects, using a series of examples to support her causal analysis. Trace this strategy through the essay, trying to determine where language is a cause, an effect, or both.

4. How logical do you find Lakoff's article, and why? Do you think that she succumbs to any logical fallacies or exaggerates in order to make a point? Justify your response.

5. How effective do you find Lakoff's attempt to link the language stemming from the war in Iraq with that of the language used to invoke the "enemy" in wars stretching back in history to ancient Greece? Is this sufficient support for her thesis or claim? Explain.

Responding in Writing

6. Select one word that appears prominently in discussions of the war in Iraq (or Afghanistan, or both), and demonstrate the ways in which government and the press invoke this word to influence public attitudes.

7. Write a cause-and-effect essay in which you demonstrate the ways in which language can stereotype certain types of people—for example, immigrants, Muslims, gays, Africans.

8. Argue for or against the proposition that Lakoff presents a convincing argument in "The Power of Words in Wartime." Refer to specific strategies she employs to support your position.

Networking

9. Lakoff refers to Konrad Lorenz in paragraph 11. With one other class member, go online and find out more about this person. Then explain in class discussion why you think Lakoff refers to him in her essay.

10. Go online to find out more about Abu Ghraib, a topic that Lakoff injects into her essay. Download at least three images of this episode, and then write a brief essay, with illustrations, highlighting Lakoff's claim about the "psychological chasm between 'us' and 'them.'"

Easy, Tiger

DAVID SEDARIS | David Sedaris was born in 1956. Before he achieved success as a writer, he cleaned houses in New York City. Sedaris is best known as a personal essayist, often injecting broad humor and satire into narratives that typically involve family members, friends, and his partner Hugh. He can often be heard on National Public Radio. Sedaris's essays have been collected in *Naked* (1997), *Me Talk Pretty One Day* (2000), *Dress Your Family in Corduroy and Denim* (2004), and *When You Are Engulfed in Flames* (2008). In this essay that was published in *The New Yorker* in 2011, Sedaris offers a humorous account of "learning" languages while touring the globe.

Before Reading

When traveling abroad—or when you simply head to a local ethnic restaurant or grocery store—do you make an attempt to learn a few basic words in the native language? Or do you simply speak English, assuming that English is now the common mode of global communication?

On a recent flight from Tokyo to Beijing, at around the time that my lunch tray was taken away, I remembered that I needed to learn Mandarin. "Goddammit," I whispered. "I knew I forgot something." 1

David Sedaris, "Easy, Tiger," first published by *The New Yorker* and reprinted by permission of Don Congdon Associates, Inc. Copyright © 2011 by David Sedaris.

Normally, when landing in a foreign country, I'm prepared to say, at   2
the very least. "Hello" and "I'm sorry." This trip, though, was a two-
parter, and I'd used my month of prep time to bone up on my Japanese.
For this, I returned to the Pimsleur audio program I'd relied on for my
previous two visits. I'd used its Italian version as well, and had noted
that they followed the same basic pattern. In the first thirty-minute lesson, a man approaches a strange woman, asking, in Italian or Japanese
or whichever language you've signed up for, if she understands English.
The two jabber away for twenty seconds or so, and then an American
instructor chimes in and breaks it all down. "Say, 'Excuse me,'" he tells
you. "Ask, 'Are you an American?'" The conversations grow more complicated as you progress, and the phrases are regularly repeated so that
you don't forget them.

Not all the sentences I've learned with Pimsleur are suited to my way   3
of life. I don't drive, for example, so "Which is the road to go to Yoko-
hama?" never did me any good. The same is true of "As for gas, is it expensive?," though I have got some mileage out of "Fill her up, please,"
which I use in restaurants when getting a second cup of tea.

Thanks to Japanese I and II, I'm able to buy train tickets, count to   4
nine hundred and ninety-nine thousand, and say, whenever someone is
giving me change, "Now you are giving me change." I can manage in a
restaurant, take a cab, and even make small talk with the driver. "Do
you have children?" I ask. "Will you take a vacation this year?" "Where
to?" When he turns it around, as Japanese cabdrivers are inclined to do,
I tell him that I have three children, a big boy and two little girls. If Pimsleur included "I am a middle-aged homosexual and thus make do with
a niece I never see and a very small godson," I'd say that. In the meantime, I work with what I have.

———

Pimsleur's a big help when it comes to pronunciation. The actors are   5
native speakers, and they don't slow down for your benefit. The draw-
backs are that they never explain anything or teach you to think for
yourself. Instead of being provided with building blocks which would
allow you to construct a sentence of your own, you're left using the hundreds or thousands of sentences that you have memorized. That means
waiting for a particular situation to arise in order to comment on it; either that or becoming one of those weird non-sequitur people, the kind
who, when asked a question about paint color, answer, "There is a bank
in front of the train station," or "Mrs. Yamada Ito has been playing tennis for fifteen years."

I hadn't downloaded a Pimsleur program for China, so on the   6
flight to Beijing I turned to my Lonely Planet phrase book, knowing it
was hopeless. Mandarin is closer to singing than it is to talking, and
even though the words were written phonetically, I couldn't begin to get
the hang of them. The book was slim and palm-size, divided into short
chapters: Banking, Shopping, Border Crossing. The one titled
"Romance" included the following: "Would you like a drink?" "You're
a fantastic dancer." "You look like some cousin of mine." The latter
would work only if you were Asian, but even then it's a little creepy,
the implication being "the cousin I have always wanted to undress and
ejaculate on."

In the subchapter "Getting Closer," one learns to say, "I like you   7
very much." "You're great." "Do you want a massage?" On the following page, things heat up. "I want you." "I want to make love to you."
"How about going to bed?" And, a line that might have been written
especially for me, "Don't worry, I'll do it myself."

Oddly, the writers haven't included "Leave the light on," a must if   8
you want to actually *say* any of these things. One pictures the vacationer
naked on a bed, and squinting into his or her little book to moan, "Oh
yeah!" "Easy, tiger," "Faster," "Harder," "Slower," "Softer." "That
was . . . amazing/weird/wild." "Can I stay over?"

In the following subchapters, it all falls apart: "Are you seeing some-   9
one else?" "He/She is just a friend." "You're just using me for sex." "I
don't think it's working out." And, finally, "I never want to see you
again."

―――――

Hugh and I returned from China, and a few days later I started pre-   10
paring for a trip to Germany. The first time I went, in 1999, I couldn't
bring myself to say so much as *Guten Morgen*. The sounds felt false
coming out of my mouth, so instead I spent my time speaking English
apologetically. Not that the apologies were needed. In Paris, yes, but in
Berlin people's attitude is "Thank you for allowing me to practice my
perfect English." And I do mean perfect. "Are you from Minnesota?" I
kept asking.

In the beginning, I was put off by the harshness of German. Someone   11
would order a piece of cake and it sounded as if it were an actual order,
like "Cut the cake and lie face down in the ditch between the cobbler
and the little girl." I'm guessing this comes from having watched too
many Second World War movies. Then I remembered the umpteen Fass-
binder films I'd sat through in the eighties, and German began to sound

conflicted instead of heartless. I went back twice in 2000, and over time the sound of the language grew on me. It's like English, but sideways.

I've made at least ten trips by now, and have gone from one end of 12 the country to the other. People taught me all sorts of words, but the only ones that stuck were *Kaiserschnitt*, which means Cesarean section, and *Lebensabschnittspartner*. This doesn't translate to "lover" or "life partner" but, rather, to "the person I am with today," the implication being that things change, and you are keeping yourself open.

For this latest trip, I wanted to do better, and so I downloaded all thirty 13 lessons of Pimsleur German I, which again start off with "Excuse me, do you understand English?" As with the Japanese and the Italian versions, the program taught me to count and to tell time. Again I learned "The girl is already big" and "How are you?" (*"Wie geht es Ihnen?"*)

In Japanese and Italian, the response to the latter question is "I'm 14 fine, and you?" In German it's answered with a sigh, and a slight pause, followed by "Not so good."

I mentioned this to my German friend Tilo, who said that of course 15 that was the response. "We can't get it through our heads that people are asking that only to be polite," he said.

In Japanese I, Lesson 17, the actress who plays the wife says, *"Kai- 16 mono ga shitai n desu ga!"* ("I want to go shopping but there's a problem and you need to guess what it is.") The exercise is about numbers, so the husband asks how much money she has. She gives him a figure, and he offers to increase it incrementally.

Similarly, in the German version, the wife announces that she wants 17 to buy something. *"Ich möchte noch etwas kaufen."* Her husband asks how much money she has, and, after she answers, he responds, coldly, "I'm not giving you any more. You have enough."

There's no discord in Pimsleur's Japan, but its Germany is a moody 18 and often savage place. In one of the exercises, you're encouraged to argue with a bellhop who tries to cheat you out of your change and who ends up sneering, "You don't understand German."

"Oh, but I do," you learn to say. "I do understand German."   19

It's a program full of odd sentence combinations. "We don't live here. 20 We want mineral water" implies that if the couple *did* live in this particular town they'd be getting drunk like everyone else. Another standout is *"Der Wein ist zu teuer und Sie sprechen zu schnell."* ("The wine is too expensive and you talk too fast.") The response to this would be "Anything else, Herr Asshole?" But of course they don't teach you that.

———

On our last trip to Tokyo, Hugh and I rented an apartment in a non- 21 descript neighborhood a few subway stops from Shinjuku Station. A representative from the real-estate agency met us at the front door, and when I spoke to him in Japanese, he told me I needed to buy myself some manga. "Read those and you'll learn how people actually talk," he said. "You, you're a little too polite."

I know what he was getting at, but I really don't see this as much of 22 a problem, especially if you're a foreigner, and any perceived rudeness can turn someone not just against you but against your entire country. Here Pimsleur has it all over the phrase books of my youth, where the Ugly American was alive, and kicking people. "I didn't order this!" he raged in Greek and Spanish. "Think you can cheat me, do you?" "Go away or I'll call the police."

Now for the travelling American there's less of a need for phrase 23 books. Not only do we expect everyone to speak our language; we expect everyone to be fluent. I rarely hear an American vacationer say to a waiter or a shopkeeper in Europe, "Your English is so good." Rather, we act as if it were part of his job, like carrying a tray or making change. In this respect, the phrase books and audio programs are an almost charming throwback, a suggestion that *the traveller* put himself out there, that *he* open himself to criticism and not the person who's just trying to scrape by selling meatballs in Bumfucchio, Italy.

One of the things I like about Tokyo is the constant reinforcement 24 one gets for trying. "You are very skilled at Japanese," everyone keeps telling me. I know people are just being polite, but it spurs me on, just as I hoped to be spurred on in Germany. To this end, I've added a second audio program, one by a man named Michel Thomas, who works with a couple of students, a male and a female. At the start, he explains that German and English are closely related and thus have a lot in common. In one language, the verb is "to come," and in the other it's "*kommen*." English "to give" is German "*geben*," Boston's "That is good" is Berlin's "*Das ist gut*." It's an excellent way to start, and leaves the listener thinking, *Hey, Ich kann do dis.*

———

Unlike the nameless instructor in Pimsleur, Herr Thomas explains 25 things—the fact, for example, that if there are two verbs in a German sentence one of them comes at the end. He doesn't give you phrases to memorize. In fact, he actively discourages study. "How would you say, 'Give it to me?'" he asks the female student. She and I correctly answer, and then he turns to the male. "Now try "I would like for you to give it to me.'"

Ten minutes later, we've graduated to "I can't give it to you today, 26
because I cannot find it." To people who speak nothing but English, this
might seem easy enough, but anyone else will appreciate how difficult it is:
negatives, multiple uses of "it," and the hell that breaks loose following the
German "because." The thrill is that you're actually figuring it out on your
own. You're engaging with another language, not just parroting it.

Walking through the grocery store with Pimsleur *und* Thomas on my 27
iPod, I picture myself pulling up to my Munich hotel with my friend
Ulrike, who's only ever known me to say "Cesarean section" and "the
person I am with until someone better comes along."

"*Bleiben wir hier heute Abend?*" I plan to say. "*Wieviele Nächte?* 28
Zwei? Das ist teuer, nicht wahr?"

She's a wonderful woman, Ulrike, and if that's all I get out of this— 29
seeing the shock register on her face as I natter on—it'll be well worth
my mouth of study.

Perhaps that evening after dinner, I'll turn on the TV in my hotel room. 30
And maybe, if I'm lucky, I'll understand one out of every two hundred
words. The trick, ultimately, is not to let that discourage me, to think, Oh,
well. That's more than I understood the last time I watched TV in Germany. That was a few years back, in Stuttgart. There was a television
mounted on a perch in my room, and I turned it on to find a couple having
sex. This wasn't on pay-per-view but just regular Sunday-night TV. And I
meant these two were really going at it. If I'd had the Lonely Planet guide to
German, I might have recognized "Please don't stop!" "That was amazing/
weird." With Herr Thomas, I could understand "I just gave it to you," and,
with Pimsleur, "I would like to come now."

I watched this couple for a minute or two, and then I advanced to 31
the next channel, which was snowed out unless you paid for it. What
could they possibly be doing here that they weren't doing for free on the
other station? I asked myself. Turning each other inside out?

———

And isn't that the joy of foreign travel—there's always something to 32
scratch your head over. You don't have to be fluent in order to wonder.
Rather, you can just sit there with your mouth open, not exactly dumb,
just speechless.

Thinking about the Essay

1. Does this essay have a conventional thesis statement? Why or why not?
   What is the main point that Sedaris wants to convey to his readers?

2. A narrative essay often makes its points in a different way from an analytical or argumentative paper. In his narrative, Sedaris employs humor to tell connected stories about his "mastery" of foreign languages. Locate at least three examples of Sedaris's comic narrative technique, and explain their purpose.

3. How many sections does Sedaris divide his essay into? Why does he organize the essay this way? How does he achieve unity and coherence as he moves from section to section?

4. How does Sedaris craft a **persona** or self-image for himself? Does he invite us to take him seriously, or does he present his attempt to learn languages as one big joke? Justify your response with specific references to the text and an explanation of the tone Sedaris creates as he moves through various nations and languages.

5. What is the purpose of the concluding paragraph? What point is Sedaris trying to make, and in your opinion, is he successful?

Responding in Writing

6. Write a narrative essay in which you relate a comic episode or series of episodes involving your attempt to learn a foreign language.

7. Write an essay analyzing the various comic techniques used by Sedaris in "Easy, Tiger."

8. Argue for or against the proposition that one should attempt to learn a few basic words in the native language when traveling abroad.

Networking

9. In groups of four, exchange your narrative essays. After each paper has been read once by each member, discuss each essay as a group, commenting on the effectiveness of the narrative, suggesting ideas for how to improve certain elements, and especially paying attention to the tone and level of humor.

10. Go online and locate a recording of Sedaris reading one of his essays. Next write an analysis of the way in which his spoken presentation informs your understanding and appreciation of "Easy, Tiger."

5

Global Relationships: Are Sex and Gender Roles Changing?

As we move into the twenty-first century, the roles of men and women in the United States and around the world are in flux. In the United States, there are increasing numbers of American women in many professional fields—medicine, law, education, politics, and corporate life. And, with more men—"Mr. Moms"—staying home and caring for their children, either by preference or necessity, there is greater equality in domestic responsibilities. At the same time, a woman's right to choose or even obtain social services is under attack. And it was only in the summer of 2003 that the United States Supreme Court struck down a Texas law that had made sex between consenting adult males in the privacy of their homes a crime.

This national opposition in certain quarters to equality of rights in human relations is reflected in reactionary global attitudes and practices. Issues of race, sexual orientation, and ethnicity complicate the roles of women and men on a global scale. In certain nations, women can still be stoned to death for sexual "crimes"; in others, homosexuality can be punished by incarceration and even execution. Slave trafficking in women and children fuels a vibrant sex industry here and around the world. And children—stolen, bought, or extorted from poor parents from South America to Southeast Asia—can wind up in the United States as "adopted" boys and girls.

American women do seem to have advantages over many of their global counterparts, for when we consider the situation of women globally, the issue of equal rights and human rights becomes acute. From increasing acquired immunodeficiency syndrome (AIDS) rates among global women, to their exploitation as cheap labor or sex workers, to female infanticide, to the continuing resistance of men in traditional societies to any thought of gender equality, the lives of women in many parts of the world are perilous. Gendered value systems in traditional

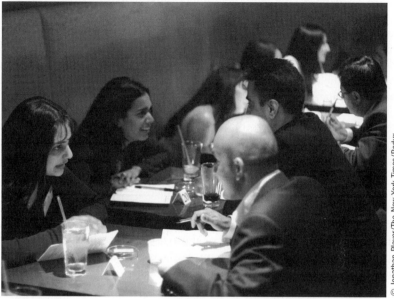

Hindu women take part in a speed-dating event at a London nightclub. Daters meet for a few minutes before moving on to the next date. Traditionally, relationships and marriages in this community were arranged by the families of the potential bride and groom.

Thinking about the Image

1. You probably know how awkward it can be to meet someone new. How do you think this photographer captured such an intimate, difficult moment between these two people?

2. What key characteristics do you see that distinguish groups of people or ethnicities in this photograph?

3. This photograph originally accompanied "Arranged Marriages Get a Little Reshuffling" by Lizette Alvarez on the following page. How accurately does the photograph illustrate the article? Newspaper editors have a limited amount of space to fill each day—why do you think this newspaper's editors wanted to include a photograph with this story?

4. If you could take a snapshot of dating culture in your own social group, what would you need to include in order to best capture its essence? Describe the image using very specific language.

societies change glacially, and often under only the most extreme conditions. For example, before the massacre of more than 800,000 Tutsi by their Hutu neighbors in Rwanda in 1993, women could not work or appear alone in the market; with the killing of so many of the men, Rwandan women suddenly had to assume responsibility for tasks they formerly had been excluded from. Women are the ones who are displaced disproportionately by wars, ethnic conflicts, famine, and environmental crises.

In this new global era, the destinies of women and men around the world are intertwined. Global forces have brought them together. The role of democracy in promoting human rights, the challenge to spread wealth from North to South and West to East, the need to prevent wars, and even the degradation of the environment have notable implications for men and women. Some argue that global forces—which we will detect in some essays in this chapter and study in detail in the next chapter—are notably hostile to women. Others argue that to the extent that nations can promote peace and democracy, produce prosperity, improve health and the environment, and reduce racism and ethnocentrism, both women and men will be the beneficiaries.

The essays in this chapter present insights into the roles of men and women around the world. The writers inquire into the impact of economics, politics, race, gender and sexual orientation, and culture on the lives of women and men. They invite us to reconsider the meaning of human rights, self-determination, and equality from a gendered perspective. In the twenty-first century, new ideas have emerged about the roles and rights of women and men. The essays that follow reveal some of the challenges that must be overcome before the concept of equal rights and opportunities for women and men can be realized.

Arranged Marriages Get a Little Reshuffling

LIZETTE ALVAREZ

In the following article, which appeared in *The New York Times* in 2003, Lizette Alvarez, a journalist for the newspaper, examines the changing attitudes and rituals concerning the traditional practice of arranged marriages. Writing from London, she focuses on "young, hip, South Asians." These young people do not reject traditions governing relations between the sexes. Instead, they "reshuffle" these conventions so that they may work successfully for them in the twenty-first century.

Before Reading

What is your attitude toward arranged marriage? In many Western nations, divorce rates approach 50 percent. Why not try arranged marriage if choosing your own mate is so frustrating and perilous?

They are young, hip, South Asians in their 20s who glide seamlessly 1 between two cultures, carefully cherry picking from the West to modernize the East.

They can just as easily listen to Justin Timberlake, the pop star, as 2 Rishi Rich, the Hindu musical dynamo. They eat halal meat but wear jeans and T-shirts to cafes.

Now these young Indians and Pakistanis are pushing the cultural 3 boundaries created by their parents and grandparents one step further: they are reshaping the tradition of arranged marriages in Britain.

While couples were once introduced exclusively by relatives and 4 friends, the Aunt Bijis, as Muslims call their matchmakers, are now being slowly nudged out by a boom in Asian marriage Web sites, chat rooms and personal advertisements. South Asian speed dating—Hindus one night, Muslims the next—is the latest phenomenon to hit London, with men and women meeting each other for just three minutes at restaurants and bars before moving on to the next potential mate.

Arranged marriages are still the norm within these clannish, tight- 5 knit communities in Britain, but, with the urging of second- and third-generation children, the nature of the arrangement has evolved, mostly by necessity.

What the young Indians and Pakistanis of Britain have done, in 6 effect, is to modernize practices that had evolved among the urban middle class in India in recent decades, allowing the prospective bride and groom a little more than one fleeting meeting to make up their minds.

The relaxation that had crept in since the 1960s allowed the couple, 7 after an initial meeting before their extended families, to meet alone several times, either with family members in another room or at a restaurant, before delivering a verdict. Now, the meetings take place in public venues without the family encounter first.

"The term we use now is 'assisted' arranged marriage," said Maha 8 Khan, a 23-year-old London Muslim woman. "The whole concept has changed a lot. Parents have become more open and more liberal in their concept of marriage and courtship."

Gitangeli Sapra, a trendy, willowy British Sindhu who at 25 jokes   9 that she is on her way to spinsterhood, is an avid speed dater with no qualms about advertising her love of modern arranged marriages. She even wrote a column about it for *The Sunday Times*.

"It's not based on love," she said, "which can fizzle out."   10

Ms. Sapra had attended 10 of the more formal arranged meetings—   11 awkward, drawn-out affairs in which the young man, his mother and several other relatives came over to meet the young woman and her family. She wore her best Indian outfit, a sari or elegant Indian pants and top. She sat quietly, which is almost impossible to fathom, considering her chattiness. When called upon, she poured tea, and then talked briefly to her potential mate in a side room.

"The matriarchs do the talking," she said over a glass of wine at an Ital-   12 ian restaurant. "You sit there looking cute and like the ideal housewife."

"To be honest, it's an easy way to get a rich man, with my mother's   13 blessing," she added, with a laugh.

None of them worked out, though, and Ms. Sapra has moved on to   14 speed dating with the blessings of her mother.

The very concept raises the hackles of some more old-fashioned parents,   15 but many are coming around, in part out of desperation. If Ms. Sapra finds someone on a speed date, she will quickly bring him home to her mother.

The abiding principles behind an arranged marriage still remain   16 strong—lust does not a lasting marriage make and family knows best. But parents and elders, eager to avoid alienating their children, making them miserable or seeing them go unmarried, have shown considerable flexibility. This is especially pronounced among the middle class, whose members tend to have integrated more into British life.

"The notion of arrangement has become more fluid," said Yunas   17 Samad, a sociology professor at Bradford University, who has studied marriage in the Muslim community. "What is happening is that the arranged marriage is becoming a bit more open and children are getting a bit more say in this so it becomes a nice compromise. There is the comfort of family support and a choice in what they are doing."

"It's a halfway house, not completely traditional and not completely   18 the same as what is happening in British society," he added.

To the surprise of parents and elders, this new hybrid between East   19 and West has actually stoked enthusiasm for an age-old tradition that many young people privately viewed as crusty and hopelessly unhip.

Now they see it as an important way to preserve religion and iden- 20
tity, not to mention a low-maintenance way of finding a mate. "It's like
your parents giving you a black book of girls," said Ronak Mashru, 24,
a London comedian whose parents are from India.

The young people also recognize that arranged marriages—in which 21
similar education and income levels, religious beliefs and character
outweigh the importance of physical attraction—can well outlast love
marriages.

"The falling-in-love system has failed," said Rehna Azim, a Pakistani 22
family lawyer who founded an Asian magazine, *Memsahib*.

South Asian unions are viewed as marriages between families, not 23
individuals. Divorce is anathema, while respect and standing within a
community are paramount. A lot of people have much invested in making a match work.

Similarly, several customs have survived dating: decisions have to be 24
made relatively quickly, often after the second or third meeting, and,
Ms. Sapra said, "once you've said yes, there is no turning back."

Dowries remain common and background still matters, too.   25

"Our mums look at the C.V.'s," said Vani Gupta, 30, a speed dater. 26
"They figure out whether we're compatible on paper—right job, right
background, right caste. It's nice to know your parents have done the
work for you. You feel more secure."

These middle-class women, most of them educated professionals or 27
university students, are looking for more modern men, who accept working wives and help around the house. But a "mechanic won't try for a
lawyer and a lawyer would not look for a mechanic," she said.

Ms. Sapra, for example, is looking for a fellow Sindhu, and a Gujar- 28
ati Indian typically seeks another Gujarati.

Muslims still keep it mostly within the family and the same region of 29
Pakistan. Cousins still frequently marry cousins, or at least second or
third cousins, and many British Pakistanis still find their brides back in
Pakistan. But now more men are marrying white British women who
convert to Islam, and others insist on finding a Muslim bride there who
speaks English, eats fish and chips and watches *East Enders*, a popular
soap opera.

Parents and elders have had to adapt, in large part because the num- 30
ber of potential partners is much smaller here than in their home countries. Rather than see an educated daughter go unwed, parents and
elders have accepted these more modern approaches, "Women are not
going to be put back in some kind of bottle," Professor Samad said.

Ms. Azim said, "Parents can say my child had an arranged marriage, 31
and he can say, 'Yeah, it's arranged. But I like her.'"

Thinking about the Essay

1. Writing for *The New York Times*, Alvarez knows her primary audience. What assumptions does she make about this audience? What secondary audiences would be interested in her topic, and why?

2. Does this article have a thesis? If so, where is it? If not, why not?

3. How does this essay reflect journalistic practice? Point to aspects of style, paragraph organization, article length, and other journalistic features. Is the tone of the article strictly neutral and objective (one aspect of journalistic method), or does it shade toward commentary or perhaps even contain an implicit argument? Explain.

4. How many people were interviewed for this article? Who are they, and what are their backgrounds? Taken together, how do they embody some of the main points that Alvarez wants to make about courtship practices among some Asians today?

5. What rhetorical practices—for example, definition, comparison and contrast, process and causal analysis—can you locate in this essay? Toward what purpose does the writer use them?

Responding in Writing

6. What is the difference between people who use Internet dating sites to make their own contacts and establish their own relationships and people from traditional societies who use the Internet to "cherry pick" prospective mates, whom they then present to their parents for appraisal? Which method strikes you as safer or potentially more successful, and why?

7. What is so great about "modern" dating and courtship practices if they often end in frustration and failure? Why not try something old, tried, and tested—like arranged marriage? Imagine that your parents insist on an arranged marriage for you. Write a personal response to this situation. Do not write that you would try to subvert the entire ritual. Instead, explain how you might "manage" this process to make the outcome acceptable.

8. Alvarez, presenting one principle behind the need for arranged marriages, writes that "lust does not a lasting marriage make" (paragraph 16). Do you agree or disagree with this claim? Provide at least three reasons to justify your response.

Networking

9. In class discussion, design a questionnaire about attitudes toward arranged marriage. Aim for at least five questions that can be answered briefly. Then have each class member obtain several responses to the questionnaire from other students. Compile the results, discuss them, and arrive at conclusions.

10. Investigate an Internet dating site. Sign up for it if you feel comfortable, or simply monitor the site for information. Report your findings to the class.

In Africa, AIDS Has a Woman's Face

KOFI A. ANNAN

Kofi A. Annan was born in the Gold Coast, as Ghana was known under British rule, in 1938. The son of a Fonte nobleman, he graduated in 1957 from Mfantsipim, a prestigious boarding school for boys that had been founded by the Methodist Church; Ghana won its independence from Great Britain that same year. After studies at the University of Science and Technology in Kumasi, Annan came to the United States on a Ford Foundation fellowship in 1959, completing his degree in economics at Macalester College in St. Paul, Minnesota. He also has a master's degree in management from the Massachusetts Institute of Technology (1972). Annan has worked for the United Nations in various capacities for four decades and was secretary-general of the United Nations from 1997 to 2006. He shared the Nobel Peace Prize in 2001 with the United Nations. In the following essay, which appeared in *The New York Times* in 2002, he writes about one of the many "problems without borders" that he believes we must deal with from an international perspective.

Before Reading

Consider the impact that AIDS has on a developing nation or an entire region. What are the economic consequences of the AIDS epidemic in these countries? What happens to the condition of women in such societies?

A combination of famine and AIDS is threatening the backbone of Africa—the women who keep African societies going and whose work makes up the economic foundation of rural communities. For decades, we have known that the best way for Africa to thrive is to ensure that its women have the freedom, power and knowledge to make decisions affecting their own lives and those of their families and communities. At the United Nations, we have always understood that our work for development depends on building a successful partnership with the African farmer and her husband.

Study after study has shown that there is no effective development strategy in which women do not play a central role. When women are fully involved, the benefits can be seen immediately: families are healthier; they are better fed; their income, savings and reinvestment go up. And, what is true of families is true of communities and, eventually, of whole countries.

But today, millions of African women are threatened by two simultaneous catastrophes: famine and AIDS. More than 30 million people are now at risk of starvation in southern Africa and the Horn of Africa. All of these predominantly agricultural societies are also battling serious AIDS epidemics. This is no coincidence: AIDS and famine are directly linked.

Because of AIDS, farming skills are being lost, agricultural development efforts are declining, rural livelihoods are disintegrating, productive capacity to work the land is dropping and household earnings are shrinking—all while the cost of caring for the ill is rising exponentially. At the same time, H.I.V. infection and AIDS are spreading dramatically and disproportionately among women. A United Nations report released last month shows that women now make up 50 percent of those infected with H.I.V. worldwide—and in Africa that figure is now 58 percent. Today, AIDS has a woman's face.

AIDS has already caused immense suffering by killing almost 2.5 million Africans this year alone. It has left 11 million African children orphaned since the epidemic began. Now it is attacking the capacity of these countries to resist famine by eroding those mechanisms that enable populations to fight back—the coping abilities provided by women.

In famines before the AIDS crisis, women proved more resilient than men. Their survival rate was higher, and their coping skills were stronger. Women were the ones who found alternative foods that could sustain their children in times of drought. Because droughts happened once a decade or so, women who had experienced previous droughts were able to pass on survival techniques to younger women. Women are the ones who nurture social networks that can help spread the burden in times of famine.

But today, as AIDS is eroding the health of Africa's women, it is eroding the skills, experience and networks that keep their families and communities going. Even before falling ill, a woman will often have to care for a sick husband, thereby reducing the time she can devote to planting, harvesting and marketing crops. When her husband dies, she is often deprived of credit, distribution networks or land rights. When she dies, the household will risk collapsing completely, leaving children to fend for themselves. The older ones, especially girls, will be taken out of school to work in the home or the farm. These girls, deprived of education and opportunities, will be even less able to protect themselves against AIDS. 7

Because this crisis is different from past famines, we must look beyond relief measures of the past. Merely shipping in food is not enough. Our effort will have to combine food assistance and new approaches to farming with treatment and prevention of H.I.V. and AIDS. It will require creating early-warning and analysis systems that monitor both H.I.V. infection rates and famine indicators. It will require new agricultural techniques, appropriate to a depleted work force. It will require a renewed effort to wipe out H.I.V.-related stigma and silence. 8

It will require innovative, large-scale ways to care for orphans, with specific measures that enable children in AIDS-affected communities to stay in school. Education and prevention are still the most powerful weapons against the spread of H.I.V. Above all, this new international effort must put women at the center of our strategy to fight AIDS. 9

Experience suggests that there is reason to hope. The recent United Nations report shows that H.I.V. infection rates in Uganda continue to decline. In South Africa, infection rates for women under 20 have started to decrease. In Zambia, H.I.V. rates show signs of dropping among women in urban areas and younger women in rural areas. In Ethiopia, infection levels have fallen among young women in the center of Addis Ababa. 10

We can and must build on those successes and replicate them elsewhere. For that, we need leadership, partnership and imagination from the international community and African governments. If we want to save Africa from two catastrophes, we would do well to focus on saving Africa's women. 11

Thinking about the Image

1. Although the map on the facing page did not appear with Kofi Annan's editorial, it was produced by a United Nations group formed to educate people about, and actively combat, H.I.V./AIDS. In what ways does this map visually represent the trends Annan describes? How does the map make the urgency of his argument more immediate?

2. Is there any information on the map that surprises you?

3. If you were a delegate to the United Nations from an African or Asian nation, what questions or responses would you have for Secretary-General Kofi Annan?

4. Use the information in this map to support your answer to any of the "Responding in Writing" questions.

Thinking about the Essay

1. What is the tone of Annan's introductory paragraph and the entire essay? What is his purpose? Point to specific passages to support your answer.

2. Annan employs causal analysis to develop this essay. Trace the causes and effects that he presents. What are some of the primary causes and effects? What secondary causes and effects does he mention?

3. This essay is rich in the use of examples. What types of illustration does Annan present to support his thesis?

4. Locate other rhetorical strategies—for example, comparison and contrast—that appear as structuring devices in this essay.

5. This essay presents a problem and offers a solution. Explain this strategy, paying careful attention to how the pattern evolves.

Responding in Writing

6. In a brief essay, explain what you have learned about AIDS in Africa from Annan's essay. Do you share his sense of optimism about the ability of the nations involved and the international community to solve the problem? Why or why not?

7. Explain your personal viewpoint on the increase of AIDS among the women of the world—not just in Africa but in Asia, Russia, Europe, and elsewhere.

8. Write an essay on another threat to women—either in a particular country or region, or around the world.

FIGURE 5.1   Regional Estimates of H.I.V./AIDS Infection as of December 2010

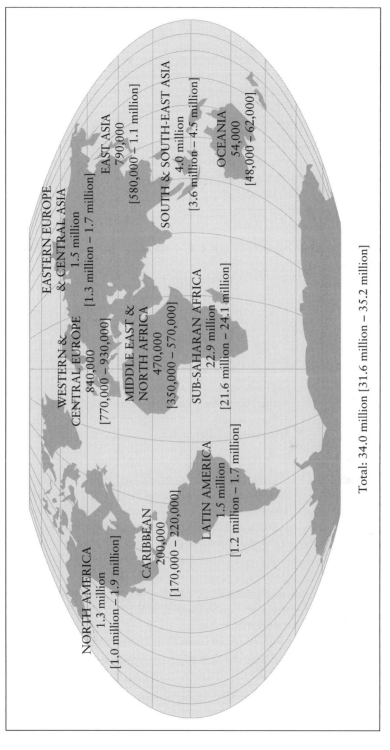

NORTH AMERICA
1.3 million
[1.0 million – 1.9 million]

CARIBBEAN
200,000
[170,000 – 220,000]

LATIN AMERICA
1.5 million
[1.2 million – 1.7 million]

WESTERN &
CENTRAL EUROPE
840,000
[770,000 – 930,000]

EASTERN EUROPE
& CENTRAL ASIA
1.5 million
[1.3 million – 1.7 million]

MIDDLE EAST &
NORTH AFRICA
470,000
[350,000 – 570,000]

SUB-SAHARAN AFRICA
22.9 million
[21.6 million – 24.1 million]

EAST ASIA
790,000
[580,000 – 1.1 million]

SOUTH & SOUTH-EAST ASIA
4.0 million
[3.6 million – 4.5 million]

OCEANIA
54,000
[48,000 – 62,000]

Total: 34.0 million [31.6 million – 35.2 million]

Source: UNAIDS, *2011 World AIDS Day Report.* Reprinted with permission.

Networking

9. Form working groups of four or five class members, and draw up an action plan to solicit funds on your campus for United Nations AIDS relief efforts in sub-Saharan Africa. Then create a master plan based on the work of other class groups. Decide if you want to present this plan to the campus administration for approval.

10. Search the Internet for information on the United Nations programs to alleviate the AIDS epidemic around the world. Then write a letter to your congressional representative explaining why (or why not) Congress should support these efforts.

The French, the Veil, and the Look

ELAINE SCIOLINO

> Elaine Sciolino is currently Paris correspondent for *The New York Times*. After receiving an M.A. from New York University in 1971, she began a distinguished career in journalism, first working for *Newsweek* from 1972 to 1984 as a foreign correspondent and Rome bureau chief. Since 1985, Sciolino has been employed by *The New York Times* as a reporter, senior writer, and chief diplomatic correspondent—the first woman to hold that position at the newspaper. Sciolino has covered the Iranian revolution, Iran hostage crisis, the Iran–Iraq War, the U.S. invasion of Grenada, and other global crises. Her books include *Outlaw State: Saddam Hussein's Quest for Power and the Gulf Crisis* (1991), *Persian Mirrors* (2000), and *La Seduction: How the French Play the Game of Life* (2011). In this essay from the April 17, 2011, issue of *The New York Times*, Sciolino examines the causes behind French hostility to the facial veil.

Before Reading

Should women and men be permitted by law to dress as they wish in any society, or should restrictions be placed on the ways in which people dress in public?

P ARIS — Many scholars of Islam will tell you that nothing in the   1
Koran requires a Muslim woman to cover her face—that its rules for

© AP Photo/Claude Paris

In this June 19, 2009, file photo, two women, one wearing the niqab, a veil worn by conservative Muslims that exposes only a woman's eyes, right, walk side by side in the Belsunce district of downtown Marseille, France. A popular Muslim cleric in Saudi Arabia, Sheik Aedh al-Garni, has issued a ruling, or fatwa, saying it is permissible for Muslim women to reveal their faces in countries where the Islamic veil is banned, while criticizing efforts in Europe to outlaw the garment.

proper Islamic dress are ambiguous and limited. "Say to the believing women that they should lower their gaze and guard their modesty," it says. It adds, "They should draw their veils over their bosoms and not display their ornaments."

Even Khadija, the first wife of the prophet Muhammad and a successful 2 businesswoman, who surely guarded her modesty, is believed to have bared her face in public. Historically, in the Middle East, it was often tribal Bedouin women who covered their faces, sometimes with decorative masklike veils dripping with coins that announced the value of their bank accounts.

Westerners became sensitive to the image of faceless Muslim women 3 largely through the use of the burqa by the Taliban to oppress women in Afghanistan. That garment functions like a body tent, with an eye screen to allow some vision. Years before it became an issue in the United States, French feminists fulminated against the burqa, and later against other radical interpretations of Islam in Afghanistan, including public stoning for adultery, the demolition of Buddhist shrines and the banning of music. And now, the French government has officially banned the wearing of full-face veils.

But the face-covering veils in France are different. Even though many here mistakenly call it a burqa, the garment worn by women here is a niqab, an improvised cover in black with no religious or traditional significance beyond what a wearer or observer gives it. Some of these women may be rebels, demanding control over their bodies and recognition within a Western culture whose social values they reject. Some may have been forced into covering their faces by domineering men; others may believe they are better Muslims because they hide their faces in public. Some are French converts from Christianity.   4

France's ideal of a secularized republic theoretically leaves it blind to color, ethnicity and religion, and makes everyone equal under the law; there is no census or reliable poll data on why these women veil, or even how many do. (The government's best estimate is 2,000 at most.)   5

So why all the fuss, on both sides of this question, about a tiny minority of women who wear odd-looking dress in a country that is the world's creative headquarters for odd-looking fashion? One explanation is cultural. In French culture, the eyes are supposed to meet in public, to invite a conversation or just to exchange a visual greeting with a stranger. Among Muslims, the eyes of men and women are not supposed to meet, even by chance, and especially not in public or between strangers.   6

"Le regard"—the look exchanged by two people—is a classic component of French literature, developed centuries ago in the love poetry of the troubadours. Especially in Paris, a stare in public is not usually taken as a sign of rudeness, and can be accepted as a warm compliment. You never walk alone here, it seems. "The visual marketplace of seduction" is how Pascal Bruckner and Alain Finkielkraut define public space in their 1977 book, "The New Love Disorder."   7

In another book, "Galanterie Française," Claude Habib, a specialist in 18th-century literature, argues that the centuries-old French tradition of gallantry "presupposes a visibility of the feminine" and "a joy of being visible—the very one that certain young Muslim girls cannot or do not want to show."   8

French tradition has also long encouraged mixing of the sexes in social situations. "The veil," Ms. Habib continues, "interrupts the circulation of coquetry and of paying homage, in declaring that there is another possible way for the sexes to coexist: strict separation."   9

A more familiar explanation for French antagonism to the facial veil is historical and political: the deep-rooted French fear, resentment and   10 rejection of the "other"—the immigrant, the invader, the potential terrorist or abuser of human rights who eats, drinks, prays and dresses differently, and refuses to assimilate in the French way. Some of the French, particularly on the far right, still believe that France's colonial "civilizing mission" was a noble one, and that the people of former colonies, including the Arabs of North Africa, have clung to backward ways that they are now exporting to France. "The veil's presence reminds French people daily that that mission failed," said Rebecca Ruquist, an American scholar of race and religion in modern France. "It has been seen as a sartorial rejection of the values of the French republic."

By donning an all-encompassing black garment that covers all but 11 the eyes, these women seem to want their coverings, not their faces, to be noticed. Their veils are generally fixed in place, cut or shaped in such a way that they hide all but their eyes.

In some parts of the Islamic world, however, women opt for more 12 fluidity. In Saudi Arabia, for example, where Muslim women are required to keep their bodies and hair under wraps in public, facial covering is neither obligatory nor banned and can be used in a kind of cat-and-mouse game with strangers. One favorite head covering is a long black scarf that becomes opaque when doubled over. It is worn with one end hanging down in front, the other over the shoulder. Should a strange man look at her, a woman might take the hanging end of the scarf and flip it up to cover her face. She can see out, but no one can see in.

France's officials and legislators have used an amalgam of arguments 13 to defend their new law. Interior Minister Claude Guéant said it defends "two fundamental principles: secularism and the principle of equality between man and woman." A stronger argument is that any hidden face is a potential security risk, and it is on that basis that the law does not single out Islamic veils by name, but rather all facial coverings in public.

In theory, that means that anyone wearing a balaclava, a fencing 14 mask or a motorcycle helmet with a full-face visor could be punished. But will they? The French might be shocked if they were. And there are exemptions, for Santa Clauses and carnivalgoers, for example.

Here's another question: Will lavish-spending female tourists from 15 gulf Arab states be forced to bare their faces on the Champs-Elysées? (In Switzerland, Justice Minister Eveline Widmer-Schlumpf wants to ban facial veils, but has said that gulf tourists will be exempt.) Perhaps, as some have suggested, it will be rare for anyone to be penalized in France, given how difficult it is to enforce the law fairly and uniformly.

Meanwhile, France will remain France—the land where the uncov- 16
ered body is celebrated. Billboards and posters on Paris streets regularly
feature naked breasts and buttocks. To encourage women over the age
of 40 to get mammograms, 10 prominent women, including the two-
starred Michelin chef Hélène Darroze and Nathalie Rykiel, director of
the Sonia Rykiel fashion house, posed topless in Marie Claire magazine
two years ago.

And one of the most colorful images of protest against labor reform 17
in 2006 was of a flag-waving student in Bordeaux dressed as Marianne,
in a red Phrygian cap and white peasant blouse. As in the 19th-century
painting by Eugène Delacroix that hangs in the Louvre, her breasts were
exposed. Marianne remains, as she has always been, the French republic's idealized national symbol.

Thinking about the Essay

1. What is Sciolino's thesis? Where does she state her main idea, or does she imply it? Explain.

2. Why does Sciolino begin her essay with a discussion of the Koran and Islam? Which paragraphs constitute her introduction, and what facts does she present?

3. The writer uses several comparative methods in this essay. Identify the paragraphs where comparison and contrast exist, and explain the purpose of this strategy. What types of evidence does she use to support her comparative strategy?

4. Trace the pattern of cause and effect that Sciolino develops.

5. Where does Sciolino use definition as a rhetorical strategy? Do you find this strategy effective? Why or why not?

Responding in Writing

6. Compose an argumentative essay in which you defend or support the proposition that a secular society should have the right to impose dress restrictions on residents who dress according to religious guidelines.

7. Write your own extended definition of "the look," connecting it to a specific ethnic, racial, or national culture.

8. Analyze the impact of religion on relationships between men and women. Focus on one religious group—for example, Catholics, Christian Evangelicals, fundamentalist Muslims—and explain how these groups attempt to regulate moral behavior.

Networking

9. Exchange your essay with another class member. Peer critique your partner's essay, focusing on his or her use of various rhetorical strategies to develop the paper.

10. Locate online at least three reviews of Elaine Sciolino's most recent book, *La Seduction*. Then write a summary presenting your findings.

Legal in Unlikely Places

JOSEPH CONTRERAS

> Joseph Contreras, a native Californian, joined the staff of *Newsweek* in 1980 as a correspondent in the magazine's Los Angeles bureau. His reporting on world issues is truly global in scope: Contreras has served as *Newsweek* bureau chief in Miami, Mexico City, Buenos Aires, Johannesburg, and Jerusalem. Contreras, who is known for his expertise on Latin American issues, established his early reputation with a series on the Colombian drug wars of the 1980s and the revolution in Peru. As Jerusalem bureau chief, Contreras reported on the political rise of Benjamin Netanyahu in the 1990s and the deterioration of the Middle East peace process in the years following Israel's 1996 election. As Miami bureau chief, he covered the Elián Gonzalez custody battle and the controversy over the 2000 U.S. presidential election. He was appointed *Newsweek*'s Latin America regional editor in 2002, and he is currently stationed in southern Sudan where he serves as a public information officer for a U.N. peacekeeping mission. In the following selection from the September 17, 2007, issue of *Newsweek International*, Contreras examines gay power in global—and especially Latin American—perspective.

Before Reading

What does "machismo" mean? How might one think that machismo might likely clash with gay rights?

A fter eight years together, Gilberto Aranda and Mauricio List walked   1
into a wedding chapel in the Mexico City neighborhood of Coyoacan

last April and tied the knot in front of 30 friends and relatives. Aranda's disapproving father was not invited to the springtime nuptials. For the newlyweds, the ceremony marked the fruit of the gay-rights movement's long struggle to gain recognition in Mexico. The capital city had legalized gay civil unions only the month before. "After all the years of marches and protests," says Aranda, 50, a state-government official, "a sea change was coming."

The sea change spreads beyond Mexico City, a cosmopolitan capital   2
that is home to a thriving community of artists and intellectuals.

The growing maturity of the gay-rights movement in the West is hav-   3
ing a marked effect on the developing world. In the United States, the Republican Party is in trouble in part because it has made a fetish of its opposition to gay marriage. At least some gays in big cities like New York question why they are still holding "pride" parades, as if they were still a closeted minority and not part of the Manhattan mainstream. Since 2001, Western European countries like Belgium, the Netherlands and Spain have gone even farther than the United States, placing gay and lesbian partners on the same legal footing as their heterosexual counterparts. And now, the major developing powers of Asia, Latin America and Africa are following the liberal road—sometimes imitating Western models, sometimes not—but in all cases setting precedents that could spread to the remaining outposts of official homophobia.

In Mexico, the declining clout and prestige of the Roman Catholic   4
Church have emboldened gay-rights activists and their allies in state legislatures and city councils to pass new laws legalizing same-sex civil unions, starting with Mexico City in November. The rising influence of tolerant Western pop culture has encouraged gay men and lesbians to proclaim their sexuality in gay-pride marches like the one in the Brazilian city of Sao Paulo in June, which drew 3 million participants, according to the event's organizers. It was the largest ever in Brazil.

Western models also helped inspire South Africa to legalize civil   5
unions in November 2006, thus becoming the first country in the developing world to do so. In China, the trend goes back to the climate of economic reform that took hold in the 1980s, ending the persecution of the era of Mao Zedong, who considered homosexuals products of the "moldering lifestyle of capitalism."

Among left-wing movements in many developing countries, globaliza-   6
tion is a favorite scapegoat for all of the planet's assorted ills. But even those who resist the West's basically conservative free-market economic orthodoxy are quick to acknowledge the social liberalism—including

respect for the rights of women and minorities of all kinds—that is the West's main cultural and legal export. "I think it helped that Spain and other parts of Europe had passed similar laws," says longtime Mexican gay-rights activist Alejandro Brito. "These types of laws are becoming more about human rights than gay issues."

Key people have hastened the trend in some countries. Some activists 7 single out a few political celebrities for de-stigmatizing their cause, including Nelson Mandela, who readily embraced British actor Sir Ian McKellen's suggestion that he support a ban on discrimination on the basis of sexual preference in South Africa's first post-apartheid constitution, and former prime minister Tony Blair, whose government was the first to recognize civil partnerships between same-sex couples. They also point to activist judges in Brazil, South Africa, and the European Court of Human Rights, who have handed down landmark rulings that unilaterally granted gay, lesbian and transgender communities new rights. These include a judicial order that gays be admitted into the armed forces of European Union member states.

The biggest and perhaps most surprising change is in Latin America, 8 the original home of machismo. In 2002, the Buenos Aires City Council approved Latin America's first-ever gay-civil-union ordinance, and same-gender unions are the law of the land in four Brazilian states today. Last year an openly homosexual fashion designer was elected to Brazil's National Congress with nearly half a million votes. In August a federal-court judge in the Brazilian state of Rio Grande do Sul broke new legal ground when he ordered the national-health-care system to subsidize the cost of sex-change operations in public hospitals, thereby putting sexual "reassignment" on par with heart surgery, organ transplants and AIDS treatment as medical procedures worthy of taxpayer support.

By the year-end, Colombia could become the first country in Latin 9 America to grant gay and lesbian couples full rights to health insurance, inheritance and social-security benefits. A bill containing those reforms is working its way through the National Congress at present. And even Cuba has turned a corner. In the 1960s and early 1970s homosexuals in Cuba were blacklisted or even banished to forced-labor camps along with Jehovah's Witnesses, Catholic priests and other so-called social misfits. HIV patients were locked away in sanitariums as recently as 1993. Several Cuban cities now host gay and lesbian film festivals. The hit TV program on the island's state-run airwaves last year was *The Hidden Side of the Moon*, a soap opera about a married man who falls in love with a man and later tests positive for HIV.

The push for "more modern ways of thinking" about minorities, fem- 10
inists and homosexuals has roots that go back to the political ferment
that shook the region in the late 1960s and 1970s, says Braulio Peralta,
author of the 2006 book on gay rights in Mexico, *The Names of the
Rainbow*. But it has gained in recent years, due in part to troubles in the
Roman Catholic Church, which includes eight out of 10 Mexicans and
long stood opposed to any attempt to redefine marriage laws. Last November, the Mexico City Legislature took up the civil-union law just as
the country's top cardinal, Norberto Rivera Carrera, was facing charges
that he had sheltered a Mexican priest accused of sexually abusing children in California. The prelate chose to stay under the radar as the vote
loomed. "The Catholic Church was facing a credibility crisis," says longtime Mexico City–based gay-rights activist Brito. "So many of its leaders
including Rivera knew that if they fiercely opposed the gay-union law,
the news media would eat them alive."

The change in attitudes is most vivid in the sparsely populated border 11
state of Coahuila, an unlikely setting for blazing trails on gay rights. The
left-wing political party that rules the national capital has made few
inroads here. Yet soon after the state's young governor, Humberto Mor-
eira Valdes, was elected in 2006, he backed a civil-union bill modeled on
France's pacts of civil solidarity, and in the state capital of Saltillo the
progressive Catholic bishop added his support. The 62-year-old prelate,
Raul Vera, says he was comfortable doing so in part because the bill
stopped short of calling for same-sex marriage. "As the church I said we
could not assume the position of homophobes," he says. "We cannot
marginalize gays and lesbians. We cannot leave them unprotected."

That seems to be the prevailing consensus in South Africa's ruling 12
party. The constitution adopted by South Africa after the African
National Congress (ANC) took power in 1994 was the world's first political charter to outlaw discrimination on the basis of sexual orientation.
In November 2006, the national Parliament overwhelmingly approved a
civil-union bill after the country's constitutional court called for amend-
ments to a 44-year-old marriage law that denied gay and lesbian couples
the legal right to wed. In pushing for approval of the Civil Union Act,
the ruling ANC shrugged off both conservative opposition parties and
religious leaders, some of whom accused the government of imposing the
morality of a "radical homosexual minority" on South Africans. President Thabo Mbeki had been blasted by gay rights activists in the past
for trying to downplay his country's raging HIV/AIDS epidemic, but on
the issue of same-sex civil unions his government stood firm.

The sweeping terms of the 2006 Civil Union Act placed South Africa in 13 a select club of nations that have enacted similar laws and that, until last year, included only Canada, Belgium, Spain and the Netherlands. But there are glimmers of change in other nations. China decriminalized sodomy a decade ago and removed homosexuality from its list of mental disorders in 2001. Police broke up a gay and lesbian festival in Beijing in 2005 but took no action last February against an unauthorized rally in support of legalizing gay marriage. The Chinese Communist Party has established gay task forces in all provincial capitals to promote HIV/AIDS awareness and prevention. And in April a Web site launched a weekly hour-long online program called Connecting Homosexuals with an openly gay host. It is the first show in China to focus entirely on gay issues.

Tolerance, however, by no means spans the globe. Homosexuality 14 remains taboo throughout the greater Middle East. In most of the Far East, laws permitting gay and lesbian civil unions are many years if not decades away. In Latin America, universal acceptance of homosexuality is a long way off. Jamaica is a hotbed of homophobia. Even in Mexico, the first couple to take advantage of Coahuila's new civil-union statute were fired from their jobs as sales clerks after their boss realized they were lesbians. The new Mexico City law grants same-gender civil unions property and inheritance rights, but not the right to adopt children.

Even Mexican gays who still struggle against daily bias see signs of 15 improvement, however. In 2003 Jose Luis Ramirez landed work as a buyer at the Mexico City headquarters of a leading department-store chain, and things were going swimmingly until he brought his boyfriend to a company-hosted dinner with clients. "My boss's face just dropped," recalls Ramirez. Ramirez was subsequently denied promotions and left the company last year. But sexuality "isn't an issue" with his current employer, a new household-furnishings retailer.

Tolerance is now the majority, at least among the young. A 2005 poll by 16 the Mitofsky market-research firm found that 50 percent of all Mexicans between the ages of 18 and 29 supported proposals to allow gay marriage. Karla Lopez met Karina Almaguer on the assembly line of a Matamoros auto-stereo factory. The two became the first Mexican couple to marry under the civil-union bill; Lopez, now 30, is a mother of three. She urges more gays and lesbians to follow her example and come out publicly. "I felt strange at first because people would judge us and look at us from head to toe," she says. "But I now feel more secure and at ease." If more political leaders, clergymen and judges act to legitimize folks like Karla Lopez, the new mood of tolerance will surely proliferate across the planet in her lifetime.

Thinking about the Essay

1. What is Contreras's purpose in this essay? Does he want to inform, shock, persuade, or argue, or a combination of these? Point to words and phrases that support your position.

2. In your own words, state the thesis that emerges from Contreras's essay. Does the thesis emerge from the title? Why or why not? How does the title reflect the writer's overall purpose?

3. Explain the use of exemplification or illustration to structure and unify the essay. Is there a pattern to this use of illustration, or does Contreras simply hop from one example to the next?

4. What comparative and causal patterns of development can you detect in this essay? Why are they effective—or do you think they are not?

5. How are the introductory and concluding paragraphs linked? Why does Contreras frame his essay in this manner?

Responding in Writing

6. Are you convinced that acceptance of gay rights is growing globally? Answer this question in a brief argumentative essay, referring to Contreras's essay if you wish.

7. Write a personal essay explaining your own attitude toward gay rights.

8. Write an essay of causal analysis in which you explain why global gay rights is part of the larger effort to promote universal human rights.

Networking

9. Working in small groups, collaborate in finding out more about the position of the Catholic Church—a subject that Contreras alludes to in his essay—on homosexuality and gay rights. Appoint one member of your group to join a class panel discussing this topic.

10. If your class has a virtual whiteboard, participate in listing all the examples that Contreras introduces in his essay. Contribute to a general discussion of the use of examples in essay writing.

A Dark Window on Human Trafficking

MIKE CEASER | Mike Ceaser is a journalist who writes frequently for *The Chronicle of Higher Education*. He specializes in Latin American affairs. Ceaser also has written for

> *Americas, The Lancet, National Catholic Reporter,* and other publications. In the following essay, published in the *Chronicle* on July 25, 2008, Ceaser investigates the unsavory world of human trafficking in young girls across South American and North American borders.

Before Reading

How would you define "human trafficking"? Why has this phenomenon become such a recent problem worldwide?

P olice-car lights flashed and prostitutes, pimps, reporters, and police 1 officers milled about. One by one, the neon signs displaying scantily clad women went dark. Finally, the police sealed the gates beneath the billboard of two naked women amid the moon and stars.

While the police closed the La Luna nightclub for employing under- 2 age girls as prostitutes, a pair of graduate students from Dominican University, near Chicago, stood by urging them on. For the students, the shuttering of the club was a personal victory.

"I don't think that prostitution can be a choice that you make," said 3 Tracy O'Dowd, who, along with Sergio Velarde, had assisted in winning the court battle against the owners of the nightclub. "I think you're brought there one way or another."

Ms. O'Dowd and Mr. Velarde, both master's-degree students in 4 social work, had come here three months earlier, in late January, to work as interns at the Our Youth Foundation, which is based in Ecuador and battles the exploitation of children. Concerned about human trafficking and interested in Latin America, both had studied the issue of trafficking at Dominican. Before leaving home, they learned that the sexual exploitation of minors was common in Ecuador, and that the country's corrupt and inefficient legal system rarely took action against those responsible.

Only in 2005 did Ecuador pass its first major law against human 5 trafficking; in 2007 the United States' "Trafficking in Persons Report" said that Ecuador "does not fully comply with the minimum standards for the elimination of trafficking," though the report also noted improvements in prosecutions, public education, and support for victims.

Mr. Velarde, whose parents and grandparents emigrated from Mex- 6 ico to the United States, speaks passionately about the challenges faced by migrants, who are often exploited even when they are not the victims of traffickers. Once, while visiting relatives in the Mexican state of Chihuahua, his family encountered immigrants from Central America who had been abandoned there and told they were in the United States. The many fast-food restaurants made the locale resemble a U.S. city.

Mr. Velarde believes that in "individualistic" American society, people are leery of supporting and assisting immigrants—even those who were brought to the United States against their will.   7

"Once the stigma is placed on immigrants, it doesn't matter how you got there," Mr. Velarde says. "If you got there on your free will or against your free will, you're always going to have that stigma."   8

But he and Ms. O'Dowd found that human trafficking in Ecuador differs fundamentally from what they'd read about in other nations, and soon found themselves swept up in a landmark legal battle against traffickers. Human trafficking generally refers to the carrying of people across borders deceitfully or against their will, for prostitution or forced labor. While that happens to Ecuadoreans, here the crime most commonly consists of forcing young girls into brothels, through coercion or outright kidnapping. Sometimes young men seek out girls from poor, troubled families and pretend to fall in love with them—and then "sell" them to brothel owners.   9

"Here, they do this whole fantasy couple, fantasy relationship, and then all of a sudden, 'I don't have any more money, so you have to work,'" says Mr. Velarde. "But the girl still believes they're a couple, and he still kind of treats them as a couple."   10

It's an often-invisible crime.   11

Mr. Velarde says that in his visits to poor communities, he discovered that people often don't know that such cases involve human trafficking, or are so poor that they assume their absent daughters must be better off.   12

Most families never imagine that their daughters have ended up at a place like La Luna, a complex of three huge nightclub-brothels, which had come to represent both the crime and the legal invulnerability often enjoyed by the perpetrators. Adult prostitution is legal in Ecuador, but La Luna was notorious for employing underage girls. In January 2006, pressured by the Our Youth Foundation and others, the police finally raided the club and rescued 11 girls ages 13 through 17, who were taken to a safe house operated by the foundation.   13

The trial of the club's five owners, repeatedly postponed, dragged on until this March. Ms. O'Dowd and Mr. Velarde met three of the victims, now ages 15 through 17, when the girls prepared to testify for the   14 prosecution. Then the two demonstrated in front of the courthouse in support of the victims—and faced off against a group backing the brothel owners.

"We stood outside the courtroom for three hours," Ms. O'Dowd 15 wrote in the blog she posted as part of her course work. "There were about 50 people there to support these girls, and there were about 20 supporting the traffickers. We waited with posters saying 'No to sexual exploitation,' 'Justice that comes late isn't justice.'"

In the first days of April, the court issued its verdict: All the men 16 were guilty.

"The five men on trial were sentenced to 16 years," Mr. Velarde 17 blogged on April 4, "and it was a huge win."

Children's-rights advocates called the club's shuttering in April a 18 landmark because of its size and wealth. And officials present at the closing vowed that it was the start of a crackdown on brothels employing minors.

But while La Luna became the face of exploitation here, the crime's 19 roots lie in the city's poor and socially troubled barrios. And it was there that the Dominican interns did the nitty-gritty and often frustrating work intended to prevent the children of vulnerable families from ever being misled into prostitution.

The interns did this in places like a nondescript neighborhood of 20 brick and concrete houses that Ms. O'Dowd visited one overcast day.

She knocked on the door of a home where the father had been 24 imprisoned for sexually abusing one of his daughters. Then, surrounded by children, Ms. O'Dowd sat on a couch with the mother in the tidy living room and asked about the family's situation and needs: How were they doing financially? Did the children need notebooks for school? Would they like counseling? But the woman seemed resigned and hopeless. Between sobs, she described how the absence of her husband, an auto mechanic, had left the family financially devastated. She was even hostile to the Our Youth Foundation, which she blamed for taking him away.

"What I want is for you to help me, to get my husband out of jail," 22 she pleaded. Ms. O'Dowd left feeling frustrated by the mother's attitude and lack of appreciation for the danger to her daughters.

Even united families face the threat of trafficking because of the pov- 23 erty and social dislocation caused by Ecuador's heavy migration from the country side to the wealthier cities.

Another morning, Mr. Velarde rode a series of buses and then a   24
pickup truck up a dirt road to a neighborhood of crude homes scattered
among bushes on a mountainside high above Quito, the capital. In a
house of uninsulated brick and concrete lived an indigenous family who
had migrated from the coast in search of work. The mother cleans
houses when pain from a kidney stone permits, while the children's stepfather earns about $30 per month as a security guard.

Inside the home, Mr. Velarde and an intern from an Ecuadorean uni-   25
versity interviewed the family and left satisfied that they were making do
with their limited resources. But while the group waited for a bus back
down the mountainside, the mother unexpectedly mentioned that two
years earlier her daughter, now 14 years old, was kidnapped by a family
acquaintance, who raped her and held her captive for eight days while
trying to "sell" her to a brothel.

Although the family succeeded in rescuing the girl, she is still afraid to   26
leave the house. Then the mother described how the local schoolteacher
accosts female students, forcing the family to send their daughters to a more
distant school—which means a perilous walk back home every evening.

"Sometimes I think about the other girls who are getting bigger,"   27
their mother worried, "that the same thing could happen to them."

The interns reported the family's situation to the foundation, for   28
follow-up assistance. "That her daughter was kidnapped—that just
changes the whole situation," Mr. Velarde observed afterward. "Research
says that if they've had such a thing with a sister, a cousin, . . . then
they're vulnerable."

Ms. O'Dowd and Mr. Velarde returned to Chicago this spring feeling   29
hopeful that Ecuador was taking real steps against trafficking, through
both police actions and new laws. But the court case against the club fell
short of being a complete victory: The owners' sentences were slashed
from 16 years to six.

Their Ecuadorean experience left the Dominican students with hopes   30
of continuing to fight human trafficking, either in the United States,
where they feel the problem has received too little attention, or back in
Latin America. But the visit to Ecuador also changed them both, making
them more interested in preventing the circumstances that make people
vulnerable to trafficking. Although thousands of people are believed to
be victims of human trafficking into the United States each year, the
United States does not include itself in its own annual trafficking report.

"As a country, I think we've focused more on everyone else," says   31
Mr. Velarde, "and when you have eyes on everybody else, you don't
have eyes on your own situation."

Thinking about the Essay

1. How does Ceaser devise his introduction? What techniques does he use to create a dramatic situation throughout the essay? Are these strategies effective? Why or why not?

2. Ceaser profiles two students. Who are they, and what do we learn about them? What is the writer's attitude toward them? Justify your response.

3. Does Ceaser have a thesis or claim in this essay? Explain.

4. Ceaser wrote this article for a specialized audience—college teachers and administrators. Why would this readership be interested in the subject? Why might the essay appeal to a broader audience?

5. In analyzing the trafficking of young South American girls to the United States for the purpose of prostitution, Ceaser relies on causal analysis. Examine the causes and effects—both primary and secondary—that the writer traces.

Responding in Writing

6. In an investigative essay, analyze the causes behind the increase in the trafficking of women across international borders.

7. Argue for or against the proposition that American society is too tolerant of human trafficking for the purpose of prostitution, especially if the victims are undocumented immigrants.

8. Do you believe that we are responsible collectively for such realities as human trafficking? Write a persuasive essay in which you respond to this question.

Networking

9. In small groups, discuss Ceaser's assertion that "individualistic" American society creates the conditions that foster a tolerance for human trafficking.

10. Go online and find out more about human trafficking in girls and young women from South America to the United States. Write an investigative report based on your findings.

Hear Her Roar

RANA FOROOHAR

Rana Foroohar graduated from Barnard College in 1992. Today she is the assistant managing editor in charge of economics and business at *Time* magazine.

Previously she was the deputy editor for international business and economics coverage at *Newsweek*. While at *Newsweek*, Foroohar wrote cover stories, opinion pieces, and a weekly column, and also covered Europe and the Middle East for that publication. Moreover, she has contributed essays to *Forbes* and other magazines and also writes for the online news website *The Daily Beast*. In this essay from a 2009 issue of *Newsweek*, Foroohar examines the rising influence of women in the global economy.

Before Reading

Do you think that female employment is rising or falling in light of continuing problems in the global economy? Explain why you think it is rising or falling.

It hasn't been easy to find a bright spot in the global economy for a couple of years now. Growth markets, once as numerous as no-interest mortgage options, have grown scarce. But in the last few months, economists, consultants, and other business types have begun to track the rise of a new emerging market, one that may end up being the largest and most powerful of all: women. According to a new study by the Boston Consulting Group, women are now poised to drive the post-recession world economy, thanks to an estimated $5 trillion in new female-earned income that will be coming on line over the next five years. Worldwide, total income for men ($23.4 trillion) is still more than double that for women ($10.5 trillion), but the gap is poised to shrink significantly because the vast majority of new income growth over the next few years will go to women, due to a narrowing wage gap and rising female employment. That means women will be the ones driving the shopping— and, economists hope, the recovery. That growth represents the biggest emerging market in the history of the planet—more than twice the size of the two hottest developing markets, India and China, combined. 1

It's seismic stuff, and the impact of the shift—one that few leaders, either in the political world or in business, have fully grasped—will be broad and deep. An August report by Goldman Sachs entitled "The Power of the Purse" proclaims women the economic engine of the future, noting that future spending by women, which tends to focus more on health, education, and children's well-being, "should support the development of 2 human capital" to a greater extent than spending by men, thus "fueling economic growth in the years ahead." At the same time, the report notes, economic growth continues to bolster gender equality, a virtuous circle that has already had massive impacts on the status of women around the world.

While most of us know intuitively that women's place in the world   3 has risen in the last several decades, a look at the hard data is startling, in a good way. Huge improvements in female access to education around the world mean that the literacy rates for young women, which used to trail those of men by 30 percent or more, are now almost universally within a single digit of men's. In the U.S. and the EU, most college students are already women, and even in most of the key developing countries, girls now fare nearly as well as boys in primary- and secondary-school enrollment. Labor-force participation, already high in rich countries, has jumped exponentially in large swaths of the developing world over the last few years; 70 percent of women in countries like China and Vietnam now work. Health has improved dramatically, and fertility rates have dropped.

While women are still underrepresented in politics, there have been   4 significant gains in recent years, most notably in poor nations—countries like Uganda, Burundi, and Macedonia are among those that now have more than 30 percent female legislatures, thanks largely to the implementation of quotas.

Around the world, nations are changing laws to give women more   5 equal standing in areas like property, inheritance, and divorce rights. In many cases, technology and globalization have played an important role in changing attitudes. A 2007 study by the National Bureau of Economic Research on rural India found that within six to seven months of getting cable TV, men and women alike had become more open to the idea of women's autonomy, and more accepting of female participation in household decision making.

In fact, women already make the majority of the world's purchasing   6 decisions. BCG estimates that they control some $12 trillion of the world's $18.4 trillion in annual consumer spending, and that percentage will likely rise as a new upwardly mobile class of young female professionals overtakes their male peers in wealth and status. In developed countries, there is already an elite cadre of urban women who are more powerful than their male counterparts. "If you walk down the streets of Manhattan, London, or Frankfurt today," notes BCG senior partner Michael J. Silverstein, "and you ask 100 single men and women between the ages of 25 and 30 what they make, the women will make more." It's nothing less than the entry of a new generation of potential leaders onto the world stage. "The shift is statistical," says Silverstein. "Older women who tended to be paid less are retiring, and a new group of younger women, who had equal education and started with roughly equal wages are rising." Silverstein believes that if this new group, now rising through middle management, stays on the fast track, the number of Fortune 500 CEOs who are women could rise from 38 today to over 100 in the next 10 years.

Higher female earners in the developed world, coupled with growing   7
female employment participation in poorer countries, is the reason that women's earned income is growing at 8.1 percent versus 5.8 percent for men. The financial crisis has widened this gap, by hitting male jobs hardest. Some 80 percent of job losses in the U.S. during the downturn have befallen men, in part because male-dominated areas like manufacturing and financial services have been gutted during the recession. But the rise of female earning power is a deeper shift that has gone hand in hand with the other economic megatrend of our era: the advancement of emerging markets. As Goldman's report makes clear, improving gender equality has coincided with the rapid growth of the global middle class. From about 1.7 billion people today, this middle class is expected to reach approximately 3.6 billion by 2030, and 85 percent of the newly wealthy will live in the world's major developing nations.

The rise of women as a grand, cross-border emerging market could   8
have implications as profound as the rise of India and China. There's a wide body of research to suggest that women's spending patterns may be exactly what the world needs at this moment. "Economists have studied how women spend in comparison to men, and they tend to spend more on things that are linked to people's well-being, like health and education. They also tend to save more, and exhibit less risky financial behavior," notes Yassine Fall, senior economic adviser for UNIFEM, the U.N. agency dedicated to women. The fallout for business and investors could be significant. Goldman Sachs estimates, for example, that more male-oriented product categories like alcohol and tobacco may show slower growth rates than areas like consumer durables, food, health care, and child care—in short, all the stuff that women spend their money on.

Women may also play an important role in reshaping industries like   9
financial services. The female propensity to save may fuel growth of banking services in countries such as India, where roughly half of all household assets are currently held in physical categories like land and machinery. The vast unmet desire among Western women for more

simple, understandable financial products and services could also help make retail investing in countries like the U.S. more accessible and transparent. Analysts say companies like Visa, Wal-Mart, Nestle, Johnson & Johnson, and others that already have a strong leg up in the women's market stand to prosper further from the female consumer boom.

Meanwhile, as women gain greater power at the political level, there   10 will also likely be macroeconomic spending shifts. A study last year of Britain's Parliament found that since 1997, when the country doubled its female representation in Parliament to 18.2 percent, family issues such as tax credits, health care, child care, and education have received more money and more attention. Likewise, in India, where a 1992 law mandated increased levels of female participation in local government, female council leaders have taken on 60 percent more water projects than their male counterparts. Of course, there's widespread consensus now that government spending on health, education, and social safety nets are exactly what the world needs to get growth back on track. If women can help do that, with political power as well as the power of the purse, they may be the catalyst for any number of new growth markets.

Thinking about the Essay

1. How does the writer's title reflect her opinion of the role of women in today's global economy?

2. What is Foroohar's thesis, and where does she state it most clearly? Do you detect an argument or claim underlying her thesis? Justify your response by referring to specific parts of the essay.

3. Examine the writer's topic sentences. How do they serve as models for paragraph development?

4. Foroohar draws on several bodies of evidence to support her key statements. What varieties of evidence can you locate, and how effective do you find these supporting facts?

5. Evaluate the rhetorical strategies—for instance comparison and contrast and causal analysis—that Foroohar uses to develop key topics in her essay.

Responding in Writing

6. Write a 100-word summary of Foroohar's essay, capturing all important topics that she presents.

7. Take one major point that Foroohar makes in this essay, and write your own paper on it. For instance, you might focus on women's access to

education, changing laws affecting women, or women's growing purchasing power.

8. Compose an argumentative essay in which you agree or disagree with Foroohar's claim that women's global economic condition is improving.

Networking

9. Participate in a class debate, using Foroohar's essay as a reference point, in which you argue for or against the writer's claim that the global women's collective voice in economic affairs is becoming more powerful and influential.

10. Read three of Foroohar's contributions to *The Daily Beast*. Provide a précis of your research, highlighting the topics that Foroohar tends to focus on.

Life on the Global Assembly Line

BARBARA EHRENREICH AND ANNETTE FUENTES

Barbara Ehrenreich was born in 1941 in Butte, Montana. She attended Reed College (B.A., 1963) and Rockefeller University (Ph.D. in biology, 1968). A self-described socialist and feminist, Ehrenreich uses her scientific training to investigate a broad range of social issues: health care, the plight of the poor, and the condition of women around the world. Her scathing critiques of American health care in such books as *The American Health Empire* (with John Ehrenreich, 1970), *Complaints and Disorders: The Sexual Politics of Sickness* (with Deirdre English, 1973), and *For Her Own Good* (with English, 1978) established her as an authority in the field. In her provocative *The Hearts of Men: American Dreams and the Flight from Commitment* (1983), Ehrenreich surveys the decline of male investment in the family from the 1950s to the 1980s. A prolific writer during the 1980s and 1990s, Ehrenreich most recently published the award-winning book *Nickel and Dimed: On (Not) Getting By in America* (2001) and *Bait and Switch: The (Futile) Pursuit of the American Dream* (2005). She is also a frequent contributor to magazines, including *The Nation, Esquire, Radical America, The New Republic*, and *The New York Times*, while serving as a contributing editor to *Ms.* and *Mother Jones*. The classic essay that appears here, written for *Ms.* in 1981 with Annette Fuentes, a New York–based journalist and adjunct professor at

Columbia University, was among the first articles to expose the plight of working women around the world.

Before Reading

What experiences or expectations do you bring to a new job? What happens if you discover you are being exploited?

Ms.; 1981 January   1
flash forward   2

Globalization has changed the rules of the game. The nation-state   3
as we understand it is a state that is bargaining, struggling, being
swallowed up by the forces of globalization. In 1985, on the eve of
the Nairobi conference, our message about development was really
new, that you can't just talk about gender equality without considering equality of what. Do you want equal shares of a poisoned pie?
It was a message that had a galvanizing effect on people, because by
Beijing, globalization issues had become part of everyone's vocabulary. No longer was it a situation where the North worries about
gender equality and the South about development.

—Economist Gita Sen, *Ford Foundation Report*, Winter 2000

Every morning, between four and seven, thousands of women head   4
out for the day shift. In Ciudad Juarez, they crowd into *ruteras* (run-down
vans) for the trip from the slum neighborhoods to the industrial parks on
the outskirts of the city. In Penang they squeeze, 60 or more at a time,
into buses for the trip to the low, modern factory buildings of the Bayan
Lepas free trade zone. In Taiwan, they walk from the dormitories—where
the night shift is already asleep in the still-warm beds—through the checkpoints in the high fence surrounding the factory zone.

This is the world's new industrial proletariat: young, female, Third   5
World. Viewed from the "first world," they are still faceless, genderless
"cheap labor," signaling their existence only through a label or tiny
imprint "made in Hong Kong," or Taiwan, Korea, the Dominican
Republic, Mexico, the Philippines. But they may be one of the most strategic blocs of womanpower in the world. Conservatively, there are 2 million Third World female industrial workers employed now, millions
more looking for work, and their numbers are rising every year.

It doesn't take more than second-grade arithmetic to understand   6
what's happening. In the U.S., an assembly-line worker is likely to earn,
depending on her length of employment, between $3.10 and $5 an hour.

In many Third World countries, a woman doing the same work will earn $3 to $5 a day.

And so, almost everything that can be packed up is being moved out to the Third World: garment manufacture, textiles, toys, footwear, pharmaceuticals, wigs, appliance parts, tape decks, computer components, plastic goods. In some industries, like garment and textile, American jobs are lost in the process, and the biggest losers are women, often black and Hispanic. But what's going on is much more than a matter of runaway shops. Economists are talking about a "new international division of labor," in which the process of production is broken down and the fragments are dispersed to different parts of the world, while control over the overall process and technology remains safely at company headquarters in "first world" countries.   7

The American electronics industry provides a classic example: circuits are printed on silicon wafers and tested in California; then the wafers are shipped to Asia for the labor-intensive process by which they are cut into tiny chips and bonded to circuit boards; final assembly into products such as calculators or military equipment usually takes place in the United States. Garment manufacture too is often broken into geographically separated steps, with the most repetitive, labor-intensive jobs going to the poor countries of the southern hemisphere.   8

So much any economist could tell you. What is less often noted is the gender breakdown of the emerging international division of labor. Eighty to 90 percent of the low-skilled assembly jobs that go to the Third World are performed by women in a remarkable switch from earlier patterns of foreign-dominated industrialization. Until now, "development" under the aegis of foreign corporations has usually meant more jobs for men and—compared to traditional agricultural society—a diminished economic status for women. But multinational corporations and Third World governments alike consider assembly-line work—whether the product is Barbie dolls or missile parts—to be "women's" work.   9

It's an article of faith with management that only women can do, or will do, the monotonous, painstaking work that American business is exporting to the Third World. The personnel manager of a light assembly plant in Taiwan told anthropologist Linda Gail Arrigo, "Young male workers are too restless and impatient to do monotonous work with no career value. If displeased, they sabotage the machines and even threaten the foreman. But girls? At most, they cry a little."   10

A top-level management consultant who specializes in advising American companies on where to relocate, gave us this global generalization: 11

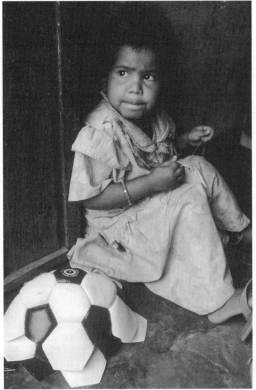

This three-year-old in India helps her mother and sisters make soccer balls—for 75 cents a day.

"The [factory] girls genuinely enjoy themselves. They're away from their families. They have spending money. Of course it's a regulated experience too—with dormitories to live in—so it's a healthful experience."

What is the real experience of the women in the emerging Third World 12 industrial work force? Rachael Grossman, a researcher with the Southeast Asia Resource Center, found women employees of U.S. multinational firms in Malaysia and the Philippines living four to eight in a room in boarding-houses, or squeezing into tiny extensions built onto squatter huts near the factory. Where companies do provide dormitories, they are not of the "healthful," collegiate variety. The American Friends Service Committee reports that dormitory space is "likely to be crowded—while one shift works, another sleeps, as many as twenty to a room."

Living conditions are only part of the story. The work that multina- 13 tional corporations export to the Third World is not only the most tedious, but often the most hazardous part of the production process. The countries they go to are, for the most part, those that will guarantee no interference from health and safety inspectors, trade unions, or even freelance reformers.

Consider the electronics industry, which is generally thought to be 14 the safest and cleanest of the exported industries. The factory buildings are low and modern, like those one might find in a suburban American industrial park. Inside, rows of young women, neatly dressed in the company uniform or T-shirt, work quietly at their stations. There is air conditioning (not for the women's comfort, but to protect the delicate semiconductor parts they work with), and high-volume piped-in Bee Gees hits (not so much for entertainment, as to prevent talking).

For many Third World women, electronics is a prestige occupation, at 15 least compared to other kinds of factory work. They are unlikely to know that in the United States the National Institute on Occupational Safety and Health (NIOSH) has placed electronics on its select list of "high health-risk industries using the greatest number of toxic substances." If electronics assembly work is risky here, it is doubly so in countries where there is no equivalent of NIOSH to even issue warnings. In many plants toxic chemicals and solvents sit in open containers, filling the work area with fumes that can literally knock you out. "We have been told of cases where ten to twelve women passed out at once," an AFSC field worker in northern Mexico told us, "and the newspapers report this as 'mass hysteria.'"

Some of the worst conditions have been documented in South Korea, 16 where the garment and textile industries have helped spark that country's "economic miracle." Workers are packed into poorly lit rooms, where summer temperatures rise above 100 degrees. Textile dust, which can cause permanent lung damage, fills the air. Management may require forced overtime of as much as 48 hours at a stretch, and if that seems to go beyond the limits of human endurance, pep pills and amphetamine injections are thoughtfully provided. In her diary (originally published in a magazine now banned by the South Korean government), Min Chong Suk, 30, a sewing-machine operator, wrote of working from 7 A.M. to 11:30 P.M. in a garment factory: "When [the apprentices] shake the waste threads from the clothes, the whole room fills with dust, and it is hard to breathe. Since we've been working in such dusty air, there have been increasing numbers of people getting tuberculosis, bronchitis, and eye diseases. Since we are women, it makes us so sad when we have pale, unhealthy, wrinkled faces like dried-up spinach. It seems to me that no one knows our blood dissolves into the threads and seams, with sighs and sorrow."

In all the exported industries, the most invidious, inescapable health 17 hazard is stress. Lunch breaks may be barely long enough for a woman to stand in line at the canteen or hawkers' stalls. Visits to the bathroom are treated as privileges. Rotating shifts—the day shift one week, the night shift the next—wreak havoc with sleep patterns. Because inaccuracies or failure to meet production quotas can mean substantial pay losses, the pressures are quickly internalized; stomach ailments and nervous problems are not unusual.

As if poor health and the stress of factory life weren't enough to 18 drive women into early retirement, management actually encourages a high turnover in many industries. "As you know, when seniority rises, wages rise," the management consultant to U.S. multinationals told us. He explained that it's cheaper to train a fresh supply of teenagers than to pay experienced women higher wages. "Older" women, aged 23 or 24, are likely to be laid off and not rehired.

The lucky ones find husbands. The unlucky ones find themselves at 19 the margins of society—as bar girls, "hostesses," or prostitutes.

There has been no international protest about the exploitation of 20 Third World women by multinational corporations—no thundering denunciations from the floor of the United Nations' General Assembly, no angry resolutions from the Conference of the Non-Aligned Countries. Sociologist Robert Snow, who has been tracing the multinationals on their way south and eastward for years, explained why. "The Third World governments want the multinationals to move in. There's cutthroat competition to attract the corporations."

The governments themselves gain little revenue from this kind of 21 investment—especially since most offer tax holidays and freedom from export duties in order to attract the multinationals in the first place. Nor do the people as a whole benefit, according to a highly placed Third World woman within the U.N. "The multinationals like to say they're contributing to development," she told us, "but they come into our countries for one thing—cheap labor. If the labor stops being so cheap, they can move on. So how can you call that development? It depends on the people being poor and staying poor." But there are important groups that do stand to gain when the multinationals set up shop in their countries: local entrepreneurs who subcontract to the multinationals; "technocrats" who become local management; and government officials who specialize in cutting red tape for an "agent's fee" or an outright bribe.

In the competition for multinational investment, local governments 22
advertise their women shamelessly. An investment brochure issued by the
Malaysian government informs multinational executives that: "the manual dexterity of the Oriental female is famous the world over. Her hands
are small, and she works fast with extreme care. . . . Who, therefore,
could be better qualified by nature and inheritance, to contribute to the
efficiency of a bench-assembly production line than the Oriental girl?"

Many "host" governments are willing to back up their advertising 23
with whatever brutality it takes to keep "their girls" just as docile as
they look in the brochures. Even the most polite and orderly attempts to
organize are likely to bring down overkill doses of police repression:

In Guatemala in 1975 women workers in a North American–owned 24
garment factory drew up a list of complaints that included insults by
management, piecework wages that turned out to be less than the legal
minimum, no overtime pay, and "threats of death." In response, the
American boss called the local authorities to report that he was being
harassed by "Communists." When the women reported for work the
next day they found the factory surrounded by two fully armed contin-
gents of military police. The "Communist" ringleaders were picked out
and fired.

In the Dominican Republic in 1978, workers who attempted to 25
organize at La Romana industrial zone were first fired, then obligingly
arrested by the local police. Officials from the AFL-CIO have described
the zone as a "modern slave-labor camp," where workers who do not
meet their production quotas during their regular shift must stay and put
in unpaid overtime until they do meet them, and many women workers
are routinely strip-searched at the end of the day. During the 1978
organizing attempt, the government sent in national police in full combat
gear armed with automatic weapons. Gulf & Western supplements the
local law with its own company-sponsored motorcycle club, which specializes in terrorizing suspected union sympathizers.

In Inchon, South Korea, women at the Dong-II Textile Company 26
(which produces fabrics and yarn for export to the United States) had
succeeded in gaining leadership in their union in 1972. But in 1978 the
government-controlled, male-dominated Federation of Korean Trade
Unions sent special "action squads" to destroy the women's union.
Armed with steel bars and buckets of human excrement, the goons broke
into the union office, smashed the office equipment, and smeared the
excrement over the women's bodies and in their hair, ears, eyes, and
mouths.

Crudely put (and incidents like this do not inspire verbal delicacy), 27
the relationship between many Third World governments and the multinational corporations is not very different from the relationship between
a pimp and his customers. The governments advertise their women, sell
them, and keep them in line for the multinational "johns." But there are
other parties to the growing international traffic in women—such as the
United Nations' Industrial Development Organization (UNIDO), the
World Bank, and the United States government itself.

UNIDO has been a major promoter of "free trade zones." These are 28
enclaves within nations that offer multinationals a range of creature
comforts, including: freedom from paying taxes and export duties; low-
cost water, power, and buildings; exemption from whatever labor laws
may apply in the country as a whole; and, in some cases, such security
features as barbed-wire, guarded checkpoints, and government-paid
police.

Then there is the World Bank, which over the past decade has lent 29
several billion dollars to finance the roads, airports, power plants, and
even the first-class hotels that multinational corporations need in order
to set up business in Third World countries.

But the most powerful promoter of exploitative conditions for Third 30
World women workers is the United States government itself. For example, the notoriously repressive Korean textile industry was developed
with the help of $400 million in aid from the U.S. State Department.
Malaysia became a low-wage haven for the electronics industry thanks
to technical assistance financed by AID and to U.S. money (funneled
through the Asian Development Bank) to set up free trade zones.

But the most obvious form of United States involvement, according 31
to Lenny Siegel, the director of the Pacific Studies Center, is through
"our consistent record of military aid to Third World governments that
are capitalist, politically repressive, and are not striving for economic
independence."

What does our government have to say for itself? According to AID 32
staffer Emmy Simmons, "we can get hung up in the idea that it's exploitation without really looking at the alternatives for women. These people
have to go somewhere."

Anna, for one, has nowhere to go but the maquiladora. Her family 33
left the farm when she was only six, and the land has long since been
bought up by a large commercial agribusiness company. After her father
left to find work north of the border, money was scarce for years.
So when the factory where she now works opened, Anna felt it was "the

best thing that had ever happened" to her. As a wage-earner, her status rose compared to her brothers with their on-again, off-again jobs. Partly out of her new sense of confidence she agreed to meet with a few other women one day after work to talk about wages and health conditions. That was the way she became what management called a "labor agitator" when, six months later, 90 percent of the day shift walked out in the company's first south-of-the-border strike.

Women like Anna need their jobs desperately. They know the risks 34 of organizing. Beyond that—if they do succeed in organizing—the company can always move on in search of a still-docile, job-hungry work force. Yet thousands of women in the Third World's industrial work force have chosen to fight for better wages and working conditions.

One particularly dramatic instance took place in South Korea in 35 1979. Two hundred young women employees of the YH textile-and-wig factory staged a peaceful vigil and fast to protest the company's threatened closing of the plant. On the fifth day of the vigil, more than 1,000 riot police, armed with clubs and steel shields, broke into the building where the women were staying and forcibly dragged them out. Twenty-one-year-old Kim Kyong-suk was killed during the melee. It was her death that touched off widespread rioting throughout Korea that many thought led to the overthrow of President Park Chung Hee.

So far, feminism, first-world style, has barely begun to acknowledge 36 the Third World's new industrial womanpower. Jeb Mays and Kathleen Connell, cofounders of the San Francisco–based Women's Network on Global Corporations, are two women who would like to change that: "There's still this idea of the Third World woman as 'the other'—someone exotic and totally unlike us," Mays and Connell told us. "But now we're talking about women who wear the same styles in clothes, listen to the same music, and may even work for the same corporation. That's an irony the multinationals have created. In a way, they're drawing us together as women."

Saralee Hamilton, an AFSC staff organizer says: "The multinational 37 corporations have deliberately targeted women for exploitation. If feminism is going to mean anything to women all over the world, it's going to have to find new ways to resist corporate power internationally." She envisions a global network of grass-roots women capable of sharing experiences, transmitting information, and—eventually—providing direct support for each other's struggles. It's a long way off; few women anywhere have the money for intercontinental plane flights or even long-distance calls, but at least we are beginning to see the way. "We all have the same hard life," wrote Korean garment worker Min Chong Suk. "We are bound together with one string."

Thinking about the Essay

1. Describe the writers' argumentative purpose in this essay. Is it to convince or persuade—or both? Explain.

2. Who is the intended audience for this essay? What is the level of diction? How are the two connected?

3. Examine the writers' use of illustration in this essay. How do they use these illustrations to support a series of generalizations? Ehrenreich and Fuentes cite various studies and authorities. Identify these instances and explain the cumulative effect.

4. Ehrenreich and Fuentes draw on a number of rhetorical strategies to advance their argument. Explain their use of comparison and cause-and-effect analysis.

5. Evaluate the writers' conclusion. Does it effectively reinforce their argument? Why or why not?

Responding in Writing

6. Ehrenreich and Fuentes wrote this article originally for *Ms.* magazine. Why would the essay appeal to the *Ms.* audience? What elements would also appeal to a general audience? Write a brief essay that answers these questions, providing specific examples from the text.

7. Write a personal essay in which you describe a job that you had (or have) in which you were exploited. Provide sufficient illustrations to support your thesis.

8. The writers imply that workforce women around the world are exploited more than men. Write an essay in which you agree or disagree with their claim.

Networking

9. Form small groups, and read the drafts of each other's essays. After general comments about how to improve the first draft, concentrate on ways to provide even greater illustration to support each writer's thesis or claim.

10. With another class member, do a Web search for new examples of the global exploitation of working women. Limit your focus to one of the countries mentioned by Ehrenreich and Fuentes. Think about whether the conditions that the two writers exposed more than twenty years ago are better or worse today. Share your conclusions with the rest of the class.

6

CHAPTER

The Challenge of Globalization: What Are the Consequences?

Quick! Where was your cell phone manufactured? What is the
origin of the clothes you are wearing today—and how much do
you think the workers were paid to produce it? What will your
lunch or dinner consist of: pizza, fried rice, tacos, a California
roll? The ordinary features of our daily lives capture the forces of
globalization that characterize our new century and our changed
world. *The New York Times* columnist Thomas Friedman, who writes
persuasively on the subject—and who has an essay in this chapter—
terms globalization the "super-story," the one all-embracing subject
that dominates national and transnational developments today. As we
see from the essays in this chapter, the concept of globalization already
influences many major trends in economic, social, cultural, and
political life in the twenty-first century.

It could be argued, of course, that globalization is nothing new: after
all, Greece "globalized" much of the known world as far as India. Then
Rome created its global dominion from England to Persia. More recently, for almost three centuries—from the seventeenth to the twentieth—
England ruled the waves and a majority of the world's nations. And
from the twentieth century to the present, the United States has assumed
the mantle of the world's major globalizing power. (Some critics claim
that globalization might simply be a mask for "Americanization.") With
antiglobalization demonstrations and riots now commonplace in the
United States, Europe, and the Third World, we have to acknowledge
that there *is* something about contemporary globalization that prompts
debate and demands critical analysis. Lawyer, consumer advocate,
writer, and three-time presidential candidate Ralph Nader states the
case against globalization boldly: "The essence of globalization is a
subordination of human rights, of labor rights, consumer rights, environmental rights, democracy rights, to the imperatives of global trade

168

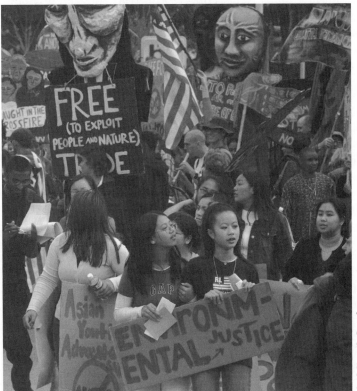

A multiethnic group of protesters representing a wide range of causes marches in Richmond, California, to protest globalization.

Thinking about the Image

1. How many different ideas or causes do you see represented in this photograph? What does that suggest about this particular protest? About the antiglobalization movement in general?

2. What is the photographer's perspective on this event? Is anyone looking directly at the lens? Would your response to the photograph—or the story it tells—be different if there was a focus on just one or two people? If the photographer was farther away and captured a larger crowd in the frame?

3. What other kinds of images do you associate with street protests? Based on the fact that this one photograph was chosen to represent an entire day of protest, what can you infer about the tone of the protest and the response of the community?

4. Street protest is a kind of rhetoric, in that the demonstrators have a purpose and an audience. How clear is the purpose of these protesters? Who is their audience? Do you think such protests will make any difference to people like the child on p. 165?

and investment." But is Nader correct? Robert Rubin, who was secretary of the treasury during the Clinton administration and a prominent figure in the financial community, objects: "I think a healthy economy is the best environment in which to pursue human rights." The oppositional viewpoints of Nader and Rubin suggest that discussion of globalization often produces diverse opinions and that consequently we must think carefully and openly about the globalizing trends molding our lives today.

One trend that is clear today, as the twenty-first century begins, is that capitalism has triumphed over all its main rivals: communism, fascism, and socialism. Thus capitalism is the dominant if not the sole model of development for the nations of the world. Where capitalism collides with alternative visions of development—for example, Islamic economics in Iran—the result proves disastrous. The question that many people—especially young people on college and university campuses around the world—ask is whether or not capitalism can meaningfully address the numerous questions of social justice raised by globalization. If, for example, the environmental policy of the United States aids the interests of its energy companies, can this policy benefit others in the developing world? Or does the policy exclude almost everyone in a developing nation? Such questions can be asked about virtually every key issue raised by Ralph Nader and others who are skeptical of globalization as an overpowering economic force around the world.

The writers in this chapter and the next offer a variety of perspectives and critical insights into the nature and effects of globalization trends. Because of developments in information technology, people in the most distant parts of the world now are as close to us as someone in the dorm room next door—and perhaps more compelling. We certainly see poverty, famine, the degradation of the environment, and civil wars close-up. But is all this suffering the result of predatory multinational corporations and runaway capitalism? After all, both globalization *and* civil society are increasing worldwide, and the connections between the two require subtle critical analysis. The writers in this chapter bring such critical ability to their treatment of the social implications of current globalization trends.

Prologue: The Super-Story

Thomas L. Friedman

A noted author, journalist, and television commentator, and currently an op-ed contributor to *The New York Times*, Thomas L. Friedman writes and speaks knowledgeably about contemporary trends in politics and global development. He was born in Minneapolis, Minnesota, in 1953, and was educated at Brandeis University (B.A., 1975) and St. Anthony's College (M.A., 1978).

Friedman covered the Middle East for *The New York Times* for ten years, and for five years, he was bureau chief in Beirut, writing about both the Lebanese civil war and the Israel–Palestine conflict. He recorded these experiences in *From Beirut to Jerusalem* (1989), for which he won the National Book Award for nonfiction. A strong proponent of American intervention to solve seemingly intractable problems like the Arab–Israeli conflict, Friedman writes at the end of *From Beirut to Jerusalem*, "Only a real friend tells you the truth about yourself. An American friend has to help jar these people out of their fantasies by constantly holding up before their eyes the mirror of reality." In 2002, Friedman received the Pulitzer Prize for Commentary for his reports on terrorism for *The New York Times*. His other books include *The Lexus and the Olive Tree: Understanding Globalization* (2000), *The World Is Flat* (2005), *Hot, Flat, and Crowded* (2008), and *That Used to Be Us: How America Fell Behind in the World It Invented and How We Can Come Back* (2011). Friedman also has published a collection of articles and essays, *Longitudes and Attitudes: Exploring the World After September 11* (2002), where the following selection serves as the book's **prologue**.

Before Reading

How would you define the word *globalization*? Is it simply a trend in which nations interrelate economically, or are other forces involved? Do you think that globalization is good or bad? Justify your response.

I am a big believer in the idea of the super-story, the notion that we all   1
carry around with us a big lens, a big framework, through which we look at the world, order events, and decide what is important and what is not. The events of 9/11 did not happen in a vacuum. They happened in the context of a new international system—a system that cannot explain everything but *can* explain and connect more things in more places on more days than anything else. That new international system is called globalization. It came together in the late 1980s and replaced the previous international system, the cold war system, which had reigned since the end of World War II. This new system is the lens, the super-story, through which I viewed the events of 9/11.

I define globalization as the inexorable integration of markets, trans-   2
portation systems, and communication systems to a degree never witnessed before—in a way that is enabling corporations, countries, and
individuals to reach around the world farther, faster, deeper, and
cheaper than ever before, and in a way that is enabling the world to
reach into corporations, countries, and individuals farther, faster, deeper,
and cheaper than ever before.

Several important features of this globalization system differ from those   3
of the cold war system in ways that are quite relevant for understanding
the events of 9/11. I examined them in detail in my previous book, *The
Lexus and the Olive Tree*, and want to simply highlight them here.

The cold war system was characterized by one overarching feature—   4
and that was *division*. That world was a divided-up, chopped-up place,
and whether you were a country or a company, your threats and opportunities in the cold war system tended to grow out of who you were divided from. Appropriately, this cold war system was symbolized by a
single word—*wall*, the Berlin Wall.

The globalization system is different. It also has one overarching   5
feature—and that is *integration*. The world has become an increasingly
interwoven place, and today, whether you are a company or a country,
your threats and opportunities increasingly derive from who you are connected to. This globalization system is also characterized by a single
word—*web*, the World Wide Web. So in the broadest sense we have gone
from an international system built around division and walls to a system
increasingly built around integration and webs. In the cold war we
reached for the hotline, which was a symbol that we were all divided but
at least two people were in charge—the leaders of the United States and
the Soviet Union. In the globalization system we reach for the Internet,
which is a symbol that we are all connected and nobody is quite in charge.

Everyone in the world is directly or indirectly affected by this new   6
system, but not everyone benefits from it, not by a long shot, which is
why the more it becomes diffused, the more it also produces a backlash
by people who feel overwhelmed by it, homogenized by it, or unable to
keep pace with its demands.

The other key difference between the cold war system and the global-   7
ization system is how power is structured within them. The cold war system was built primarily around nation-states. You acted on the world in
that system through your state. The cold war was a drama of states confronting states, balancing states, and aligning with states. And, as a system, the cold war was balanced at the center by two superstates, two
superpowers: the United States and the Soviet Union.

The globalization system, by contrast, is built around three balances, 8
which overlap and affect one another. The first is the traditional balance
of power between nation-states. In the globalization system, the United
States is now the sole and dominant superpower and all other nations
are subordinate to it to one degree or another. The shifting balance of
power between the United States and other states, or simply between
other states, still very much matters for the stability of this system. And
it can still explain a lot of the news you read on the front page of the paper, whether it is the news of China balancing Russia, Iran balancing
Iraq, or India confronting Pakistan.

The second important power balance in the globalization system is 9
between nation-states and global markets. These global markets are
made up of millions of investors moving money around the world with
the click of a mouse. I call them the Electronic Herd, and this herd gath-
ers in key global financial centers—such as Wall Street, Hong Kong,
London, and Frankfurt—which I call the Supermarkets. The attitudes
and actions of the Electronic Herd and the Supermarkets can have a
huge impact on nation-states today, even to the point of triggering the
downfall of governments. Who ousted Suharto in Indonesia in 1998? It
wasn't another state, it was the Supermarkets, by withdrawing their support for, and confidence in, the Indonesian economy. You also will not
understand the front page of the newspaper today unless you bring the
Supermarkets into your analysis. Because the United States can destroy
you by dropping bombs, but the Supermarkets can destroy you by
downgrading your bonds. In other words, the United States is the dominant player in maintaining the globalization game board, but it is hardly
alone in influencing the moves on that game board.

The third balance that you have to pay attention to—the one that is 10
really the newest of all and the most relevant to the events of 9/11—is
the balance between individuals and nation-states. Because globalization
has brought down many of the walls that limited the movement and
reach of people, and because it has simultaneously wired the world
into networks, it gives more power to *individuals* to influence both
markets and nation-states than at any other time in history. Whether
by enabling people to use the Internet to communicate instantly at
almost no cost over vast distances, or by enabling them to use the
Web to transfer money or obtain weapons designs that normally would
have been controlled by states, or by enabling them to go into a hardware store now and buy a five-hundred-dollar global positioning device, connected to a satellite, that can direct a hijacked airplane—
globalization can be an incredible force-multiplier for individuals.

Individuals can increasingly act on the world stage directly, unmediated by a state.

So you have today not only a superpower, not only Supermarkets, 11 but also what I call "super-empowered individuals." Some of these super-empowered individuals are quite angry, some of them quite wonderful—but all of them are now able to act much more directly and much more powerfully on the world stage.

Osama bin Laden declared war on the United States in the late 1990s. 12 After he organized the bombing of two American embassies in Africa, the U.S. Air Force retaliated with a cruise missile attack on his bases in Afghanistan as though he were another nation-state. Think about that: on one day in 1998, the United States fired 75 cruise missiles at bin Laden. The United States fired 75 cruise missiles, at $1 million apiece, at a person! That was the first battle in history between a superpower and a super-empowered angry man. September 11 was just the second such battle.

Jody Williams won the Nobel Peace Prize in 1997 for helping to 13 build an international coalition to bring about a treaty outlawing land mines. Although nearly 120 governments endorsed the treaty, it was opposed by Russia, China, and the United States. When Jody Williams was asked, "How did you do that? How did you organize one thousand different citizens' groups and nongovernmental organizations on five continents to forge a treaty that was opposed by the major powers?" she had a very brief answer: "E-mail." Jody Williams used e-mail and the networked world to super-empower herself.

Nation-states, and the American superpower in particular, are still 14 hugely important today, but so too now are Supermarkets and super-empowered individuals. You will never understand the globalization system, or the front page of the morning paper—or 9/11—unless you see each as a complex interaction between all three of these actors: states bumping up against states, states bumping up against Supermarkets, and Supermarkets and states bumping up against super-empowered individuals—many of whom, unfortunately, are super-empowered angry men.

Thinking about the Essay

1. Friedman constructs this essay and entitles it a "prologue." What is the purpose of a prologue? What subject matter does the writer provide in his prologue?

2. The writer is not afraid to inject the personal "I" into his analysis—a strategy that many composition teachers will warn you against. Why does Friedman start with his personal voice? Why can he get away with it? What does the personal voice contribute to the effect of the essay?

3. In addition to his personal voice, what other stylistic features make Friedman's essay, despite its complicated subject matter, accessible to ordinary readers? How does he establish a colloquial style?

4. This essay offers a series of definitions, comparisons, and classifications as structuring devices. Locate instances of these three rhetorical strategies and explain how they complement each other.

5. Friedman uses September 11 as a touchstone for his essay. Why does he do this? What is the effect?

Responding in Writing

6. Write a 250-word summary of Friedman's essay, capturing all the important topics that he presents.

7. Take one major point that Friedman makes in this essay and write a paper on it. For example, you might want to discuss why September 11 represents a key transition point in our understanding of globalization. Or you might focus on the concept of the Supermarket or the Electronic Herd.

8. Think about the world today, and write your own "super-story" in which you define and classify its primary features.

Networking

9. Divide into two roughly equal groups, and conduct a debate on whether or not globalization is a good or bad phenomenon. Use Friedman's essay as a reference point. Your instructor should serve as the moderator for this debate.

10. Join the Electronic Herd and develop a list of links to sites that deal with globalization. Contribute your list to the others generated by class members in order to create a superlist for possible future use.

Brave, New Social World

DENNIS MCCAFFERTY

Dennis McCafferty is a technology writer living in Washington, DC. He contributes to the "Society" page of the professional journal *Communications of the ACM*, where this article featuring the use of Facebook, Twitter, and other social media tools in three countries—Brazil, Egypt, and Japan—appeared in the July 2011 issue.

Before Reading

List the ways in which social media tools promote globalization trends.

Source: Dennis McCafferty "Brave New Social World," Communications of the ACM, Vol. 54:7, © 2011 Association for Computing Machinery, Inc. Reprinted by permission. http://dl.acm.org/citation.cfm?doid=1965724.1965732.

Today, social media is emerging as a dominant form of instant global   1
communication. Growing more addictively popular by the day—nearly
two-thirds of Internet users worldwide use some type of social media,
according to an industry estimate—Facebook, Twitter, and other easily
accessible online tools deepen our interaction with societies near and far.

Consider these numbers: Facebook is poised to hit 700 million users   2
and, as seven of 10 Facebook members reside outside the U.S., more
than 70 global-language translations. Twitter's user numbers will reportedly hit 200 million later this year, and users can tweet in multiple languages. In terms of daily usage, Facebook generates the second-most
traffic of any site in the world, according to Alexa.com, a Web information company, at press time. (Google is number one.) As for blogging,
which now seems likes a relatively old-fashioned form of social media,
the dominant site, blogger.com, ranks eighth. As for Twitter, it's now
11th—and climbing.

The top five nations in terms of social media usage are the U.S.,   3
Poland, Great Britain, South Korea, and France, according to the Pew
Research Center. But beyond international rankings and traffic numbers,
there's much diversity in the manner in which the citizens of the world
take advantage of these tools, according to *Blogging Around the Globe:
Motivations, Privacy Concerns and Social Networking,* an IBM Tokyo
research report. In Japan, blogs often serve as outlets for personal expression and diary-style postings. In the U.S., it's mostly about earning income
or promoting an agenda. In the U.K., it's a combination of these needs, as
well as professional advancement and acting as a citizen journalist.

Communications connected with three citizens in three different   4
nations, each of whom are finding their own individual voice through
these resources. In fact, we depended primarily upon social media to initially reach them. One is a Japanese female blogger who segues seamlessly from pop-culture observations to revealing reflections on the
nation's recent earthquake, tsunami, and nuclear disaster. Another is a
Brazilian businesswoman who uses multiple digital outlets to expand her
marketing reach throughout the world. The third is an Egyptian news-
man who is helping record history with his dispatches of daily life in a
region undergoing dramatic political change. (In terms of social media
usage, Brazil ranks eighth, Japan 12th, and Egypt 18th, according to
Pew.) Here are their stories.

Me and Tokyo

The contrast is striking: Before March 11, Mari Kanazawa's blog, Wata-   5
shi to Tokyo (translation: Me and Tokyo), waxes whimsically about a

recent tweet in Japanese by the band Radiohead, as well as consumer products such as Wasasco, a wasabi-flavored Tabasco.

After March 11, however, the conversation takes an abrupt turn. The day after the devastating Tōhoku earthquake and tsunami, Kanazawa writes this unsettling passage: "Earthquake, tsunami, fire and now we have a nuclear meltdown . . . I was in the Midtown Tower when it happened. Japanese people are used to earthquakes, we can usually sense them because the building sways, but this time it was shaking up and down. Some people screamed and some hid under their desks." 6

Within a week, Kanazawa casts a sense of humor about the situation: "I really don't need to check Geiger counters and don't need a lot of toilet paper because earthquakes [don't] make me [go to the bathroom] more than usual." 7

Blogs: Motivations for writing and readership levels by region.

Region	Motivation	Readership
Japan	Personal diary, self-expression	74% Internet users, average 4.54 times/week, 25% daily, highest in world
Korea	Personal diary, personal scrapbook, online journalism	43% Internet users, average 2.03 times/week, ages 8–24: 4 times/week ages 25–34: 3 times/week
China	96% personal blogs loaded with photos, audio, animations	Highest for ages 18–24 (less than 3 times/week), probably friends
U.S.	Make money, promote political or professional agenda	27% Internet users, average 0.9 times/week, lower than Asia, higher than Europe
Germany	For fun, like to write, personal diary	Bloggers are regular readers of other blogs on average 21.15 (std dev 39, med 10)
U.K.	Connect with others, express opinions/vent, make money, citizen journalist, validation, professional advancement	23% Internet users, average 0.68 times/week
Poland	Self-expression, social interaction, entertainment	Not available

Source: Mei, Kobayashi, *Blogging Around the Globe: Motivations, Privacy Concerns and Social Networking*, IBM Research-Tokyo, 2010.

A high-profile cyberpersonality in Japan, Kanazawa has always per-   8
ceived her blog as equal parts diary and cultural commentary. She was
one of the rare Japanese citizens who wrote a blog in English when she
started in 2004, so her traffic numbers have spiked to a healthy 2,000
unique visitors a-day. A Web site manager, Kanazawa prefers the free-
form creativity of a blog, as opposed to the restrictive 140-character
count of Twitter. "It doesn't fit me," she says of the latter. "My blog
is an information hub for Japanese subculture. That's my style. I
wanted to tell people that we have more interesting, good things than
sushi, sumo, tempura, geishas, and ninjas."

Since the disaster, like many Japanese citizens posting blogs and Face-   9
book status updates, Kanazawa has sought and published information
about the nation's recovery efforts. "These tools are so effective in this
disaster," she says. "People need to check for things such as the transportation situation and where the evacuation areas are. In Tōhoku, when
someone tweeted 'We need 600 rice balls here,' they were delivered
within an hour. Social media went from being a communication tool to
a lifeline."

Brazil—and Beyond

In generations past, it would be difficult for a self-described life coach   10
like Lygya Maya of Salvador, Brazil, to interact with a motivational-
speaking giant like Tony Robbins, an American who has more than 200
books, audio CDs, and other products listed on Amazon.com. Perhaps
she would have needed to take a trip to the U.S. in hopes of speaking
with Robbins at one of his tour stops. Or write him a letter and hope he
would answer with something beyond a polite thank you.

But this is the 21st century, and Maya takes full advantage of the   11
digital age to engage with high-profile leaders such as Robbins and Mark
Victor Hansen, co-author of the bestselling *Chicken Soup for the Soul*
books. Robbins and Hansen are now Facebook friends with Maya, who
they have advised and encouraged to push beyond perceived limitations
in her work.

Such international collaborations have enabled Maya to create her   12
own signature style to market herself, which she calls a "Brazilian Carni-
val Style" approach to guide clients to enjoying a happy, productive, and
empowering life. Maya now sees up to 300 clients a year in private sessions, and hosts as many as 500 group sessions annually.

"I use blogs, Facebook, Twitter, and Plaxo [an online address book]   13
to promote my business," Maya says. "I am about to start podcasting, as
well as making YouTube videos on every channel that I can find on the

Internet. Social media has opened up my business on many different levels. I am now able to promote it literally to the world, free of charge."

Maya has also established more than 2,500 personal connections via 14 Facebook, LinkedIn, and other sites. She'll send tweets several times a day, offering reflections like "When truthfully expressed, words reflect our core value and spirit." All of this has helped Maya promote her budding empire of services and products, which will soon include a book, *Cheeka Cheeka BOOM Through Life!: The Luscious Story of a Daring Brazilian Woman.* It's gotten to the point where—like some of her counterparts in the U.S.— she must subcontract work just to keep up with it all.

"I'm about to hire a team to work with me on Twitter and all the 15 social media out there that we can use to support campaigns," Maya says. "You must have a great team to share quality work. Otherwise, you will have stress. This allows me to promote my services and products 24/7—and that includes while I'm sleeping."

A Witness in Egypt

Amr Hassanein lists *Babel, Fantasia,* and *The Last Temptation of Christ* 16 as his favorite movies on his Facebook page. And his organizations/ activities of interest include Hands Along the Nile Development Services, a nonprofit organization that promotes intercultural understanding between the U.S. and his native Egypt. Now working as a freelance producer for ABC News, Hassanein is also using Facebook as a vehicle to showcase his own firsthand accounts of political unrest in the Middle East. Recently, for example, ABC sent him to Libya to assist with news coverage of the nation's conflict.

"My usage of social media tools is from a neutral side," says Hassa- 17 nein, sounding very much like an objective news reporter. "Social media makes me feel like an observer. It gives me a sense of what's going on around me at all times. The impact events here in Egypt, like the demonstrations, were organized and known through Facebook."

Still, it's impossible to live through these times without getting caught 18 up in the politics. His sympathies remain with We Are All Khaled Said, an anti-torture group that uses social media to allow voices of the Arab uprisings to be heard. (Sample Facebook post from the group: "Gaddafi has vowed it will be a 'long war' in Libya. Let's hope his [sic] wrong & Gaddafi's massacre of his people will end very soon.")

Hassanein recognizes that social media provides an opportunity to 19 deliver an unfiltered message to the world about local developments, as well as debunk stereotypes about people of the Middle East. Yet, aside from this bigger-picture purpose, these tools allow him to easily remain in close contact with loved ones and work associates.

Actions taken by the Egyptian government to block access to Face-   20
book and Twitter significantly backfired during its recent conflict, further
fueling the resolve of the freedom movement, he says. "The impact was
clear: What were normal demonstrations became a revolution. It made
me think about the consequences of blocking people from information."

That said, some of the "anything goes" aspects of social media make   21
Hassanein feel uncomfortable. "When you watch a news channel that
presents a direction you don't like," he says, "you have the ability not to
watch. In social media, there is no uni-direction you can refuse or reject.
People are the senders and the receivers. Inputs need to be self-filtering
and self-censoring. For me, I will use my head."

Thinking about the Essay

1. What is McCafferty's thesis? What does he mean by "instant global communication" (paragraph 1)? How do the three people McCafferty profiles
illuminate his thesis?

2. What is the allusion that the writer embeds in the title? How does this
allusion influence the writer's tone?

3. McCafferty contributed this article to a magazine for technology and communications professionals. How does he adjust his style to address the interests of this audience? What is his purpose in attaching a photograph and
a graph?

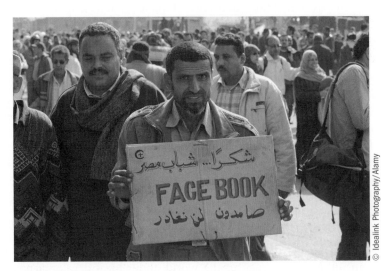

An anti-Mubarak protestor holds a sign praising Facebook for helping to
organize the protest in Tahrir Square, Cairo, Egypt.

4. How effective do you find the writer's decision to divide this essay into sections with subtitles? Justify your answer by referring to specific rhetorical strategies—for instance, classification—that you detect.

5. Evaluate McCafferty's conclusion. Why does he end the essay with a quotation?

Responding in Writing

6. Compose a classification essay in which you examine the types of social media tools available to people today and how these tools might contribute to globalization trends.

7. Argue for or against the proposition that social media tools can lead to social and political change.

8. Write a personal essay in which you discuss your own use of social media tools and what your motivation might be in maintaining a blog.

Networking

9. In a group of five, review the writer's table "Blogs: Motivations for writing and readership levels by region." Then have each person list his or her own motivation for engaging in social media writing and communication. Draw up a list of all these reasons, and report to the class.

10. Check one of the blogs or websites mentioned in this article. Write a summary of your findings.

How to Raise a Global Kid

LISA MILLER

Lisa Miller is a senior writer and religion editor at *Newsweek*. After graduating from Oberlin College in 1984, Miller worked for the *Harvard Business Review*. Before joining *Newsweek*, she also held positions at *The New Yorker* and *The Wall Street Journal*. In the following essay, which appeared in the July 25, 2011, edition of *Newsweek*, Miller discusses the challenge facing American children who must have international experience in order to compete in the global economy.

Before Reading

Does your college offer study abroad opportunities? If so, do you plan to spend a term or academic year abroad? Do you think that study abroad programs help students to succeed in the global economy? Why or why not?

Happy Rogers, age 8, stands among her classmates in the schoolyard   1
at dismissal time, immune, it seems, to the cacophonous din. Her parents and baby sister are waiting outside, but still she lingers, engrossed in conversation. A poised and precocious blonde, Hilton Augusta Parker Rogers, nicknamed Happy, would be at home in the schoolyard of any affluent American suburb or big-city private school. But here, at the elite, bilingual Nanyang Primary School in Singapore, Happy is in the minority, her Dakota Fanning hair shimmering in a sea of darker heads. This is what her parents have traveled halfway around the world for. While her American peers are feasting on the idiocies fed to them by junk TV and summer movies, Happy is navigating her friendships and doing her homework entirely in Mandarin.

Fluency in Chinese, she says—in English—through mouthfuls of spa-   2
ghetti bolognese at a Singapore restaurant, "is going to make me better and smarter."

American parents have barely recovered from the anxiety attacks   3
they suffered at the hands of the Tiger Mom—oh, no, my child is already 7 and she can't play a note of Chopin—and now here comes Happy's father, the multimillionaire American investor and author Jim Rogers, to give them something new to fret about. It is no longer enough to raise children who are brave, curious, hardworking, and compassionate. Nor is it sufficient to steer them toward the right sports, the right tutors, the right internships, and thus engineer their admittance to the right (or at least a good enough) college. According to Rogers, who in 2007 left New York's Upper West Side to settle in Singapore with his wife, Paige Parker, and Happy (Beeland Anderson Parker Rogers, called Baby Bee, was born the next year), parents who really care about their children must also ponder this: are we doing enough to raise "global" kids?

"I'm doing what parents have done for many years," Jim Rogers   4
says. "I'm trying to prepare my children for the future, for the 21st century. I'm trying to prepare them as best I can for the world as I see it." Rogers believes the future is Asia—he was recently on cable television flogging Chinese commodities. "The money is in the East, and the debtors are in the West. I'd rather be with the creditors than the debtors," he adds.

It has become a convention of public discourse to regard rapid 5 globalization—of economies and business; of politics and conflict; of fashion, technology, and music—as the great future threat to American prosperity. The burden of meeting that challenge rests explicitly on our kids. If they don't learn—now—to achieve a comfort level with foreign people, foreign languages, and foreign lands, this argument goes, America's competitive position in the world will continue to erode, and their future livelihood and that of subsequent generations will be in jeopardy. Rogers is hardly the only person who sees things this way. "In this global economy, the line between domestic and international issues is increasingly blurred, with the world's economies, societies, and people interconnected as never before," said U.S. Education Secretary Arne Duncan in remarks in the spring of 2010 at the Asia Society in New York. "I am worried that in this interconnected world, our country risks being disconnected from the contributions of other countries and cultures."

Despite Duncan's articulate urgency (and the public example of Rog- 6 ers and a few others like him), America is so far utterly failing to produce a generation of global citizens. Only 37 percent of Americans hold a passport. Fewer than 2 percent of America's 18 million college students go abroad during their undergraduate years—and when they do go, it's mostly for short stints in England, Spain, or Italy that are more like vacations. Only a quarter of public primary schools offer any language instruction at all, and fewer high schools offer French, German, Latin, Japanese, or Russian than they did in 1997. The number of schools teaching Chinese and Arabic is so tiny as to be nearly invisible.

Meanwhile, 200 million Chinese schoolchildren are studying English. 7 South Korean parents recently threw a collective hissy fit, demanding that their children begin English instruction in first grade, rather than in second. Nearly 700,000 students from all over the world attended U.S. universities during the 2009–10 school year, with the greatest increases in kids from China and Saudi Arabia. "Not training our kids to be able to work and live in an international environment is like leaving them illiterate," says David Boren, the former U.S. senator and current president of the University of Oklahoma. The gap between our ambition and reality yawns wide.

There is no consensus on remedies. According to a white paper issued 8 in 2009 by the Institute on International Education, most colleges and universities say they want to increase participation in study-abroad programs, but only 40 percent are actually making concerted efforts to do so. Long immersion programs are expensive, and in an environment of tough statewide budget cuts, students and professors are too crunched for time to make international experience a priority. Educators disagree on which kinds of experiences are most advantageous for kids—or even what advantageous means. Is it enough for a teenager who has never traveled farther than her grandma's house to get a passport and order a pint in a London pub? Or does she have to spend a year in Beijing, immersed in Mandarin and economic policy? Is the goal of foreign experience to learn a language or gain some special expertise—in auto engineering or peace mediation? Or is it to be of service to others by giving mosquito nets to poor children in an African village?

Jim Rogers sees an America in decline, and his solution has been to immerse himself in the countries and cultures that are ascendant. "We think we're the world leader, but we're not," he says. "I don't like saying that. I'm an American. I vote. I pay taxes. But the level of knowledge is not very high, and that's going to hurt us, I'm afraid." In the Rogers family's five-bedroom bungalow, there is no TV. Instead, there are more than a dozen globes to look at and maps to ponder, a nanny and a maid who speak only Mandarin to the kids, bicycles to ride, and a new karaoke machine so the girls can learn Chinese songs.

A generation ago and as far back as Thomas Jefferson, a certain kind of child from a certain kind of family went abroad because it was done; a sojourn in Europe was as crucial to becoming a cultivated person as knowing the works of Mozart or Rembrandt. The point was to see the Great Museums, of course, but also to breathe the air—to learn to converse in another tongue, to adapt to the rhythms of another place. Hemingway did this, of course, but so did Benjamin Franklin and Johnny Depp. This is what Pamela Wolf, who just returned to New York City with her husband and children from a year in Barcelona, did. She enrolled her teenagers in an international school, where they made friends with kids from around the world and learned to speak fluent Spanish. Her children have a global perspective not only because of their language skills but also because arriving in a new place, knowing no one, forced them to be resilient. "It's pushing yourself out of your comfort zone," Wolf says. "It builds a very compassionate child. While, yes, grades and academics are as important to me as anyone, you need resilience to understand and have sympathy for other people."

Such lengthy sojourns, though, are available to only a few: the very adventurous or the very rich. Wolf and her husband are both self-employed. "Financially," she says, "we have the great privilege of earning money while we're away."

Without resources and connections, a foreign experience can be a misery. Two years ago, Maribeth Henderson moved from San Antonio with her husband, her college-age son, and her adopted 5-year-old daughter, Wei Wei, to a remote part of China, in Guangdong province. Wei Wei didn't learn much Mandarin—her school taught mainly Cantonese—and Henderson felt lonely and alienated. "It was so Chinese that I couldn't assimilate and feel comfortable," she says. "I couldn't speak the language; it was hard for us to even order food in a restaurant. If you ordered a chicken, they would literally hand you a chicken. You were lucky if it wasn't alive." Henderson abandoned ship, returning to Texas with Wei Wei ahead of schedule and leaving her husband and son in Guangzhou. Now, though, she's planning to try again. This summer she and Wei Wei will move to Beijing, and Henderson hopes the big city will ameliorate her former isolation. About her goal—helping Wei Wei learn Chinese— Henderson has no doubts. "For children to be competitive and successful in a global economy," she says, "it's important for them to be bilingual."

For parents who want to give their children global experience while   13 keeping them safely on the straight and narrow American path of PSATs, SATs, and stellar extracurriculars, there's an ever-growing field of options. Immersion schools have exploded over the past 40 years, grow- ing from none in 1970 to 440 today, according to the Center for Applied Linguistics, and Mandarin, especially, is seen among type-A parents as a twofer: a child who learns Mandarin starting at 5 increases her brain capacity and is exposed to the culture of the future through language. (One mom in San Francisco laughs when she recalls that her daughter learned about Rosa Parks and the Montgomery bus boycott in Chinese.) The education entrepreneur Chris Whittle and colleagues recently announced plans for the new Avenues school, to open in New York City in September 2012 and designed to compete with the city's most exclusive (and expensive) private schools. Its curriculum will be fully bilingual— parents choose a Mandarin or Spanish track when their kids are 3— providing the Happy Rogers experience but with all the conveniences of home. "We think that any child that graduates from high school a mono- glot is automatically behind," Whittle says. Fourteen months before the school's doors open, Avenues has already received 1,200 applications.

Study abroad is now a prerequisite on some college campuses, and a   14 few professional schools, especially in business and engineering, have begun to require international study as part of their curricula. Nursing students at a community college in Utah must all spend a month at a hospital in Vietnam as part of their training. But Margaret Heisel, direc- tor of the Center for Capacity Building in Study Abroad, believes that a real global education comes from a long stay in a strange place; it gives kids skills that no amount of study can teach.

My own experience proves this point. During my sophomore year in 15 high school, my father, a university professor, moved our entire family to Amsterdam for his sabbatical year and enrolled my brothers and me in local public schools. During that glorious year, I rode my bike through city streets, learned to roll a cigarette one-handed, and eventually spoke Dutch like a 15-year-old native. (I can still say "That's so stupid" and "This is so boring.") We saw Stonehenge and the Rijksmuseum and drove to Burgundy for the grape harvest, but the real impact of that adventure was that I learned a degree of self-reliance—a 15-year-old girl needs to make friends and will cross any cultural boundary to do so— that I didn't know I had.

"I think it's liberating to some extent," Heisel says. "It touches people in places that being in a familiar place doesn't. It requires versatility, flexibility. It's a different culture and it's pressing on kids in different ways." Baby Bee is equally at home on visits to the U.S. and in Singapore, where her father rides her to school each day on his personal pedicab. There she sings the Singapore national anthem and pledges the Singapore flag. "She's no different from the Chinese kids," says her teacher, Fu Su Qin. "And her Chinese is just as good."

Thinking about the Essay

1. Consider Miller's title and the promise it holds that readers will discover how to raise a global kid. Does Miller actually follow through on the promise implied by this title? Why or why not? Refer to specific aspects of the essay to justify your response.

2. What is the writer's thesis? Is this main idea stated or implied? Explain. What major topics inform Miller's thesis?

3. Why does Miller start her essay with a profile of Happy Rogers and her family? Which paragraphs constitute the writer's introduction? What is Miller's tone here and throughout the essay?

4. How does Miller employ the comparative method in order to organize her essay? What specific topics is she comparing and contrasting?

5. What conclusions does Miller draw about the challenges facing American students as they prepare for lives in a global economy?

Responding in Writing

6. Write a process paper in which you explain how you plan to prepare for the challenge of competing for work in an increasingly globalized world and economy.

7. In an argumentative essay, take up Miller's assertion that the United States is falling behind in the preparation of "global kids," agreeing or disagreeing with her opinion.

8. Find out more about "Tiger Mom" tactics, and write an essay about this topic and its relation to the education of global kids. (To prepare for this assignment, read the essays by Amy Chua and Patricia Williams in Chapter 7.)

Networking

9. In groups of four or five, draft an article for your college newspaper in which you argue for increased opportunities to study abroad—or the creation of a study abroad program if one doesn't exist on your campus. Revise your paper, paying close attention to the logic and tone of your argument, before submitting the article for possible publication.

10. Consult the Institute for International Education's (IIE) website. Write a summary of your findings about the IIE's programs to strengthen international education.

The Noble Feat of Nike

JOHAN NORBERG

Johan Norberg, a Swedish writer and leading European intellectual, contributed this article to London's *The Spectator* in June 2003. In the essay, he takes issue with those who think that globalization is the invention of "ruthless international capitalists." In arguing his case, Norberg centers his discussion on one symbol of globalization—Nike—suggesting that we simply have to look at our "feet" to understand Nike's "feat" in advancing a benign form of globalization. Norberg is the author of *In Defense of Global Capitalism*, and writer and presenter of the recent documentary *Globalization Is Good*. Since 2007, Norberg has been associated with the Cato Institute, a conservative Washington, DC, think tank.

Before Reading

Check your sneakers. Where were they made? What do you think the workers earned to manufacture them? Do you think they were exploited? Explain your response.

Nike. It means victory. It also means a type of expensive gym shoe. In   1
the minds of the anti-globalisation movement, it stands for both at
once. Nike stands for the victory of a Western footwear company over the
poor and dispossessed. Spongy, smelly, hungered after by kids across the
world, Nike is the symbol of the unacceptable triumph of global capital.

A Nike is a shoe that simultaneously kicks people out of jobs in the   2
West, and tramples on the poor in the Third World. Sold for 100 times
more than the wages of the peons who make them, Nike shoes are hate-
objects more potent, in the eyes of the protesters at this week's G8 riots,
than McDonald's hamburgers. If you want to be trendy these days, you
don't wear Nikes; you boycott them.

So I was interested to hear someone not only praising Nike sweat-   3
shops, but also claiming that Nike is an example of a good and responsible business. That someone was the ruling Communist party of Vietnam.

Today Nike has almost four times more workers in Vietnam than in   4
the United States. I travelled to Ho Chi Minh to examine the effects of
multinational corporations on poor countries. Nike being the most notorious multinational villain, and Vietnam being a dictatorship with a
documented lack of free speech, the operation is supposed to be a classic
of conscience-free capitalist oppression.

In truth the work does look tough, and the conditions grim, if we   5
compare Vietnamese factories with what we have back home. But that's
not the comparison these workers make. They compare the work at Nike
with the way they lived before, or the way their parents or neighbours
still work. And the facts are revealing. The average pay at a Nike factory
close to Ho Chi Minh is $54 a month, almost three times the minimum
wage for a state-owned enterprise.

Ten years ago, when Nike was established in Vietnam, the workers   6
had to walk to the factories, often for many miles. After three years on
Nike wages, they could afford bicycles. Another three years later, they
could afford scooters, so they all take the scooters to work (and if you
go there, beware; they haven't really decided on which side of the road
to drive). Today, the first workers can afford to buy a car.

But when I talk to a young Vietnamese woman, Tsi-Chi, at the fac-   7
tory, it is not the wages she is most happy about. Sure, she makes five
times more than she did, she earns more than her husband, and she can
now afford to build an extension to her house. But the most important
thing, she says, is that she doesn't have to work outdoors on a farm any
more. For me, a Swede with only three months of summer, this sounds
bizarre. Surely working conditions under the blue sky must be superior to
those in a sweatshop? But then I am naively Eurocentric. Farming means

10 to 14 hours a day in the burning sun or the intensive rain, in rice fields with water up to your ankles and insects in your face. Even a Swede would prefer working nine to five in a clean, air-conditioned factory.

Furthermore, the Nike job comes with a regular wage, with free or 8 subsidised meals, free medical services and training and education. The most persistent demand Nike hears from the workers is for an expansion of the factories so that their relatives can be offered a job as well.

These facts make Nike sound more like Santa Claus than Scrooge. 9 But corporations such as Nike don't bring these benefits and wages because they are generous. It is not altruism that is at work here; it is globalisation. With their investments in poor countries, multinationals bring new machinery, better technology, new management skills and production ideas, a larger market and the education of their workers. That is exactly what raises productivity. And if you increase productivity— the amount a worker can produce—you can also increase his wage.

Nike is not the accidental good guy. On average, multinationals in 10 the least developed countries pay twice as much as domestic companies in the same line of business. If you get to work for an American multinational in a low-income country, you get eight times the average income. If this is exploitation, then the problem in our world is that the poor countries aren't sufficiently exploited.

The effect on local business is profound: "Before I visit some foreign 11 factory, especially like Nike, we have a question. Why do the foreign factories here work well and produce much more?" That was what Mr. Kiet, the owner of a local shoe factory who visited Nike to learn how he could be just as successful at attracting workers, told me: "And I recognise that productivity does not only come from machinery but also from satisfaction of the worker. So for the future factory we should concentrate on our working conditions."

If I was an antiglobalist, I would stop complaining about Nike's 12 bad wages. If there is a problem, it is that the wages are too high, so that they are almost luring doctors and teachers away from their important jobs.

But—happily—I don't think even that is a realistic threat. With grow- 13 ing productivity it will also be possible to invest in education and healthcare for Vietnam. Since 1990, when the Vietnamese communists began to liberalise the economy, exports of coffee, rice, clothes and footwear have surged, the economy has doubled, and poverty has been halved. Nike and Coca-Cola triumphed where American bombs failed. They have made Vietnam capitalist.

I asked the young Nike worker Tsi-Chi what her hopes were for her   14
son's future. A generation ago, she would have had to put him to work on
the farm from an early age. But Tsi-Chi told me she wants to give him a
good education, so that he can become a doctor. That's one of the most
impressive developments since Vietnam's economy was opened up. In ten
years 2.2 million children have gone from child labour to education. It
would be extremely interesting to hear an antiglobalist explain to Tsi-Chi
why it is important for Westerners to boycott Nike, so that she loses her
job, and has to go back into farming, and has to send her son to work.

The European Left used to listen to the Vietnamese communists when   15
they brought only misery and starvation to their population. Shouldn't
they listen to the Vietnamese now, when they have found a way to
improve people's lives? The party officials have been convinced by Nike
that ruthless multinational capitalists are better than the state at providing workers with high wages and a good and healthy workplace. How
long will it take for our own anticapitalists to learn that lesson?

Thinking about the Essay

1. Examine the writer's introduction. Why is it distinctive? How does
   Norberg ''hook'' us and also set the terms of his argument? Why is Nike
   an especially potent symbol around which to organize an essay on
   globalization?

2. Explain the writer's claim and how he defends it. Identify those instances in
   which he deals with the opposition. How effective do you think his argument
   is? Justify your answer.

3. What is the writer's tone in this essay? Why is the tone especially effective
   in conveying the substance of Norberg's argument?

4. Analyze the writer's **style** and how it contributes to his argument. Identify
   specific stylistic elements that you consider especially effective.

5. To a large extent, the writer bases his argument on direct observation. How
   can you tell that he is open-minded and truthful in the presentation of
   facts? What is the role of a newspaper or journal in claiming responsibility
   for the accuracy of this information?

Responding in Writing

6. Select a symbol of globalization and write an essay about it. You may use
   Nike if you wish, or Coca-Cola, McDonald's, or any other company that has
   a global reach.

7. Write a **rebuttal** to Norberg's essay. Try to answer him point by point.

8. Why have clothing manufacturing and other forms of manufacturing fled from the United States and other industrialized nations to less developed parts of the world? Write a causal analysis of this trend, being certain to state a thesis or present a claim that illustrates your viewpoint on the issue.

Networking

9. In groups of four, examine your clothes. List the countries where they were manufactured. Share the list with the class, drawing a global map of the countries where the various items were produced.

10. Check various Internet sites for information on Nike and its role in globalization. On the basis of your findings, determine whether or not this company is sensitive to globalization issues. Participate in a class discussion of this topic.

Globalization Rocked the Ancient World Too

JARED DIAMOND

Jared Diamond is an internationally acclaimed professor and writer whose interests and expertise span many fields including geography, evolutionary biology, ecology, physiology, history, and economics. Born in Boston in 1937, Diamond received his B.A. from Harvard University (1958) and a Ph.D. from Cambridge University (1961). Currently he is a professor of geography at the University of California, Los Angeles (UCLA). Diamond is known for his work as a conservationist and as a director of the World Wildlife Fund. His field experience includes numerous expeditions to New Guinea and neighboring islands, where he helped to establish Indonesian New Guinea's national park system. His book *Guns, Germs, and Steel: The Fate of Human Societies* was awarded the Pulitzer Prize in 1998. He has also written the best-selling *Collapse: How Societies Choose to Fail or Succeed* (2004). In this essay, which appeared in the *Los Angeles Times* on September 4, 2003, Diamond explores globalization from a unique historical perspective.

Before Reading

Do you think that the current debate over globalization is a new phenomenon, or might globalization have roots in older societies and civilizations?

We tend to think of globalization as uniquely modern, a product of   1
20th century advances in transportation, technology, agriculture and communications. But widespread dispersal, from a few centers, of culture, language, political ideas and economic systems—even genetically modified foods—is actually quite an ancient phenomenon.

The first wave of globalization began around 8500 BC, driven pri-   2
marily by genetically modified foods created in the Mideast and China, and to a lesser extent Mexico, the Andes and Nigeria. As those foods spread to the rest of the world, so did the cultures that created them, a process that reshaped the ancient world in much the same way the U.S., Europe and Japan are reshaping today's world.

Our ancient ancestors' method of genetically modifying food was of   3
course much different from the way it is done today. When humans lived as hunters and gatherers, they had to make do with whatever wild plants and animals they found. It turned out, though, that some of the wild species upon which humans relied for food could be domesticated. Early farmers soon learned not only how to cultivate the resulting crops and raise livestock but also how to select the traits they valued, thereby genetically modifying foods.

In choosing to sow seeds from wild plants with particularly desirable   4
traits—often the result of mutations—early farmers changed genetically, albeit unconsciously, the foods they raised.

Take the case of peas. Most wild pea plants carry a gene that makes   5
their pods pop open on the stalk, causing the peas to spill onto the ground. It is no surprise that early farmers sought out mutant plants with a gene for pods that stayed closed, which made for an easier harvest. As a consequence of their preference, by selecting, over many generations, seeds from the plants that best served them, they ended up with a genetically modified variety of peas.

Would-be farmers in some regions had a huge advantage. It turned   6
out that only a few species of wild plants and animals could be domesticated, most of them native to the Mideast, China, Mexico, the Andes or Nigeria—precisely those places that became ancient centers of power. The crops and livestock of those five restricted homelands of agriculture still dominate our foods today. Many of the lands most productive for modern agriculture—including California, Europe, Japan and Java—contributed no species that were domesticated.

Ancient people lucky enough to live in one of the few areas with wild 7
plants that could be domesticated radically altered their societies. Hunters and gatherers traded their nomadic lifestyles for safer, more settled
lives in villages near their gardens, orchards and pastures. Agricultural
surpluses, like wheat and cheese, could be stored for winter or used to
feed inventors and bureaucrats. For the first time in history, societies
could support individuals who weren't directly involved in producing
food and who therefore had time to govern or to figure out how to smelt
iron and steel. As a result of all the extra food and stability, farming
societies increased in population density a thousandfold over neighboring
hunter-gatherers.

Ultimately, ancient genetically modified foods conferred military and 8
economic might on the societies that possessed them. It was easy for
armies of 1,000 farmers, brandishing steel swords and led by a general,
to kill or drive out small bands of nomads armed only with wooden
spears. The result was globalization, as early farmers spread out from
those first five homelands, carrying their genes, foods, technologies, cultures, scripts and languages around the world.

It is because of this first wave of globalization that almost every liter- 9
ate person alive today uses one of only two writing systems: an alphabet
derived from the first Mideastern alphabet or a character-based language
that grew out of Chinese. This is also why more than 90% of people
alive today speak languages belonging to just a half-dozen language families, derived thousands of years ago from a half-dozen languages of the
five ancient homelands. The Indo-European family that includes English,
for example, originated in the Mideast. But then as now, there was also
a cost: Countless other ancient languages and cultures were eliminated as
the early farmers and their languages spread.

The first wave of globalization moved faster along east-west axes 10
than along north-south axes. The explanation is simple: Regions lying
due east or west of one another share the same latitude, and therefore
the same day length and seasonality. They are also likely to share similar
climates, habitats and diseases, all of which means that crops, livestock
and humans can spread east and west more easily, since the conditions
to which they have adapted are similar. Conversely, crops, animals and
technologies adapted to one latitude spread only with difficulty north or
south to another latitude with a different seasonality and climate.

There are certainly differences between modern globalization and 11
that first ancient wave. Today, crops are deliberately engineered in the
laboratory rather than unconsciously in the field. And globalizing
influences spread much more quickly by plane, phone and Internet

than they did on foot and horseback. But the basic similarity remains: Now, as then, a few centers of innovation and power end up dominating the world.

Even in our modern wave of globalization, genetically modified crops   12 tend to spread along an east-west rather than a north-south axis. That's because crops still remain as tied to particular climates as in ancient times. Plant breeders at U.S. firms like Monsanto concentrate on genetically modifying wheat, corn and other temperate-zone crops rather than coconuts, oil palms and other plants that grow in the tropics. That makes good business sense for American plant breeders, because the rich farmers who can afford their products live in the temperate zone, not in the tropics. But it also contributes to the widening gap between rich and poor countries.

Does this mean that tropical Paraguay and Zambia are eternally   13 cursed, and that their citizens should accept poverty as fate? Of course not. Europeans and Americans themselves enjoy no intrinsic biological advantages: They just had the good luck to acquire useful technologies and institutions through accidents of geography. Anyone else who now acquires those same things can reap the same benefits. Japan, Malaysia, Singapore, South Korea and Taiwan already have; China and others are trying and will probably succeed. In addition, some poor countries that don't acquire enough technology to become rich can still acquire enough technology (like a few nukes, missiles, chemical weapons, germs or boxcutters) to cause a lot of trouble.

The biggest problem with today's wave of globalization involves dif-   14 ferences between the First and Third worlds. Today, citizens in North America, Europe and Japan consume, on average, 32 times more resources (and produce 32 times more waste) than the billions of citizens of the Third World. Thanks to TV, tourism and other aspects of globalization, though, people in less affluent societies know about our lifestyle, and of course they aspire to it.

Vigorous debates are going on today about whether our world could   15 sustain double its present population (along with its consumption and waste), or even whether our world's economy is sustainable at its present level. Yet those aren't the biggest risks. If, through globalization, everyone living on Earth today were to achieve the standard of living of an average American, the effect on the planet would be some 10 times what it is today, and it would certainly be unsustainable.

We can't prevent people around the world from aspiring to match   16 our way of life any more than the exporters of culture during the first wave of globalization could expect other cultures not to embrace the farming way of life. But since the world couldn't sustain even its present population if all people lived the way that those in the First World do now, we are left with a paradox. Globalization, most analysts feel, is unstoppable. But its consequences may overtax the Earth's ability to support us. That's a paradox that needs resolving.

Thinking about the Essay

1. What is Diamond's claim, and how does he support it with evidence? What are the key fields of knowledge that he taps for facts and information?

2. Explain the tone of Diamond's essay and the way in which he establishes his authority as an expert. Do you think he is objective or subjective in the presentation of his argument? Justify your response by referring to specific words, sentences, and paragraphs.

3. Which paragraphs constitute Diamond's introduction? How does he link these paragraphs to the conclusion?

4. Do you think that Diamond's comparative method is effective? Why or why not? How is the comparative method reflected in the organization of the essay?

5. How does cause and effect analysis interact with Diamond's other key rhetorical strategies, notably illustration and comparison and contrast?

Responding in Writing

6. Respond in an argumentative essay to Diamond's assertion that globalization widens the gap between rich and poor nations. Be certain to provide adequate evidence to support your position.

7. Write an analysis of Diamond's essay that focuses on the types of evidence the writer uses to support his argument and the relative effectiveness of this strategy.

8. Compose an essay in which you present your opinion about genetically modified foods. Use sufficient evidence to support your thesis or claim.

Networking

9. With two other class members, write a letter to the editor of your college newspaper in which you discuss the impact of globalization on your campus.

10. Conduct research on the impact of globalization on the "First" and "Third" Worlds. Based on this research, compose a brief documented essay that lays out the conflicts between First and Third World nations over the impact of globalization on their societies and cultures.

Slumdog Millionaire

ROBERT KOEHLER

> Robert Koehler is a film and culture critic who writes for *Variety, Cinema Scope, The Christian Science Monitor*, and other publications. He also blogs on *filmjourney.org*. In his film criticism, as the following essay demonstrates, Koehler typically ranges beyond the specific film under discussion to place it in broader cultural, literary, and historical contexts. His approach to *Slumdog Millionaire*, the "feel-good" movie of 2008 that won the Academy Award for Best Picture, reflects this in-depth analytical approach. Koehler's provocative essay appeared in *CINEASTE*'s Spring 2009 issue.

Before Reading

How does film reflect the forces of globalization today? Can films made in India or elsewhere ever be as popular as American films that appear overseas? Why or why not?

D anny Boyle's *Slumdog Millionaire* is the film of the moment for the   1 "new middlebrow"—that audience able to perceive momentous changes in the world and culture when they're reported in, say, *The New York Times*, but one, at the same time, that wouldn't have the slightest clue that the most thrilling new rushes of creative filmmaking since the nouvelle vague originate in the apartments and editing rooms of Manila, Kuala Lumpur, Barcelona, and Buenos Aires. This new middlebrow has a fresh object of adoration in Boyle's entertainment, since it quite conveniently summarizes and expresses so many wishes, hopes, and romantic yearnings of the West toward what is perceived as the troubled East—with today's West resembling nothing so much as the West of the Sixties and its taste for turning Indian style into various forms of Hippie Chic. (*Slumdog* is paisley cinema, pure and simple.) Boyle's feverish, woozy, drunken, and thoroughly contrived picaresque film also conveniently packages misperceptions about India (and the East) that continue to support the dominant Western view of the Subcontinent, making the film a potent object to examine not only what is cockeyed about an outsider's view (particularly, an Englishman's view) of India, but even more, what is misperceived by a middlebrow critical establishment and audience about what comprises world cinema.

Suitably then, the creative godfather of *Slumdog*, more than Bolly- 2
wood musical fantasies, is Charles Dickens. Certain Bollywood tropes
are obediently followed, such as the innocent hero rising above terrible
circumstances, the determined pursuit of a love against all odds and that
stock Bollywood type, the snarling (often mustachioed) nemesis. But,
including the much discussed group-dance finale, these are tropes
included almost by necessity and play onscreen in a notably rote fashion.
They are alien to Boyle, which is why the Dickens model is more culturally and even cinematically germane when addressing the issues inside
Slumdog. Dickens's picaresque novels about young underdog heroes
struggling and managing to eventually thrive in social settings weighed
heavily against them were grist for, first, Vikas Swarup's novel, *Q & A*,
and then, Simon Beaufoy's loosely adapted screenplay, which greatly
compresses the novel's episodes and sections, renames characters and—
for as outlandish as the final film is—actually tones down the adventure's more incredible events and coincidences.

If Dickens's milieu was the early years of the Industrial Revolution, 3
the film's setting is the new era of globalism, in which India is undergoing its own revolution. Jamal (Dev Patel) is Pip, Nicholas Nickleby,
and Oliver Twist rolled into one, a lad who by sheer gumption has managed to land a spot as a contestant on the hugely popular *Who Wants
to Be a Millionaire?* even though he's a humble (but oh so smart) chai
wallah (or tea servant) at a cell-phone sales center. When he's first seen
on screen, though, Jamal is in trouble: A fat cop is abusing him in a
police station, though that's nothing next to the electrocution he receives
from the chief inspector (veteran Indian actor Irrfan Khan), who's convinced that Jamal has cheated on the show. How, his caste-based logic
goes, could a "slumdog" like Jamal have won ten million rupees (and
only one question away from winning 100 million) without cheating?
Even the most scurrilous and bigoted of Mumbai cops likely wouldn't
go all Abu Ghraib on a poor teen boy for cheating on TV, and it's just
the start of the film's endless supply of stunning exaggeration-for-effect
gambits that are more like a two-by-four upside the head than anything
that might be termed in polite company as "dramatic touches." Boyle
appears to have absorbed this exaggeration into his directorial blood-
stream, since, in at least the film's first half and lingering long into the
second, he indulges in a rush of shots filmed with an obsessively canted
camera, the technique lovingly nurtured by Orson Welles to convey
states of eruption and dislocation, but grievously abused by Boyle
through repetitive excess until it reeks of desperation.

Publicity shot from *Slumdog Millionaire*.

So, we get it: Jamal has everything stacked against him as he must   4
convince these thugs with badges how he knew the questions thrown to
him by the show's supercilious and remarkably condescending host,
Prem (Anil Kapoor), and that he will—it is written—prevail. From here,
the rest of the movie comprises Jamal's case, which begins with the
wildly implausible notion that Jamal remembers more or less everything
in his life inside the framework of a Dickens novel, and ends with his
endless and, um, dogged pursuit of his only true love, the beautiful (can
she be anything else?) Latika (Frieda Pinto). Of course, wild implausibil-
ity has been Boyle's general stock-in-trade for some time, beginning with
his *Clockwork Orange* pastiche, *Trainspotting* (which followed his Ham-
mer pastiche, *Shallow Grave*, and preceded his Roland Emmerich pastiche, *The Beach*, a film so awful that it would have killed many lesser
mortals' directing careers on the spot, and nearly killed Boyle's). *28 Days
Later* was intrinsically implausible—about zombies apparently ready to
race Usain Bolt in the Olympics—but so burly, aggressive, and spectacularly rude that it didn't allow a moment's pause for reflection. Is Boyle's
last movie, *Sunshine*, about a space crew on a mission straight for the
sun, any more ridiculous than *Slumdog Millionaire*, which suggests that
a little Muslim boy raised in Mumbai's worst hellholes can become rich
and famous? (Well, maybe a little more.)

Because *Slumdog* isn't conceived as a genre piece with its own built-in conventions (horror, sci-fi) but is rather a self-consciously contrived picaresque situated in the real world of Indian class structure, Muslim/ Hindu religious conflicts, underworld crime rings, and pop media, the sheer impulse to push the story into a frothy romance functions as a betrayal of its fundamental material. In the end, when Jamal has won (because, as the viewer is reminded more times than is worth counting, his victory is destined to happen), he becomes India's new superstar, its latest populist hero, a seeming sensation, a bolt out of the blue. So where is he? Squatting ever so quietly, alone, unmolested, unnoticed by anyone in Mumbai's central train station, where he spots Latika, also alone, and where they then run to each other and break into a Bollywood-style number. The effect of this scene turned the first audience at Telluride, based on eyewitness accounts, all goofy in the head. ("I wanted to run outside and scream and holler at the mountains," one starry-eyed survivor told me.)

It's hard to argue against such sentiment or reaction: for sure, early viewers of Julie Andrews running down that Austrian meadow in *The Sound of Music* were similarly nutty. Some are just mad for *Slumdog Millionaire*—including far, far too many critics—and they won't hear a discouraging word. As the cultlike object of many in the new middlebrow, no argument is heard, and some express outright shock when their beloved new movie is broken apart, knocked, or outright dismissed as what it is—a really, really minor movie, with really, really big problems. Just as the score by composer A.R. Rahman, a crafty and fairly cynical Bollywood hand, is bogus "Indian" music from top to bottom, with an excess of quasi-hip-hop stylings, electronic beat patterns and vocalese gumming up the works and sounding like the kind of backgrounds one might hear in a TV travel advert, so the closing number is bogus Bollywood following on the heels of bogus social drama.

The problem, for the fresh-scrubbed middlebrow and for the rest of us, is that if the real thing isn't known—that is, genuinely Indian cinema— how to judge the Fox Searchlight facsimile?

Really, though, *Slumdog* is fun, so let your quibbles just drift away, sit back, relax and let it spill all over you like a nice mango lassi. That's certainly the refrain of too many of the post-Telluride reviews, which recognized Boyle's brazen manipulations and absurd storytelling jumps of even marginal logic for what they were but still joined in the cheering (a word that I counted in at least ten reviews). And they're right; it is fun—fun as a cultural fabrication to question. Consider this overlooked yet central aspect of the film's many conceits: *Slumdog* uses TV as a national arena, and precisely as the medium wherein Jamal not only escapes his class, but (when the show is reviewed on tape during the police station interrogation) uses it as a tool to justify his existence. The film at once reinforces the myths of reality game show TV as actual rather than manufactured suspense and as a machine for getting rich quick, while—in total contradiction—suggesting that TV can also be a partner with the police in torture. As at so many other points, Boyle and Beaufoy try to have it both ways: Jamal proves his mettle by deploying his life experiences in order to be the ideal game show star, while the show itself (via Prem, who says that he "owns" the show and reveals that he's also from the slums) collaborates with police to persecute and torture Jamal, even though Prem also knows—an important point—that Jamal isn't cheating. The basis for arranging for Jamal's arrest is a collapsing house of cards on close inspection, since the arrest is not only a surprise to the show's producer, but couldn't have possibly been managed by Prem, who has after all been on the show during airtime.

Perhaps Prem is jealous of his fellow slumdog? An interesting, even   9
profound, character point—one that's right there, hanging like ripe narrative fruit, and which would have been even more interesting had Beaufoy and Boyle bothered to pluck it. The Dickensian sensibility, with its ironies and coincidences, is imposed here but never truly developed and only selectively applied—Dickens's picaresque tales, laden with social criticism and narrative athleticism, never fail to point a harsh finger at unjust authority (something Boyle is clearly uncomfortable doing) through a romance of the hero's ultimately improbable triumph over odds (something Boyle bases his whole movie on, culminating with the ersatz Bollywood finale). As a result, the exchanges of colonialism in *Slumdog Millionaire* are too delicious not to notice. In a single film, we have: the celebration of the export of a British gameshow to the Indian viewing public; a narrative structured on the show itself and the (British) Dickens picaresque; a disastrously tone-deaf and colorblind depiction of the world experienced by Muslim lower classes as decorated in gloriously erotic and lush colors as perhaps only a European-based director (Boyle) and cinematographer (the usually brilliant and ingenious Anthony Dod Mantle) could manage; a British-themed call center as the opening of opportunity and upward mobility for Jamal.

In its expressly liberal intentions to depict an India in which a single   10
Muslim boy can win a nation's heart, *Slumdog Millionaire* massages the Western viewer's gaze on a country and culture they barely know, save for a vague sense of cultural exports like the occasional Bollywood

movie or song. Perhaps especially now, after the fearsome attacks by Islamist extremists on Mumbai's most cherished institutions and on Western tourists, Boyle's film is just the soft pillow for concerned Western viewers to plump their heads; surely, there's hope, when even a Muslim lad who is abused, scorned, and rejected can recover his dignity, win the girl and thrive in a world free of terror. It's precisely the India of which Westerners, starting with its former British masters, heartily dream, an India where everything is possible.

The Indian reality, of course, is far more complex, and it has taken 11 filmmakers of sublime artistry and a subtle grasp of the huge Indian spectrum like Mani Ratnam, Shonali Bose, Buddhadeb Dasgupta, Girish Kasaravalli, and Murali Nair to express that complexity on screen. Opportunities for lower classes to free themselves from the old constraints are indeed greater now in India than ever before, largely through the jobs created by the nation's exploding high-tech and manufacturing sectors, which have literally created a middle class where one barely existed before. That new middle class is full of Jamals, using the new social streams fostered by computers and the Web to find types of work that simply never existed before in the Indian economy. The now infamous call centers—an aspect Boyle's film hardly glances at—are mere slivers of this new economy. But it is new, and therefore has only just begun to make its presence felt in a nation of such vast stretches and distances of geography, culture, religious traditions, and economic status.

It's here that Boyle's vision of India goes truly south, since it rein- 12 forces his target audience's general ignorance of reference points in Indian cinema. An affectionate nod in an early sequence to the Bollywood spectacles starring Amitabh Bachchan is typical: His enduring superstar status aside, the particular Amitabh movies visually cited in *Slumdog Millionaire* are actually too old for Jamal—a lower-class boy born in the late Eighties—to have seen (except, perhaps, on videotape). The brief Amitabh film reel in *Slumdog* is more properly seen as reflective of Boyle's own personal memory bank of the Bollywood movies seen in his youth, and therefore useful for Boyle's purposes, since Amitabh remains the one Bollywood superstar widely known in the West. (He's also something of an insider's joke here, since he was the original host of the Indian *Millionaire* show titled, *Kaun Banega Crorepati? (Who Will Become a Crorepati?)*.

Slumdog Millionaire may be minor, but in one way it's important: It 13 serves as the ideal vehicle for the new middlebrow's perception of what makes up world cinema. For starters, as a non-Indian movie with Indian actors (pros based in the U.K. and India, plus newcomers and nonpros), dialog, settings and music, it provides a comfortable substitute for a genuine Indian film (say, by the above-mentioned, neglected and under-seen Ratnam, Dasgupta, or Nair). The new middlebrow can thus say they've covered their current Indian cinema; after all, they've seen—and enjoyed—*Slumdog Millionaire*.

Boyle's film has been celebrated as an expression of globalization, and it's certainly true that the story itself couldn't exist in a world before globalization took effect in once-protectionist India, and that Jamal's progress is globalization incarnate. But a truer manifestation of globalization is the explosion of world cinema itself, and how the past decade and a half has seen the spread of national cinemas to an unmatched degree in the art form's history. This has been possible only through the combined forces of globalization and the absorption of previous experimentation in film grammar and theory; the ways in which local filmmakers in their local conditions have responded to the challenges of making cinema on their own terms has made the current period probably the most exciting ever from a global perspective.   14

India is an interesting example in this regard, since its many languages and regions have produced a wide range of filmmaking styles and voices, most of which continue to struggle (like Ratnam, who himself dances between more genres and forms than Steven Soderbergh) to be seen abroad. We're living in the midst of a paradoxical climate, however: Just as world cinema and its locally-based voices (and not glib fly-by-night tourists like Boyle) are more aggressively active than ever, and more exciting in their expressions, the outlets in the U.S. for this work are shrinking. Distributors, burned by too many subtitled films that bomb at the box office, have narrowed their shopping lists at festivals and markets. Alternative outlets, from festivals to pay-per-view, can contain only so many titles. Video is the last refuge, meaning that cinema made by artists ends up being seen (if at all) on TV.   15

Boyle is obviously keenly aware of this condition in his own film about characters raised speaking Hindu: He manages to compress the Hindu dialogue into about fifteen minutes' total running time (a fraction of the full running time of 116 minutes), and then offer up subtitles for the Hindu in distractingly snazzy lines of text that dance all over the screen like a hyperkinetic TV ad—apparently the perfect solution for otherwise worldly minded folks who hate reading subtitles. In the future, *Slumdog Millionaire* might be seen as a talisman of a potentially degraded film culture, in which audiences were sufficiently dumbed-down to accept   16 the fake rather than the real thing, and in a new middlebrow haze, weren't able to perceive the difference.

Thinking about the Essay

1. What are Koehler's major complaints against *Slumdog Millionaire*? What is his purpose in using such sharp language to register his complaints? Cite examples of his biting, ironic (even sarcastic) style and tone, and explain why or why not you think style and tone reinforce his purpose and claim.

2. Koehler introduces his essay by describing the "new middlebrow." How does he describe or define this audience? Where else in the essay does he allude to it? What is his intention? Do you find his statements about "new middlebrow" to be potentially offensive? Why or why not?

3. Explain the ways in which Koehler places *Slumdog Millionaire* within the context of globalization. What does he have to say about this interrelationship? How does he lay out his case?

4. Where does Koehler allude to Charles Dickens, and why does he establish this analogy between the nineteenth-century British novelist and a twenty-first-century film?

5. Does Koehler make any concessions about *Slumdog Millionaire*? Why or why not? Would further concessions—or a more temperate style and tone—have strengthened his argument? Explain.

Responding in Writing

6. Do you think Koehler makes a strong case against *Slumdog Millionaire*? Respond to this question in an argumentative essay.

7. Write your own extended definition of "new middlebrow," relating it to types of films that have global or international settings and themes.

8. Rent *Slumdog Millionaire*. After viewing it, write a review for your college newspaper that focuses on the ways the film touches on issues of globalization.

Networking

9. Help to organize a forum of four or five class members who will present their responses to Koehler's essay, concentrating on the provocative ways in which he attacks *Slumdog Millionaire* (and its "new middlebrow" audience).

10. Go online and find five reviews of *Slumdog Millionaire*. Write a critique in which you identify the reasons why some critics liked the film, others disliked it, and still others had mixed responses.

Fear Not Globalization

Joseph S. Nye Jr.

Joseph Samuel Nye Jr. was born in South Orange, New Jersey, in 1937. He received undergraduate degrees from Princeton University (1958) and Oxford University (1960) and a Ph.D. degree from Harvard University (1964) in political science. Nye is University Distinguished Service Professor and former Dean of the Kennedy School of Government at Harvard University. A prolific writer and well-known authority in international relations, Nye has served in the U.S. Department of State and on the committees of such prominent organizations as the Ford Foundation and the Carnegie Endowment for International Peace. A frequent guest on television programs, including *Nightline* and *The NewsHour with Jim Lehrer*, Nye also writes frequently for *The New York Times, The Christian Science Monitor, Atlantic Monthly,* and *The New Republic.* His most recent book is *The Future of Power* (2011). The title of the following essay, which appeared in *Newsday* on October 8, 2002, captures Nye's essential thesis about the forces of globalization in today's world.

Before Reading

Is globalization a force for good or bad? Will it turn all nations, cultures, and peoples into reflections of each other?

When anti-globalization protesters took to the streets of Washington recently, they blamed globalization for everything from hunger to the destruction of indigenous cultures. And globalization meant the United States.

The critics call it Coca-Colonization, and French sheep farmer Jose Bove has become a cult figure since destroying a McDonald's restaurant in 1999.

Contrary to conventional wisdom, however, globalization is neither homogenizing nor Americanizing the cultures of the world.

To understand why not, we have to step back and put the current period in a larger historical perspective. Although they are related, the

"Fear Not Globalization" by Joseph S. Nye, Jr. author of *The Paradox of American Power.* Reprinted by permission.

long-term historical trends of globalization and modernization are not the same. While modernization has produced some common traits, such as large cities, factories and mass communications, local cultures have by no means been erased. The appearance of similar institutions in response to similar problems is not surprising, but it does not lead to homogeneity.

In the first half of the 20th century, for example, there were some   5 similarities among the industrial societies of Britain, Germany, America and Japan, but there were even more important differences. When China, India and Brazil complete their current processes of industrialization and modernization, we should not expect them to be replicas of Japan, Germany or the United States.

Take the current information revolution. The United States is at the   6 forefront of this great movement of change, so the uniform social and cultural habits produced by television viewing or Internet use, for instance, are often attributed to Americanization. But correlation is not causation. Imagine if another country had introduced computers and communications at a rapid rate in a world in which the United States did not exist. Major social and cultural changes still would have followed. Of course, since the United States does exist and is at the leading edge of the information revolution, there is a degree of Americanization at present, but it is likely to diminish over the course of the 21st century as technology spreads and local cultures modernize in their own ways.

The lesson that Japan has to teach the rest of the world is that even a   7 century and a half of openness to global trends does not necessarily assure destruction of a country's separate cultural identity. Of course, there are American influences in contemporary Japan (and Japanese influences such as Sony and Pokémon in the United States). Thousands of Japanese youths are co-opting the music, dress and style of urban black America. But some of the groups they listen to dress up like samurai warriors on stage. One can applaud or deplore such cultural transfers, but one should not doubt the persistence of Japan's cultural uniqueness.

The protesters' image of America homogenizing the world also   8 reflects a mistakenly static view of culture. Efforts to portray cultures as unchanging more often reflect reactionary political strategies than descriptions of reality. The Peruvian writer Mario Vargas Llosa put it well when he said that arguments in favor of cultural identity and against globalization "betray a stagnant attitude toward culture that is not borne out by historical fact. Do we know of any cultures that have remained unchanged through time? To find any of them one has to travel to the small, primitive, magico-religious communities made up of people . . . who, due to their primitive condition, become progressively more vulnerable to exploitation and extermination."

Vibrant cultures are constantly changing and borrowing from other cultures. And the borrowing is not always from the United States. For example, many more countries turned to Canada than to the United States as a model for constitution-building in the aftermath of the Cold War. Canadian views of how to deal with hate crimes were more congenial to countries such as South Africa and the post-Communist states of Eastern Europe than America's First Amendment practices.   9

Globalization is also a two-edged sword. In some areas, there has been not only a backlash against American cultural imports, but also an effort to change American culture itself. American policies on capital punishment may have majority support inside the United States, but they are regarded as egregious violations of human rights in much of Europe and have been the focus of transnational human rights campaigns. American attitudes toward climate change or genetic modification of food draw similar criticism. More subtly, the openness of the United States to the world's diasporas both enriches and changes American culture.   10

Transnational corporations are changing poor countries but not homogenizing them. In the early stages of investment, a multinational company with access to the global resources of finance, technology and markets holds the high cards and often gets the best of the bargain with the poor country. But over time, as the poor country develops a skilled workforce, learns new technologies, and opens its own channels to global finance and markets, it is often able to renegotiate the bargain and capture more of the benefits.   11

As technical capabilities spread and more and more people hook up to global communications systems, the U.S. economic and cultural preponderance may diminish. This in turn has mixed implications for American "soft" power, our ability to get others to do what we want by attraction rather than coercion. Less dominance may mean less anxiety about Americanization, fewer complaints about American arrogance and a little less intensity in the anti-American backlash. We may have less control in the future, but we may find ourselves living in a world somewhat more congenial to our basic values of democracy, free markets and human rights.   12

Thinking about the Essay

1. What is Nye's purpose in writing this article? How can you tell? What type of audience does Nye have in mind for his essay? Why does he produce such an affirmative tone in dealing with his subject?

2. Which paragraphs constitute Nye's introduction? Where does he place his thesis, and how does he state it?

3. Break down the essay into its main topics. How does Nye develop these topics? What strategies does he employ—for example, causal analysis, comparison and contrast, illustration—and where?

4. Analyze Nye's topic sentences for his paragraphs. How do they serve as clear guides for the development of his paragraphs? How do they serve to unify the essay?

5. How does Nye's concluding paragraph serve as an answer both to the issue raised in his introduction and to other concerns expressed in the body of the essay?

Responding in Writing

6. From your own personal experience of globalization, write an essay in which you agree or disagree with Nye's assertion that there is little to fear from globalization.

7. Try writing a rebuttal to Nye's argument, explaining why there is much to fear about globalization. Deal point by point with Nye's main assertions. Be certain to provide your own evidence in support of your key reasons.

8. Write an essay that responds to the following topic sentence in Nye's essay: "Vibrant cultures are constantly changing and borrowing from other cultures" (paragraph 9). Base your paper on personal experience, your reading, and your knowledge of current events.

Networking

9. With four other classmates, imagine that you have to teach Nye's essay to a class of high school seniors. How would you proceed? Develop a lesson plan that you think would appeal to your audience.

10. With the entire class, arrange a time when you can have an online chat about Nye's essay. As a focal point for your discussion, argue for or against the idea that he does not take the dangers of globalization seriously enough.

7

Culture Wars: Whose Culture Is It, Anyway?

A s we have seen in earlier chapters, the power and influence of the United States radiate outward to the rest of the world in many ways. Nowhere is this more visible than in the impact of various American cultural manifestations—ranging from food, to clothing, to music, to television, and film—on other countries. When a French farmer burns down a McDonald's, terrorists destroy a disco in Bali, or clerics in Iran attempt to ban Barbie dolls from stores, we sense the opposition to American cultural hegemony. Conversely, when Iranians do find ways to buy Barbies and also turn on their banned satellite systems to catch the latest episode of *Big Bang Theory*, or when street merchants in Kenya sell University of Michigan T-shirts, we detect the flip side of the culture wars—the mesmerizing power of American culture throughout the world. Sometimes it seems that American culture, wittingly or unwittingly, is in a battle for the world's soul.

We also have to acknowledge that the culture wars color American life as well. At home, current debates over immigration, affirmative action, gay marriage, and much more impinge on our daily lives and dominate media presentations. It might be fashionable to say that we all trace our DNA to Africa and that ideally we are all citizens of the world, but the issue of what sort of culture we represent individually or collectively is much more complicated. Barack Obama might be the icon for the New American or the new Universal Person, but his slightest actions and words can prompt cultural controversy. American culture cuts many ways; it is powerful, but also strange and contradictory.

The culture wars take us to the borders of contradiction both at home and abroad. It is too facile to say that we are moving "beyond" monoculturalism at home or that the rest of the world doesn't have to embrace American culture if it doesn't want to. What is clear is that the very *idea* of American culture, in all its diversity, is so pervasive

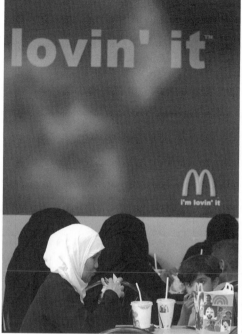

Muslim tourists eat in a McDonald's restaurant
in the Egyptian Red Sea resort of Sharmel-Sheikh.

Thinking about the Image

1. If McDonald's is stereotypically American, what is stereotypically
   Egyptian about this image? Why do you think the photographer is
   emphasizing those stereotypes?

2. Think about other images of globalization you have seen in this
   book. How effective is the "rhetoric" of globalization here?

3. Why is something so seemingly basic as food such a potent symbol
   of cultural meaning and pride? Does this photograph capture this
   symbolism effectively? Why or why not?

that it spawns numerous viewpoints and possibilities for resolution. After
all, culture is a big subject: it embraces one's ethnic, racial, class, religious,
sexual, and national identity. We can't be uncritical about culture. We have
to understand how culture both molds and reflects our lives.

The writers in this chapter offer perspectives—all of them provocative
and engaging—on national and transnational culture. They deal with the
ironies of culture at home and the paradoxes of American cultural influence

abroad. Some of the writers engage in self-reflection, others in rigorous analysis. All refuse to view culture in simplistic terms. In reading them, you might discover that whether you grew up in the United States or another country, culture is at the heart of who you are.

First, They'll Come for the Burkas

DIANA WAGMAN

> Diana Wagman is a novelist, screenwriter, essayist, and reviewer who lives in Los Angeles. She received an M.A. from American University. Wagman is the author of three novels: *Skin Deep* (1997), *Spontaneous* (2000), and *Bump* (2003), which was shortlisted for the Dublin Literary Prize. She wrote the screenplay for *Delivering Milo* (2001), starring Albert Finney and Bridget Fonda. Wagman has taught fiction and screenwriting at UCLA Writer's Extension, Loyola Marymount University, California Institute of the Arts, and the California State Universities, Long Beach and San Bernardino. She writes frequently for the *Los Angeles Times*, where this selection appeared on July 24, 2011.

Before Reading

Is wearing a burka in public any more unusual or offensive than wearing short-shorts? Why or why not? And who, if anyone, should make a judgment about the way people dress in society?

E very summer when the temperature goes up, people start stripping   1
down. At the risk of sounding like a prude, I find it unseemly. Toddlers look cute in just a pair of shorts. Middle-aged men do not. Most women don't look good in shorts, period.

Yes, there are starlets strutting down Sunset Boulevard beautiful in   2
little short-shorts, but they're the exception. I don't see them at my local grocery store leaning over the frozen food case. What I see reaching for the ice cream is just way too much. I'm not talking about age. I'm not talking about weight. I'm just asking for modesty. I don't want to be confronted with body parts best seen only by your doctor.

But America is a free country, and imposing any kind of dress code   3
starts us down a very slippery slope.

I was hiking in Griffith Park with a friend and she told me how 4
happy she was about the law in France prohibiting Islamic full-face veils
in public. I was appalled. It's freedom of religion, I said, and freedom of
speech. It's oppression of women, she replied. How do you know? I
asked.

At that moment, two young women jogged past us in tiny, stretchy 5
shorts and bikini tops. Nothing was left to the imagination. They were
fit and attractive, but I found myself thinking I'd almost rather my teenage daughter wore a burka. One outfit is as extreme as the other. Both
get second and third looks. Each conveys an image of the woman wearing it, a supposition that may or may not be true.

As for oppression, what sort of response will the girls in bikinis get, 6
especially from men? To be ogled and objectified doesn't do much for wom-
en's equality. You could argue, as my friend did, neither does a religion that
requires women to be completely covered. But in a democratic society,
America or France, people should be free to wear whatever they want.

Driving in the Fairfax district, I love to watch Orthodox Jewish fami- 7
lies walking to temple. The men in their long coats and big hats, the
women in tailored suits and wigs, and especially the little boys with curl-
ing payos and yarmulkes and the tassels of their prayer shawls flapping.

There is a Buddhist temple in my neighborhood, and the monks wear 8
wonderful orange robes and shave their heads, men and women alike.

I lived in Utah for seven years, and Mormon "garments," worn 9
under clothing, cover more skin than what most people wear in my
Trader Joe's. I would find their nylon jumpsuits oppressive, but it's none
of my business.

If we outlaw burkas, then we should ban all manner of religious 10
dress, including nuns' habits and priests' collars. And if we're suppressing that personal expression, where will it end?

A 20-year-old college football player got on a plane in San Francisco 11
reportedly wearing his pants so low his whole butt—in tight black briefs,
according to one account—showed. I don't know how he walked to his
seat, but it was a fashion statement: He must have thought he looked
cool. A flight attendant took exception and asked him to pull up his
pants. What happened next is in some dispute, but eventually he was
arrested. He missed his flight, but he wasn't charged.

Just days earlier, same airline, an older man, white-haired, got on a 12
flight wearing blue women's underwear, a matching spaghetti-strap, mid-
riff-baring top, a cropped see-through sweater and black thigh highs and
high heels. Airline personnel didn't say a word.

Now, it was the white-haired man's right to look ridiculous (up to a   13
point, which no one has said he crossed), but the same right was not
extended to the football player. Was it because the football player was
black? Was it because he was young? Was it because he looked "gang-
sta"? The flight attendant made a judgment based at least in part on a
pair of sagging sweatpants. Isn't that repression?

When does one person's "expression" become more important than   14
another's? An 11-year-old was sent home from school for wearing a
T-shirt that read "Obama a Terrorist's Best Friend." If another kid wore
a shirt reading "Obama the Best President Ever," some might disagree,
but who would prevent him from sharing his opinion?

At the mall some years ago I passed a young woman wearing a   15
T-shirt bearing a vulgar message about President Bush almost impossible
to explain to your 9-year-old. But I absolutely defend her right to wear it.

I think France is wrong. President Nicolas Sarkozy said, "The full veil   16
is contrary to the dignity of women," but laws about what we can and
cannot wear degrade everyone's dignity.

Yes, I wish my across-the-street neighbor would put on a shirt when   17
he stands in his driveway to smoke a cigarette. His sweaty chest hair
over man-boobs is a sight I could live without. But then I remind myself:
Summer won't last forever.

Thinking about the Essay

1. How does Wagman begin her essay? What tone does she establish?

2. Is Wagman writing exclusively for a Los Angeles audience or might she
   appeal to a secondary audience as well? Justify your response.

3. What evidence does Wagman provide to reinforce her claim? Does she offer
   sufficient evidence to make her argument convincing? Why or why not?

4. How much space does Wagman devote to burkas? What is her purpose in
   raising the topic?

5. Explain how the author uses the comparative method to develop her essay.

Responding in Writing

6. Write a comparative essay about dress codes between one specific group
   in the United States and dress codes in one other country.

7. Compose a classification essay in which you discuss fashion styles around
   the world.

8. Argue for or against the proposition that there should be restrictions on the
   way people dress in public.

Networking

9. In small groups, discuss the tone of Wagman's essay and how it contributes to her argument. Summarize your conclusions for the class.

10. Conduct online research on the conflict over the burka in France. Write a précis that captures the essence of this debate.

Whose Culture Is It, Anyway?

HENRY LOUIS GATES JR.

Henry Louis Gates Jr. is one of the most respected figures in the field of African-American studies. Born in 1950 in Keyser, West Virginia, he received a B.A. degree (summa cum laude) from Harvard University (1973) and M.A. (1974) and Ph.D. degrees (1979) from Clare College, Cambridge University. A recipient of numerous major grants, including the prestigious MacArthur Prize Fellowship, and a professor at Harvard University, Gates in numerous essays and books argues for a greater diversity in arts, literature, and life. In one of his best-known works, *Loose Canons: Notes on the Culture Wars* (1992), Gates states, "The society we have made simply won't survive without the values of tolerance. And cultural tolerance comes to nothing without cultural understanding." Among his many publications are *The Signifying Monkey: Toward a Theory of Afro-American Literary Criticism* (1988), which won both a National Book Award and an American Book Award; *Colored People, A Memoir* (1994); *The Future of the Race* (with Cornel West, 1996); *Wonders of the African World* (1999); and *In Search of Our Roots* (2009), which won an NAACP Image Award in 2010. In the following essay, which appeared originally in *The New York Times* on May 4, 1991, Gates analyzes the cultural diversity movement in American colleges and universities.

Before Reading

Gates argues elsewhere that we must reject "ethnic absolutism" of all kinds. What do you think he means by this phrase? Exactly how does a college or university—perhaps your institution—transcend this problem?

I recently asked the dean of a prestigious liberal arts college if his school   1
would ever have, as Berkeley has, a 70 percent non-white enrollment.
"Never," he replied. "That would completely alter our identity as a center of the liberal arts."

The assumption that there is a deep connection between the shape of   2
a college's curriculum and the ethnic composition of its students reflects
a disquieting trend in education. Political representation has been
confused with the "representation" of various ethnic identities in the
curriculum.

The cultural right wing, threatened by demographic changes and the   3
ensuing demands for curricular change, has retreated to intellectual protectionism, arguing for a great and inviolable "Western tradition," which
contains the seeds, fruit and flowers of the very best thought or uttered in
history. (Typically, Mortimer Adler has ventured that blacks "wrote no
good books.") Meanwhile, the cultural left demands changes to accord
with population shifts in gender and ethnicity. Both are wrongheaded.

I am just as concerned that so many of my colleagues feel that the ra-   4
tionale for a diverse curriculum depends on the latest Census Bureau
report as I am that those opposed see pluralism as forestalling the possibility of a communal "American" identity. To them, the study of our
diverse cultures must lead to "tribalism" and "fragmentation."

The cultural diversity movement arose partly because of the fragmen-   5
tation of society by ethnicity, class and gender. To make it the culprit
for this fragmentation is to mistake effect for cause. A curriculum that
reflects the achievement of the world's great cultures, not merely the
West's, is not "politicized"; rather it situates the West as one of a community of civilizations. After all, culture is always a conversation among
different voices.

To insist that we "master our own culture" before learning others—   6
as Arthur Schlesinger Jr. has proposed—only defers the vexed question:
What gets to count as "our" culture? What has passed as "common culture" has been an Anglo-American regional culture, masking itself as
universal. Significantly different cultures sought refuge underground.

Writing in 1903, W. E. B. Du Bois expressed his dream of a high cul-   7
ture that would transcend the color line: "I sit with Shakespeare and he
winces not." But the dream was not open to all. "Is this the life you
grudge us," he concluded, "O knightly America?" For him, the humanities were a conduit into a republic of letters enabling escape from racism
and ethnic chauvinism. Yet no one played a more crucial role than he in
excavating the long buried heritage of Africans and African-Americans.

The fact of one's ethnicity, for any American of color, is never neu- 8
tral: One's public treatment, and public behavior, are shaped in large
part by one's perceived ethnic identity, just as by one's gender. To
demand that Americans shuck their cultural heritages and homogenize
themselves into a "universal" WASP culture is to dream of an America
in cultural white face, and that just won't do.

So it's only when we're free to explore the complexities of our 9
hyphenated culture that we can discover what a genuinely common
American culture might actually look like.

Is multiculturalism un-American? Herman Melville didn't think so. 10
As he wrote: "We are not a narrow tribe, no. . . . We are not a nation,
so much as a world." We're all ethnics; the challenge of transcending
ethnic chauvinism is one we all face.

We've entrusted our schools with the fashioning and refashioning of 11
a democratic polity. That's why schooling has always been a matter of
political judgment. But in a nation that has theorized itself as plural from
its inception, schools have a very special task.

Our society won't survive without the values of tolerance, and cul- 12
tural tolerance comes to nothing without cultural understanding. The
challenge facing America will be the shaping of a truly common public
culture, one responsive to the long-silenced cultures of color. If we relin-
quish the ideal of America as a plural nation, we've abandoned the very
experiment America represents. And that is too great a price to pay.

Thinking about the Essay

1. Gates poses a question in his title. How does he answer it? Where does he
   state his thesis?

2. The essay begins with an anecdote. How does it illuminate a key aspect of
   the problem Gates analyzes?

3. Gates makes several references to other writers—Mortimer Adler, Arthur
   Schlesinger Jr., W. E. B. Du Bois, and Herman Melville. Who are these
   figures, and how do they provide a frame or context for Gates's argument?

4. How does the writer use comparison and contrast and causal analysis to
   advance his argument?

5. How does the concluding paragraph serve as a fitting end to the writer's
   argument?

Responding in Writing

6. Write a comparative essay in which you analyze the respective approaches
   to multiculturalism by Diana Wagman and Gates.

7. Gates speaks of "our hyphenated culture" (paragraph 9). Write a paper examining this phrase and applying it to your own campus.

8. Are you on "the cultural left" or "the cultural right" (to use Gates's words in paragraph 3), or somewhere in the middle? Write a personal essay responding to this question.

Networking

9. Form four working groups of classmates. Each group should investigate the ethnic composition of your campus, courses, and programs designed to foster pluralism and multiculturalism and the institution's policy on affirmative action. Draft a document in which you present your findings and conclusions concerning the state of the cultural diversity movement on your campus.

10. Search the World Wide Web for sites that promote what Gates terms "'universal' WASP culture" (paragraph 8). What sort of ideology do they promote? Where do they stand in terms of the culture wars? What impact do you think they have on the course of contemporary life in the United States?

Why Chinese Mothers Are Superior

AMY CHUA

Amy Chua was born in Champaign, Illinois, in 1962. Her parents were ethnic Chinese from the Philippines who emigrated to the United States. Chua graduated from Harvard College in 1984 and received her J.D. from Harvard Law School in 1987. She is a professor of law at Yale Law School. Chua's first two books, *World on Fire* (2003) and *Day of Empire* (2007), deal with ethnic economic conflicts in a global context. With her next book, *Battle Hymn of the Tiger Mother* (2011), Chua was catapulted to fame and controversy for her comic explanation of why Chinese mothers are superior to their American counterparts. This excerpt from her third book appeared in the January 8, 2011, edition of *The Wall Street Journal*.

Before Reading

What might a parent's motivations be in preventing a child from appearing in a school play, indulging in computer games, or selecting her own extracurricular activities? Do you think such parental control is beneficial or harmful? Explain.

Source: From *Battle Hymn of the Tiger Mother* by Amy Chua pp. 3–5, 29, 50–53, 60–63. © 2011 by Amy Chua. Used by permission of The Penguin Press, a division of Penguin Group (USA) Inc.

Alot of people wonder how Chinese parents raise such stereotypically   1
successful kids. They wonder what these parents do to produce so
many math whizzes and music prodigies, what it's like inside the family,
and whether they could do it too. Well, I can tell them, because I've
done it. Here are some things my daughters, Sophia and Louisa, were
never allowed to do:

- attend a sleepover
- have a playdate
- be in a school play
- complain about not being in a school play
- watch TV or play computer games
- choose their own extracurricular activities
- get any grade less than an A
- not be the No. 1 student in every subject except gym and drama
- play any instrument other than the piano or violin
- not play the piano or violin.

I'm using the term "Chinese mother" loosely. I know some Korean,   2
Indian, Jamaican, Irish and Ghanaian parents who qualify too. Conversely, I know some mothers of Chinese heritage, almost always born
in the West, who are not Chinese mothers, by choice or otherwise. I'm
also using the term "Western parents" loosely. Western parents come in
all varieties.

All the same, even when Western parents think they're being strict,   3
they usually don't come close to being Chinese mothers. For example,
my Western friends who consider themselves strict make their children
practice their instruments 30 minutes every day. An hour at most. For a
Chinese mother, the first hour is the easy part. It's hours two and three
that get tough.

Despite our squeamishness about cultural stereotypes, there are tons   4
of studies out there showing marked and quantifiable differences
between Chinese and Westerners when it comes to parenting. In one
study of 50 Western American mothers and 48 Chinese immigrant mothers, almost 70% of the Western mothers said either that "stressing academic success is not good for children" or that "parents need to foster
the idea that learning is fun." By contrast, roughly 0% of the Chinese
mothers felt the same way. Instead, the vast majority of the Chinese
mothers said that they believe their children can be "the best" students,
that "academic achievement reflects successful parenting," and that if
children did not excel at school then there was "a problem" and parents
"were not doing their job." Other studies indicate that compared to

Western parents, Chinese parents spend approximately 10 times as long every day drilling academic activities with their children. By contrast, Western kids are more likely to participate in sports teams.

What Chinese parents understand is that nothing is fun until you're   5 good at it. To get good at anything you have to work, and children on their own never want to work, which is why it is crucial to override their preferences. This often requires fortitude on the part of the parents because the child will resist; things are always hardest at the beginning, which is where Western parents tend to give up. But if done properly, the Chinese strategy produces a virtuous circle. Tenacious practice, practice, practice is crucial for excellence; rote repetition is underrated in America. Once a child starts to excel at something—whether it's math, piano, pitching or ballet—he or she gets praise, admiration and satisfaction. This builds confidence and makes the once not-fun activity fun. This in turn makes it easier for the parent to get the child to work even more.

Chinese parents can get away with things that Western parents can't.   6 Once when I was young—maybe more than once—when I was extremely disrespectful to my mother, my father angrily called me "garbage" in our native Hokkien dialect. It worked really well. I felt terrible and deeply ashamed of what I had done. But it didn't damage my self-esteem or anything like that. I knew exactly how highly he thought of me. I didn't actually think I was worthless or feel like a piece of garbage.

As an adult, I once did the same thing to Sophia, calling her garbage   7 in English when she acted extremely disrespectfully toward me. When I mentioned that I had done this at a dinner party, I was immediately ostracized. One guest named Marcy got so upset she broke down in tears and had to leave early. My friend Susan, the host, tried to rehabilitate me with the remaining guests.

The fact is that Chinese parents can do things that would seem   8 unimaginable—even legally actionable—to Westerners. Chinese mothers can say to their daughters, "Hey fatty—lose some weight." By contrast, Western parents have to tiptoe around the issue, talking in terms of "health" and never ever mentioning the f-word, and their kids still end up in therapy for eating disorders and negative self-image. (I also once heard a Western father toast his adult daughter by calling her "beautiful and incredibly competent." She later told me that made her feel like garbage.)

Chinese parents can order their kids to get straight As. Western   9 parents can only ask their kids to try their best. Chinese parents can say, "You're lazy. All your classmates are getting ahead of you." By contrast, Western parents have to struggle with their own conflicted feelings about achievement, and try to persuade themselves that they're not disappointed about how their kids turned out.

I've thought long and hard about how Chinese parents can get away 10 with what they do. I think there are three big differences between the Chinese and Western parental mind-sets.

First, I've noticed that Western parents are extremely anxious about 11 their children's self-esteem. They worry about how their children will feel if they fail at something, and they constantly try to reassure their children about how good they are notwithstanding a mediocre performance on a test or at a recital. In other words, Western parents are concerned about their children's psyches. Chinese parents aren't. They assume strength, not fragility, and as a result they behave very differently.

For example, if a child comes home with an A-minus on a test, a 12 Western parent will most likely praise the child. The Chinese mother will gasp in horror and ask what went wrong. If the child comes home with a B on the test, some Western parents will still praise the child. Other Western parents will sit their child down and express disapproval, but they will be careful not to make their child feel inadequate or insecure, and they will not call their child "stupid," "worthless" or "a disgrace." Privately, the Western parents may worry that their child does not test well or have aptitude in the subject or that there is something wrong with the curriculum and possibly the whole school. If the child's grades do not improve, they may eventually schedule a meeting with the school principal to challenge the way the subject is being taught or to call into question the teacher's credentials.

If a Chinese child gets a B—which would never happen—there would 13 first be a screaming, hair-tearing explosion. The devastated Chinese mother would then get dozens, maybe hundreds of practice tests and work through them with her child for as long as it takes to get the grade up to an A.

Chinese parents demand perfect grades because they believe that their 14 child can get them. If their child doesn't get them, the Chinese parent assumes it's because the child didn't work hard enough. That's why the solution to substandard performance is always to excoriate, punish and shame the child. The Chinese parent believes that their child will be strong enough to take the shaming and to improve from it. (And when Chinese kids do excel, there is plenty of ego-inflating parental praise lavished in the privacy of the home.)

Second, Chinese parents believe that their kids owe them everything. 15 The reason for this is a little unclear, but it's probably a combination of

Confucian filial piety and the fact that the parents have sacrificed and done so much for their children. (And it's true that Chinese mothers get in the trenches, putting in long grueling hours personally tutoring, training, interrogating and spying on their kids.) Anyway, the understanding is that Chinese children must spend their lives repaying their parents by obeying them and making them proud.

By contrast, I don't think most Westerners have the same view of   16 children being permanently indebted to their parents. My husband, Jed, actually has the opposite view. "Children don't choose their parents," he once said to me. "They don't even choose to be born. It's parents who foist life on their kids, so it's the parents' responsibility to provide for them. Kids don't owe their parents anything. Their duty will be to their own kids." This strikes me as a terrible deal for the Western parent.

Third, Chinese parents believe that they know what is best for their   17 children and therefore override all of their children's own desires and preferences. That's why Chinese daughters can't have boyfriends in high school and why Chinese kids can't go to sleepaway camp. It's also why no Chinese kid would ever dare say to their mother, "I got a part in the school play! I'm Villager Number Six. I'll have to stay after school for rehearsal every day from 3:00 to 7:00, and I'll also need a ride on weekends." God help any Chinese kid who tried that one.

Don't get me wrong: It's not that Chinese parents don't care about   18 their children. Just the opposite. They would give up anything for their children. It's just an entirely different parenting model.

Here's a story in favor of coercion, Chinese-style. Lulu was about 7,   19 still playing two instruments, and working on a piano piece called "The Little White Donkey" by the French composer Jacques Ibert. The piece is really cute—you can just imagine a little donkey ambling along a country road with its master—but it's also incredibly difficult for young players because the two hands have to keep schizophrenically different rhythms.

Lulu couldn't do it. We worked on it nonstop for a week, drilling   20 each of her hands separately, over and over. But whenever we tried putting the hands together, one always morphed into the other, and everything fell apart. Finally, the day before her lesson, Lulu announced in exasperation that she was giving up and stomped off.

"Get back to the piano now," I ordered.   21

"You can't make me."   22

"Oh yes, I can."   23

Back at the piano, Lulu made me pay. She punched, thrashed and   24 kicked. She grabbed the music score and tore it to shreds. I taped the score back together and encased it in a plastic shield so that it could never be destroyed again. Then I hauled Lulu's dollhouse to the car and told her I'd donate it to the Salvation Army piece by piece if she didn't have "The Little White Donkey" perfect by the next day. When Lulu said, "I thought you were going to the Salvation Army, why are you still here?" I threatened her with no lunch, no dinner, no Christmas or Hanukkah presents, no birthday parties for two, three, four years. When she still kept playing it wrong, I told her she was purposely working herself into a frenzy because she was secretly afraid she couldn't do it. I told her to stop being lazy, cowardly, self-indulgent and pathetic.

Jed took me aside. He told me to stop insulting Lulu—which I wasn't 25 even doing, I was just motivating her—and that he didn't think threatening Lulu was helpful. Also, he said, maybe Lulu really just couldn't do the technique—perhaps she didn't have the coordination yet—had I considered that possibility?

"You just don't believe in her," I accused.   26

"That's ridiculous," Jed said scornfully. "Of course I do."   27

"Sophia could play the piece when she was this age."   28

"But Lulu and Sophia are different people," Jed pointed out.   29

"Oh no, not this," I said, rolling my eyes. "Everyone is special in 30 their special own way," I mimicked sarcastically. "Even losers are special in their own special way. Well don't worry, you don't have to lift a finger. I'm willing to put in as long as it takes, and I'm happy to be the one hated. And you can be the one they adore because you make them pancakes and take them to Yankees games."

I rolled up my sleeves and went back to Lulu. I used every weapon 31 and tactic I could think of. We worked right through dinner into the night, and I wouldn't let Lulu get up, not for water, not even to go to the bathroom. The house became a war zone, and I lost my voice yelling, but still there seemed to be only negative progress, and even I began to have doubts.

Then, out of the blue, Lulu did it. Her hands suddenly came 32 together—her right and left hands each doing their own imperturbable thing—just like that.

Lulu realized it the same time I did. I held my breath. She tried it ten- 33 tatively again. Then she played it more confidently and faster, and still the rhythm held. A moment later, she was beaming.

"Mommy, look—it's easy!" After that, she wanted to play the piece 34 over and over and wouldn't leave the piano. That night, she came to sleep in my bed, and we snuggled and hugged, cracking each other up.

When she performed "The Little White Donkey" at a recital a few weeks later, parents came up to me and said, "What a perfect piece for Lulu— it's so spunky and so her."

Even Jed gave me credit for that one. Western parents worry a lot 35 about their children's self-esteem. But as a parent, one of the worst things you can do for your child's self-esteem is to let them give up. On the flip side, there's nothing better for building confidence than learning you can do something you thought you couldn't.

There are all these new books out there portraying Asian mothers as 36 scheming, callous, overdriven people indifferent to their kids' true interests. For their part, many Chinese secretly believe that they care more about their children and are willing to sacrifice much more for them than Westerners, who seem perfectly content to let their children turn out badly. I think it's a misunderstanding on both sides. All decent parents want to do what's best for their children. The Chinese just have a totally different idea of how to do that.

Western parents try to respect their children's individuality, encourag- 37 ing them to pursue their true passions, supporting their choices, and providing positive reinforcement and a nurturing environment. By contrast, the Chinese believe that the best way to protect their children is by preparing them for the future, letting them see what they're capable of, and arming them with skills, work habits and inner confidence that no one can ever take away.

Thinking about the Essay

1. How would you characterize the tone of Chua's introductory paragraph? What is her purpose here?

2. What is Chua's claim, and what evidence does she provide to support it?

3. Explain the pattern of comparison and contrast that the writer develops in this essay. What are the major comparative topics that she presents?

4. Why does Chua focus on her daughter Lulu in the second half of the essay? Do you find this strategy to be effective? Why or why not?

5. How does Chua's conclusion both reinforce and alter her argument?

Responding in Writing

6. Write an argumentative essay in which you either support or reject Chua's claim.

7. Compose an essay of comparison and contrast in which you examine with an objective tone two different approaches to raising children.

8. Write a classification essay in which you analyze the ways in which various ethnic and racial groups approach childrearing.

Networking

9. Exchange your essay with another class member and offer a peer critique of his or her essay. Focus on how effectively the writer develops the key rhetorical strategy—argumentation, comparison and contrast, or classification—called for by the assignment.

10. Consult Amy Chua's website and *The Wall Street Journal* website, which offer reader responses to Chua's essay. Explain the tone of these exchanges in a brief essay.

The Tiger Mama Syndrome

Patricia J. Williams

Patricia J. Williams, who was born in 1951, is an American legal scholar and an expert in critical race theory—a line of argument claiming that race is a main determinant of the nation's legal system. Williams received her B.A. from Wellesley College in 1972 and earned a J.D. from Harvard Law School in 1975. She is currently a professor of law at Columbia University, where she has taught since 1991. Her books include *The Alchemy of Race and Rights* (1991), *The Rooster's Egg* (1995), *Seeing a Color-Blind Future* (1997), and *Open House* (2004). Williams writes a column for *The Nation* magazine, "Diary of a Mad Law Professor," where this article appeared on February 21, 2011.

Before Reading

Based on your reading of the previous essay by Amy Chua, how would you define a "Tiger Mama syndrome"? What, exactly, is a syndrome? Must a syndrome always be harmful or negative in connotation? Why or why not?

A my Chua does not hold the patent on prejudice. There are lots of ways to spin a stereotype, and that she calls herself a "Chinese" mother in her hotly debated book on parenting, *Battle Hymn of the Tiger Mother*, plays well against cultural anxieties about American economic status. But for heaven's sake—the woman was born in Illinois!

1

Patricia J. Williams, "The Tiger Mama Syndrome." Reprinted with permission from the February 21, 2011 issue of *The Nation*. For subscription information, call 1-800-333-8536. Portions of each week's *Nation* magazine can be accessed at http://www.thenation.com.

No doubt that Chua and her daughters have put in the requisite   2
10,000 hours it takes to be fluent in any subject, but the Ivy League is
chock-full of accomplished people who put in such hours. They come
from all over the United States and all over the world. Some growing
percentage of them are the products of yuppie, buppie, narcissistic heli-
copter parents—hockey dads, stage moms, the kind of people who
would rather see their child drop dead of heatstroke while running a race
than see that child give up. Like Chua, they do so in the name of all
sorts of higher values—family honor, Catholic guilt, team spirit, Texan
bragging rights, Jamaican superiority, Jewish destiny, women's equality,
Norwegian sang-froid, black pride, Hindu nationalism, immigrant striving, Protestant ethic, true grit. The world is a queasy, uncertain place
right now, and what it takes to compete in the rat race exposes our kids
to ever-increasing rates of depression, mental illness and substance
abuse.

That said, the Ivy League is also home to a much larger group of   3
people who work hard, who love their chosen pursuits, who are happily
well-adjusted, yet who did not acquire their highly effective study habits
by being turned out into the snow when they were 2 years old—a form
of "discipline" Chua brags about. Some of them are even Chinese. Likewise, there are many Ivy Leaguers who do not believe that their accom-
plishment makes them less "American" or "Western." They don't spend
time worrying, as Chua does, that if they "feel that they have individual
rights guaranteed by the US Constitution" they will be "much more
likely to disobey their parents and ignore career advice."

So let's not spend too much time wondering why Chua assigns her   4
neurosis to her Chinese-ness rather than to her aspirational American
upper-middle-class-ness. What I find more intriguing is not so much her
obsession with academic success but her pathological yearning for dominance, control, standing and respect. Chua does not just want perfect
scores; she is desperately afraid that she and her daughters will be
drowned in the cold goop of what she endlessly refers to as "decline."

Chua's fears are not confined by race, ethnicity or personal effort   5
alone. After all, in Greece and France students have been rioting because
of the rising costs of a good education and the paucity of jobs. In Akron,
Ohio, an African-American tiger mother named Kelley Williams-Bolar
was recently prosecuted for lying about where she lived so she could get
her children into a decent school district. In California, immigrant kids of
Mexican parents are battling for the right to pay in-state tuition at public
universities. In Memphis there are fights about whether integrating a poor

school district with a wealthier suburban one would constitute a "theft" of education. In London, a woman named Mrinal Patel was accused of fraud for misrepresenting her address so as to qualify her child for a better school. There are few places, in other words, where people are not worried about the quality of life and distribution of resources on a crowded planet.

At the same time, if Singapore, China and Hong Kong are produc- 6 ing a greater number of students with musical proficiency and excellent test scores, it's because they have made huge public investments in education. They make musical instruments available to students—as the United States once did in the first part of the twentieth century. They have teachers certified in the subjects they teach—as was the case in Russian schools during the Sputnik era. "Westerners" are not nearly as lacking in work ethic as Chua maintains; but you don't get to Yale if your elementary school has no books. You don't rank first in the world in science if, as in the United States, 60 percent of your biology teachers are reluctant to teach evolution—and 13 percent teach creationism instead.

It would be so deliciously convenient if calling your kids "garbage"— 7 another parenting trick Chua boasts about—actually turned them into little engines that could. But our larger educational crisis will involve a public investment that simply does not correlate with shooting down the self-esteem of children or disrespecting the "Western-ness" of the parents who struggle to raise them.

Finally, Amy Chua exhibits an excruciating self-consciousness 8 about how she is seen in a racialized public imagination. She is riddled with angst about not betraying her status as a "model minority" who's "supposed" to be smart in music, math and science. She even "disciplines" one of her daughters by threatening to adopt a "real" Chinese kid. Even as her narrative is swaddled in Dragon Lady analogies, every line is inflected by very American prejudices and divisive ethnic generalizations. Indeed, if you take away the peculiarly manic quality that is Chua's alone, her anxieties are no different from a lot of "buffer" groups whose inroads on the edges of assimilation mark them, and whose successes are watched reproachfully, jealously by the larger society. The Kennedys walked this walk for the Irish. Fiorello La Guardia complained of it when he was the "breakthrough" Italian. Condoleezza Rice's and Michelle Obama's parents toiled and pushed for them in ways typical of a generation of civil rights babies. In other words, this tensely, needily overachieving mentality is hardly unique. It is not necessarily or even probably generated from Chua's romanticized motherland. Our collective dilemma, and the most poignant challenge presented by her book, is how to survive in a world where the slightest nonconformity risks landing you outside—of a home, of a job, of a life—and left to stand by yourself, alone in the freezing cold.

Thinking about the Essay

1. According to Williams, what is Amy Chua's problem or the basic outlines of her syndrome? How does Williams present her argument in order to explain this syndrome? What is the writer's purpose and tone? Does she establish her claim in a single sentence or develop it incrementally? Explain.

2. Consider the writer's authority and how this influences a reader's response to her argument. How would you describe the elements of ethos and pathos inherent in her argument?

3. How does Williams employ both comparison and contrast and classification to develop the essay?

4. Why might this essay be considered an example of extended definition? Respond to this question with reference to specific aspects of the text.

5. How effective is Williams's conclusion? Does her ending serve to confirm her claim? Why or why not?

Responding in Writing

6. Write a classification essay in which you explain the types of students you have encountered in high school or college.

7. Compose a comparative essay in which you analyze the two essays by Amy Chua and Patricia J. Williams.

8. In a persuasive essay, argue for or against the proposition that certain cultures prepare their children for education better than others.

Networking

9. As a class, set up a chat room or blog, and discuss the differences in cultural perspectives highlighted in the essays by Chua and Williams. Use hyperlinks to guide the discussion to additional sources.

10. Conduct an online survey for reliable information on Patricia J. Williams. Keeping track of your sources, write a brief research paper on Williams's perspective on race, ethnicity, and American culture.

It's a Mall World After All

MAC MARGOLIS

In the following piece, which appeared in the December 5, 2005, *Newsweek International*, columnist Mac Margolis defends a much maligned and distinctively American export to the world by looking at the variety of its manifestations around the world and its almost inadvertent role as a social and political institution. Margolis is a recipient of the Maria Moors Cabot Prize for outstanding reporting on Latin America—the oldest international award in journalism. He is a contributor to *The Economist, The Washington Post,* and *The Christian Science Monitor.*

Before Reading

In what sense do you regard malls as an institution? Do you associate malls with democratic or other values?

When the Los Angeles firm Altoon + Porter Architects set out to   1
design a shopping arcade in Riyadh, Saudi Arabia, a few years ago, it faced a delicate mission: to raise a glitzy pleasure dome full of Western temptations in the maw of fundamentalist Islam. Not that the Saudis were consumer innocents; King Khalid airport in Riyadh fairly hums with wealthy Arabs bound for the lavish shops of Paris and London. But the trick was to lure women buyers—the royalty of retail—who are not allowed to shed their veils in public. "Women can't be expected to buy anything if they can't try it on," says architect Ronald Altoon, managing partner of the firm. So Altoon + Porter came up with an ecumenical solution: the Kingdom Centre, a three-story glass-and-steel Xanadu of retail with an entire floor—Women's Kingdom—devoted exclusively to female customers. "We took the veil off the women and put it on the building," says Altoon.

The modest proposal paid off. In Women's Kingdom, Saudi women   2
can shop, schmooze, dine or even loll about at the spa without upsetting the sheiks or subverting Sharia, the country's strict Islamic laws. Normally the third level of any mall is a dud, but it's become the most profitable floor in the whole arcade. The Kingdom Centre may not be

revolutionary; no one is burning veils at the food court. Still, it represents a small but meaningful freedom for Saudi women. And its success points to the irrepressible global appetite for consumer culture, as well as to the growing role that the right to shop plays in fostering democratization and development.

It's been more than two decades since John B. Hightower, the director   3
of New York City's South Street Seaport Museum, a combination cultural center and shopping arcade, brazenly declared that "shopping is the chief cultural activity of the United States." Since then, it has also become one of America's chief exports: shopping malls, once a peculiarly American symbol of convenience and excess, now dot the global landscape from Santiago to St. Petersburg and Manila to Mumbai. In 1999, India boasted only three malls. Now there are 45, and the number is expected to rise to 300 by 2010. The pint-size Arab Emirate of Dubai, sometimes known as the Oz of malls, clocked 88.5 million mall visitors last year; nearly 180 million Brazilians mob shopping arcades every month—almost as many as in the United States. Where elephants and giraffes once gamboled along the Mombasa road leading into Nairobi, the African mall rat is now a far more common sight, with four gleaming new malls to scavenge in at the Kenyan capital and three more in the works. And no one can keep pace with China, where foreign investors are scrambling to get a piece of a real-estate boom driven in part by mall mania. "The same energy and dynamism that the shopping industry brought to North America 30, 40 years ago is now reaching overseas," says Michael Kercheval, head of the International Council of Shopping Centers, an industry trade association and advisory group. "Now it's reached the global masses."

Indeed, the planet appears deep in the grip of the retail version of an   4
arms race. For years, the West Edmonton Mall in Alberta, Canada, with 20,000 parking spaces, an ice-skating rink, a miniature-golf course and four submarines (more than in the Canadian Navy) on display, had reigned as the grandest in the world. Last October it was overtaken by the $1.3 billion Golden Resources Shopping Center in northwest Beijing, with 20,000 employees and nearly twice the floor space of the Pentagon. Developers in Dubai are breaking ground on not one but two malls they claim will be even bigger, one of which boasts a man-made, five-run ski slope. Yet all these have been eclipsed by the behemoth South China Mall, which opened its doors in the factory city of Dongguan this year. By the end of the decade, China is likely to have at least seven of the world's 10 largest malls—many of them equipped with hotels, on the theory that no one can possibly see everything in a single day.

To those who malign malls as the epitome of all that is wrong with   5
American culture, their spread is like a pestilence upon the land. Dissi-
dent scholars churn out one dystopian tract—"One Nation Under
Goods," "The Call of the Mall"—after another. Critics despair of whole
nations willing to cash in their once vibrant downtowns and street markets for a wasteland of jerry-built nowhere, epic traffic jams and mar-
quees ablaze with fatuous English names (Phoenix High Street, Palm
Springs Life Plaza and Bairong World Trade Center Phase II). To some,
this is an assault on democracy itself. "Shopping malls are great for dictatorships," says Emil Pocock, a professor of American studies at Eastern
Connecticut State University, who takes students on field trips to malls
to study consumer society. "What better way to control folks than to
put them under a dome and in enclosed doors?" The "malling of America," in the words of author and famous mall-basher William Kowinski,
has become the malling of the world.

As it turns out, that may not be such a bad thing. Rather than pre-   6
sage or hasten the decline of the traditional downtown, as many critics
fear, the rise of the mall is actually serving as a catalyst for growth, especially in developing nations. In China, the booming retail sector has
sucked in a fortune in venture capital and spawned dozens of joint ven-
tures with international investors looking to snap up Chinese urban
properties. In late July, the Simon Property Group, a major U.S. devel-
oper, teamed up with Morgan Stanley and a government-owned Chinese
company to launch up to a dozen major retail centers throughout China
over the next few years. Malls are a leading force in driving India's $330
billion retailing industry, which already accounts for a third of national
GDP and recently overtook Russia's. Similarly, a burst of consumer
spending in the Philippines—thanks to overseas nationals who send
between $6 billion and $7 billion back every year—has fueled a real-
estate boom, led by megamalls.

Most developing-world malls are integrated in the heart of the inner   7
cities instead of strewn like beached whales along arid superhighways.
"In China, 80 percent of shoppers walk to the mall," says Kercheval of
the ICSC. In some megacities, including New Delhi, Nairobi and Rio,
urban sprawl has flung customers into outlying neighborhoods, many of
which spring up around brand-new shopping centers. That means malls
are no longer catering just to the elite. "We used to talk exclusively
about A-class shoppers," says Kercheval. "Now we are seeing the arrival
of B-, C- and D-class customers. The developing-world mall is becoming
more democratic."

In many places, malls are welcome havens of safety and security. In 8 Rio, where teenagers (especially young men) are the main victims of street crime, parents breathe easier when they know their kids are at play in the mall, some of which deploy 100 or more private police. "Safety is one of our biggest selling points," says Paulo Malzoni Filho, president of the Brazilian Association of Shopping Centers. "When I enter into one of these malls, it feels like I have landed in a foreign country," says Parag Mehta, a regular at the Inorbit mall in the busy northern Mumbai suburb of Malad.

And as malls break new ground around the world, the one-size-fits- 9 all business model created in North American suburbia is giving way to regionalized versions. Malls may conjure up the specter of a flood of U.S. brands and burgers, but in reality, local palates and preferences often prevail. On a recent evening in Beijing's Golden Resources Shopping Center, Kentucky Fried Chicken and Papa John's were nearly deserted, while the Korean restaurant just around the corner was packed. Chile has long welcomed foreign investors, yet the leading retailers at malls in Santiago are two local chains, Falabella and Almacenes Paris. In San Salvador, capital of El Salvador, the Gallerias shopping arcade houses a Roman Catholic church that holds mass twice a day—an intriguing metaphysical twist on the concept of the anchor store. In many developing countries, malls have attracted banks, art galleries, museums, car-rental agencies and even government services such as passport offices and motor-vehicle departments, becoming de facto villages instead of just shopping centers.

For residents of the developing world, malls increasingly serve as 10 surrogate civic centers, encouraging social values that go beyond conspicuous spending. China is home to some 168 million smokers, but they are not allowed to partake at the smoke-free malls. That's not the only environmental plus; many Chinese malls are equipped with a soft-switching system that stabilizes the electrical current and conserves energy. In the Middle East, arcades such as Riyadh's Kingdom Centre are among the few public spaces where women can gather, gab or just walk about alone in public. "Malls are not just places to shop, they are places to imagine," says Xia Yeliang, a professor at Beijing University's School of Economics. "They bring communities together that might not otherwise encounter one another and create new communities."

For some societies, malls even offer a communal respite from the 11 past. In Warsaw, where World War II demolished most of the historic shopping district—and dreary chockablock communist-era architecture finished the job—one of the most revered public spaces around is the local mall. "For decades Poles dressed up for Sunday mass," says Grzegorz Makowski, a sociologist at Warsaw University and expert on consumer culture. "Now they dress for a visit to the shopping mall."

Still, for some critics, no amount of social or economic development 12 can hide the fact that all modern malls are at heart temples of rampant consumerism. Jan Gehl, a leading Danish champion of urban renaissance and a professor of architecture at the Royal Academy of Fine Arts in Copenhagen, likes to show his students pictures of malls around the world and ask them where each one is located. Many look so indistinguishable that they can't tell. (Only now are some clues beginning to appear.) Even Victor Gruen, the Viennese Jewish émigré who fled Hitler's Europe and created the first indoor-shopping arcade in the Minneapolis suburbs in the 1950s, eventually grew disgusted by the soulless concrete-box-with-parking monstrosities rendered in his name. "I refuse to pay alimony to these bastards of development," he growled during a 1978 speech in London, fleeing back to Europe. By then there was no escape; malls were already marching on the Old World.

Half a century on, some of the resistance to malls speaks more to 13 nostalgia for an illusory past than a rejection of the present. Ancient Turkey certainly had its bazaar rats. And what is the contemporary shopping center if not a souk with a Cineplex? "Maybe the mall is just a modern and more comfortable version of what has always been," says Stephen Marshall of the Young Foundation, a London think tank. "It's quite possible the ancients would have seen our malls with all that technology as terrific places."

Certainly mall developers seem to have learned from their early 14 excesses. Instead of garish bunkers with blind walls and plastic rain forests, newer malls boast sculpture gardens, murals, belvederes and gentle lighting. Lush creepers, great ferns, cacti and feathery palms tumble down the interior of the Fashion Mall, a boutique arcade, in Rio de Janeiro. The Kingdom Centre in Riyadh won an international design award in 2003. And while "big" may still be beautiful in mallworld, more and more developers are launching arcades built to modest scale, deliberately emulating yesterday's main streets or the Old World piazzas they replaced. This may not be the much-vaunted consumer's arcadia the mallmeisters had always hoped for, but global malls seem oddly to come closer to the bold democratic ideal than the originals ever did. And when it rains, everybody stays dry.

Thinking about the Essay

1. Highlight three passing allusions that occur in the essay (the allusion to Xanadu in the opening paragraph, for example). Is there a chain of association between the series of allusions you see in the essay?

2. Why does Margolis focus on the "ecumenical solution" devised by the architectural firm Altoon + Porter in his beginning paragraph? How does this illustration serve to set up the other examples in the essay?

3. Where in the essay does Margolis address critics of malls as a cultural phenomenon? What is his response to these critics?

4. How does Margolis connect the "right to consumer culture" with democratic rights and values? Do you feel he is successful in making this connection? Why or why not?

5. Margolis concludes the piece by asserting that "global malls seem oddly to come closer to the bold democratic ideal than the originals ever did." Where in the essay has Margolis considered those precedents? Do you feel he has offered enough historical evidence to support his conclusion?

Responding in Writing

6. Do you see evidence in your own community that mall developers "have learned from their early excesses"? Write a brief critique of the architectural style and layout of your local mall.

7. Respond to Margolis's observation in paragraph 11 that malls "offer a communal respite from the past." Do you see this as a stereotypically American attitude toward the past? Would you characterize what malls offer as a "respite from the past" or as an "*escape* from the past"?

8. In a brief essay, reflect on the reasons for your own resistance to or enthusiasm for malls. Would you describe your feelings in terms of nostalgia for a past model in the process of being replaced or in terms of progress? What is the nature of this progress? What is lost or gained in the move to a new model of commerce?

Networking

9. In groups of three or four, list at least three "social values" (i.e., not consumer values) that are promoted or made possible by your local mall.

10. Go online and look up images of at least five different malls located in five different countries. What signs of individual character do you see?

Does the World Still Care About American Culture?

RICHARD PELLS | Richard Pells, who was born in Kansas City, Missouri, in 1941, studied at Rutgers University (B.A., 1963) and Harvard University (M.A., 1964; Ph.D., 1969). He is a professor of history at the University of Texas at Austin. His books include *Radical Visions and American Dreams* (1973), *Not Like Us: How Europeans Have Loved, Hated, and Transformed American Culture Since World War II* (1997), and *Modernist America: Art, Music, Movies, and the Globalization of American Culture* (Yale University Press, 2011). In the following article from the March 6, 2009, issue of *The Chronicle of Higher Education*, Pells examines the causes behind the decline of global interest in American culture.

Before Reading

Do you accept the premise that the rest of the world is less interested in American culture today than it was during most of the twentieth century?

For most of the 20th century, the dominant culture in the world was   1
American. Now that is no longer true. What is most striking about attitudes toward the United States in other countries is not the anti-Americanism they reflect, or the disdain for former President George W. Bush, or the opposition to American foreign policies. Rather, people abroad are increasingly indifferent to America's culture.

America's culture used to be the elephant in everyone's living room.   2
Whether people felt uncomfortable with the omnipresence of America's high or popular culture in their countries, they could not ignore its power or its appeal. American writers and artists were superstars—the objects of curiosity, admiration and envy. Today they are for the most part unnoticed or regarded as ordinary mortals, participants in a global rather than a distinctively American culture.

America's elections still matter to people overseas. As someone who   3
has taught American studies in Europe, Latin America and Asia, I received e-mail messages from friends abroad asking me who I thought would win the presidency in November. But I rarely get queries about

Richard Pells, "Does the World Still Care About American Culture?" Originally appeared in *The Chronicle of Higher Education*, March 6, 2009, Volume 55, Issue 26, p. B4. Reprinted by permission of the author.

what I think of the latest American movie. Nor does anyone ask me about American novelists, playwrights, composers or painters.

Imagine any of these events or episodes in the past happening now: In 1928, fresh from having written "Rhapsody in Blue" and the "Piano Concerto in F Major," George Gershwin traveled to Paris and Vienna. He was treated like an idol. As America's most famous composer, he met with many of the leading European modernists: Schoenberg, Stravinsky, Prokofiev, Ravel. At one point, Gershwin asked Stravinsky if he could take lessons from the great Russian. Stravinsky responded by asking Gershwin how much money he made in a year. Told the answer was in six figures, Stravinsky quipped, "In that case . . . I should study with you." 4

In the 1930s, Louis Armstrong and Duke Ellington toured throughout Europe, giving concerts to thousands of adoring fans, including members of the British royal family. In the 1940s and '50s, Dave Brubeck, Miles Davis, Dizzy Gillespie, Benny Goodman and Charlie Parker often gave concerts in Western and Eastern Europe, the Soviet Union, the Middle East, Africa, Asia and Latin America. The Voice of America's most popular program in the 1960s was a show called Music USA, specializing in jazz, with an estimated 100 million listeners around the world. In the 1940s and '50s as well, Leonard Bernstein was invited to conduct symphony orchestras in London, Moscow, Paris, Prague, Tel Aviv and Milan. 5

If you were a professor of modern literature at a foreign university, your reading list had to include Bellow, Dos Passos, Faulkner, Hemingway and Steinbeck. If you taught courses on the theater, it was obligatory to discuss *Death of a Salesman, The Iceman Cometh, Long Day's Journey Into Night* and *A Streetcar Named Desire.* 6

If you wanted to study modern art, you did not—like Gene Kelly in *An American in Paris*—journey to the City of Light (all the while singing and dancing to the music of Gershwin) to learn how to become a painter. Instead you came to New York, to sit at the feet of Willem de Kooning and Jackson Pollock. Or later you hung out at Andy Warhol's "factory," surrounded by celebrities from the arts and the entertainment world. 7

If dance was your specialty, where else could you find more creative choreographers than Bob Fosse or Jerome Robbins? If you were an aspiring filmmaker in the 1970s, the movies worth seeing and studying all originated in America. What other country could boast of such cinematic talent as Woody Allen, Robert Altman, Francis Ford Coppola, George Lucas, Martin Scorsese and Steven Spielberg? 8

Of course, there are still American cultural icons who mesmerize a global audience or whose photos are pervasive in the pages of the world's tabloid newspapers. Bruce Springsteen can always pack an arena wherever he performs. The Broadway musical *Rent* has been translated into more than 20 languages. Hollywood's blockbusters still make millions of dollars abroad. America's movie stars remain major celebrities at international film festivals. 9

But there is a sense overseas today that America's cultural exports are not as important, or as alluring, as they once were. When I lecture abroad on contemporary American culture, I find that few of America's current artists and intellectuals are household names, luminaries from whom foreigners feel they need to learn. The cultural action is elsewhere—not so much in Manhattan or San Francisco but in Berlin (the site of a major film festival) and Mumbai (the home of Indian filmmakers and media entrepreneurs who are now investing in the movies of Spielberg and other American directors). The importance of Mumbai was reinforced, spectacularly, when *Slumdog Millionaire* won the Oscar for best picture. 10

What accounts for the decline of interest in American art, literature and music? Why has American culture become just another item on the shelves of the global supermarket? 11

The main answer is that globalization has subverted America's influence. During the 1990s, many people assumed that the emergence of what they called a global culture was just another mechanism for the "Americanization" of the world. Be it Microsoft or McDonald's, Disney theme parks or shopping malls, the movies or the Internet, the artifacts of American culture seemed ubiquitous and inescapable. 12

Yet far from reinforcing the impact of American culture, globalization has strengthened the cultures of other nations, regions and continents. Instead of defining what foreigners want, America's cultural producers find themselves competing with their counterparts abroad in shaping people's values and tastes. What we have in the 21st century is not a hegemonic American culture but multiple forms of art and entertainment—voices, images and ideas that can spring up anywhere and be disseminated all over the planet. 13

American television programs like *Dallas* and *Dynasty* were once the most popular shows on the airwaves, from Norway to New Zealand. Now many people prefer programs that are locally produced. Meanwhile, cable and satellite facilities permit stations like Al-Jazeera to define and interpret the news from a Middle Eastern perspective for people throughout the world. 14

Since 2000, moreover, American movies have steadily lost market share 15
in Europe and Asia. In 1998, the year *Titanic* was released abroad, American films commanded 64 percent of the ticket sales in France. Ten years
later, Hollywood's share of the French market has fallen to 50 percent.
Similarly, in 1998, American films accounted for 70 percent of the tickets
sold in South Korea. Today that figure has fallen to less than 50 percent.

As in the case of television programs, audiences increasingly prefer 16
movies made in and about their own countries or regions. Indian films
are now more popular in India than are imports from Hollywood. At
the same time, American moviegoers are increasingly willing to sample
films from abroad (and not just in art houses), which has led to the popularity in the United States of Japanese cartoons and animated films as
well as recent German movies like *The Lives of Others*.

After World War II, professors and students from abroad were eager 17
to study in the United States. America was, after all, the center of the
world's intellectual and cultural life. Now, with the rise of continental
exchange programs and the difficulties that foreign academics face
obtaining U.S. visas, it is often easier for a Dutch student to study in
Germany or France or for a Middle Eastern student to study in India,
than for either of them to travel to an American university. That further
diminishes the impact of American culture abroad.

Crowds, especially of young people, still flock to McDonald's— 18
whether in Beijing, Moscow or Paris. But every country has always had
its own version of equally popular fast food. There are wurst stands in
Germany and Austria, fish-and-chips shops in England, noodle restaurants in South Korea and Singapore, kabob outlets on street corners in
almost any city (including in America), all of which remain popular and
compete effectively with the Big Mac.

Finally, cellphones and the Internet make information and culture 19
instantly available to anyone, without having to depend any longer on
American definitions of what it is important to know. Indeed, globalization has led not to greater intellectual and political uniformity but to the
decentralization of knowledge and culture. We live today in a universe
full of cultural options, and we are therefore free to choose what to
embrace and what to ignore.

I am not suggesting that America's culture is irrelevant. It remains 20
one—but only one—of the cultural alternatives available to people
abroad and at home. Moreover, it is certainly conceivable that President
Barack Obama will improve America's currently dreadful image in the
world, encouraging people to pay more attention not only to American

policies but also to American culture—which the Bush administration, despite its efforts at cultural diplomacy, was never able to do.

But it is doubtful that America will ever again be the world's pre- 21 eminent culture, as it was in the 20th century. That is not a cause for regret. Perhaps we are all better off in a world of cultural pluralism than in a world made in America.

Thinking about the Essay

1. What claim does Pells establish in his introductory paragraph? What minor propositions does he provide to support his claim?

2. Where does Pells inject information about himself into this essay? What is his purpose? Do you think his strategy is effective? Justify your response.

3. Does Pells ever establish a clear definition of American culture or does he force us to induce it? Explain. Could there be alternative definitions of American culture that compete with Pells's understanding of the word? Why or why not?

4. Trace the pattern of cause and effect that Pells establishes. According to Pells, what are the primary and secondary causes for the decline of global interest in American culture?

5. Pells alludes to numerous cultural figures and artistic works in this essay. What expectations does he have of his audience here? Would readers be less likely to relate to his essay—or accept his argument—if they were not familiar with Gene Kelly or had not read or seen *The Iceman Cometh*? Explain.

Responding in Writing

6. Write an argumentative essay in which you attempt to refute Pells's claim that the world is losing interest in American culture. Provide supporting points and examples to buttress your argument.

7. Write a causal analysis of the impact of globalization on the dissemination of American culture around the world.

8. Reverse Pells's claim and write an essay contending or explaining why Americans are far more interested in the cultures of other nations and regions than they were in the past.

Networking

9. Working in small groups, develop a list of all the references and allusions in Pells's essay and then identify as many as possible. Based on this list, establish what your group thinks that Pells means by American culture.

10. Conduct online research on one American musician, writer, artist, filmmaker, or actor mentioned in the essay—for example, Louis Armstrong, Ernest Hemingway, or Woody Allen—and explore the reception of this individual overseas. What conclusions can you draw from your research?

On Seeing England for the First Time

JAMAICA KINCAID

Jamaica Kincaid was born Elaine Potter Richardson in 1949 in St. John's, Antigua, in the West Indies. After emigrating to the United States, she became a staff writer for *The New Yorker*, with her short stories also appearing in *Rolling Stone, The Paris Review*, and elsewhere. She has taught at Harvard University and other colleges while compiling a distinguished body of fiction and nonfiction, notably *Annie John* (1985), *A Small Place* (1988), *Lucy* (1991), *The Autobiography of My Mother* (1996), and *Among Flowers: A Walk in the Himalaya* (2005). The stories collected in *At the Bottom of the River* (1984) won the Morton Dauwen Zabel Award from the American Academy and Institute of Arts and Letters. Although Kincaid has turned recently in her writing to the relatively peaceful world of gardening, the typical tone of her fiction and essays is severely critical of the social, cultural, and political consequences of colonialism and immigration. In "On Seeing England for the First Time," published in *Transition* in 1991, Kincaid thinks about the time when Great Britain was associated with the forces of globalization throughout the world.

Before Reading

It was once said that the sun never sets on the British Empire. What does this statement mean? Could the same be said of the United States today?

When I saw England for the first time, I was a child in school sitting   1
at a desk. The England I was looking at was laid out on a map gently, beautifully, delicately, a very special jewel; it lay on a bed of sky blue—the background of the map—its yellow form mysterious, because though it looked like a leg of mutton, it could not really look like anything so familiar as a leg of mutton because it was England—with shadings of pink and green, unlike any shadings of pink and green I had seen

before, squiggly veins of red running in every direction. England was a special jewel all right, and only special people got to wear it. The people who got to wear England were English people. They wore it well and they wore it everywhere: in jungles, in deserts, on plains, on top of the highest mountains, on all the oceans, on all the seas, in places where they were not welcome, in places they should not have been. When my teacher had pinned this map up on the blackboard, she said, "This is England"—and she said it with authority, seriousness, and adoration, and we all sat up. It was as if she had said, "This is Jerusalem, the place you will go to when you die but only if you have been good." We understood then—we were meant to understand then—that England was to be our source of myth and the source from which we got our sense of reality, our sense of what was meaningful, our sense of what was meaningless—and much about our own lives and much about the very idea of us headed that last list.

At the time I was a child sitting at my desk seeing England for the first time, I was already very familiar with the greatness of it. Each morning before I left for school, I ate a breakfast of half a grapefruit, an egg, bread and butter and a slice of cheese, and a cup of cocoa; or half a grapefruit, a bowl of oat porridge, bread and butter and a slice of cheese, and a cup of cocoa. The can of cocoa was often left on the table in front of me. It had written on it the name of the company, the year the company was established, and the words "Made in England." Those words," Made in England," were written on the box the oats came in too. They would also have been written on the box the shoes I was wearing came in; a bolt of gray linen cloth lying on the shelf of a store from which my mother had bought three yards to make the uniform that I was wearing had written along its edge those three words. The shoes I wore were made in England; so were my socks and cotton undergarments and the satin ribbons I wore tied at the end of two plaits of my hair. My father, who might have sat next to me at breakfast, was a carpenter and cabinet maker. The shoes he wore to work would have been made in England, as were his khaki shirt and trousers, his underpants and undershirt, his socks and brown felt hat. Felt was not the proper material from which a hat that was expected to provide shade from the hot sun should be made, but my father must have seen and admired a picture of an Englishman wearing such a hat in England, and this picture that he saw must have been so compelling that it caused him to wear the wrong hat for a hot climate most of his long life. And this hat—a brown felt hat—became so central to his character that it was the first thing he

2

put on in the morning as he stepped out of bed and the last thing he took off before he stepped back into bed at night. As we sat at breakfast a car might go by. The car, a Hillman or a Zephyr, was made in England. The very idea of the meal itself, breakfast, and its substantial quality and quantity was an idea from England; we somehow knew that in England they began the day with this meal called breakfast and a proper breakfast was a big breakfast. No one I knew liked eating so much food so early in the day; it made us feel sleepy, tired. But this breakfast business was Made in England like almost everything else that surrounded us, the exceptions being the sea, the sky, and the air we breathed.

At the time I saw this map—seeing England for the first time—I did not say to myself, "Ah, so that's what it looks like," because there was no longing in me to put a shape to those three words that ran through every part of my life, no matter how small; for me to have had such a longing would have meant that I lived in a certain atmosphere, an atmosphere in which those three words were felt as a burden. But I did not live in such an atmosphere. My father's brown felt hat would develop a hole in its crown, the lining would separate from the hat itself, and six weeks before he thought that he could not be seen wearing it—he was a very vain man—he would order another hat from England. And my mother taught me to eat my food in the English way: the knife in the right hand, the fork in the left, my elbows held still close to my side, the food carefully balanced on my fork and then brought up to my mouth. When I had finally mastered it, I overheard her saying to a friend, "Did you see how nicely she can eat?" But I knew then that I enjoyed my food more when I ate it with my bare hands, and I continued to do so when she wasn't looking. And when my teacher showed us the map, she asked us to study it carefully, because no test we would ever take would be complete without this statement: "Draw a map of England."

I did not know then that the statement "Draw a map of England" was something far worse than a declaration of war, for in fact a flat-out declaration of war would have put me on alert, and again in fact, there was no need for war—I had long ago been conquered. I did not know then that this statement was part of a process that would result in my erasure, not my physical erasure, but my erasure all the same. I did not know then that this statement was meant to make me feel in awe and small whenever I heard the word "England": awe at its existence, small because I was not from it. I did not know very much of anything then—certainly not what a blessing it was that I was unable to draw a map of England correctly.

After that there were many times of seeing England for the first time.   5
I saw England in history. I knew the names of all the kings of England. I
knew the names of their children, their wives, their disappointments,
their triumphs, the names of people who betrayed them; I knew the dates
on which they were born and the dates they died. I knew their conquests
and was made to feel glad if I figured in them; I knew their defeats. I
knew the details of the year 1066 (the Battle of Hastings, the end of the
reign of the Anglo-Saxon kings) before I knew the details of the year
1832 (the year slavery was abolished). It wasn't as bad as I make it
sound now; it was worse. I did like so much hearing again and again
how Alfred the Great, traveling in disguise, had been left to watch cakes,
and because he wasn't used to this the cakes got burned, and Alfred
burned his hands pulling them out of the fire, and the woman who had
left him to watch the cakes screamed at him. I loved King Alfred. My
grandfather was named after him; his son, my uncle, was named after
King Alfred; my brother is named after King Alfred. And so there are
three people in my family named after a man they have never met, a
man who died over ten centuries ago. The first view I got of England
then was not unlike the first view received by the person who named my
grandfather.

This view, though—the naming of the kings, their deeds, their   6
disappointments—was the vivid view, the forceful view. There were
other views, subtler ones, softer, almost not there—but these were the
ones that made the most lasting impression on me, these were the ones
that made me really feel like nothing. "When morning touched the sky"
was one phrase, for no morning touched the sky where I lived. The
mornings where I lived came on abruptly, with a shock of heat and loud
noises. "Evening approaches" was another, but the evenings where I
lived did not approach; in fact, I had no evening—I had night and I had
day and they came and went in a mechanical way: on, off; on, off. And
then there were gentle mountains and low blue skies and moors over
which people took walks for nothing but pleasure, when where I lived a
walk was an act of labor, a burden, something only death or the automobile could relieve. And there were things that a small turn of a head
could convey—entire worlds, whole lives would depend on this thing, a
certain turn of a head. Everyday life could be quite tiring, more tiring
than anything I was told not to do. I was told not to gossip, but they
did that all the time. And they ate so much food, violating another of
those rules they taught me: do not indulge in gluttony. And the foods
they ate actually: if only sometime I could eat cold cuts after theater,
cold cuts of lamb and mint sauce, and Yorkshire pudding and scones,

and clotted cream, and sausages that came from up-country (imagine, "up-country"). And having troubling thoughts at twilight, a good time to have troubling thoughts, apparently; and servants who stole and left in the middle of a crisis, who were born with a limp or some other kind of deformity, not nourished properly in their mother's womb (that last part I figured out for myself; the point was, oh to have an untrustworthy servant); and wonderful cobbled streets onto which solid front doors opened; and people whose eyes were blue and who had fair skins and who smelled only of lavender, or sometimes sweet pea or primrose. And those flowers with those names: delphiniums, foxgloves, tulips, daffodils, floribunda, peonies; in bloom, a striking display, being cut and placed in large glass bowls, crystal, decorating rooms so large twenty families the size of mine could fit in comfortably but used only for passing through. And the weather was so remarkable because the rain fell gently always, only occasionally in deep gusts, and it colored the air various shades of gray, each an appealing shade for a dress to be worn when a portrait was being painted; and when it rained at twilight, wonderful things happened: people bumped into each other unexpectedly and that would lead to all sorts of turns of events—a plot, the mere weather caused plots. I saw that people rushed: they rushed to catch trains, they rushed toward each other and away from each other; they rushed and rushed and rushed. That word: rushed! I did not know what it was to do that. It was too hot to do that, and so I came to envy people who would rush, even though it had no meaning to me to do such a thing. But there they are again. They loved their children; their children were sent to their own rooms as a punishment, rooms larger than my entire house. They were special, everything about them said so, even their clothes; their clothes rustled, swished, soothed. The world was theirs, not mine; everything told me so.

If now as I speak of all this I give the impression of someone on the outside looking in, nose pressed up against a glass window, that is wrong. My nose was pressed up against a glass window all right, but there was an iron vise at the back of my neck forcing my head to stay in place. To avert my gaze was to fall back into something from which I had been rescued, a hole filled with nothing, and that was the word for everything about me, nothing. The reality of my life was conquests, subjugation, humiliation, enforced amnesia. I was forced to forget. Just for instance, this: I lived in a part of St. John's, Antigua, called Ovals. Ovals was made up of five streets, each of them named after a famous English seaman—to be quite frank, an officially sanctioned criminal: Rodney

7

Street (after George Rodney), Nelson Street (after Horatio Nelson), Drake Street (after Francis Drake), Hood Street, and Hawkins Street (after John Hawkins). But John Hawkins was knighted after a trip he made to Africa, opening up a new trade, the slave trade. He was then entitled to wear as his crest a Negro bound with a cord. Every single person living on Hawkins Street was descended from a slave. John Hawkins's ship, the one in which he transported the people he had bought and kidnapped, was called *The Jesus*. He later became the treasurer of the Royal Navy and rear admiral.

Again, the reality of my life, the life I led at the time I was being 8 shown these views of England for the first time, for the second time, for the one-hundred-millionth time, was this: the sun shone with what sometimes seemed to be a deliberate cruelty; we must have done something to deserve that. My dresses did not rustle in the evening air as I strolled to the theater (I had no evening, I had no theater; my dresses were made of a cheap cotton, the weave of which would give way after not too many washings). I got up in the morning, I did my chores (fetched water from the public pipe for my mother, swept the yard), I washed myself, I went to a woman to have my hair combed freshly every day (because before we were allowed into our classroom our teachers would inspect us, and children who had not bathed that day, or had dirt under their fingernails, or whose hair had not been combed anew that day, might not be allowed to attend class). I ate that breakfast. I walked to school. At school we gathered in an auditorium and sang a hymn, "All Things Bright and Beautiful," and looking down on us as we sang were portraits of the Queen of England and her husband; they wore jewels and medals and they smiled. I was a Brownie. At each meeting we would form a little group around a flagpole, and after raising the Union Jack, we would say, "I promise to do my best, to do my duty to God and the Queen, to help other people every day and obey the scouts' law."

Who were these people and why had I never seen them, I mean really 9 seen them, in the place where they lived? I had never been to England. No one I knew had ever been to England, or I should say, no one I knew had ever been and returned to tell me about it. All the people I knew who had gone to England had stayed there. Sometimes they left behind them their small children, never to see them again. England! I had seen England's representatives. I had seen the governor general at the public grounds at a ceremony celebrating the Queen's birthday. I had seen an old princess and I had seen a young princess. They had both been extremely not beautiful, but who of us would have told them that? I had never seen England, really seen it, I had only met a representative, seen a picture, read books, memorized its history. I had never set foot, my own foot, in it.

The space between the idea of something and its reality is always   10 wide and deep and dark. The longer they are kept apart—idea of thing, reality of thing—the wider the width, the deeper the depth, the thicker and darker the darkness. This space starts out empty, there is nothing in it, but it rapidly becomes filled up with obsession or desire or hatred or love—sometimes all of these things, sometimes some of these things, sometimes only one of these things. The existence of the world as I came to know it was a result of this: idea of thing over here, reality of thing way, way over there. There was Christopher Columbus, an unlikable man, an unpleasant man, a liar (and so, of course, a thief) surrounded by maps and schemes and plans, and there was the reality on the other side of that width, that depth, that darkness. He became obsessed, he became filled with desire, the hatred came later, love was never a part of it. Eventually, his idea met the longed-for reality. That the idea of something and its reality are often two completely different things is something no one ever remembers; and so when they meet and find that they are not compatible, the weaker of the two, idea or reality, dies. That idea Christopher Columbus had was more powerful than the reality he met, and so the reality he met died.

And so finally, when I was a grown-up woman, the mother of two   11 children, the wife of someone, a person who resides in a powerful country that takes up more than its fair share of a continent, the owner of a house with many rooms in it and of two automobiles, with the desire and will (which I very much act upon) to take from the world more than I give back to it, more than I deserve, more than I need, finally then, I saw England, the real England, not a picture, not a painting, not through a story in a book, but England, for the first time. In me, the space between the idea of it and its reality had become filled with hatred, and so when at last I saw it I wanted to take it into my hands and tear it into little pieces and then crumble it up as if it were clay, child's clay. That was impossible, and so I could only indulge in not-favorable opinions.

There were monuments everywhere; they commemorated victories,   12 battles fought between them and the people who lived across the sea from them, all vile people, fought over which of them would have dominion over the people who looked like me. The monuments were useless to them now, people sat on them and ate their lunch. They were like markers on an old useless trail, like a piece of old string tied to a finger to jog the memory, like old decoration in an old house, dirty, useless, in the way. Their skins were so pale, it made them look so fragile, so weak, so ugly. What if I had the power to simply banish them from their land, send boat after boatload of them on a voyage that in fact had no destination, force them to live in a place where the sun's presence was a constant? This would rid them of their pale complexion and make them look more like me, make them look more like the people I love and treasure and hold dear, and more like the people who occupy the near and far reaches of my imagination, my history, my geography, and reduce them and everything they have ever known to figurines as evidence that I was in divine favor, what if all this was in my power? Could I resist it? No one ever has.

And they were rude, they were rude to each other. They didn't like 13 each other very much. They didn't like each other in the way they didn't like me, and it occurred to me that their dislike for me was one of the few things they agreed on.

I was on a train in England with a friend, an English woman. Before 14 we were in England she liked me very much. In England she didn't like me at all. She didn't like the claim I said I had on England, she didn't like the views I had of England. I didn't like England, she didn't like England, but she didn't like me not liking it too. She said, "I want to show you my England, I want to show you the England that I know and love." I had told her many times before that I knew England and I didn't want to love it anyway. She no longer lived in England; it was her own country, but it had not been kind to her, so she left. On the train, the conductor was rude to her; she asked something, and he responded in a rude way. She became ashamed. She was ashamed at the way he treated her; she was ashamed at the way he behaved. "This is the new England," she said. But I liked the conductor being rude; his behavior seemed quite appropriate. Earlier this had happened: we had gone to a store to buy a shirt for my husband; it was meant to be a special present, a special shirt to wear on special occasions. This was a store where the Prince of Wales has his shirts made, but the shirts sold in this store are beautiful all the same. I found a shirt I thought my husband would like and I wanted to buy him a tie to go with it. When I couldn't decide which one to choose, the salesman showed me a new set. He was very pleased with these, he said, because they bore the crest of the Prince of Wales, and the Prince of Wales had never allowed his crest to decorate an article of clothing before. There was something in the way he said it; his tone was slavish, reverential, awed. It made me feel angry; I wanted to hit him. I didn't do that. I said, my husband and I hate princes, my husband would never wear anything that had a prince's anything on it. My friend stiffened. The salesman stiffened. They both drew themselves in, away from me. My friend told me that the prince was a symbol of her Englishness, and I could see that I had caused offense. I looked at her. She was an English person, the sort of English person I used to know at home, the sort who was nobody in England but somebody when they came to live among the people like me. There were many people I could have seen England with; that I was seeing it with this particular person, a person who reminded me of the people who showed me England long ago as I sat in church or at my desk, made me feel silent and afraid, for I wondered if, all these years of our friendship, I had had a friend or had been in the thrall of a racial memory.

I went to Bath—we, my friend and I, did this, but though we were together, I was no longer with her. The landscape was almost as familiar as my own hand, but I had never been in this place before, so how could that be again? And the streets of Bath were familiar, too, but I had never walked on them before. It was all those years of reading, starting with Roman Britain. Why did I have to know about Roman Britain? It was of no real use to me, a person living on a hot, drought-ridden island, and it is of no use to me now, and yet my head is filled with this nonsense, Roman Britain. In Bath, I drank tea in a room I had read about in a novel written in the eighteenth century. In this very same room, young women wearing those dresses that rustled and so on danced and flirted and sometimes disgraced themselves with young men, soldiers, sailors, who were on their way to Bristol or someplace like that, so many places like that where so many adventures, the outcome of which was not good for me, began. Bristol, England. A sentence that began "That night the ship sailed from Bristol, England" would end not so good for me. And then I was driving through the countryside in an English motorcar, on narrow winding roads, and they were so familiar, though I had never been on them before; and through little villages the names of which I somehow knew so well though I had never been there before. And the countryside did have all those hedges and hedges, fields hedged in. I was marveling at all the toil of it, the planting of the hedges to begin with and then the care of it, all that clipping, year after year of clipping, and I wondered at the lives of the people who would have to do this, because wherever I see and feel the hands that hold up the world, I see and feel myself and all the people who look like me. And I said, "Those hedges" and my friend said that someone, a woman named Mrs. Rothchild,

15

worried that the hedges weren't being taken care of properly; the farmers couldn't afford or find the help to keep up the hedges, and often they replaced them with wire fencing. I might have said to that, well if Mrs. Rothchild doesn't like the wire fencing, why doesn't she take care of the hedges herself, but I didn't. And then in those fields that were now hemmed in by wire fencing that a privileged woman didn't like was planted a vile yellow flowering bush that produced an oil, and my friend said that Mrs. Rothchild didn't like this either; it ruined the English countryside, it ruined the traditional look of the English countryside.

It was not at that moment that I wished every sentence, everything I 16 knew, that began with England would end with "and then it all died; we don't know how, it just all died." At that moment, I was thinking, who are these people who forced me to think of them all the time, who forced me to think that the world I knew was incomplete, or without substance, or did not measure up because it was not England; that I was incomplete, or without substance, and did not measure up because I was not English. Who were these people? The person sitting next to me couldn't give me a clue; no one person could. In any case, if I had said to her, I find England ugly, I hate England; the weather is like a jail sentence, the English are a very ugly people, the food in England is like a jail sentence, the hair of English people is so straight, so dead looking, the English have an unbearable smell so different from the smell of people I know, real people of course, she would have said that I was a person full of prejudice. Apart from the fact that it is I—that is, the people who look like me—who made her aware of the unpleasantness of such a thing, the idea of such a thing, prejudice, she would have been only partly right, sort of right: I may be capable of prejudice, but my prejudices have no weight to them, my prejudices have no force behind them, my prejudices remain opinions, my prejudices remain my personal opinion. And a great feeling of rage and disappointment came over me as I looked at England, my head full of personal opinions that could not have public, my public, approval. The people I come from are powerless to do evil on grand scale.

The moment I wished every sentence, everything I knew, that began 17 with England would end with "and then it all died, we don't know how, it just all died" was when I saw the white cliffs of Dover. I had sung hymns and recited poems that were about a longing to see the white cliffs of Dover again. At the time I sang the hymns and recited the poems, I could really long to see them again because I had never seen them at all, nor had anyone around me at the time. But there we were, groups of people longing for something we had never seen. And so there they were, the white cliffs, but they were not that pearly majestic thing I used to sing about, that thing that created such a feeling in these people that when they died in the place where I lived they had themselves buried facing a direction that would allow them to see the white cliffs of Dover when they were resurrected, as surely they would be. The white cliffs of Dover, when finally I saw them, were cliffs, but they were not white; you would only call them that if the word "white" meant something special to you; they were dirty and they were steep; they were so steep, the correct height from which all my views of England, starting with the map before me in my classroom and ending with the trip I had just taken, should jump and die and disappear forever.

Thinking about the Essay

1. Based on your careful reading of this essay, summarize Kincaid's understanding of cultural imperialism. Does the fact that she writes about England and not the United States diminish the importance of her argument? Explain.

2. Kincaid divides her essay into two major parts. What is her intention? What is the effect?

3. Kincaid establishes several contrasts between England and Antigua. What are they? How does this comparative method serve to organize the essay?

4. The writer's paragraphs tend to be quite long. Analyze the way she develops her introductory and concluding paragraphs. Also examine the longest paragraph in the essay (paragraph 6), and explain how she achieves coherence in the presentation of her ideas.

5. How does Kincaid's use of the personal voice—the "I" point of view—affect the tone and purpose of her essay? By adopting this personal perspective, what does Kincaid want the audience to infer about her and her experience of cultural imperialism?

Responding in Writing

6. Write an account of your early education. What did you learn about the country where you were born and its relationship to the rest of the world? How did your early education influence or mold your global understanding today?

7. Write an essay analyzing Kincaid's various views on England and what they ultimately mean to her. Has she convinced you about her perspective on the subject? Why or why not? Be certain to deal with her concluding paragraph and her reference to the "white cliffs of Dover."

8. Imagine that you live in a country that has a history of colonization. (Perhaps you or your family has actually experienced this condition.) What would your attitude toward the colonizing or globalizing power be? Write a paper exploring this real or imaginary situation.

Networking

9. With three other class members, draw up a complete list of the contrasts that Kincaid establishes between Antigua and England. Arrive at a consensus about why she is so preoccupied with England—not just as a child but also as an adult writing about the experience. Select one member of your group as a representative in a class panel discussion that talks about these contrasts.

10. Go online and find information about Antigua. Evaluate Kincaid's impressions of her native island with what you have learned about it.

The Clash of Civilizations: Is Conflict Avoidable?

The spread of Coca-Cola, Hollywood films, and rock and roll around the world—all the trappings of American popular culture—combined with the broader economic and political forces generated by America's superpower status has helped fuel what we call the "clash of civilizations." The phrase, coined by the American political scientist Samuel Huntington, who has an essay in this chapter, suggests that we are in a new era in which the forces of globalization have brought entire civilizations, rather than separate nations, into conflict with each other. The nature of this conflict goes to the heart of what we mean by cultural identity—who am I, and where do I belong?—and how we see ourselves in relation to our civilization and other civilizations we come into contact with.

According to Huntington, whose long article appeared in the summer 1993 issue of *Foreign Affairs* and subsequently in an expanded book, *The Clash of Civilizations and the Remaking of World Order* (1996), the world can be divided into seven or perhaps eight contemporary civilizations: Western, Latin American, Islamic, Sinic or Chinese (which includes China, Taiwan, Korea, and Vietnam), Japanese, Hindu, Orthodox (Russia, Serbia, and Greece), and African. "Human history," writes Huntington, "is the history of civilizations. It is impossible to think of the development of humanity in any other terms." Historically there have been numerous conflicts between and among these civilizations. However, Huntington's thesis is that with the rise of the West since 1500, other civilizations—notably the Islamic and Chinese—have resented this "rise" and reacted against it. Furthermore, in the inevitable cycles of history, other civilizations will rise in reaction to the dominance of the Western world and become dominant themselves, thus leading to a new clash with global consequences.

Palestinian schoolgirls walk past Israeli soldiers in Hebron, one of the most contested and violent cities of the West Bank—a region jointly controlled by Israel and the Palestinian Authority. The tomb of Abraham, considered the patriarch of both Judaism and Islam, is located in Hebron; rivalries here extend for millennia.

Thinking about the Image

1. What elements make this photograph especially compelling? Consider the expressions on the faces of the schoolgirls, the size and positioning of the soldiers, and the details of the setting.

2. Do you think that the photographer reinforces conventional depictions of the Arab–Israeli conflict in the American media, or is the photographer trying to present a different perspective? Explain your response.

3. Do you believe that the photographer advances an argument concerning Israel's occupation of the West Bank? Why or why not?

Huntington's broad thesis has come under scrutiny and attack on all sides, and some of his critics appear in this chapter. Yet it could be argued that what we see most clearly in the world today—the conflict between the Western and Islamic worlds or the gradual ascendancy of China as the next major world power—confirms Huntington's basic claim. Conversely, if you think that reality actually contradicts Huntington's thesis, then you could argue that Western forms of culture, democracy, and modernization actually are cutting across all civilizations and triumphing over them. The social scientist Benjamin Barber maintains that there will be raging conflicts among civilizations in the future, but that "McWorld," as he terms the West, will triumph over "Jihad." Thus Western civilization will not decline but will defeat the forces of fundamentalism and totalitarianism.

The essays in this chapter deal with the clash of civilizations from a variety of perspectives. We can't deny that conflicts among civilizations exist; some are religious, others ethnic, still others cultural. The writers invite us to consider our own loyalties, and whether we associate with one culture, nation, or civilization or with many. Are there commonalities among civilizations, or must we be forever in conflict? Must we always deal with threats to our gods, our ancestors, our civilization? Or, in a world of seven billion people, are there tangible signs that we needn't think of "inferior" and "superior" civilizations but rather of a world showing signs of heightened tolerance, integration, and harmony? The way we answer these questions will determine the fabric of future civilizations.

American Dream Boat

K. OANH HA

K. Oanh Ha was born in Vietnam in 1973. As she relates in the following essay, she left Vietnam with her family in July 1979, journeying with other "boat people" to the United States. Raised in California, she covered globalization for KQED Radio in San Francisco. In 2010 Ha joined Bloomberg News as its Vietnam Bureau Chief. Her stories explore the business of globalization as well as its social and cultural impact. Prior to working in radio, she was a staff writer for the *San Jose Mercury News*. She is working on a novel that is based loosely on her family's escape from Vietnam. In this personal narrative that she published in *Modern Maturity* in 2002, Ha provides a gentle affirmation of how—when it comes to love—civilizations need not clash.

Before Reading

Have you dated someone whose background represents a culture or civilization entirely different from yours? If not, do you know of a couple who signify this coming together of civilizations? How do you—or they—work out any "clashes"?

The wedding day was only two weeks away when my parents called with yet another request. In accordance with Vietnamese custom, they fully expected Scott Harris, my fiancé, and his family to visit our family on the morning of the wedding, bearing dowry gifts of fruit, candies, jewelry, and a pig, in an elaborate procession. 1

"But it's not going to mean anything to Scott or his family. They're not Vietnamese!" I protested. My parents were adamant: "Scott is marrying a Vietnamese. If he wants to marry you, he'll honor our traditions." 2

Maybe there's no such thing as a stress-free wedding. Small or large, there's bound to be pressure. But our February 12 wedding was a large do-it-yourselfer that required a fusion of Vietnamese and American traditions—a wedding that forced me and my parents to wrestle with questions about our identities, culture, and place in America. After nearly 20 years here, my family, and my parents in particular, were determined to have a traditional Vietnamese wedding of sorts, even if their son-in-law and Vietnam-born, California-raised daughter are as American as they can be. 3

And so I grudgingly called Scott that night to describe the wedding procession and explain the significance of the ritual. It's a good thing that he is a patient, easygoing man. "I'll bring the pig," he said, "but I'm worried it'll make a mess in the car." 4

"Oh! It's a *roasted* pig," I told him, laughing. 5

I was six years old when my family fled Vietnam in July 1979, just one family among the thousands who collectively became known as the "boat people," families who decided it was better to risk the very real possibility of death at sea than to live under Communist rule. But, of course, I never understood the politics then. I was just a child following my parents. 6

My memories are sketchy. There was the time that Thai pirates wielding saber-like machetes raided our boat. Two years ago, I told my mother, Kim Hanh Nguyen, how I remembered a woman dropping a handful of jewelry into my rice porridge during the raid with the instructions to keep eating. "That was no woman," my mother said. "That was me!" When we reached the refugee camp in Kuala Lumpur, my mother used the wedding ring and necklace to buy our shelter. 7

In September 1980, we arrived in Santa Ana, California, in Orange County, now home to the largest Vietnamese community outside of Vietnam. Those who had left in 1975, right after the end of the war and the American withdrawal, had been well-educated, wealthy, and connected with the military. My family was part of the wave of boat people—mostly middle-class and with little education—who sought refuge in America. 8

For nearly a year after we arrived, we crowded into the same three-bedroom apartment, all 13 of us: brothers, sisters, cousins, uncles, aunts, sisters-in-law, and my father's mother. There were only four of us children in my immediate family then, three born in Vietnam and one born shortly after our resettlement in the U.S.

We started school and watched Mr. Rogers on PBS in the afternoons, grew to love hamburgers and ketchup and longed to lose our accents. We older kids did lose our accents—and those who came later never had accents to begin with because they were born here. When we first came, I was the oldest of three children, all born in Vietnam. Now I have seven siblings, 22 years separating me from my youngest brother, who will start kindergarten in the fall.

In some ways, I was the stereotypical Asian nerd. I took honors classes, received good grades, and played the violin and cello. But there was a part of me that also yearned to be as American as my blond-haired neighbors across the street. I joined the school's swim and tennis teams, participated in speech competitions (which were attended by mostly white students) and worshipped Esprit and Guess. My first serious boyfriend was white but most of my friends were Asians who were either born in the U.S. or immigrated when they were very young. None of us had accents and we rarely spoke our native languages around one another. The last thing we wanted to be mistaken for was FOBs—fresh off the boat. I even changed my name to Kyrstin, unaware of its Nordic roots.

I wanted so badly to be a full-fledged American, whatever that meant. At home though, my parents pushed traditional Vietnamese values. I spent most of my teenage years baby-sitting and had to plead with my then overly strict parents to let me out of the house. "Please, please. I just want to be like any other American kid."

My parents didn't understand. "You'll always be Vietnamese. No one's going to look at you and say you're an American," was my mother's often-heard refrain.

I saw college as my escape, the beginning of the trip I would undertake on my own. We had come to America as a family but it was time I navigated alone. College was my flight from the house that always smelled of fish sauce and jasmine tea.

At UCLA, I dated the man who would become my husband. Though he's 17 years older than I am, my parents seemed to be more concerned with the cultural barriers than our age difference. "White Americans are fickle. They don't understand commitment and family responsibility like we Asians do," I was told.

Soon after I announced my engagement, my father, Minh Phu Ha, 16
and I had a rare and intimate conversation. "I'm just worried for you,"
he said. "All the Vietnamese women I know who have married whites
are divorced from them. Our cultures are too far apart."

My father, I think, is worried that none of his kids will marry Viet- 17
namese. My sisters are dating non-Vietnamese Asians while my brother
is dating a white American. "It's just that with a Vietnamese son-in-law,
I can talk to him," my father explained to me one day. "A Vietnamese
son-in-law would call me '*Ba*' and not by my first name."

Although my parents have come to terms with having Scott as their 18
son in-law and to the prospect of grandchildren who will be racially
mixed, there are still times when Scott comes to visit that there are awkward silences. There are still many cultural barriers.

I still think of what it all means to marry a white American. I worry 19
that my children won't be able to speak Vietnamese and won't appreciate that part of their heritage. I also wonder if somehow this is the ultimate fulfillment of a latent desire to be "American."

Vietnamese-Americans, like Chinese-Americans, Indian-Americans, 20
and other assimilated immigrants, often speak of leading hyphenated
lives, of feet that straddle both cultures. I've always been proud of being
Vietnamese. As my family and I discussed and heatedly debated what
the wedding event was going to look like, I began to realize just how
"American" I had become.

And yet there was no denying the pull of my Vietnamese roots. Four 21
months before the wedding, I traveled back to Vietnam for the second
time since our family's escape. It was a trip I had planned for more than
a year. I was in Saigon, the city of my birth, to research and write a
novel that loosely mirrors the story of my own family and our journey
from Vietnam. The novel is my tribute to my family and our past. I'm
writing it for myself as much as for my younger siblings, so they'll know
what our family's been through.

I returned to Vietnam to connect with something I can't really name 22
but know I lost when we left 20 years ago. I was about to start a new
journey with the marriage ahead, but I needed to come back to the place
where my family's journey began.

Scott came along for the first two weeks and met my extended fam- 23
ily. They all seemed to approve, especially when he showed he could eat
pungent fish and shrimp sauce like any other Vietnamese.

During my time there I visited often with family members and talked 24
about the past. I saw the hospital where I was born, took a walk

through our old house, chatted with my father's old friends. The gaps in the circle of my hyphenated life came closer together with every new Vietnamese word that I learned, with every Vietnamese friend that I made.

I also chose the fabric for the tailoring of the *ao dai*, the traditional   25 Vietnamese dress of a long tunic over flowing pants, which I would change into at the reception. I had my sisters' bridesmaid gowns made. And I had a velvet ao dai made for my 88-year-old maternal grandmother, *Bâ Ngoai,* to wear to the wedding of her oldest grandchild. "My dream is to see you on your wedding day and eat at your wedding feast," she had told me several times.

Bâ Ngoai came to the U.S. in 1983, three years after my family   26 landed in Orange County as war refugees. As soon as we got to the United States, my mother filed immigration papers for her. Bâ Ngoai made that journey at age 73, leaving the only home she had known to be with my mother, her only child. Bâ Ngoai nurtured and helped raise us grandchildren.

I had extended my stay in Vietnam. Several days after my original de-   27 parture date, I received a phone call. Bâ Ngoai had died. I flew home carrying her ao dai. We buried her in it.

In Vietnamese tradition, one is in mourning for three years after the   28 loss of a parent or grandparent. Out of respect and love for the deceased, or *hieu*, decorum dictates that close family members can't get married until after the mourning period is over. But my wedding was only a month and a half away.

On the day we buried my grandmother, my family advised me to   29 burn the white cloth headband that symbolized my grief. By burning it, I ended my official mourning.

Through my tears I watched the white cloth become wispy ashes. My   30 family was supportive. "It's your duty to remember and honor her," my father told me. "But you also need to move forward with your life."

On the morning of our wedding, Scott's family stood outside our   31 house in a line bearing dowry gifts. Inside the house, Scott and I lighted incense in front of the family altar. Holding the incense between our palms, we bowed to my ancestors and asked for their blessings. I looked at the photo of Bâ Ngoai and knew she had to be smiling.

Thinking about the Essay

1. How do you interpret the title? What aspects of the essay does it capture?

2. There are several characters in this essay. Who are they? How are they described? What sort of persona does Ha create for herself as the "I" narrator?

3. Why does Ha begin the essay in the present and then shift to the past? Trace the narrative pattern throughout her essay.

4. Often when you write a personal essay, it is valuable to create a central conflict. What is the conflict (or conflicts) in this selection? How does Ha develop and resolve it? Does this conflict lead to a thesis? Why or why not?

5. Explain the various moods and tones that Ha imbues her narrative with. Do they "clash" or not? Are they finally reconciled? Justify your response.

Responding in Writing

6. In a brief essay, explain why Ha's essay tells us about the clash of civilizations and how we might resolve it.

7. Write a narrative essay in which you tell of a relationship in which the people come from different civilizations. You can base this essay on personal experience, the experience of family or friends, or a situation drawn from television or film.

8. Do you think that the narrator and her husband will have a happy marriage? Why or why not? Cite what you have learned about them in the essay as support for your response.

Networking

9. In a group of four, discuss the relationship between Scott and "Kyrstin" Oanh. Do you think it is healthy and viable, or do you sense potential problems? Summarize your decision for the rest of the class.

10. Search the Internet for more information on the Vietnamese boat people. Where have they settled in the United States? How do they preserve their culture and civilization? How often do they intermarry with Americans outside their background? Discuss your findings with the class.

The West and the Rest: Intercivilizational Issues

SAMUEL P. HUNTINGTON

The late Samuel Phillips Huntington was born in New York City in 1927. He received his education at Yale University (B.A., 1946), the University of Chicago (M.A., 1948), and Harvard University (Ph.D., 1951). A leading authority on international affairs, Huntington worked and consulted for numerous government and private organizations, including the National Security

Council, the National War College, and the Office of the Secretary of Defense. He was professor of government at Harvard University and director of its Center for Strategic Studies up to the time of his death in 2008. Among his many books are *The Soldier and the State* (1957), *Political Order in Changing Societies* (1968), *American Military Strategy* (1986), and *The Clash of Civilizations and the Remaking of World Order* (1996), from which this essay is taken.

Before Reading

Do you think that Western civilization is under assault from Islamic, Chinese, or other civilizations? Why or why not?

Western Universalism

In the emerging world, the relations between states and groups from different civilizations will not be close and will often be antagonistic. Yet some intercivilization relations are more conflict-prone than others. At the micro level, the most violent fault lines are between Islam and its Orthodox, Hindu, African, and Western Christian neighbors. At the macro level, the dominant division is between "the West and the rest," with the most intense conflicts occurring between Muslim and Asian societies on the one hand, and the West on the other. The dangerous clashes of the future are likely to arise from the interaction of Western arrogance, Islamic intolerance, and Sinic assertiveness. 1

Alone among civilizations the West has had a major and at times devastating impact on every other civilization. The relation between the power and culture of the West and the power and cultures of other civilizations is, as a result, the most pervasive characteristic of the world of civilizations. As the relative power of other civilizations increases, the appeal of Western culture fades and non-Western peoples have increasing confidence in and commitment to their indigenous cultures. The central problem in the relations between the West and the rest is, consequently, the discordance between the West's—particularly America's—efforts to promote a universal Western culture and its declining ability to do so. 2

The collapse of communism exacerbated this discordance by reinforcing in the West the view that its ideology of democratic liberalism 3 had triumphed globally and hence was universally valid. The West, and especially the United States, which has always been a missionary nation, believe that the non-Western peoples should commit themselves to the Western values of democracy, free markets, limited government, human rights, individualism, the rule of law, and should embody these values in their institutions. Minorities in other civilizations embrace and promote these values, but the dominant attitudes toward them in non-Western cultures range from widespread skepticism to intense opposition. What is universalism to the West is imperialism to the rest.

The West is attempting and will continue to attempt to sustain its pre-eminent position and defend its interests by defining those interests as the interests of the "world community." That phrase has become the euphemistic collective noun (replacing "the Free World") to give global legitimacy to actions reflecting the interests of the United States and other Western powers. The West is, for instance, attempting to integrate the economies of non-Western societies into a global economic system which it dominates. Through the IMF and other international economic institutions, the West promotes its economic interests and imposes on other nations the economic policies it thinks appropriate. In any poll of non-Western peoples, however, the IMF undoubtedly would win the support of finance ministers and a few others but get an overwhelmingly unfavorable rating from almost everyone else, who would agree with Georgi Arbatov's description of IMF officials as "neo-Bolsheviks who love expropriating other people's money, imposing undemocratic and alien rules of economic and political conduct and stifling economic freedom."[1]

Non-Westerners also do not hesitate to point to the gaps between Western principle and Western action. Hypocrisy, double standards, and "but nots" are the price of Universalist pretensions. Democracy is promoted but not if it brings Islamic fundamentalists to power; nonproliferation is preached for Iran and Iraq but not for Israel; free trade is the elixir of economic growth but not for agriculture; human rights are an issue with China but not with Saudi Arabia; aggression against oil-owning Kuwaitis is massively repulsed but not against non-oil-owning Bosnians. Double standards in practice are the unavoidable price of universal standards of principle.

Having achieved political independence, non-Western societies wish to free themselves from Western economic, military, and cultural domination. East Asian societies are well on their way to equaling the West economically. Asian and Islamic countries are looking for shortcuts to

1. Georgi Arbatov, "Neo-Bolsheviks of the I.M.F.," *New York Times*, 7 May 1992, p. A27.

balance the West militarily. The universal aspirations of Western civilization, the declining relative power of the West, and the increasing cultural
assertiveness of other civilizations ensure generally difficult relations
between the West and the rest. The nature of those relations and the
extent to which they are antagonistic, however, vary considerably and
fall into three categories. With the challenger civilizations, Islam and
China, the West is likely to have consistently strained and often highly
antagonistic relations. Its relations with Latin America and Africa,
weaker civilizations which have in some measure been dependent on the
West, will involve much lower levels of conflict, particularly with Latin
America. The relations of Russia, Japan, and India to the West are likely
to fall between those of the other two groups, involving elements of
cooperation and conflict, as these three core states at times line up with
the challenger civilizations and at times side with the West. They are the
"swing" civilizations between the West, on the one hand, and Islamic
and Sinic civilizations, on the other.

Islam and China embody great cultural traditions very different from   7
and in their eyes infinitely superior to that of the West. The power and
assertiveness of both in relation to the West are increasing, and the conflicts between their values and interests and those of the West are multi-
plying and becoming more intense. Because Islam lacks a core state, its
relations with the West vary greatly from country to country. Since the
1970s, however, a fairly consistent anti-Western trend has existed,
marked by the rise of fundamentalism, shifts in power within Muslim
countries from more pro-Western to more anti-Western governments, the
emergence of a quasi war between some Islamic groups and the West, and
the weakening of the Cold War security ties that existed between some
Muslim states and the United States. Underlying the differences on specific
issues is the fundamental question of the role these civilizations will play
relative to the West in shaping the future of the world. Will the global
institutions, the distribution of power, and the politics and economies of
nations in the twenty-first century primarily reflect Western values and
interests or will they be shaped primarily by those of Islam and China? . . .

The issues that divide the West and these other societies are increas-   8
ingly important on the international agenda. Three such issues involve the
efforts of the West: (1) to maintain its military superiority through policies
of nonproliferation and counter proliferation with respect to nuclear, biological, and chemical weapons and the means to deliver them; (2) to promote Western political values and institutions by pressing other societies
to respect human rights as conceived in the West and to adopt democracy

on Western lines; and (3) to protect the cultural, social, and ethnic integrity of Western societies by restricting the number of non-Westerners admitted as immigrants or refugees. In all three areas the West has had and is likely to continue to have difficulties defending its interests against those of non-Western societies. . . .

The changing balance of power among civilizations makes it more 9 and more difficult for the West to achieve its goals with respect to weapons proliferation, human rights, immigration, and other issues. To minimize its losses in this situation requires the West to wield skillfully its economic resources as carrots and sticks in dealing with other societies, to bolster its unity and coordinate its policies so as to make it more difficult for other societies to play one Western country off against another, and to promote and exploit differences among non-Western nations. The West's ability to pursue these strategies will be shaped by the nature and intensity of its conflicts with the challenger civilizations, on the one hand, and the extent to which it can identify and develop common interests with the swing civilizations, on the other.

Thinking about the Essay

1. How would you characterize the tone of this essay? Does Huntington present himself as argumentative, opinioned, objective, fair-minded, liberal, conservative, or what? Identify words, sentences, and passages that support your assessment of the writer's voice.

2. Summarize Huntington's argument. What is his thesis or claim? What types of support does he provide?

3. What aspects of Huntington's language tell you that he writes for an audience that can follow his rapid sweep of the civilizations and institutions of the world? To what extent does he employ "loaded" language to advance his argument? Explain.

4. Huntington employs numerous rhetorical strategies to develop his argument, among them comparison and contrast, classification, and illustration. Locate examples of these strategies in the essay.

5. What, in Huntington's view, is the answer to the clash of civilizations? How does he prepare the reader for his answer? Trace the "logic" of his answer through the essay.

Responding in Writing

6. Compare and contrast the essays by Ha and Huntington. Establish a clear thesis concerning their views about the conflict of civilizations, and the different ways they approach the subject. Develop at least three key topics.

7. Do you agree or disagree with Huntington's analysis and argument? Explain your response in an argumentative paper of your own.

8. Respond in an analytical essay to Huntington's statement, "Alone among civilizations the West has had a major and at times devastating impact on every other civilization."

Networking

9. Discuss Huntington's essay in groups of three or four. Draw up a list of all the key elements in his argument. Then join a general class discussion on why his argument has caused so much controversy.

10. Go online and conduct an advanced search on "Samuel Huntington" AND "Clash of Civilizations." How has the debate developed since the time Huntington first published his ideas? Summarize the controversy in a brief paper.

The Light

HISHAM MATAR

Hisham Matar is a Libyan novelist, poet, and essayist who was born in New York City in 1950, the son of an official who worked for the Libyan mission to the United Nations. At the age of three, Hisham returned with his parents to Tripoli, but in 1979, his father fled to Cairo with the family in order to avoid persecution by the Gaddafi regime. (Libyan agents kidnapped his father in Cairo in 1990; he has not been seen since.) In 1986, Matar moved to London where he completed an undergraduate degree in architecture and an M.A. in design. His debut novel, *In the Country of Men*, was shortlisted for England's prestigious Man Booker Prize in 2006. Matar's second novel, *Anatomy of a Disappearance*, was published in 2011 at a time when he was a visiting professor at Barnard College in Manhattan. Matar's essays have appeared in several major journals in the United States and Great Britain. In this essay from the September 12, 2011, issue of *The New Yorker*, Hisham uses a vivid poetic style in order to expose conflicts between and within clashing civilizations.

Before Reading

Can a landscape—a sunny seashore or a bleak stretch of terrain—affect one's thoughts and emotions? Can the environment also influence one's cultural and political behavior? Why or why not?

There is an hour in the Arab Mediterranean when the sun, as if in a state of indecision, hovers a palm's length above the horizon. What a few hours earlier was a blinding star is now weak enough to look at directly. Its sideways light holds everything in a soft orange glow: the color of reticence and doubt, the color of my generation of Libyans and the historical moment we inherited. But it also signals hope, the possibility of a different future, where we might one day live free from totalitarian rule, and independent of the intrusive foreign powers that colluded with our dictators. For our entire lives we have been held between these two forces, and this late-afternoon light, different from anywhere else in the world, seemed suggestive both of our entrapment and of our yearning.

We lived out our lives in a theatre of the macabre and the absurd. We would listen to endless speeches, and we would clap. We endured the disappearances, the assassinations, and never managed to completely ignore the sweet-colored posters of our grinning leaders. On the outside, the countries we admired, Europe and America, paid us the insult of befriending our dictators and, when it came to our suffering, looking the other way. It did not escape us that these external powers exercised a new form of political control over our affairs. We called it "remote-control colonialism." I still remember a speech by the late Egyptian President Anwar al-Sadat. I was a boy, and we were by the sea. Someone was grilling fish—I remember the smell of fish. Of the speech itself, all that remains in my head is one line, spoken by Sadat in the tone of an irritated adult: "99.9 per cent of the playing cards are with America." I remembered the shared silence among the people sitting around me, and what it meant—the realization that America's blessing was needed for all Egypt's dealings with the world. Even I understood the metaphor: the "playing cards" were not only our present but also our future—in short, our fate.

Save for a few extraordinary exceptions—Palestine, for example—my generation was born well after foreign occupiers had left our lands. Yet the independence we inherited was elusive, as elusive as our late afternoons. The older and bloodier our dictators became, the more grandiose was their language. To maintain their legitimacy, they liked to recall darker times, when the "boot of the European pressed on our necks." The words they chose, their posturing, smothered us. Our leaders were not only violent; they also corrupted our imagination. Dictatorship is the triumph of kitsch, as Ryszard Kapuscinski noted, and my generation has been aggressively and comprehensively exposed to the conning powers of this sort of bloodstained kitsch. Our lives have been lived within its logic. It decided what we read, watched, and heard. It influenced even the words we chose to express love, or how we felt about the moon and the sunset. It intervened whenever we veered off the path. It spoke in one note, monotonous and intolerant. When we hesitated, it did not explain; it simply repeated its orders, with greater ferocity. Worst of all, we slowly learned to obey.

Even when I was a young boy playing in the garden of our house in 4 Tripoli in the late afternoon, while my family and the whole world, it seemed, napped, I found that afternoon light both mesmeric and unsettling. It was only during this hour that the audacious yet cynical political language of our leaders fell silent. It was the hour most appropriate for contemplating the conundrum we were in; for realizing that the dictator had perfected his art and that, paradoxically, now that we were "independent," foreign intrusion in our politics and our economics was even more sinister, because it seemed impossible to resist. These circumstances inspired self-loathing in us, a sort of Beckettian pessimism: We can't be tools, we are tools, we will be tools.

One of the more perverse symptoms of this despair was extremism: 5 inarticulate, devastating, and violent. It expressed, in the most grotesque way, our hopelessness as well as the bleak landscape of our political imagination. It disturbed us and silenced us, making us even more reticent in the modern world. In hindsight, shame was not an inappropriate response.

Like picadors taunting a wounded bull, we watched as all the West- 6 ern silliness that we were already used to grew more heightened. We saw Western commentators become hysterical whenever the subject of Islam came up. Reductive interpreters of Arab life and history, people such as Bernard Lewis, were suddenly in vogue again. But, at last, when our isolation and our despondency became utterly desperate, we rose.

The Arab Spring is a powerful and compelling response not only to 7 an age of tyranny but also to the remnant chains of imperial influence. The final outcome—if there ever is such a thing as a final outcome in history—of our revolutions remains unclear. We might not succeed in building a better future. But no one can question the authenticity of our desire, or how much we are prepared to sacrifice for the opportunity to gain self-determination, dignity, and justice. Although the light persists, it is no longer melancholy. It suddenly seems an ally, its weak warmth on the skin comforting. When the sun sets now, our nights are calm. And we pray; farewell to the abyss.

Thinking about the Essay

1. In what way is the title for the essay symbolic? What types of **figurative language** does Matar use to develop and enhance his key symbol? How does his focus on the light of the Arab Mediterranean produce a specific mood?

2. State Matar's claim or major proposition. Where does his claim appear most clearly? What minor propositions does he develop?

3. What purpose might he have for incorporating anecdotes from his childhood?

4. Explain the allusions to Anwar al-Sadat (paragraph 2), Ryszard Kapuscinski (paragraph 3), ''Beckettian pessimism'' (paragraph 4), and Bernard Lewis (paragraph 6). How do these allusions contribute to your understanding of the writer and his goal in composing this essay?

5. Analyze the comparative framework of this essay. What are the main elements and ideas that Matar compares and contrasts?

Responding in Writing

6. Write an expository essay in which you respond to Matar's statement, ''The Arab Spring is a powerful and compelling response not only to an age of tyranny but also to the remnant chains of imperial influence.''

7. Argue for or against the proposition that environment is destiny.

8. Write a narrative and descriptive essay in which you tell of a time and event that helped you to understand conflicts between peoples, cultures, and civilizations.

Networking

9. In small groups, discuss the interaction of poetry and prose in ''The Light.'' Evaluate the success of Matar's approach to writing, and share your evaluation with the class.

10. With several classmates, create a Facebook group that raises awareness about political conditions in one nation affected by the Arab Spring.

When Afghanistan Was at Peace

MARGARET ATWOOD

> Margaret Atwood, born in 1939, is a Canadian novel-
> ist, poet, short story writer, essayist, and literary critic
> whose work explores the troubled contours of the mod-
> ern world. Atwood's second collection of poetry, *The
> Circle Game* (1966), was published to critical acclaim.
> Equally impressive is a distinguished series of novels,
> including *Life Before Man* (1979), *The Handmaid's
> Tale* (1986), *Cat's Eye* (1988), *The Blind Assassin*
> (2000), *The Penelopiad* (2005), and *The Year of the
> Flood* (2009). Atwood's writing often blends the
> intensely personal experience with global realities. In
> "When Afghanistan Was at Peace," published in October
> 2001 in *The New York Times Magazine*, Atwood
> describes a world ruined by clashing civilizations.

Before Reading

Reflect on what you know about Afghanistan. How many "civilizations" have
attempted to conquer and control it? Why is the United States fighting in
Afghanistan today? What problems do you foresee for Afghanistan's future?

In February 1978, almost 23 years ago, I visited Afghanistan with my 1
spouse, Graeme Gibson, and our 18-month-old daughter. We went
there almost by chance: we were on our way to the Adelaide literary festival in Australia. Pausing at intervals, we felt, would surely be easier on a
child's time clock. (Wrong, as it turned out.) We thought Afghanistan
would make a fascinating two-week stopover. Its military history
impressed us—neither Alexander the Great nor the British in the 19th century had stayed in the country long because of the ferocity of its warriors.

"Don't go to Afghanistan," my father said when told of our plans. 2
"There's going to be a war there." He was fond of reading history
books. "As Alexander the Great said, Afghanistan is easy to march into
but hard to march out of." But we hadn't heard any other rumors of
war, so off we went.

We were among the last to see Afghanistan in its days of relative 3
peace—relative, because even then there were tribal disputes and superpowers in play. The three biggest buildings in Kabul were the Chinese

Source: From *Writing with Intent* by Margaret Atwood. Copyright © 2006 Margaret Atwood.
Reprinted by permission of Basic Books, a member of the Perseus Books Group.

Embassy, the Soviet Embassy and the American Embassy, and the head of the country was reportedly playing the three against one another.

The houses of Kabul were carved wood, and the streets were like a living "Book of Hours": people in flowing robes, camels, donkeys, carts with huge wooden wheels being pushed and pulled by men at either end. There were few motorized vehicles. Among them were buses covered with ornate Arabic script, with eyes painted on the front so the buses could see where they were going.

4

We managed to hire a car in order to see the terrain of the famous and disastrous British retreat from Kabul to Jalalabad. The scenery was breathtaking: jagged mountains and the "Arabian Nights" dwellings in the valleys—part houses, part fortresses—reflected in the enchanted blue-green of the rivers. Our driver took the switchback road at breakneck speed since we had to be back before sundown because of bandits.

5

The men we encountered were friendly and fond of children: our curly-headed, fair-haired child got a lot of attention. The winter coat I wore had a large hood so that I was sufficiently covered and did not attract undue notice. Many wanted to talk; some knew English, while others spoke through our driver. But they all addressed Graeme exclusively. To have spoken to me would have been impolite. And yet when our interpreter negotiated our entry into an all-male teahouse, I received nothing worse than uneasy glances. The law of hospitality toward visitors ranked higher than the no-women-in-the-teahouse custom. In the hotel, those who served meals and cleaned rooms were men, tall men with scars either from dueling or from the national sport, played on horseback, in which gaining possession of a headless calf is the aim.

6

Girls and women we glimpsed on the street wore the chador, the long, pleated garment with a crocheted grill for the eyes that is more comprehensive than any other Muslim cover-up. At that time, you often saw chic boots and shoes peeking out from the hem. The chador wasn't obligatory back then; Hindu women didn't wear it. It was a cultural custom, and since I had grown up hearing that you weren't decently dressed without a girdle and white gloves, I thought I could understand such a thing. I also knew that clothing is a symbol, that all symbols are ambiguous and that this one might signify a fear of women or a desire to protect them from the gaze of strangers. But it could also mean more negative things, just as the color red can mean love, blood, life, royalty, good luck—or sin.

7

I bought a chador in the market. A jovial crowd of men gathered around, amused by the spectacle of a Western woman picking out such

8

a non-Western item. They offered advice about color and quality. Purple was better than light green or the blue, they said. (I bought the purple.) Every writer wants the Cloak of Invisibility—the power to see without being seen—or so I was thinking as I donned the chador. But once I had put it on, I had an odd sense of having been turned into negative space, a blank in the visual field, a sort of antimatter—both there and not there. Such a space has power of a sort, but it is a passive power, the power of taboo.

Several weeks after we left Afghanistan, the war broke out. My   9 father was right, after all. Over the next years, we often remembered the people we met and their courtesy and curiosity. How many of them are now dead, through no fault of their own?

Six years after our trip, I wrote *The Handmaid's Tale*, a speculative   10 fiction about an American theocracy. The women in that book wear outfits derived in part from nuns' costumes, partly from girls' schools' hemlines and partly—I must admit—from the faceless woman on the Old Dutch Cleanser box, but also partly from the chador I acquired in Afghanistan and its conflicting associations. As one character says, there is freedom to and freedom from. But how much of the first should you have to give up in order assuring the second? All cultures have had to grapple with that and our own—as we are now seeing—is no exception. Would I have written the book if I never had visited Afghanistan? Possibly. Would it have been the same? Unlikely.

Thinking about the Essay

1. Does Atwood provide a thesis sentence in this essay? Why or why not? How does her title imply a thesis? If you were writing a thesis sentence of your own for this essay, what would it be?

2. What is Atwood's purpose in writing this narrative essay? Consider that this essay was published shortly after the events of 9/11. Is narration an appropriate strategy for her purpose? Why or why not?

3. Narrative essays typically use description to flesh out the story. Find descriptive details that Atwood provides, and explain what these details contribute to the overall effect.

4. Analyze the point of view in this essay. Is Atwood an observer, a participant, or both? Is she neutral or involved? Support your opinion.

5. Consider the relationship of the introductory paragraphs to the conclusion. Why does Atwood use the introduction and conclusion to expand the time frame of her main narrative?

Responding in Writing

6. Write an **editorial** for your college newspaper supporting or attacking the role of Western powers in Afghanistan today.

7. Imagine that you are traveling to Afghanistan on assignment for a newspaper. Report back, telling readers about what you see and where you go. Feel free to research the subject prior to writing the essay.

8. What does Atwood say about the clash of civilizations in this essay? Answer this question by analyzing the strategies she uses to convey her thesis.

Networking

9. In groups of two or three, pool your knowledge of Afghanistan. Prepare a brief report to be presented to the class.

10. In her essay, Atwood alludes to some of the nations and civilizations that have tried to conquer Afghanistan over the centuries. For research, conduct a library or Internet search on the history of Afghanistan and how it has been a crossroads in the clash of civilizations. Prepare a brief report on your findings.

Fundamentalism Is Here to Stay

KAREN ARMSTRONG

Karen Armstrong is one of the most highly regarded commentators on religion in North America and Europe. She currently teaches Christianity at the Leo Baeck College Centre for Jewish Education in London. Armstrong joined a Catholic convent at the age of seventeen but left her order after seven years. Her experience as a nun, and her departure from the Catholic Church, are recounted in the autobiographical *Through the Narrow Gates* (1982). Armstrong now describes herself as a "freelance monotheist" and compares religion to a raft: "Once you get across the river, moor the raft and go on. Don't lug it with you if you don't need it anymore." Armstrong's recent books include *The Battle for God: A History of Fundamentalism* (2001), *Islam: A Short History* (2001), and *The Great Transformation: The Beginning of Our Religious Traditions* (2006). In the following essay, which appeared on globalagendamagazine.com in 2005, Armstrong defines religious fundamentalism as a reaction to—and a clash with—the perceived values of a secular modernity.

Source: Karen Armstrong, "Fundamentalism Is Here to Stay" © 2005 Karen Armstrong and reprinted by kind permission of the author.

Before Reading

How do you define *fundamentalism*? Do you see the fundamentalist impulse as a feature common to all religions? Are there differences in degree or kind?

In the middle of the 20th century, it was generally assumed that secu-   1
larism was the coming ideology and that religion would never again play a major role in world events. Today, religion dominates the headlines, and this is due in no small part to the militant piety that has developed in every single major world faith over the past century.

We usually call it "fundamentalism." Fundamentalist groups have   2
staged revolutions, assassinated presidents, carried out terrorist atrocities and become an influential political force in strongly secularist nations. There has, for example, been much discussion about the role of Protestant fundamentalism in the recent American elections. It is no longer possible to dismiss fundamentalism as a passing phase.

Fundamentalism Is Not . . .

We should begin by defining what fundamentalism is not. First, it should   3
not be equated with religious conservatism. Leading American religious revivalist Billy Graham, for example, is not a fundamentalist.

Second, fundamentalism should not be linked automatically with vio-   4
lence. Only a tiny proportion of fundamentalists worldwide take part in acts of terror. The rest are simply struggling to live what they regard as a good religious life in a world that seems increasingly inimical to faith.

Third, fundamentalism is not an exclusively Islamic phenomenon.   5
There are fundamentalist Jews, Christians, Hindus, Buddhists, Sikhs and Confucians, who all challenge the secular hegemony of the modern world. In fact, Islam developed a fundamentalist strain long after it had erupted in Judaism and Christianity.

Fundamentalism Is . . .

So what is fundamentalism? It is essentially a revolt against modern secu-   6
lar society. Wherever a western polity has been established that separates religion and politics, fundamentalist movements have sprung up in protest. Whatever the politicians or the pundits claim, people worldwide are demonstrating that they want to see religion reflected more prominently in public life. As part of their campaign, fundamentalists tend to withdraw from mainstream society to create enclaves of pure faith.

Typical examples are the Ultra-orthodox Jewish communities in New   7
York or the fundamentalist Christianity of Bob Jones University in South

Carolina. Here fundamentalists build a counterculture, in conscious defiance of the godless world that surrounds them, and from these communities some undertake a counteroffensive designed to drag God or religion back to centre stage from the wings to which they have been relegated in modern secular culture.

This campaign is rarely violent. It usually consists of a propaganda 8 or welfare effort. In the United States, for example, the fundamentalist riposte attempts to reform school textbooks or to get Christian candidates elected to government posts. But if warfare is endemic in a region and has become chronic—as in the Middle East or Afghanistan—fundamentalists can get sucked into the violence that pervades the whole of society. In this way, originally secular disputes such as the Arab-Israeli conflict have been sacralized, on both sides.

The Road to Modernity

The ubiquity of the fundamentalist revolt shows that there is widespread 9 disappointment with modernity. But what is it about the modern world that has provoked such rage and distress? In the 16th century, the peoples of the west began to develop a new type of civilization unprecedented in world history. Instead of basing their economy on a surplus of agricultural produce, as did all premodern cultures, they relied increasingly on technology and the constant reinvestment of capital, which freed them from the inherent limitations of agrarian society. This demanded radical change at all levels of society—intellectual, political, social and religious. A wholly new way of thinking became essential, and new forms of government had to evolve to meet these altered conditions. It was found by trial and error that the best way of creating a productive society was to create a secular, tolerant, democratic polity.

It took Europe some 300 years to modernize, and the process was 10 wrenching and traumatic, involving bloody revolutions, often succeeded by reigns of terror, brutal holy wars, dictatorships, cruel exploitation of the workforce, the despoliation of the countryside, and widespread alienation and anomie.

We are now witnessing the same kind of upheaval in developing 11 countries presently undergoing modernization. But some of these countries have had to attempt this difficult process far too rapidly and are forced to follow a western program, rather than their own.

This accelerated modernization has created deep divisions in developing nations. Only an elite has a western education that enables them to understand the new modern institutions. The vast majority remains 12 trapped in the premodern ethos. They experience the incomprehensible change as profoundly disturbing, and cling to traditional religion for support. But as modernization progresses, people find that they cannot be religious in the old way and try to find new means of expressing their piety. Fundamentalism is just one of these attempts, and it therefore develops only after a degree of modernization has been achieved.

The modern spirit that developed in the west had two essential char-   13 acteristics: independence and innovation. Modernization in Europe and America proceeded by declarations of independence on all fronts— religious, political and intellectual—as scientists and inventors demanded the freedom to develop their ideas without interference from religious or political authorities. Further, despite the trauma of modernization, it was exciting, because the western countries were continually meeting new challenges and creating something fresh. But in some developing countries, modernization came not with independence, but with colonial dependence and subjugation, and the west was so far ahead that these could not innovate but only imitate. So they find it difficult to develop a truly modern spirit. A nation such as Japan, which was not colonized, was able to make its own distinctive contribution to the modern economy in a way that some Middle Eastern countries have not been able to do.

A Fight for Survival

Culture is always contested, and fundamentalists are primarily concerned   14 with saving their own society. Protestant fundamentalists in the United States want America to be a truly Christian nation, not a secular, pluralist republic. In Palestine, Hamas began by attacking the Palestine Liberation Organization, because it wanted the Palestinian resistance to be inspired by an Islamic rather than a secular polity. Osama bin Laden started by targeting the Saudi royal family and such secularist rulers as Saddam Hussein. Only at a secondary stage—if at all—do fundamentalists begin to attack a foreign foe. Thus fundamentalism does not represent a clash between civilizations, but a clash within civilizations.

Perhaps the most important factor to understand about this wide-   15 spread religious militancy is its rootedness in a deep fear of annihilation. Every fundamentalist movement I have studied in Judaism, Christianity and Islam is convinced that modern secular society wants to wipe out religion—even in America. Fundamentalists, therefore, believe they are fighting for survival, and when people feel that their backs are to the wall, some can strike out violently. This profound terror of annihilation is not as paranoid as it may at first appear. Jewish fundamentalism, for example, gained fresh momentum after World War II, when Hitler had tried to exterminate European Jewry, and after the 1973 October War, when Israelis felt vulnerable and isolated in the Middle East.

In some Muslim countries, modernization has usually been so accelerated that secularism has been experienced as an assault. When Mustafa Kemal Ataturk created modern secular Turkey, he closed down all the madrasahs (traditional institutes for higher education in Islamic studies) and abolished the Sufi orders. He also forced all men and women to wear Western dress. Reformers such as Ataturk wanted their countries to look modern. In Iran, the shahs used to make their soldiers walk through the streets with their bayonets out, tearing off women's veils and ripping them to pieces. In 1935, Shah Reza Pahlavi gave his soldiers orders to shoot at unarmed demonstrators in Mashhad (one of the holiest shrines in Iran), who were peacefully protesting against obligatory Western clothes. Hundreds of Iranians died that day. In such circumstances, secularism was not experienced as liberating and civilized, but as wicked, lethal and murderously hostile to faith.

The main fundamentalist ideology of Sunni Islam developed in the concentration camps in Egypt in which president Jamal Abd al-Nasser had incarcerated thousands of members of the Muslim Brotherhood in the late 1950s, without trial and often for doing nothing more incriminating than attending a meeting or handing out leaflets. One of these prisoners was Sayyid Qutb, who was executed by Nasser in 1966. Qutb went into the camp as a moderate and a liberal. But in these vile prisons, watching the Brothers being executed and subjected to mental and physical torture, and hearing Nasser vowing to relegate Islam to a marginal role in Egypt, he came to regard secularism as a great evil. He developed an ideology of committed armed struggle against this threat to the faith. His chief disciple today is Osama bin Laden.

Thus fundamentalism usually develops in a symbiotic relationship with a secularism that is experienced as hostile and invasive. Every fundamentalist movement I have studied in each of the three monotheistic traditions has developed in direct response to what is perceived as a secularist attack. The more vicious the assault, the more extreme the fundamentalist riposte is likely to be. Because fundamentalists fear that secularists want to destroy them, aggressive and military action will only serve to confirm this conviction and exacerbate their fear, which can spill over into ungovernable rage.

Thus membership of al-Qaeda has increased since the recent Gulf   19
War. The offensive has convinced many Muslims that the West has
really inaugurated a new crusade against the Islamic world. In the
United States, Protestant fundamentalists in the smaller towns and rural
areas often feel "colonized" by the alien ethos of Harvard, Yale and
Washington, DC. They feel that the liberal establishment despises them,
and this has resulted in a fundamentalism that has gone way beyond
Jerry Falwell and the Moral Majority of the 1970s. (Falwell is an American fundamentalist Baptist pastor, televangelist and founder of the
Moral Majority—a group dedicated to promoting its conservative and
religious Christian-centric beliefs via support of political candidates.)
Some groups, such as the Christian Reconstructionists, look forward to
the imminent destruction of the federal government; the blazing towers
of the World Trade Center would not be alien to their ideology. When
liberals deplore the development and persistence of fundamentalism in
their own societies and worldwide, they should be aware that the
excesses of secularists have all too often been responsible for this radical
alienation.

Here to Stay

Fundamentalism is not going to disappear, as secularists once imagined   20
that religion would modestly retreat to the sidelines and confine itself to
private life. Fundamentalism is here to stay, and in Judaism, Christianity
and Islam, at least, it is becoming more extreme. Fundamentalism is not
confined to the "other" civilizations. A dangerous gulf has appeared,
dividing many societies against themselves. In the Middle East, India,
Pakistan, Israel and the United States, for example, fundamentalists and
secular liberals form two distinct camps, neither of which can understand
the other.

In the past, these movements were often dismissed with patrician dis-   21
dain. This has proved to be short-sighted. We have to take fundamentalism very seriously. Had the US made a greater effort to understand
Shiite Islam, for example, it might have avoided unnecessary errors in
the lead-up to the Iranian Revolution of 1978 to 79. The first step must
be to look beneath the bizarre and often repulsive ideology of these
movements to discern the disquiet and anger that lie at their roots. We
must no longer deride these theologies as the fantasies of a lunatic fringe,
but learn to decode their ideas and imagery. Only then can we deal crea-
tively with fears and anxieties that, as we have seen to our cost, no society can safely ignore.

Thinking about the Essay

1. Why does Armstrong define fundamentalism first by stating what it is *not*? How do you respond to this tactic as a reader?

2. Where does Armstrong shift in the essay from definition to process analysis? How does Armstrong link the historical and economic factors that gave rise to modernity with the secular values that came to be associated with modernity? How is fundamentalism a response to modernity as both a process and a set of values?

3. Why does Armstrong make a point, throughout the essay, of dissociating the concept of fundamentalism from violence?

4. What examples does Armstrong give to acknowledge the militancy of twentieth century attempts at rapid modernization? Do these examples strengthen or weaken her definition of fundamentalism? How has Armstrong prepared for this acknowledgment earlier in the essay?

5. Describe the symbiotic relationship between fundamentalist terrorism and secular modernity.

Responding in Writing

6. Respond to the term *militant piety*, which some would read as an oxymoron. How can piety take this form? In a brief essay, consider some examples of militant piety and explain why the term would, in your opinion, apply in each case.

7. Fundamentalism, according to Armstrong, "does not represent a clash between civilizations, but a clash within civilizations." How does Armstrong's concept of fundamentalism refute or qualify Samuel P. Huntington's "clash of cultures" theory? In an evaluative essay, point to some limitations that you see in both theories.

8. In a brief essay, offer some advice to American foreign policymakers on how to promote modernization in a Middle Eastern nation (like Iraq) so that it would not be experienced or perceived as an "assault."

Networking

9. In groups of three or four, make a list of three religious leaders or public figures in the United States whose views everyone in the group agrees would qualify as "fundamentalist" (according to Armstrong's definition). Share the list with the class, and justify the application of the label to each person on the list.

10. Go online and read at least three reviews of Armstrong's *The Battle for God: A History of Fundamentalism*. Do any of the reviewers take exception to her definition of *fundamentalism*?

A World Not Neatly Divided

AMARTYA SEN | Amartya K. Sen, the 1998 Nobel Prize winner in economics, was born in 1933 in Santiniketan, India. After studying at Presidency College in Calcutta, Sen emigrated to England, where he received B.A. (1955), M.A., and Ph.D. (1959) degrees from Trinity College, Cambridge. Master of Trinity College since 1998, Sen also has taught at Oxford University, the London School of Economics, Harvard University, and Cornell University. Sen is credited with bringing ethical considerations into the study of economics. He has done groundbreaking work in establishing techniques for assessing world poverty and the relative wealth of nations, the causes of famine, and the economic impact of health and education on developing societies. His study, *Collective Choice and Social Welfare* (1970), in which he uses the tools of economics to study such concepts as fairness, liberty, and justice, brings to economic theory a dimension of moral philosophy that has made Sen an influential figure in contemporary thought. Other notable works include *Poverty and Famines: An Essay on Entitlement and Deprivation* (1981), *On Ethics and Economics* (1987), *Development as Freedom* (1999), *The Argumentative Indian: Writings on Indian History, Culture and Identity* (2005), *The Idea of Justice* (2009), and *Peace and Democratic Society* (2011). As this essay from *The New York Times,* published on November 23, 2001, demonstrates, Sen commands a lucid prose style that enables him to make complex issues accessible to general readers. Here, he argues for a more nuanced approach to the idea of civilization than the one posed by Samuel Huntington.

Before Reading

Is it necessary to divide the world into various types of civilizations? What is the purpose of such classification, and what are the possible results?

W hen people talk about clashing civilizations, as so many politicians   1
and academics do now, they can sometimes miss the central issue. The inadequacy of this thesis begins well before we get to the question

of whether civilizations must clash. The basic weakness of the theory lies in its program of categorizing people of the world according to a unique, allegedly commanding system of classification. This is problematic because civilizational categories are crude and inconsistent and also because there are other ways of seeing people (linked to politics, language, literature, class, occupation or other affiliations).

The befuddling influence of a singular classification also traps those 2 who dispute the thesis of a clash: To talk about "the Islamic world" or "the Western world" is already to adopt an impoverished vision of humanity as unalterably divided. In fact, civilizations are hard to partition in this way, given the diversities within each society as well as the linkages among different countries and cultures. For example, describing India as a "Hindu civilization" misses the fact that India has more Muslims than any other country except Indonesia and possibly Pakistan. It is futile to try to understand Indian art, literature, music, food or politics without seeing the extensive interactions across barriers of religious communities. These include Hindus and Muslims, Buddhists, Jains, Sikhs, Parsees, Christians (who have been in India since at least the fourth century, well before England's conversion to Christianity), Jews (present since the fall of Jerusalem), and even atheists and agnostics. Sanskrit has a larger atheistic literature than exists in any other classical language. Speaking of India as a Hindu civilization may be comforting to the Hindu fundamentalist, but it is an odd reading of India.

A similar coarseness can be seen in the other categories invoked, like 3 "the Islamic world." Consider Akbar and Aurangzeb, two Muslim emperors of the Mogul dynasty in India. Aurangzeb tried hard to convert Hindus into Muslims and instituted various policies in that direction, of which taxing the non-Muslims was only one example. In contrast, Akbar reveled in his multiethnic court and pluralist laws, and issued official proclamations insisting that no one "should be interfered with on account of religion" and that "anyone is to be allowed to go over to a religion that pleases him."

If a homogeneous view of Islam were to be taken, then only one of 4 these emperors could count as a true Muslim. The Islamic fundamentalist would have no time for Akbar; Prime Minister Tony Blair, given his insistence that tolerance is a defining characteristic of Islam, would have to consider excommunicating Aurangzeb. I expect both Akbar and Aurangzeb would protest, and so would I. A similar crudity is present in the characterization of what is called "Western civilization." Tolerance and individual freedom have certainly been present in European history. But there is no dearth of diversity here, either. When Akbar was making his pronouncements on religious tolerance in Agra, in the 1590's, the Inquisitions were still going on; in 1600, Giordano Bruno was burned at the stake, for heresy, in Campo dei Fiori in Rome.

Dividing the world into discrete civilizations is not just crude. It propels us into the absurd belief that this partitioning is natural and necessary and must overwhelm all other ways of identifying people. That imperious view goes not only against the sentiment that "we human beings are all much the same," but also against the more plausible understanding that we are diversely different. For example, Bangladesh's split from Pakistan was not connected with religion, but with language and politics.   5

Each of us has many features in our self-conception. Our religion, important as it may be, cannot be an all-engulfing identity. Even a shared poverty can be a source of solidarity across the borders. The kind of division highlighted by, say, the so-called "anti-globalization" protesters— whose movement is, incidentally, one of the most globalized in the world—tries to unite the underdogs of the world economy and goes firmly against religious, national or "civilizational" lines of division.   6

The main hope of harmony lies not in any imagined uniformity, but in the plurality of our identities, which cut across each other and work against sharp divisions into impenetrable civilizational camps. Political leaders who think and act in terms of sectioning off humanity into various "worlds" stand to make the world more flammable—even when their intentions are very different. They also end up, in the case of civilizations defined by religion, lending authority to religious leaders seen as spokesmen for their "worlds." In the process, other voices are muffled and other concerns silenced. The robbing of our plural identities not only reduces us; it impoverishes the world.   7

Thinking about the Essay

1. How does Sen begin his essay? What is his argument, and how does he present it in the opening paragraph?

2. Sen uses several illustrations to support his argument about "singular classification." Locate three of these examples and explain how they advance his claim.

3. Any discussion of types—whether types of civilizations or types of teachers—lends itself to classification. How does Sen use classification and **division** to organize his argument and his essay?

4. What transitional devices serve to unify this essay?

5. Does Sen's concluding paragraph serve to confirm his thesis or claim? Explain your answer.

Responding in Writing

6. What is so wrong about "singular classification," especially when considering nations, cultures, and civilizations? Write a response to this question, referring to Sen's essay in the process.

7. Write a complete analysis of the ways in which Sen composes his argument in "A World Not Neatly Divided."

8. Write a comparative paper analyzing the essays by Sen and Samuel Huntington.

Networking

9. In small groups, select a city, region, country, or civilization, and then draw up a list of traits or attributes—a singular classification—illuminating your subject. Present the list to class members, and as a group discuss the advantages and disadvantages of singular classification.

10. Conduct online research on an international city. Then write a travel blurb stressing both the singular nature of this city and also its diversity.

9

The Age of Terror: What Is the Just Response?

J ust as changes in U.S. demographics, patterns of cultural interaction, the forces of globalization, and the "clash" of civilizations have brought us into expanding contact with the peoples of the world, current events remind us that this new world can be exceedingly dangerous. Indeed, in the years since the September 11, 2001, attack, we have had to reorient our thinking about numerous critical issues: the war on terrorism; the erosion of our sense of individual and collective security; the need to achieve a balance between individual rights and common security. Above all, we now face the ethical, political, and historical challenge of dealing with the reality that although the United States is still the world's major superpower, other superpowers—notably China and India—are emerging as global rivals. There are people and nations who hate America's standing in the world. And hatred and cruelty, as Isaac Bashevis Singer, a winner of the Nobel Prize for Literature, once observed, only produce more of the same.

The 9/11 terrorist attack was so profoundly unnerving that virtually all of us can remember where we were when the planes hijacked by terrorists crashed into New York's World Trade Center and the Pentagon in Washington, DC. This was a primal national event, similar in impact to the raid on Pearl Harbor in 1941 or the assassinations of President John Kennedy and Martin Luther King Jr. in the 1960s. These prior events, whether taking the lives of thousands or just one, serve to define entire American generations. Today, the United States faces a new defining event or more accurately an unfolding series of events—first called the "war on terror" but now that phrase (as Reza Aslan explores in an essay appearing in this chapter) has been dropped by the Obama administration. Nevertheless, we do seem to be living in

Be a superpower! Destroy the Axis of Evil! One of several board
games reflecting our preoccupation with the war on terror.

Thinking about the Image

1. What is the designer's purpose in creating this image? What specific
   details support your response?

2. What is your first response to this image? Are you amused? Why or
   why not?

3. How do you think that the designer might respond to parents who
   object to this image, claiming that this "game" is inappropriate for
   children?

4. Go online and try to locate virtual games that exploit the "war on
   terror" theme. What can you conclude about terrorism's impact on
   Internet gaming and more generally on the contemporary mind?

an age of terror, and we have to find ways in which national and global
communities can deal with this unnerving reality.

In a sense, the September 11 attack and subsequent assaults—in Bali,
Spain, England, Africa, India, and elsewhere—have forced the United States
to look inward and outward for intelligent and effective responses. Looking
inward, we often have to deal with our own anger, insecurity, and hatred of
other peoples who commit these crimes against unsuspecting humanity.
These are primal emotions that affect our sense of personal identity. At the
same time, we must understand how others around the world view our
country and must gain knowledge of peoples and cultures we once knew
little or nothing about. For example, are the terrorists who planned and
launched the 9/11 attack a mere aberration—some delusional distortion of

the great culture and civilization of Islam? Or do they reflect the consensus of the Arab street? Where do college students—who should be committed to liberal learning—go to find answers to such large and complex questions? What courses exist on your campus? What organizations foster transnational or global understanding?

Ultimately—as writers in this chapter and throughout the text suggest—we have to read across cultures and nations to understand this new age of terror and its many manifestations: narcoterrorism, cyberterrorism, genocide, and more. We have to reflect on our own backgrounds. We have to be candid about how our individual experience molds our attitudes toward "others"—most of whom are like us but some of whom want to do us harm. Liberal education, as the American philosopher William James stated at the beginning of the last century, makes us less fanatical. Against the backdrop of contemporary terrorism, we have to search for wisdom and for sustaining values.

Where Nothing Says Everything

SUZANNE BERNE | Suzanne Berne, an American novelist, was born in Washington, DC, in 1961. She was educated at Wesleyan University and the Iowa Writers' Workshop. She has taught at several universities, most recently at Boston College, where she teaches creative writing. Her novels are *A Crime in the Neighborhood* (1997), *The Ghost at the Table* (1997), and *A Perfect Arrangement* (2001). Berne also has published a memoir about her grandmother, *Missing Lucile* (2010). The following essay on her visit to the devastated World Trade Center in the aftermath of 9/11, published in *The New York Times* on April 21, 2002, has become a contemporary classic.

Before Reading

Do you see yourself as part of what some commentators call the "post-9/11 generation"? Why or why not? What, in fact, do you know about September 11, 2001?

On a cold, damp March morning, I visited Manhattan's financial district, a place I'd never been, to pay my respects at what used to be the World Trade Center. Many other people had chosen to do the same that day, despite the raw wind and spits of rain, and so the first thing I   1 noticed when I arrived on the corner of Vesey and Church Streets was a crowd.

Standing on the sidewalk, pressed against aluminum police barri-   2
cades, wearing scarves that flapped into their faces and woolen hats pulled over their ears, were people apparently from everywhere. Germans, Italians, Japanese. An elegant-looking Norwegian family in matching shearling coats. People from Ohio and California and Maine. Children, middle-age couples, older people. Many of them were clutching cameras and video recorders, and they were all craning to see across the street, where there was nothing to see.

At least, nothing is what it first looked like, the space that is now   3
ground zero. But once your eyes adjust to what you are looking at, "nothing" becomes something much more potent, which is absence.

But to the out-of-towner, ground zero looks at first simply like a con-   4
struction site. All the familiar details are there: the wooden scaffolding; the cranes, the bulldozers and forklifts; the trailers and construction workers in hard hats; even the dust. There is the pound of jackhammers, the steady beep-beep-beep of trucks backing up, the roar of heavy machinery.

So much busyness is reassuring, and it is possible to stand looking at   5
the cranes and trucks and feel that mild curiosity and hopefulness so often inspired by construction sites.

Then gradually your eyes do adjust, exactly as if you have stepped   6
from a dark theater into a bright afternoon, because what becomes most striking about this scene is the light itself.

Ground zero is a great bowl of light, an emptiness that seems weirdly   7
spacious and grand, like a vast plaza amid the dense tangle of streets in lower Manhattan. Light reflecting off the Hudson River vaults into the site, soaking everything—especially on an overcast morning—with a watery glow. This is the moment when absence begins to assume a material form, when what is not there becomes visible.

Suddenly you notice the periphery, the skyscraper shrouded in black   8
plastic, the boarded windows, the steel skeleton of the shattered Winter Garden. Suddenly there are the broken steps and cracked masonry in front of Brooks Brothers. Suddenly there are the firefighters, the waiting ambulance on the other side of the pit, the police on every corner. Suddenly there is the enormous cross made of two rusted girders.

And suddenly, very suddenly, there is the little cemetery attached to   9
St. Paul's Chapel, with tulips coming up, the chapel and grounds miraculously undamaged except for a few plastic-sheathed gravestones. The

iron fence is almost invisible beneath a welter of dried pine wreaths, ban-
ners, ribbons, laminated poems and prayers and photographs, swags of
paper cranes, withered flowers, baseball hats, rosary beads, teddy bears.
And flags, flags everywhere, little American flags fluttering in the breeze,
flags on posters drawn by Brownie troops, flags on T-shirts, flags on
hats, flags streaming by, tied to the handles of baby strollers.

It takes quite a while to see all of this; it takes even longer to come   10
up with something to say about it.

An elderly man standing next to me had been staring fixedly across   11
the street for some time. Finally he touched his son's elbow and said: "I
watched those towers being built. I saw this place when they weren't
there." Then he stopped, clearly struggling with, what for him, was a
double negative, recalling an absence before there was an absence. His
son, waiting patiently, took a few photographs. "Let's get out of here,"
the man said at last.

Again and again I heard people say, "It's unbelievable." And then   12
they would turn to each other, dissatisfied. They wanted to say something more expressive, more meaningful. But it is unbelievable, to stare
at so much devastation, and know it for devastation, and yet recognize
that it does not look like the devastation one has imagined.

Like me, perhaps, the people around me had in mind images from tel-   13
evision and newspaper pictures: the collapsing buildings, the running
office workers, the black plume of smoke against a bright blue sky. Like
me, they were probably trying to superimpose those terrible images onto
the industrious emptiness right in front of them. The difficulty of this kind
of mental revision is measured, I believe, by the brisk trade in World
Trade Center photograph booklets at tables set up on street corners.

Determined to understand better what I was looking at, I decided to   14
get a ticket for the viewing platform beside St. Paul's. This proved no
easy task, as no one seemed to be able to direct me to South Street Seaport, where the tickets are distributed. Various police officers whom I
asked for directions, waved me vaguely toward the East River, differing
degrees of boredom and resignation on their faces. Or perhaps it was a
kind of incredulousness. Somewhere around the American Stock
Exchange, I asked a security guard for help and he frowned at me, saying, "You want tickets to the disaster?"

Finally I found myself in line at a cheerfully painted kiosk, watching   15
a young juggler try to entertain the crowd. He kept dropping the four
red balls he was attempting to juggle, and having to chase after them. It
was noon; the next available viewing was at 4 p.m.

Back I walked, up Fulton Street, the smell of fish in the air, to wan- 16
der again around St. Paul's. A deli on Vesey Street advertised a view of
the World Trade Center from its second-floor dining area. I went in and
ordered a pastrami sandwich, uncomfortably aware that many people
before me had come to that same deli for pastrami sandwiches who
would never come there again. But I was here to see what I could, so I
carried my sandwich upstairs and sat down beside one of the big plate-
glass windows.

And there, at last, I got my ticket to the disaster.   17

I could see not just into the pit now, but also its access ramp, which 18
trucks had been traveling up and down since I had arrived that morning.
Gathered along the ramp were firefighters in their black helmets and
black coats. Slowly they lined up, and it became clear that this was an
honor guard, and that someone's remains were being carried up the
ramp toward the open door of an ambulance.

Everyone in the dining room stopped eating. Several people stood up, 19
whether out of respect or to see better, I don't know. For a moment,
everything paused.

Then the day flowed back into itself. Soon I was outside once more, 20
joining the tide of people washing around the site. Later, as I huddled
with a little crowd on the viewing platform, watching people scrawl their
names or write "God Bless America" on the plywood walls, it occurred
to me that a form of repopulation was taking effect, with so many visitors
to this place, thousands of visitors, all of us coming to see the wide emptiness where so many were lost. And by the act of our visiting—whether
we are motivated by curiosity or horror or reverence or grief, or by something confusing that combines them all—that space fills up again.

Thinking about the Essay

1. Does Berne state her thesis or imply it? Justify your response.

2. What is Berne's primary purpose in this essay? How does her title relate to
   the purpose?

3. The writer uses vivid sensory details to set the scene at Ground Zero. How
   do these details create a specific mood? Why does this mood inform our
   understanding of the relationship between the writer, her text, and her
   audience?

4. Cite instances where Berne moves from description to reflection and medi-
   tation. What is the effect of this strategy?

5. This essay is rich in novelistic and stylistic techniques. Identify several of
   these techniques and explain their effect.

Responding in Writing

6. There have been countless essays on 9/11, but Berne's is frequently anthologized. Write your own analysis and evaluation of her essay, explaining why so many readers consider it to be outstanding.

7. How would you explain 9/11 if you were taking a group of tourists to the site today? Write a reflective essay addressing this question.

8. Argue for or against the proposition that you can learn profound truths about yourself and the world by thinking about the current "age of terror."

Networking

9. In small groups, discuss the impact that Berne's essay has had on each member. Then distill your discussion into a 200-word summary that one member of the group presents to the class.

10. Locate websites of organizations that memorialize the events of 9/11. Take notes on these organizations, and then prepare a paper on their missions and programs.

Reading a Death Warrant in Tehran

SHIRIN EBADI

Shirin Ebadi is an Iranian lawyer, former judge, and human rights activist. She was born in Hamadan, Iran, in 1947, and trained for a legal career at the University of Tehran, where she received degrees in 1969 and 1971. Ebadi became the first woman to preside over an Iranian legislative court, but after the 1979 revolution, she came under increasing pressure from conservative clergy. Her work on behalf of women, political dissidents, and prisoners made her an international celebrity—but a thorn in the side of the Islamic Republic. In 2003, Ebadi received the Nobel Peace Prize for her efforts for democracy and human rights. Following threats to her life and break-ins at her office, Ebadi went into exile. In this essay from the April 9, 2006, issue of *The New York Times Magazine*, Ebadi recounts perhaps the most harrowing episode in her career as a human rights activist.

Before Reading

Would you defend victims of human rights violations even if your efforts threatened your safety? Why or why not?

In the fall of 2000, after a decade of defending victims in the courts of 1
Iran, I faced the most harrowing days of my career. The work I typically handled—battered children, abused women, political prisoners—brought me into daily contact with human cruelty, but the case at hand was different. The government had admitted partial complicity in a few of the dozens of murders of intellectuals during the 1990's. Some were strangled while running errands, others hacked to death at home. I represented the family of two victims, a husband and wife.

The judge had granted us just 10 days to read the entire dossier, 2
thousands of pages. That would be our only access to the investigation's findings, our only chance to build our case. The disarray of the investigation, the attempts to cover up the state's hand and the mysterious prison suicide of a lead suspect compounded our difficulty in learning the truth. The stakes could not have been higher. It was the first time that the Islamic republic acknowledged it had murdered its critics—it said that a rogue squad within the Ministry of Intelligence was responsible—and that a trial would be convened to hold the perpetrators accountable. We arrived at the courthouse tense with determination.

After surveying the sheer volume of files, stacks up to our heads, we 3
realized that we would have to read them concurrently and, therefore, except for one of us, out of order. The other lawyers allowed me to start at the beginning, so each page I hurriedly turned, my eyes were the first to see.

The sun shone through the dirty windowpane as we hunched over 4
the table, silent save for the rustle of papers. The significant passages, transcripts of interrogations of the accused killers, were buried in pages of bureaucratic filler. The material was dark with descriptions of the brutal murders—one killer told of crying out "Ya Zahra," in dark homage to the Prophet Muhammad's daughter, with each stab.

Around noon, our energy lagged, and we called to the young soldier 5
in the hall for some tea. The moment the tea arrived, we bent our heads down again. I had reached a page more detailed, and more narrative, than any previous section, and I slowed down to focus. It was the transcript of a conversation between a government minister and a member of the death squad during the worst wave of killings. When my eyes first fell on the sentence that would haunt me for years to come, I thought I had misread. I blinked once, but it stared back at me from the page: "The next person to be killed is Shirin Ebadi." Me.

My throat went dry. I read the line over and over again, the printed   6
words blurring before me. The only other woman in the room, Parastou
Forouhar, whose parents had been brutally murdered, sat next to me. I
pressed her arm and nodded toward the page. She bent her veiled head
close and scanned from the top. "Did you read it? Did you read it?" she
kept whispering. We read on together. My would-be assassin went to
the minister of intelligence, requesting permission to carry out my killing.
Not during the fasting month of Ramadan, the minister replied. But they
don't fast anyway, the mercenary argued; these people have divorced
God. It was through this belief—that the intellectuals, that I, had abandoned God—that they justified the killings as religious duty. In the grisly
terminology of those who interpret Islam violently, the spilling of our
blood was considered halal, permitted by God.

The door creaked open again. More tea, flavorless cups that cluttered   7
the table but kept us alert. I distracted myself by rearranging papers, my
mind reeling. I wasn't scared, really. I remember an overwhelming disbe-
lief. Why do they hate me so much? I wondered. How have I created enemies so eager to spill my blood that they cannot wait for Ramadan to end?

We didn't stop to talk about it then. We couldn't waste any precious   8
time. I sipped my tea and went on, though I turned the pages with difficulty. It was only after we had finished for the day, as we passed
through the courtyard outside, that I told the others. They shook their
heads, murmured, "Alhamdolellah," thanks to God. I had evaded death.

I stepped into the welcoming cacophony of Tehran traffic, the wide   9
streets overrun by wheezing old cars, and got a taxi home. I ran inside,
peeled off my clothes and stayed under the shower for an hour, letting
the water cascade over me, rinsing off the filth of those files. Only after
dinner, after my daughters went to bed, did I tell my husband. So, something interesting happened to me at work today, I began.

Thinking about the Essay

1. What is the significance of the title? Does Ebadi write about one specific
   moment—the act of reading one document—or a series of related episodes? Explain.

2. Does Ebadi make a claim or develop an argument in this essay, or does
   she simply want to tell a personal story? Justify your response.

3. How does Ebadi develop and heighten the conflict underlying her narrative?
   At what point does the action reach a climax? Does she resolve the main
   conflict? Why or why not?

4. Where does Ebadi employ description to enhance the narrative? What is the
   effect?

Is Beauty Universal? Global Body Images

Not every society worships supermodels, but most societies do have notions about what constitutes beauty. Whereas a washboard stomach might set the standard for beauty for certain people in the United States, there are cultures and constituencies elsewhere that value ample stomachs and hips as the ideal body type. What one society values as beauty might not appeal—indeed might seem ridiculous—to another.

Of course, the age of globalization has spawned a fusion of styles, customs, and attitudes concerning beauty and ideal body images. Fashion magazines, advertisements, and television commercials—whether in the United States, Dubai, Japan, or anywhere on the planet—project transcultural (if not universal) standards of beauty. For example, the fashions of Africa and India adorn the bodies of Americans, and a fondness for tattoos (as one image in this portfolio reveals), appropriated from traditional societies by American teens, now seems to be spreading across continents like an unstoppable cultural virus.

The forces molding global definitions of beauty cannot escape the impact of American popular culture. Icons of American pop culture—whether Queen Latifah or Britney Spears—have an exaggerated impact on the attitudes, body styles, and beauty images of people around the world. Of course, cultural differences concerning beauty and body image persist, but the impact of American culture on how others perceive beauty can be irresistible and (as Susan Bordo observes in this book) insidious.

This portfolio presents images of the body and beauty from several cultural and transnational perspectives. These images reveal societies in transition and traditional values affected by (and at times resisting) the forces of globalization.

© Markus Cuff/Corbis

Tattoo Man.   A man displays his dragon tattoo.

Considering the Image

1. It is no longer unusual—at least in the United States—to see people with tattoos. Do you think that global culture reflects this practice, or is it more specifically American or "Western" in orientation? Explain.

2. Do you think that the photographer makes an argument for or against tattoos? Why or why not?

3. Why did the photographer choose to fill the frame with a close-up and rear view of the subject? What is the effect or dominant impression?

Kindergarten Kids.   Children pose during a model contest held for kindergarten kids in Xiamen, east China's Fujian province.

Considering the Image

1. Identify the elements in this photograph that contribute to the overall effect. What aspects of the image do you find most effective?

2. What is your response to viewing these Chinese children dressed in Western clothing and posing as if they are models on a runway in New York or Paris? Do you find the scene amusing, charming, appalling, or what? Explain your reaction.

Dubai Britney. Two Arab women in traditional black burkas walk past a picture of pop singer Britney Spears in a posh shopping center in Dubai.

Considering the Image

1. What is your reaction to this photograph? Why do you believe you respond in this manner? How might the two women in burkas and Britney Spears serve as competing cultural symbols that condition your response? If you or a family member actually wears a burka, chador, or head covering, how might your reaction differ from others in the class?

2. What "message" or argument, if any, does the photographer convey in this shot? Does the photographer advance positive or negative connotations of the women in burkas and/or Britney Spears? Might there be an element of satire in the scene? Explain your responses to these questions.

Persian Beauty. An Iranian girl, surrounded by women in chadors, awaits admission to the Jamaran mosque in Tehran. The late Ayatollah Khomeini frequently conducted Friday prayers and made important speeches at this mosque.

Considering the Image

1. How does the photographer compose this image? Why does he bathe the girl in light while the people surrounding her are cast in shadows? What appeals to logos, ethos, and pathos do you detect?

2. Compare the representation of women in this image with those appearing in the Britney Spears photo. What similar and dissimilar cultural points do the two photographers want to make?

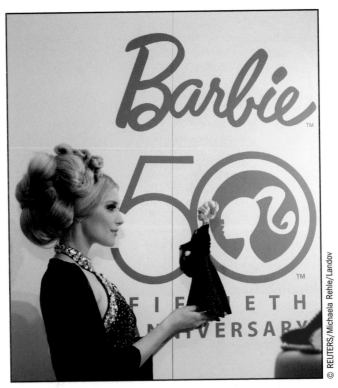

Barbie at 50.   A model poses with the world's most popular "Barbie" doll turning 50 years old, during the press preview of the 60th International Toy Fair in Nuremberg, February 4, 2009.

© REUTERS/Michaela Rehle/Landov

Considering the Image

1. Describe the composition of this image. Why is Barbie so prominently centered in the photograph?

2. Compare this image with that of Britney Spears in this portfolio. In what ways are they similar? Do they make the same point or not? Justify your response.

© David McNew/Getty Images

Equal Marriage. Lesbian couple Robin Tyler and Diane Olson hold their marriage papers as they are about to be joined in marriage by Rabbi Denise Eger in the first legally recognized same-sex marriage in Los Angeles County, at the Beverly Hills courthouse on June 16, 2008, in Beverly Hills, California.

Considering the Image

1. Analyze the composition of this photograph. What mood or dominant impression emerges from the scene? How are the two women portrayed? What do their facial expressions tell you about them?

2. What representations of gender and sexual orientation does the photographer attempt to capture? What other issues concerning beauty and body image are raised by this photograph?

7

Obese Girl Band.   Singers in a band named "Qianjin" (which in Chinese can mean both "girl" and "one ton") dance in celebration of the 2006 opening of a club for obese people in Beijing.

Considering the Image

1. Compare representations of women in this photograph with others in this portfolio, as well as with Susan Bordo's analysis in the essay that appears on pages 17–21.

2. An official at the Ministry of Health in China indicates that more than 200 million Chinese people are overweight. What cultural and economic values might serve to explain this phenomenon? How does the photograph articulate these values?

5. Evaluate the concluding paragraph. Does the writer want to resolve the conflict or sustain it? Explain.

Responding in Writing

6. Write an expository essay explaining the impact of Ebadi's article on you. What do you learn about the writer? What was her purpose in designing this text? What impressions and conclusions do you draw from this critical reading of her article?

7. Write an argumentative essay in which you argue for or against the proposition that no government has a premium on human cruelty and the manipulation of terror—that, in fact, every nation engages in it. Support your major proposition with at least three minor propositions.

8. Can you ever justify killing a person as a religious duty? Answer this question in an argumentative essay.

Networking

9. In small groups, discuss the role of the intellectual in society. Should a given society tolerate all types of intellectuals, or should certain types be monitored, controlled, imprisoned, and killed? Report your findings to the class.

10. Go online and find out more about Shirin Ebadi. (She is on Facebook, one of several sources you might want to check.) Then compose a brief biography of Ebadi.

To Any Would-Be Terrorists

Naomi Shihab Nye

Naomi Shihab Nye was born in 1952 in St. Louis, Missouri. Her family background is Palestinian American. She graduated from Trinity University (B.A., 1974) and subsequently started a career as a freelance writer and editor. Today Nye is known for her award-winning poetry, fiction for children, novels, and essays. She has been a visiting writer at the University of Texas, the University of Hawaii, the University of California at Berkeley, and elsewhere. Among Nye's books are the prize-winning poetry collection *Different Ways to Pray* (1980); several other poetry volumes, including *Yellow Glove* (1986) and *You and Yours* (2005), incorporating poems dealing with Palestinian life; a book of essays, *Never in a Hurry* (1996); and a young adult novel, *Habibi* (1997). Among her many awards are the Peter I. B. Lavin Younger Poets Award

from the Academy of American Poets and a Guggen-
heim Fellowship. Starting with the provocative title
of the following essay, Nye speaks as a Palestinian
American to an extremist audience that needs "to find
another way to live."

Before Reading

If you had an opportunity to address a terrorist or terrorist group, what would
you say and how would you say it?

I am sorry I have to call you that, but I don't know how else to get   1
your attention. I hate that word. Do you know how hard some of us
have worked to get rid of that word, to deny its instant connection to
the Middle East? And now look. Look what extra work we have.

Not only did your colleagues kill thousands of innocent, international   2
people in those buildings and scar their families forever; they wounded a
huge community of people in the Middle East, in the United States and
all over the world. If that's what they wanted to do, please know the
mission was a terrible success, and you can stop now.

Because I feel a little closer to you than many Americans could possi-   3
bly feel, or ever want to feel, I insist that you listen to me. Sit down and
listen. I know what kinds of foods you like. I would feed them to you if
you were right here, because it is very important that you listen.

I am humble in my country's pain and I am furious.   4

My Palestinian father became a refugee in 1948. He came to the   5
United States as a college student. He is 74 years old now and still home-
sick. He has planted fig trees. He has invited all the Ethiopians in his
neighborhood to fill their little paper sacks with his figs. He has written
columns and stories saying the Arabs are not terrorists; he has worked
all his life to defy that word. Arabs are businessmen and students and
kind neighbors. There is no one like him and there are thousands like
him—gentle Arab daddies who make everyone laugh around the dinner
table, who have a hard time with headlines, who stand outside in the
evenings with their hands in their pockets staring toward the far horizon.

I am sorry if you did not have a father like that.   6

I wish everyone could have a father like that.   7

My hard-working American mother has spent 50 years trying to con-   8
vince her fellow teachers and choirmates not to believe stereotypes about
the Middle East. She always told them, there is a much larger story. If

"To Any Would-Be Terrorists" by Naomi Shihab Nye. Reprinted by permission of the author.

you knew the story, you would not jump to conclusions from what you see in the news. But now look at the news. What a mess has been made.

Sometimes I wish everyone could have parents from different coun- 9
tries or ethnic groups so they would be forced to cross boundaries, to believe in mixtures, every day of their lives. Because this is what the world calls us to do. WAKE UP!

The Palestinian grocer in my Mexican-American neighborhood paints 10
pictures of the Palestinian flag on his empty cartons. He paints trees and rivers. He gives his paintings away. He says, "Don't insult me" when I try to pay him for a lemonade. Arabs have always been famous for their generosity. Remember?

My half-Arab brother with an Arabic name looks more like an Arab 11
than many full-blooded Arabs do and he has to fly every week.

My Palestinian cousins in Texas have beautiful brown little boys. 12
Many of them haven't gone to school yet. And now they have this heavy word to carry in their backpacks along with the weight of their papers and books. I repeat, the mission was a terrible success. But it was also a complete, total tragedy, and I want you to think about a few things.

1.

Many people, thousands of people, perhaps even millions of people, in 13
the United States are very aware of the long unfairness of our country's policies regarding Israel and Palestine. We talk about this all the time. It exhausts us and we keep talking. We write letters to newspapers, to politicians, to each other. We speak out in public even when it is uncomfortable to do so, because that is our responsibility. Many of these people aren't even Arabs. Many happen to be Jews who are equally troubled by the inequity. I promise you this is true. Because I am Arab-American, people always express these views to me, and I am amazed how many understand the intricate situation and have strong, caring feelings for Arabs and Palestinians even when they don't have to. Think of them, please: All those people who have been standing up for Arabs when they didn't have to.

But as ordinary citizens we don't run the government and don't get 14
to make all our government's policies, which makes us sad sometimes. We believe in the power of the word and we keep using it, even when it seems no one large enough is listening. That is one of the best things about this country: the free power of free words. Maybe we take it for granted too much. Many of the people killed in the World Trade Center probably believed in a free Palestine and were probably talking about it all the time.

But this tragedy could never help the Palestinians. Somehow, miracu-   15
lously, if other people won't help them more, they are going to have to help
themselves. And it will be peace, not violence, that fixes things. You could
ask any one of the kids in the Seeds of Peace organization and they would
tell you that. Do you ever talk to kids? Please, please, talk to more kids.

2.

Have you noticed how many roads there are? Sure you have. You must   16
check out maps and highways and small alternate routes just like anyone
else. There is no way everyone on earth could travel on the same road,
or believe in exactly the same religion. It would be too crowded: it
would be dumb. I don't believe you want us all to be Muslims. My Palestinian grandmother lived to be 106 years old and did not read or
write, but even she was much smarter than that. The only place she ever
went beyond Palestine and Jordan was to Mecca, by bus, and she was
very proud to be called a Hajji and to wear white clothes afterwards.
She worked very hard to get stains out of everyone's dresses—scrubbing
them with a stone. I think she would consider the recent tragedies a terrible stain on her religion and her whole part of the world. She would
weep. She was scared of airplanes anyway. She wanted people to worship God in whatever ways they felt comfortable. Just worship. Just
remember God in every single day and doing. It didn't matter what they
called it. When people asked her how she felt about the peace talks that
were happening right before she died, she puffed up like a proud little
bird and said, in Arabic, "I never lost my peace inside." To her, Islam
was a welcoming religion. After her home in Jerusalem was stolen from
her, she lived in a small village that contained a Christian shrine. She felt
very tender toward the people who would visit it. A Jewish professor
tracked me down a few years ago in Jerusalem to tell me she changed
his life after he went to her village to do an oral history project on
Arabs. "Don't think she only mattered to you!" he said. "She gave me a
whole different reality to imagine—yet it was amazing how close we
became. Arabs could never be just a 'project' after that."

Did you have a grandmother? Mine never wanted people to be   17
pushed around. What did yours want?

Reading about Islam since my grandmother died, I note the "toler-   18
ance" that was "typical of Islam" even in the old days. The Muslim
leader Khalidibn al-Walid signed a Jerusalem treaty which declared, "in
the name of God ... you have complete security for your churches which
shall not be occupied by the Muslims or destroyed."

It is the new millennium in which we should be even smarter than we 19
used to be, right? But I think we have fallen behind.

3.

Many Americans do not want to kill any more innocent people any- 20
where in the world. We are extremely worried about military actions
killing innocent people. We didn't like this in Iraq, we never liked it anywhere. We would like no more violence, from us as well as from you.
We would like to stop the terrifying wheel of violence, just stop it, right
on the road, and find something more creative to do to fix these huge
problems we have. Violence is not creative, it is stupid and scary, and
many of us hate all those terrible movies and TV shows made in our
own country that try to pretend otherwise. Don't watch them. Everyone
should stop watching them. An appetite for explosive sounds and top-
pling buildings is not a healthy thing for anyone in any country. The
USA should apologize to the whole world for sending this trash out into
the air and for paying people to make it.

But here's something good you may not know—one of the best- 21
selling books of poetry in the United States in recent years is the Cole-
man Barks translation of Rumi, a mystical Sufi poet of the 13th century,
and Sufism is Islam and doesn't that make you glad?

Everyone is talking about the suffering that ethnic Americans are 22
going through. Many will no doubt go through more of it, but I would
like to thank everyone who has sent me a condolence card. Americans
are usually very kind people. Didn't your colleagues find that out during
their time living here? It is hard to imagine they missed it. How could
they do what they did, knowing that?

4.

We will all die soon enough. Why not take the short time we have on 23
this delicate planet and figure out some really interesting things we might
do together? I promise you, God would be happier. So many people are
always trying to speak for God—I know it is a very dangerous thing to
do. I tried my whole life not to do it. But this one time is an exception.
Because there are so many people crying and scared and confused and
complicated and exhausted right now—it is as if we have all had a giant
simultaneous breakdown.

I beg you, as your distant Arab cousin, as your American neighbor, 24
listen to me.

Our hearts are broken: as yours may also feel broken in some ways,   25
we can't understand, unless you tell us in words. Killing people won't
tell us. We can't read that message.

Find another way to live. Don't expect others to be like you. Read   26
Rumi. Read Arabic poetry. Poetry humanizes us in a way that news, or
even religion, has a harder time doing. A great Arab scholar, Dr. Salma
Jayyusi, said, "If we read one another, we won't kill one another." Read
American poetry. Plant mint. Find a friend who is so different from you,
you can't believe how much you have in common. Love them. Let them
love you. Surprise people in gentle ways, as friends do. The rest of us
will try harder too. Make our family proud.

Thinking about the Essay

1. How does Nye address her primary audience—"would-be terrorists"? What tone or voice does she employ? What are some of the words and phrases she uses to get their attention? Of course, Nye also writes for a broader audience of readers—us. How does she make her message appealing to this larger audience?

2. Nye presents an elaborate argument in this essay. What is her central claim? What reasons or minor propositions does she give in support of her claim? How do the events of 9/11 condition the nature of her argument? What types of appeal does she make to convince her audience to think, feel, and act differently?

3. Examine the introductory paragraphs—paragraphs 1–12. Why does Nye use a first-person ("I") point of view? What is her purpose? What is the effect?

4. Analyze sections 1–4 of Nye's essay (paragraphs 13–26). What is the subject matter of each? How does the sequence of sections serve to advance the writer's argument? What transitional techniques permit essay coherence and unity?

5. Why is Nye's last paragraph a fitting conclusion to the essay? What elements from the body of the essay does this concluding paragraph reinforce and illuminate?

Responding in Writing

6. Write your own letter to any would-be terrorists. Address this audience in a personal voice. Use a variety of appeals to make your case.

7. In an analytical essay, examine the ways in which Nye tries to make her case in "To Any Would-Be Terrorists."

8. Write a letter to Naomi Shihab Nye in which you agree or disagree with the content of her essay.

Networking

9. Exchange your paper with another class member and evaluate it for content, grammar and syntax, organization, and tone. Make revisions based on your discussion.

10. Conduct online research on Rumi, and then write a paper explaining why Nye would allude to this figure in an essay on terrorism.

Now to Break the al-Qaeda Franchise

AHMED RASHID | Ahmed Rashid is a Pakistani journalist and author. He was born in 1948 in Rawalpindi, and attended colleges in Lahore and Cambridge, England. Subsequently Rashid spent ten years as a guerilla fighter attempting to overthrow Pakistan's military dictatorship before turning to journalism. He has been the Pakistan, Afghanistan, and Central Asia correspondent for London's *The Daily Telegraph* and the *Far Eastern Economic Review* for more than twenty years. Rashid is a regular contributor to BBC Online and CNN as well. His book *Taliban* (2000, 2010) has been an international best seller. Other books by Rashid include *Jihad* (2002) and *Descent into Chaos* (2008). In this essay from the May 3, 2011, issue of London's *Financial Times*, Rashid offers a cautiously optimistic assessment of al-Qaeda's waning power.

Before Reading

Do you think that al-Qaeda has been weakened or marginalized after the killing of Osama bin Laden? Why or why not?

So the world's most wanted man was finally brought down not in a 1 rugged mountain fastness but in a respectable middle-class neighbourhood in a sleepy Pakistani hill town, whose mid 19th-century colonial founders had deliberately imitated Britain's home counties. If more proof were needed of the al-Qaeda leader's lustre, the huge villa in which he had sought shelter in Abbottabad, just happened to be close to Pakistan's leading cadet college and a well-known bazaar.

For three decades Osama bin Laden has gripped the imagination of   2
Muslims across the world, and been the bane of the world's armies and
intelligence agencies. When he arrived in Peshawar in the early 1980s,
with bulldozers and his family's millions from the construction industry
to build cave shelters for the Afghan Mujahideen, nobody could suspect
that the thin, shy, but mesmerising Saudi could change the world. But
he did.

To kill nearly 3,000 people in a single blow on September 11, 2001,   3
as his followers did, and then to taunt the US to come after him took a
messianic madness. That became the al-Qaeda motto: "We love death
more than we love life." His appeal in radical circles only grew as it
seemed all the armies in the world could not counter such a war.

Evading for a decade US special forces, intelligence and drones set   4
another kind of record in jihadist circles. Jihadists believed now more
than ever that their leader was blessed and kept safe by God.

Even as al-Qaeda collapsed as a structured organisation after the   5
overthrow of the Taliban, and even as bin Laden ceased to run operations or give orders, al-Qaeda's influence spread—to Iraq, north Africa,
Europe and even the US where a handful of Muslims have tried the path
of martyrdom. But there was no al-Qaeda movement any longer, no
coherent organisation nor even a philosophy that developed. Instead,
what spread after 9/11 was the idea of death and martyrdom and taking
as many unbelievers with you as possible.

Al-Qaeda became a diffuse series of small bands, even if the threat   6
remained—and indeed remains—as just one man with a bomb in Times
Square could recreate the panic and potentially the bloodbath of 9/11.
While bin Laden stopped being a leader a long time ago, for many he
was still a symbol of martyrdom and mayhem. No one can compare to
him in the spread of Muslim history.

The chaos that he created in the Islamic world divided Muslims into   7
extremist and moderate—something no Muslim had done before on such
a scale. He further divided the faith, labelling millions of devout Muslims
as non-believers because they did not follow the reductionism of Islamic
thought to the single idea of jihad. Yet the terror his radical philosophy
evoked among autocratic Muslim rulers meant that hardly any had the
courage to stand up to him.

In fact, it is young people at the heart of the Arab revolt who are   8
rebelling not for jihad but for freedom and democracy. We should not
forget that bin Laden's failure to win support in the Arab world, despite
30 years of trying, has led to the near total rejection of the global jihadist idea by his fellow Muslims.

Nevertheless his legacy will overshadow the Muslim world for a generation. We will hear immediately from his followers, who in coming days will carry out revenge attacks around the world. In particular expect suicide attacks in Afghanistan, Pakistan and the Middle East. Second, the jihad he espoused will not disappear, for it has taken root in far too many fringe groups. Its political ambitions have been curtailed, but at a wider level it is breeding intolerance in some Muslim societies against Christians, Jews and other minority religious groups, and even beliefs within Islam such as the Sufis. 9

And yet his death offers huge opportunities across the globe. President Barack Obama needs to follow up on his promises in Cairo two years ago when he pledged to build bridges to the Muslim world. 10

The most important act for the Americans is to push for a fair and equitable settlement between Israel and the Palestinians, even as the west must redefine itself as the open-hearted friend of the new Arab societies emerging from the rubble of dictatorship. Also, bin Laden's death will make it easier for peace talks between the Taliban and the Kabul government and the Americans. The Taliban do not owe al-Qaeda anything now bin Laden is dead. 11

Al-Qaeda continued funding and training the Taliban after their collapse in 2001. But the older generation of Taliban leaders had long ago become fed up with the arrogance of Arab jihadists. The Taliban want to return home to their country free of foreigners including Americans but they don't want, for example, to bomb supermarkets or embassies in western capitals. It is worth noting that no Afghan Talib has been involved in global jihad. 12

Renouncing their links with al-Qaeda and negotiating as Afghans rather than as members of an international jihad has just become much easier for the Taliban. Nato and Afghanistan's neighbours have swiftly to take military and political measures that will help President Hamid Karzai negotiate with the Taliban to end 33 years of war. 13

Pakistan too, which has become a breeding ground for extremism and intolerance, has to seize on this as an opportunity for a new direction. The location of bin Laden's lair underlines the faultlines running through the security and intelligence forces. He was a hero to some Pakistanis because he defied the west and because the country is desperately short of heroes. Perhaps Pakistan's leaders can now have the courage to turn around the mythology and show what bin Laden really was—a political leech who introduced suicide bombing, helped to create the Pakistani Taliban and promoted intolerance in a country that was at relative peace with itself until he appeared on the scene. 14

The colonial conquests of Muslim societies by the west were followed   15
by freedom struggles and, in turn, stagnation and repression. Bin Laden
rose to prominence as Muslims were looking for a way out and he
sought to take us back many centuries.

Now Muslims have to find a way out of this extremist cul-de-sac.   16
Extremism's heroes are dead or dying and its ideology bankrupt. But the
leaders of Muslim civil society have now to give it a bold final push into
the margins, so that once again as Mohammed Ali Jinnah, the founder
of Pakistan, said in 1947—and as Arab youth are bravely urging—we
can go to mosques and temples and churches and worship and live
freely. This is a watershed moment. The question is can the west and the
Muslim world grasp it?

Thinking about the Essay

1. How would you describe the writer's audience for this essay? What impact
   would the title have on such an audience? How does Rashid adjust his
   style to meet his readership's expectations?

2. What is the author's purpose? How does his purpose inform his claim?
   Does Rashid rely on appeals to reason, emotion, or ethics, or does he combine these approaches? Justify your response.

3. Why does Rashid begin his essay with a series of paragraphs about Osama
   bin Laden? How do these lead paragraphs advance his argument concerning al-Qaeda?

4. Explain the problem-solution pattern of organization that Rashid develops in
   his article.

5. How does the end paragraph serve to underscore the tone of Rashid's
   argument?

Responding in Writing

6. Write a comparative paper analyzing the threat of al-Qaeda to both the West
   and to Islamic nations.

7. In an expository essay, present a series of solutions to Islamic terrorism.

8. Write an argumentative essay defending or rejecting the proposition that
   Islamic terrorism is a declining threat to the West.

Networking

9. In groups of three or four, discuss the last paragraph in Rashid's essay and
   the question that he poses at the very end. Try to form an answer to this
   question that reflects a consensus opinion.

10. Go online and locate at least three reviews of Rashid's book *Taliban*. Download and take notes on the reviewers' comments. Write an essay in which you analyze and evaluate these assessments of Rashid's book.

Losing the "War"

REZA ASLAN | Reza Aslan was born in Iran but immigrated to the United States when a teenager. Aslan has degrees from Santa Clara University, Harvard University, and the University of Iowa, and has pursued doctoral study at the University of California at Santa Barbara. A contributor to popular and scholarly periodicals, Aslan is also the author of *No God but God: The Origins, Evolution, and Future of Islam* (2005) and *How to Win a Cosmic War: God, Globalization, and the End of the War on Terror* (2009). In this essay from the April 8, 2009, edition of *The Los Angeles Times*, Aslan offers a critique of the "master narrative" of the war on terror.

Before Reading

Do you think that the "war on terror" is an accurate description of our common predicament, or can this phrase be a misleading or dangerous oversimplification of current global realities?

S ecretary of State Hillary Rodham Clinton let slip last week that the Obama administration has finally abandoned the phrase "war on terror." Its absence had been noted by commentators. There was no directive, Clinton said, "it's just not being used."

It may seem a trivial thing, but the change in rhetoric marks a significant turning point in the ideological contest with radical Islam. That is because the war on terror has always been a conflict more rhetorical than real. There is, of course, a very real, very bloody military component in the struggle against extremist forces in the Muslim world, though one can argue whether the U.S. and allied engagements in Iraq, Afghanistan and beyond are an integral part of that struggle, a distraction from it or, worse, evidence of its subversion and failure. But to the extent that the war on terror has been posited, from the start, as a war of ideology—a clash of civilizations—it is a rhetorical war, one fought more constructively with words and ideas than with guns and bombs.

The truth is that the phrase "war on terror" has always been prob-   3
lematic, not just because "terror," "terrorism" and "terrorist" are wastebasket terms that often convey as much about the person using them as
they do about the events or people being described, but because this was
never meant to be a war against terrorism per se. If it were, it would
have involved the Basque separatists in Spain, the Hindu/Marxist Tamil
Tigers in Sri Lanka, the Maoist rebels in eastern India, Israeli ultrana-
tionalists, the Kurdish PKK, remnants of the Irish Republican Army and
the Sikh separatist movements, and so on.

Rather, the war on terror, as conceived of by the Bush administra-   4
tion, was targeted at a particular brand of terrorism—that employed
exclusively by Islamic entities. Which is why the enemy in this ideological conflict was gradually and systematically expanded to include not
just the people who attacked the U.S. on Sept. 11, 2001, and the organizations that supported them, but an ever-widening conspiracy of disparate groups, such as Hamas in Palestine, Hezbollah in Lebanon, the
Muslim Brotherhood in Egypt, the clerical regime in Iran, the Sunni insurgency in Iraq, the Kashmiri militants, the Taliban and any other organization that declared itself Muslim and employed terrorism as a tactic.

According to the master narrative of the war on terror, these were a   5
monolithic enemy with a common agenda and a shared ideology. Never
mind that many of these groups consider one another to be a graver
threat than they consider America, that they have vastly different and
sometimes irreconcilable political yearnings and religious beliefs, and
that, until the war on terror, many had never thought of the United
States as an enemy. Give this imaginary monolith a made-up name—say,
"Islamofascism"—and an easily recognizable enemy is created, one that
exists not so much as a force to be defeated but as an idea to be opposed,
one whose chief attribute appears to be that "they" are not "us."

By lumping together the disparate forces, movements, armies, ideas   6
and grievances of the greater Muslim world, from Morocco to Malaysia;
by placing them in a single category ("enemy"), assigning them a single
identity ("terrorist"); and by countering them with a single strategy
(war), the Bush administration seemed to be making a blatant statement
that the war on terror was, in fact, "a war against Islam."

That is certainly how the conflict has been viewed by a majority in   7
four major Muslim countries—Egypt, Morocco, Pakistan and Indonesia—in a worldpublicopinion.org poll in 2007. Nearly two-thirds of
respondents said they believe that the purpose of the war on terror is to
"spread Christianity in the region" of the Middle East.

Indeed, if the war on terror was meant to be an ideological battle 8 against groups such as Al Qaeda for the hearts and minds of Muslims, the consensus around the globe seems to be that the battle has been lost.

A September 2008 BBC World Service survey of 23 countries, includ- 9 ing Russia, Australia, Pakistan, Turkey, France, Germany, Britain, the U.S., China and Mexico, found that almost 60% of all respondents said the war on terror has either had no effect or that it has made Al Qaeda stronger. Forty-seven percent said they think that neither side was winning; 56% of Americans have that view.

It is time not just to abandon the phrase "war on terror" but to 10 admit that the ideological struggle against radical Islam could never be won militarily. The battle for the hearts and minds of Muslims will take place not in the streets of Baghdad or in the mountains of Afghanistan but in the suburbs of Paris, the slums of East London and the cosmopolitan cities of Berlin and New York.

In the end, the most effective weapon in countering the appeal of 11 groups such as Al Qaeda may be the words we use.

Thinking about the Essay

1. What is Aslan's thesis, and where does it appear?

2. What does Aslan mean by "rhetoric," and how does he connect this word to "ideology," "war on terror," and "master narrative"?

3. What types of illustration does Aslan use to structure his definition and analysis of such words as "terror," "terrorism," and "terrorist"? Would you say that Aslan's definitions are universally true or stipulative (that is, strictly personal and therefore limited in application)? Explain.

4. Identify the places where Aslan uses classification and division. How does classification operate in this essay as an organizing principle?

5. Consider the conclusion of this essay. Why does Aslan end with a single sentence? What is his purpose?

Responding in Writing

6. Write your own definition of "war on terror." Be certain to use a tone that captures your feelings about this term and about how people and groups respond to it.

7. Write an argumentative essay supporting or rejecting the concept "war on terror." Refer to Aslan's article in the course of your argument.

8. Aslan uses the phrase "radical Islam." Write your own extended definition of this term, explaining why or why not it is an accurate reflection of current global realities.

Networking

9. In groups of four or five, construct your own extended definition of "the master narrative of the war on terror" (paragraph 5). Share your definition with the class.

10. Locate a "war on terror" or a "radical Islam" website. What does this website say about current global conflicts and controversies? Report your findings in class discussion.

Homeland Security Hasn't Made Us Safer

ANNE APPLEBAUM

> Anne Applebaum is a columnist for *The Washington Post* and a contributor to *Slate* magazine. In 1988, she became the Warsaw correspondent for *The Economist* and wrote about the collapse of communism across Central and Eastern Europe. Applebaum moved to London in 1992, where she wrote a weekly column on British politics and foreign affairs for *The Daily Telegraph*. During this period, she also wrote the "Foreigners" column for *Slate*. Her book *Gulag: A History* (2003) won the 2004 Pulitzer Prize for nonfiction. In the following selection, which appeared in the January/ February 2011 issue of *Foreign Policy*, Applebaum questions the effectiveness of the U.S. Department of Homeland Security.

Before Reading

What do you know about the U.S. Department of Homeland Security? Based on its name, does the organization make you feel safe from terrorism? Why or why not?

Hardly anyone has seriously scrutinized either the priorities or the   1
spending patterns of the U.S. Department of Homeland Security (DHS) and its junior partner, the Transportation Security Administration (TSA), since their hurried creation in the aftermath of the 9/11 attacks. Sure, they get criticized plenty. But year in, year out, they continue to grow faster and cost more—presumably because Americans think they

are being protected from terrorism by all that spending. Yet there is no evidence whatsoever that the agencies are making Americans any safer.

DHS serves only one clear purpose: to provide unimaginable bonan- 2
zas for favored congressional districts around the United States, most of which face no statistically significant security threat at all. One thinks of the $436,504 that the Blackfeet Nation of Montana received in fiscal 2010 "to help strengthen the nation against risks associated with potential terrorist attacks"; the $1,000,000 that the village of Poynette, Wisconsin (pop. 2,266) received in fiscal 2009 for an "emergency operations center"; or the $67,000 worth of surveillance equipment purchased by Marin County, California, and discovered, still in its original packaging, four years later. And indeed, every U.S. state, no matter how landlocked or underpopulated, receives, by law, a fixed percentage of homeland security spending every year.

As for the TSA, I am not aware of a single bomber or bomb plot 3
stopped by its time-wasting procedures. In fact, TSA screeners consistently fail to spot the majority of fake "bombs" and bomb parts the agency periodically plants to test their skills. In Los Angeles, whose airport was targeted by the "millennium plot" on New Year's 2000, screeners failed some 75 percent of these tests.

Terrorists have been stopped since 2001 and plots prevented, but 4
always by other means. After the Nigerian "underwear bomber" of Christmas Day 2009 was foiled, DHS Secretary Janet Napolitano claimed "the system worked"—but the bomber was caught by a passenger, not the feds. Richard Reid, the 2001 shoe bomber, was undone by an alert stewardess who smelled something funny. The 2006 Heathrow Airport plot was uncovered by an intelligence tip. Al Qaeda's recent attempt to explode cargo planes was caught by a human intelligence source, not an X-ray machine. Yet the TSA responds to these events by placing restrictions on shoes, liquids, and now perhaps printer cartridges.

Given this reality—and given that 9/11 was, above all, a massive 5
intelligence failure—wouldn't we be safer if the vast budgets of TSA and its partners around the world were diverted away from confiscating nail scissors and toward creating better information systems and better intelligence? Imagine if security officers in Amsterdam had been made aware of the warnings the underwear bomber's father gave to the U.S. Embassy in Abuja. Or, for that matter, if consular officers had prevented him from receiving a visa in the first place.

Better still, DHS could be broken up into its component parts, with 6
special funding and planning carried out at the federal level only for

cities and buildings that are actually at risk of terrorist attack. Here is the truth: New York City requires a lot more homeland security spending, per capita, than Poynette. Here is the even starker truth: Poynette needs no homeland security spending at all. The events of 9/11 did not prove that the United States needs to spend more on local police forces and fire brigades; they proved that Americans need to learn how to make better use of the information they have and apply it with speed and efficiency.

Thinking about the Essay

1. The writer's claim is clear from the title of her essay. Do you think that this argumentative strategy is useful and effective? Why or why not?

2. Applebaum supports her claim with various forms of evidence. What types of evidence can you identify, and how effective are these forms in bolstering her argument?

3. According to Applebaum, what are the causal connections between the Department of Homeland Security and Transportation Security Administration and the U.S. Congress? What are the effects of this relationship?

4. How does Applebaum's style suggest that she is writing for an audience that can logically follow her argument? Cite specific words and sentences to support your response.

5. To what extent is Applebaum's concluding paragraph an effective summation of her argument? Is the tone of this last paragraph in keeping with the tone of the entire essay? Why or why not?

Responding in Writing

6. Do you feel safe from terrorism knowing that the Department of Homeland Security and Transportation Security Administration maintain a constant vigil over the nation's security? Answer this question in an argumentative essay that evinces a personal tone.

7. In an illustrative essay, answer the question posed by Applebaum in paragraph 5 of her essay.

8. Select one example of a terrorist plot alluded to by Applebaum in her essay, conduct research on it, and then prepare an essay of causal analysis based on your findings.

Networking

9. In small groups, discuss how you would make homeland security more effective. Then participate in a class discussion that results in a list of all

these suggestions in order of importance. Finally, convey these recommendations to the Department of Homeland Security in an e-mail attachment.

10. Find the Department of Homeland Security website. Write a précis of your findings.

The Algebra of Infinite Justice

ARUNDHATI ROY

Arundhati Roy was born in 1959 in Shillong, India. She studied architecture in New Delhi, where she now lives. She has worked as a film designer and screenplay writer in India. Roy is the author of the novel *The God of Small Things*, for which she received the 1997 Booker Prize. The novel has been translated into dozens of languages worldwide. She has written several nonfiction books, including *The Cost of Living, Power Politics, War Talk, An Ordinary Person's Guide to Empire*, and *Public Power in the Age of Empire*. Roy was featured in the BBC television documentary *Dam/age*, which is about the struggle against big dams in India. A collection of interviews with Arundhati Roy by David Barsamian was published as *The Checkbook and the Cruise Missile*. She is a contributor to the new Verso anthology *Kashmir: The Case for Freedom*. Her newest books are *Field Notes on Democracy: Listening to Grasshoppers*, published by Haymarket Books, and *Walking with the Comrades*, published by Penguin. Roy is the recipient of the 2002 Lannan Foundation Cultural Freedom Prize. In the following essay, published in *The Progressive* in December 2001, Roy tries to explain why American foreign policy is so hated around the world.

Before Reading

Do you think that the U.S. government engages in policies around the world in order to promote "the American way of life"? Why or why not? What do you understand this term to mean? Why would peoples of other nations be skeptical of this effort?

Reprinted by Arundhati Roy, "The Algebra of Infinite Justice," *The Progressive*, Volume 65, Number 12 (December 2001), pp. 28–31. Copyright © 2001 Arundhati Roy. Online at: http://www.progressive.org/0901/roy1201.html. A full version of this essay appears in Arundhati Roy, *Power Politics*, 2nd ed. (Cambridge: South End Press, 2001), pp. 105–34.

It must be hard for ordinary Americans, so recently bereaved, to look 1
up at the world with their eyes full of tears and encounter what might
appear to them to be indifference. It isn't indifference. It's just augury.
An absence of surprise. The tired wisdom of knowing that what goes
around eventually comes around. The American people ought to know
that it is not them, but their government's policies, that are so hated.

Bush's almost god-like mission—called Operation Infinite Justice until 2
it was pointed out that this could be seen as an insult to Muslims, who
believe that only Allah can mete out infinite justice, and was renamed
Operation Enduring Freedom—requires some small clarifications. For
example, Infinite Justice/Enduring Freedom for whom?

In 1996, Madeleine Albright, then the U.S. Ambassador to the United 3
Nations, was asked on national television what she felt about the fact
that 500,000 Iraqi children had died as a result of economic sanctions
the U.S. insisted upon. She replied that it was "a very hard choice," but
that all things considered, "we think the price is worth it." Albright never
lost her job for saying this. She continued to travel the world representing
the views and aspirations of the U.S. government. More pertinently, the
sanctions against Iraq remain in place. Children continue to die.

So here we have it. The equivocating distinction between civilization 4
and savagery, between the "massacre of innocent people" or, if you like,
the "clash of civilizations" and "collateral damage." The sophistry and
fastidious algebra of Infinite Justice. How many dead Iraqis will it take
to make the world a better place? How many dead Afghans for every
dead American? How many dead children for every dead man? How
many dead mujahedeen for each dead investment banker?

The American people may be a little fuzzy about where exactly Af- 5
ghanistan is (we hear reports that there's a run on maps of the country),
but the U.S. government and Afghanistan are old friends. In 1979, after
the Soviet invasion of Afghanistan, the CIA and Pakistan's ISI (Inter-
Services Intelligence) launched the CIA's largest covert operation since
the Vietnam War. Their purpose was to harness the energy of Afghan resistance and expand it into a holy war, an Islamic jihad, which would
turn Muslim countries within the Soviet Union against the communist regime and eventually destabilize it. When it began, it was meant to be the
Soviet Union's Vietnam. It turned out to be much more than that. Over
the years, through the ISI, the CIA funded and recruited tens of thousands of radical mujahedeen from forty Islamic countries as soldiers for
America's proxy war. The rank and file of the mujahedeen were unaware
that their jihad was actually being fought on behalf of Uncle Sam.

In 1989, after being bloodied by ten years of relentless conflict, the 6
Russians withdrew, leaving behind a civilization reduced to rubble. Civil
war in Afghanistan raged on. The jihad spread to Chechnya, Kosovo,
and eventually to Kashmir. The CIA continued to pour in money and
military equipment, but the overhead had become immense, and more
money was needed.

The mujahedeen ordered farmers to plant opium as a "revolutionary 7
tax." Under the protection of the ISI, hundreds of heroin-processing laboratories were set up across Afghanistan. Within two years of the CIA's
arrival, the Pakistan/Afghanistan borderland had become the biggest producer of heroin in the world, and the single biggest source on American
streets. The annual profits, said to be between $100 and $200 billion,
were ploughed back into training and arming militants.

In 1996, the Taliban—then a marginal sect of dangerous, hard-line 8
fundamentalists—fought its way to power in Afghanistan. It was funded
by the ISI, that old cohort of the CIA, and supported by many political
parties in Pakistan. The Taliban unleashed a regime of terror. Its first
victims were its own people, particularly women. It closed down girls'
schools, dismissed women from government jobs, enforced Sharia law—
under which women deemed to be "immoral" are stoned to death and
widows guilty of being adulterous are buried alive.

After all that has happened, can there be anything more ironic than 9
Russia and America joining hands to redestroy Afghanistan? The question is, can you destroy destruction? Dropping more bombs on Afghanistan will only shuffle the rubble, scramble some old graves, and disturb
the dead. The desolate landscape of Afghanistan was the burial ground
of Soviet communism and the springboard of a unipolar world dominated by America. It made the space for neocapitalism and corporate
globalization, again dominated by America: And now Afghanistan is
poised to become the graveyard for the unlikely soldiers who fought and
won this war for America.

India, thanks in part to its geography and in part to the vision of its 10
former leaders, has so far been fortunate enough to be left out of this
Great Game. Had it been drawn in, it's more than likely that our democracy, such as it is, would not have survived. After September 11, as some
of us watched in horror, the Indian government furiously gyrated its
hips, begging the U.S. to set up its base in India rather than Pakistan.
Having had this ringside view of Pakistan's sordid fate, it isn't just odd,
it's unthinkable, that India should want to do this. Any Third World
country with a fragile economy and a complex social base should know

by now that to invite a superpower such as America in (whether it says it's staying or just passing through) would be like inviting a brick to drop through your windscreen.

Operation Enduring Freedom is being fought ostensibly to uphold the American Way of Life. It'll probably end up undermining it completely. It will spawn more anger and more terror across the world. For ordinary people in America, it will mean lives lived in a climate of sickening uncertainty: Will my child be safe in school? Will there be nerve gas in the subway? A bomb in the cinema hall? Will my love come home tonight? Being picked off a few at a time—now with anthrax, later perhaps with smallpox or bubonic plague—may end up being worse than being annihilated all at once by a nuclear bomb. 11

The U.S. government and governments all over the world are using the climate of war as an excuse to curtail civil liberties, deny free speech, lay off workers, harass ethnic and religious minorities, cut back on public spending, and divert huge amounts of money to the defense industry. To what purpose? President Bush can no more "rid the world of evildoers" than he can stock it with saints. 12

It's absurd for the U.S. government to even toy with the notion that it can stamp out terrorism with more violence and oppression. Terrorism is the symptom, not the disease. 13

Terrorism has no country. It's transnational, as global an enterprise as Coke or Pepsi or Nike. At the first sign of trouble, terrorists can pull up stakes and move their "factories" from country to country in search of a better deal. Just like the multinationals. 14

Terrorism as a phenomenon may never go away. But if it is to be contained, the first step is for America to at least acknowledge that it shares the planet with other nations, with other human beings, who, even if they are not on TV, have loves and griefs and stories and songs and sorrows and, for heaven's sake, rights. 15

The September 11 attacks were a monstrous calling card from a world gone horribly wrong. The message may have been written by Osama bin Laden (who knows?) and delivered by his couriers, but it could well have been signed by the ghosts of the victims of America's old wars: the millions killed in Korea, Vietnam, and Cambodia, the 17,500 killed when Israel—backed by the U.S.—invaded Lebanon in 1982, the tens of thousands of Iraqis killed in Operation Desert Storm, the thousands of Palestinians who have died fighting Israel's occupation of the West Bank. 16

And the millions who died, in Yugoslavia, Somalia, Haiti, Chile, Nicaragua, El Salvador, the Dominican Republic, Panama, at the hands 17 of all the terrorists, dictators, and genocidists whom the American government supported, trained, bankrolled, and supplied with arms. And this is far from being a comprehensive list.

For a country involved in so much warfare and conflict, the American people have been extremely fortunate. The strikes on September 11 were only the second on American soil in over a century. The first was Pearl Harbor. The reprisal for this took a long route, but ended with Hiroshima and Nagasaki. 18

This time the world waits with bated breath for the horrors to come. 19

Someone recently said that if Osama bin Laden didn't exist, America would have had to invent him. But in a way, America did invent him. He was among the jihadis who moved to Afghanistan in 1979 when the CIA commenced its operations there. Bin Laden has the distinction of being created by the CIA and wanted by the FBI. In the course of a fortnight, he was promoted from Suspect to Prime Suspect, and then, despite the lack of any real evidence, straight up the charts to "Wanted: Dead or Alive." 20

From what is known about bin Laden, it's entirely possible that he did not personally plan and carry out the attacks—that he is the inspirational figure, "the CEO of the Holding Company." The Taliban's response to U.S. demands for the extradition of bin Laden was uncharacteristically reasonable: Produce the evidence, then we'll hand him over. President Bush's response was that the demand was "non-negotiable." 21

(While talks are on for the extradition of CEOs, can India put in a side-request for the extradition of Warren Anderson of the USA? He was the chairman of Union Carbide, responsible for the 1984 Bhopal gas leak that killed 16,000 people. We have collated the necessary evidence. It's all in the files. Could we have him, please?) 22

But who is Osama bin Laden really? Let me rephrase that. What is Osama bin Laden? He's America's family secret. He is the American President's dark doppelgänger. The savage twin of all that purports to be beautiful and civilized. He has been sculpted from the spare rib of a world laid to waste by America's foreign policy: its gunboat diplomacy, its nuclear arsenal, its vulgarly stated policy of "full spectrum dominance," its chilling disregard for non-American lives, its barbarous military interventions, its support for despotic and dictatorial regimes, its merciless economic agenda that has munched through the economies of poor countries like a cloud of locusts, its marauding multinationals that are taking over the air we breathe, the ground we stand on, the water we drink, the thoughts we think. 23

Now that the family secret has been spilled, the twins are blurring 24 into one another and gradually becoming interchangeable. Their guns, bombs, money, and drugs have been going around in the loop for a while. Now they've even begun to borrow each other's rhetoric. Each refers to the other as "the head of the snake." Both invoke God and use the loose millenarian currency of Good and Evil as their terms of reference. Both are engaged in unequivocal political crimes. Both are dangerously armed—one with the nuclear arsenal of the obscenely powerful, the other with the incandescent, destructive power of the utterly hopeless. The fireball and the ice pick. The bludgeon and the axe.

The important thing to keep in mind is that neither is an acceptable 25 alternative to the other.

President Bush's ultimatum to the people of the world—"Either you 26 are with us or you are with the terrorists"—is a piece of presumptuous arrogance.

It's not a choice that people want to, need to, or should have to make. 27

Thinking about the Essay

1. What are the writer's political views about the United States? What aspects of Roy's essay might prompt a counterargument? Do you disagree with Roy's assessment, or do you think that the writer actually has an important argument that we should treat seriously? Explain.

2. What does the title of the essay mean? Where does Roy expand on it? Why does she equate "justice" with "algebra"?

3. Point to paragraphs and sections of this essay where the writer uses process analysis, causal analysis, and comparison and contrast to advance her argument.

4. This essay seems to hop almost cinematically from point to point. Does Roy's technique damage the organization and coherence of her essay? Why or why not?

5. In the final analysis, does Roy make a compelling or logical argument in this essay? Explain your response.

Responding in Writing

6. Do you think that people around the world hate America's policies but not Americans—as Roy asserts? Write a paper responding to this question. Provide examples to support your position.

7. Write an argumentative essay in which you either support or rebut Roy's argument. Try to proceed point by point, moving completely through Roy's main reasons in defense of her claim.

8. What does the word *justice* mean to you? Did the American nation receive its due "justice" on September 11, 2001? Write an extended-definition essay responding to this notion.

Networking

9. In small groups, discuss each member's personal impression of Roy's essay. Try to explain the thoughts and emotions it prompts. Make a list of these responses, and share them with the rest of the class.

10. Enter an Internet forum dealing with American foreign policy and monitor what participants write about it. Prepare a summary of these responses, and post them—either on your own web page or as an e-mail attachment to friends.

10

Global Aid: Can We Reduce Disease and Poverty?

Natural disasters, disease, and poverty continue to stalk the world in the twenty-first century. Moreover, the aftermath of Hurricane Katrina in 2005 was a reminder to many in the United States and around the world that major socioeconomic disparities exist even within a developed country. Poverty and a weak infrastructure made New Orleans and the surrounding region vulnerable to natural catastrophe, in much the same way that a compromised immune system invites disease. Observers compared the disaster in New Orleans to the humanitarian crises that result from floods and earthquakes in vulnerable, overpopulated Third World countries. But the fact is that most of the world's population live under conditions like those found in the slums, shantytowns, and rural backwaters of the globe and in their counterparts in the United States.

We may like to think of such conditions as the provincial vestiges of a preindustrial world that, once exposed to the light of day, will naturally be assimilated into the modern world and corrected by the natural forces of progress. But globalization has also created new forms of poverty, isolation, and dependency. The new global economy has meant a return to what some would describe as an economics of colonial exploitation—although it is not clear who is exploiting whom, or even if "exploitation" is the correct label. Globalization has changed the relationship between "rich" and "poor" countries, but it is not clear whether the forces of a global free market will tend to bridge or widen the gap between rich and poor or whether global commerce will strengthen the socioeconomic infrastructures of poor countries or mask and preserve their deficiencies. Without infrastructures of their own in place, the poorest nations in the world may become even more dependent on international aid to address poverty-related health problems. And while some blame these negative

Refugees fleeing from ongoing atrocities committed by warring factions in the Democratic Republic of Congo.

Thinking about the Image

1. How would you describe your initial response to this image? For example, do you find the image to be optimistic or depressing? Explain your position.

2. How might your response be influenced by your attitudes toward gender, sexuality, race, geography, or cultural background?

3. What point or argument do you think the photographer was trying to make?

4. Conduct research on the conflict in the Democratic Republic of the Congo, and then write a brief essay on one aspect of this problem. Insert at least three relevant images into the essay.

trends on the forces of an unregulated global free market, the philanthropic efforts of the Bill & Melinda Gates Foundation—which now spends nearly as much each year on global health projects as the World Health Organization—suggest that a corporate model of international aid may serve as a viable alternative to government-based infrastructures.

The essays in this chapter analyze global health and poverty issues in terms of a complex set of factors that have become even more challenging in recent decades with the phenomenon of globalization. For example, AIDS relief workers might distribute condoms to miners in South Africa, but the South African mines are run by unregulated transnational corporations, the miners are poor and underpaid migrant laborers, and their sex partners are often migrant workers who are forced into prostitution to feed and clothe their children. Often, the conditions that make people vulnerable to a disease are so closely connected with disease itself that cause and effect are nearly indistinguishable—hence, the term "nutritionally acquired immune deficiency syndrome" (NAIDS).

In the early nineteenth century, British economist Robert Malthus predicted that the world's population would eventually outrun the world's food supply and that hunger and famine were the natural mechanisms for adjusting supply with demand. Malthus, as many have pointed out, failed to take into account future technological innovations that would radically improve the efficiency of world food production. Today, world food supply exceeds demand. The problem of world hunger is a failure of distribution, not a failure to produce enough food. And many of the diseases that result from poverty and hunger can be treated or prevented, depending on the approach taken. Globalization reminds us that certain disparities are the result of structural failure, and that the magnitude of a natural disaster is often a function of an unnatural vulnerability.

What I Did on My Summer Vacation

JEFFREY SACHS | Jeffrey Sachs is director of the Earth Institute, Quetelet Professor of Sustainable Development, and Professor of Health Policy and Management at Columbia University. Before his move to Columbia in 2002, Sachs was director of the Center for International Development and Galen L. Stone Professor of International Trade at Harvard (where he was a faculty member for more than twenty years). Sachs serves as an economic adviser to governments in Latin America, Eastern Europe, the former Soviet Union, Asia, and Africa. He was Special Adviser to United Nations Secretary-General Kofi Annan on the set of poverty alleviation initiatives known as the Millennium Project. In the following essay, which appeared in the December 2005 issue of

Esquire magazine, Sachs describes his tour of places in
Africa where, village by village, he witnesses evidence
of the Millennium Project meeting its pragmatic goals.

Before Reading

Do you think of poverty and food shortage as world problems that, like the poor,
"will always be with us"? Can you imagine simple solutions to these problems
that are also *long-term* solutions?

This summer, from June to August, my family and I took a trip. My   1
daughter Hannah, who is ten, can now reel off the itinerary from
memory: China, Tajikistan, Israel, United Arab Emirates, Yemen, Libya,
England, Ghana, Mali, Nigeria, Kenya, Uganda, Ethiopia, Djibouti,
Rwanda, Malawi, Indonesia, Cambodia. In these places, we spent most
of our time in villages.

Throughout the world, the poor by and large live in villages. Thou-   2
sands and thousands of villages: The fact of the matter is that these villages are communities of people who want out of poverty, who want
their children to get out of poverty. They know they're poor. And they
know the whole world is not poor and that they're stuck in a situation
they don't want to be stuck in. That's the core concept of the Millennium Villages Project, which a few colleagues from the UN's Millennium
Project and the Earth Institute at Columbia University and I started
about a year ago.

Now, the basic ideas for how a poor village can be developed have   3
been known for a long time among different groups of practitioners—
those who grow food, and those who fight disease, and those who manage
water supplies. What the Millennium Project does is bring these different
groups together, because villages don't live only on farming or only on
water or only on clinics. They live as whole communities that will get out
of poverty wholly. If children are eating better because farmers are growing more food, it's going to improve the health of the children. Obviously,
it will take the burden off the clinics. If the children are healthy, they are
going to be in school. And they're going to be learning. If the children are
in school, they're going to be the ones who will bring new ideas and new
technologies to the community, so it's all mutually reinforcing.

My colleagues and I took a stand in our work several years ago that   4
we would not look for the magic bullet, because there is none. These are
just basic problems requiring basic work. Nothing magic about it. The

strategy follows from that basic idea, but the idea of approaching this on a village-by-village basis came about accidentally.

Officialdom the world over is pretty slow moving, pretty impractical, and pretty darn frustrating many ways, so even when the proof of these concepts is clear, actually getting things done is not so easy. You need a little bit of money, and donors seem utterly capable of spending it on themselves, on salaries of consultants, on meetings and seminars and workshops, but not on actually helping people not starve to death in villages. Too much of our aid money goes after an emergency comes, in shipping food aid instead of helping the farmers grow food, just as too much of it goes to razing and rebuilding a city rather than fortifying levees in advance of a disaster. Think of it as a smart investment: We can pay now or pay later. And it's a lot cheaper to pay now, and the return is incalculable. Yet this stuff doesn't actually get done, and that's why people are hungry, and that's why they're unable to access safe drinking water, and that's why they're dying by the millions.

It's not very satisfactory to see this and not act. And so in the last couple of years I've started to talk about these problems with business leaders and philanthropists, and over and over again I've heard the same response: Don't wait for the government. I'll help you. So what kind of accidentally dawned on us was that we could just go ahead and get these concepts proven on the ground. And that's what we are doing. And many philanthropists have come forward now and said, We'll give you some backing; show us what you can do.

The other day I was talking to the CEO of a major American corporation, a man who understands first and foremost the value of a good investment, and I was describing this effort to him, and he got it immediately. I hadn't even finished talking when he blurted out, "Sign me up for two villages!"

Our first village in Kenya, called Sauri, is actually a cluster of eight villages in what they call a sublocation in western Kenya, a very hungry, very disease-ridden, very isolated, extremely impoverished community. And it's a community that some of my colleagues knew because they had been analyzing the soils there and in nearby communities for many years. A colleague from Columbia University, Pedro Sanchez, who is a soils expert, felt strongly that there was an opportunity for quick development there. He told me that the soil simply lacked the nutrients to grow a proper crop. A little nitrogen, to be specific. He said to me, "You know, this situation could turn around quite quickly."

Now, when you have the experts saying that on one side and the philanthropists on the other side telling you, "Come on, let's do something," it gets pretty exciting. And that's how the Millennium Villages concept was born. The scientists said, Let's move. The philanthropists said, Let's move. A year ago we went and met with the community in Kenya and talked to people there about it. And they said, Let's move!

So we moved. 10

The trip this summer was timed to the harvest festival in Kenya, in 11 which the community celebrated the biggest harvest that it had ever had. And it's stunning how easy it was. I had told Pedro that he'd better be right about the nitrogen because a lot of people were watching, and lo and behold it was nitrogen! Putting in some basic fertilizer and helping the farmers use some improved seed varieties led to a doubling of their yields. Just like that, in one growing season. Very low cost, a few bucks per person in the village.

And we are not talking about just a few people being lifted out of 12 poverty. We're talking about five thousand people. And that cluster of villages is already serving as the model for dozens of other villages for miles around. It's exponential. It's viral. This is how the world is changed.

On my trip this summer with my family, I got to visit with the lead- 13 ership of ten African countries, from the village level to the heads of state. Each leader committed to working with us to establish ten Millennium Villages in the next year. That's a hundred altogether.

A year ago, we had two. 14

We first went to Sauri in the spring of 2004. Next, we decided to 15 work in one of the toughest places on the planet, drought-ridden Ethiopia, where it's easy to just throw up your hands and say, It's impossible. But get on the ground, talk to the community, talk to the local experts, understand their distinctive problems, put it into bite-sized units, and what looks at first to be impossible becomes solvable.

We identified an area in northern Ethiopia, Tigray province. It is an 16 hour from the regional capital, and then an hour off the road, and then an hour off the off-the-road. It's a beautiful, remote community of several thousand people in a valley that has tens of thousands of people. Again, we met with the community and found enormous enthusiasm and enormous organization—people who want to take their futures into their hands but need just a little bit of help to do it. They know about fertilizer, they know about improved seeds, they know about malaria bed nets, they know about cell phones, they know about trucks. They know they don't have any of these things. But they would like to have the chance. They're saying, Help us a bit and we can get out of this. In fact, that's what we find all over the developing world. The poor countries are saying to the rich countries: Look, we know you have an income a hundred times bigger than we have. We're starving, and you have more than enough to eat. You have everything you could ask for, and we have absolutely zero. We're not calling for revolution; we're not out to dismantle the world. We just want to have a chance to find a way over a long period of time to have some of the things that you have.

In Tigray province, their crop is a mix of teff, which is the staple 17 grain of Ethiopia; sorghum, which is a dry-season grain; a little bit of finger millet, which is another dry-season grain; and maize, which is pretty much grown all over Africa. Tree crops, papayas and mangoes, can grow in this kind of environment if there's a little bit of drip irrigation. And they provide both market opportunities and wonderful nutrition. So we started them with nurseries and improved seed. A local scientist, a wonderful young Ethiopian, was selected by the local government to head the project for us and get the community together. They built these remarkable check dams called gabions, which are just ways to preserve these mountainside villages from the short onslaught of floods and channel the water away from the crops so that the water running down the mountains doesn't create gulleys and destroy the land.

In other words, same point: simple steps, low-cost steps, all attuned 18 to the area's specific needs, led by the community, done by the community, but with a helping hand. That was early this year, and since then the local people have been out there doing the land reformation, doing reforestation, and getting ready for the planting season that was a couple months ago, and they'll be harvesting soon. In the meantime, the clinic is being built and the school is being expanded, all within a very modest budget of fifty dollars per villager per year for five years, which is our standard amount of intervention.

Then we've helped establish a local economy. And chances are, these 19 people aren't going to need us anymore. So the incessant talk in Washington about these corrupt people and their corrupt governments is just a galling excuse not to focus on practical things that we can do now to improve the world.

And for the hard-nosed among us, it bears repeating: Extreme pov- 20 erty is the best breeding ground on earth for disease, political instability, and terrorism.

Thirty-six years ago, the rich world began in earnest to figure out 21 what it would realistically take to help the poor world. A commission led by former Canadian prime minister Lester Pearson came up with the number 0.7. Here's how they arrived at that: They said that there should be a transfer of about 1 percent of GNP from the rich to the poor. That's one dollar out of every hundred. They said the public sector will do some and the private sector needs to do some, and that it should be about a seventy-thirty split. So that's where the seventy cents came from. And that was adopted by the General Assembly of the UN in 1970. The U.S. resisted for a long time. We didn't want to sign on even when the rest of the world did.

But in March 2002, the world's leaders met in Monterrey, Mexico, 22 at a conference that President Bush attended, and this conference adopted something called the Monterrey Consensus, which upheld the 0.7 target. This time, the United States signed on to it. The American signature came after a long, detailed negotiation. The U.S. finally said, Okay, it's only seventy cents. And the agreement it signed said this, in paragraph 42: "We urge developed countries that have not done so to make concrete efforts towards the target of 0.7 percent of GNP as official development assistance." Check it out, paragraph 42.

This fall at the United Nations, President Bush said that it is danger- 23 ous to American security when countries are not achieving economic development. They become unstable; they become seedbeds for terror, for violence, for the major ills of the world. The whole U.S. national-security doctrine says that development is one of the pillars of national security. There's actually nothing wrong with what these tough, self-interested types in foreign policy have been saying, because what they have been saying is that it is completely within our national interest to be helping in these circumstances.

The problem is not in the words or the logic; the problem is in our 24 lack of action. We currently give about a quarter of our pledged assistance. We've pledged to give seventy cents out of every hundred dollars of U.S. income. Instead, we give about eighteen cents. For the safety of all Americans, we must insist that our government live up to its obligation.

When President Kennedy talked about helping the people in the huts 25 and villages around the world, he said we did it not to fight communism but because it was the right thing to do. Turns out that it was right on every level, not merely morally right. It was right for our national security, for our global health, for stopping violence. It was right from a hardheaded, bottom-line, conservative standpoint, and it was right for winning hearts and minds at a time when we needed allies. And we need allies again.

This is a tiny amount of our income that could save millions of peo- 26 ple and make a safer world, and it is really a measure of our times that we ask ourselves, Why should we give a few cents out of every hundred dollars to do something like this? And yet we do ask that question.

At the beginning of July, we flew to Libya for the African Union 27 summit, where I was honored to speak to the African heads of state for the second year running.

Then on to London for the G8 summit. I didn't actually go to the 28 summit in Gleneagles but worked out of London and left the morning of the bombing.

And Tony Blair got it absolutely right that day, and President Bush 29 made a very good statement also, saying that it was all the more important to redouble our efforts in the fight against poverty and not let the terrorists take away from that agenda. And Gleneagles did produce important results: The G8 leaders committed to doubling aid to Africa. It was a welcome step in the right direction but a long way from what the world has promised.

After the G8, on to Ghana, where much interesting work is being 30 done. A lot of the agricultural concepts I am describing are drawn from Ghana's very vigorous scientific community of ecologists and agronomists, fruit growers and hydrologists. There's a tremendous amount of local research that's been done on African agriculture. And scientists there have solutions up and down the continent, and that's what they want to apply. We're not inventing any of this.

We went from Ghana to Nigeria. And Nigeria is quite another thing 31 altogether. It's the most populous country in Africa, one fifth of sub-Saharan Africa. The country has had an incredibly complex and difficult transition to democracy because it's a sprawling, multiethnic, unstable country with a long history of extreme corruption. Nigeria is led by President Obasanjo, who is fighting hard on every front to create a rule of law, decent systems, and a constitutional government.

I've been working with President Obasanjo for five years now on all 32 sorts of things. He has hosted an Africa-wide malaria conference and an Africa-wide AIDS conference that President Carter and I attended. He has hosted all sorts of other major initiatives because he's a real leader and he really understands the stakes right now. He's trying to get not only Nigeria on its feet but all of Africa.

So we will have many villages in Nigeria. In the north, we're going 33 to start one village project in Kaduna, working with the Islamic community there.

We also went south to the state of Ondo, which is led by a remark- 34 able reform-minded governor who I immediately took to. He was chairman of the geology department at Ibadan University for many years and got his Ph.D. in geology from the University of Texas. We decided together to launch a Millennium Villages project in his state. And that will be a site for two communities, Ibara and Ikaram, for about twenty thousand people, and we're getting that started right now. The governor is on e-mail with me, and he is very determined.

From Nigeria on to Mali, which is right next to Niger. People are 35 hearing about the hunger crisis in Niger, and the same basic crisis is also happening in Mali. It had a massive locust crisis last year, which ate up the crops. Timbuktu is in northern Mali. We went from the capital, Bamako, to Timbuktu, both of which are on the Niger River. Timbuktu is just at the boundary of the desert and was the way station for caravans coming from the north through the Sahara on their way to Ghana and other parts of west Africa and back again. So it's a place of intersection, of nomads and farm people as well, and it's the northern extent of settled agriculture. The villages on the south side of Timbuktu are the worst of the worst.

I asked the village chief, What are you living on now? What are you 36 going to do? It was obviously a very painful conversation. For him to be answering in front of everybody was not the easiest thing in the world, yet we needed to have the conversation. One option apparently was that they were going to borrow some seed, because they had lost everything—food, seed—to the locusts. And I asked what the terms would be. He had been looking down at the sand, and he raised his head and looked at me. The terms would be that they would have to pay it back twice, a 100 percent interest rate in one growing season, due in four months. Literally an impossible situation.

But we have an idea that we are testing. 37

A couple of months before I was in Mali, I had been to the Indian 38 state of Andhra Pradesh, which is along the Ganges River. The Ganges plain is home to hundreds of millions of people because you have intensive agriculture there. You go from farmhouse to farmhouse and everyone has a hand pump and many a treadle pump, which you use to pump water by foot. And the reason is that the water table is very close to the surface. You just dig down ten or fifteen feet and you hit water.

In Mali, you have the Niger River, but there are no pumps. And it 39 looked so familiar to me. I said, How far down is the water table? Three meters, they said.

Why don't you have a well down there?, I asked, because everyone is 40 without water. And they said, Maybe we could do that. Maybe a large project could come in. I said, But you just need treadle pumps here. This is perfect for small-scale irrigation. Now a real expert will judge this. And we have great hydrologists and agronomists on our team. So we're going to start a village in Timbuktu, and we're going to prove that along the Niger you can have irrigation.

The south of Mali is a cotton-growing area where we're also going to have a village. And it is here that you see the direct manifestation of how American cotton subsidies actually lead to the death of impoverished communities. There we had a community meeting sitting in the dirt. And I asked the people what had happened this season, and they told me something quite stunning. 41

At planting time, an agricultural collective provides some fertilizer and seed. The farmers grow the crop. And then at the end of the growing season, this enterprise buys the cotton back from the farmers at the world market price. This year, the farmers were told, Well, you've just given us your crop and now you're deeper in debt because the value of your crop is less than the input we gave you four months ago. 42

So these people literally worked for months only to be deeper in debt at the end of the season. The cotton prices are so low because we have heavily subsidized twenty-five thousand American cotton growers in a scheme that the World Trade Organization has declared illegal. Now, for cotton growers in Brazil it lowers their incomes and creates hardship, but in Mali it kills people. Because these people have no incomes, there's no nurse in the village, there's no school. And I turned to the chief. Have any children died recently? I asked. And I'll never forget his response. He waved his hand in violent disgust. "So many! *So many!*" he said before lowering his head and walking away. And then the village all piped in that they're losing children all the time because they get hungry, and then infection comes, and then the child's dead. We're not merely leaving these people to their fate but actually driving them into greater poverty without any sense of responsibility because we're not even compensating in other ways. Where's the other aid? Where's the "Oh, yes, we have to do it for our farmers, but here's what we can do for you"? 43

So that was Mali. 44

Then we flew to Kenya, and Kenya is where we started this discussion. Not only is the village process working there, but the national government is very deeply engaged, so even though it's a village program, it's also a national program. 45

We had a good meeting with the Cabinet in Nairobi and then flew to Sauri for the harvest festival. 46

And let me tell you, on that day in Kenya, the cornfields looked like 47
Illinois. And it was the most beautiful thing I ever saw in my life.

Thinking about the Essay

1. How is the essay structured as a "travelogue"? Why does Sachs open the essay with mention of his daughter?

2. How is the author's use of colloquial phrases and other language related, as a tonal gesture, to the argument of the essay?

3. Where does Sachs critique the shortcomings of the policy actions (or inaction) of nations in the developed world? What is the significance of the allusion to a recent domestic crisis in paragraph 5?

4. How does Sachs make the argument that alleviation of poverty in the developing world is in the national interest of developed nations? Where does he make this argument?

5. How does the concluding section of the essay connect with the opening paragraphs? What is the nature of the emotional appeal made in the final paragraphs of the essay?

Responding in Writing

6. In a brief essay, attempt to demystify the complexity of a current socioeconomic problem in the United States that could lead some observers to resign themselves to the problem's insolubility and to fall back upon the notion that "the poor are always with us."

7. In paragraph 25, Sachs states that John F. Kennedy's Cold War rationale for world poverty relief was "right on every level, not merely morally right." In an expository essay, consider some *non*-moral justifications for world poverty relief in the post–Cold War era.

8. Compose a letter to a local philanthropist in which you attempt to persuade him or her to contribute to a poverty relief effort like the one Sachs describes.

Networking

9. In groups of three or four, plan a group vacation with an itinerary of places in the world that members of your group think are in most dire need of assistance. Share your itinerary with the class.

10. Go online and find out information about the most recent work of the Millennium Villages Project.

A Year and a Day

EDWIDGE DANTICAT

Edwidge Danticat was born in Port-au-Prince, Haiti, in 1969, and raised by an aunt and uncle until she was twelve. At that point, she joined her parents in Brooklyn, New York. She received a B.A. from Barnard College (1990) and an M.F.A. from Brown University (1993). Her novels and short story collections, which deal with the Haitian experience, include *Krik? Krak!* (1996), *The Farming of Bones* (1998), and *The Dew Breaker* (2004). Danticat also has published children's fiction, a memoir, and a collection of essays, *Create Dangerously* (2010). In 2009, Danticat received a prestigious MacArthur Fellows Program Genius grant. In this essay from the January 17, 2011, issue of *The New Yorker*, Danticat reflects on the disastrous earthquake that leveled Port-au-Prince a year earlier, resulting in hundreds of thousands of deaths and even greater numbers of displaced Haitians.

Before Reading

Would you be willing to volunteer your time or contribute money to alleviate the suffering of people victimized by a natural disaster? Why or why not?

In the Haitian vodou tradition, it is believed by some that the souls of the   1
newly dead slip into rivers and streams and remain there, under the water, for a year and a day. Then, lured by ritual prayer and song, the souls emerge from the water and the spirits are reborn. These reincarnated spirits go on to occupy trees, and, if you listen closely, you may hear their hushed whispers in the wind. The spirits can also hover over mountain ranges, or in grottoes, or caves, where familiar voices echo our own when we call out their names. The year-and-a-day commemoration is seen, in families that believe in it and practice it, as a tremendous obligation, an honorable duty, in part because it assures a transcendental continuity of the kind that has kept us Haitians, no matter where we live, linked to our ancestors for generations.

By this interpretation of death, one of many in Haiti, more than two   2
hundred thousand souls went *anba dlo*—under the water—after the earthquake last January 12th. Their bodies, however, were elsewhere. Many were never removed from the rubble of their homes, schools,

offices, churches, or beauty parlors. Many were picked up by earth-movers on roadsides and dumped into mass graves. Many were burned, like kindling, in bonfires, for fear that they might infect the living.

"In Haiti, people never really die," my grandmothers said when I was a child, which seemed strange, because in Haiti people were always dying. They died in disasters both natural and man-made. They died from political violence. They died of infections that would have been easily treated elsewhere. They even died of chagrin, of broken hearts. But what I didn't fully understand was that in Haiti people's spirits never really die. This has been proved true in the stories we have seen and read during the past year, of boundless suffering endured with grace and dignity: mothers have spent nights standing knee-deep in mud, cradling their babies in their arms, while rain pounded the tarpaulin above their heads; amputees have learned to walk, and even dance, on their new prostheses within hours of getting them; rape victims have created organizations to protect other rape victims; people have tried, in any way they could, to reclaim a shadow of their past lives.

My grandmothers were also talking about souls, which never really die, even when the visual and verbal manifestations of their transition— the tombstones and mausoleums, the elaborate wakes and church services, the *desounen* prayers that encourage the body to surrender the spirit, the mourning rituals of all religions—become a luxury, like so much else in Haiti, like a home, like bread, like clean water.

In the year since the earthquake, Haiti has lost some thirty-five hundred people to cholera, an epidemic that is born out of water. The epidemic could potentially take more lives than the earthquake itself. And with the contagion of cholera comes a stigma that follows one even in death. People cannot touch a loved one who has died of cholera. No ritual bath is possible, no last dressing of the body. There are only more mass graves.

In the emerging lore and reality of cholera, water, this fragile veil between life and death for so many Haitians, has become a feared poison. Even as the election stalemate lingers, the rice farmers in Haiti's Artibonite Valley—the country's breadbasket—are refusing to step into the bacteria-infected waters of their paddies, setting the stage for potential food shortages and more possible death ahead, this time from hunger. In the precarious dance for survival, in which we long to honor the dead while still harboring the fear of joining them, will our rivers and streams even be trusted to shelter and then return souls?

A year ago, watching the crumbled buildings and crushed bodies that were shown around the clock on American television, I thought that I was witnessing the darkest moment in the history of the country where I was born and where most of my family members still live. Then I heard one of the survivors say, either on radio or on television, that during the earthquake it was as if the earth had become liquid, like water. That's when I began to imagine them, all these thousands and thousands of souls, slipping into the country's rivers and streams, then waiting out their year and a day before reëmerging and reclaiming their places among us. And, briefly, I was hopeful.

My hope came not only from the possibility of their and our commu- 8
nal rebirth but from the extra day that would follow the close of what has certainly been a terrible year. That extra day guarantees nothing, except that it will lead us into the following year, and the one after that, and the one after that.

Thinking about the Essay

1. At what point in the essay do you begin to sense Danticat's main purpose? What is her purpose? What type of reader might her purpose appeal to? How does she frame her thesis around this purpose?

2. Danticat provides vivid descriptive details in this essay. Which details stand out for you? How does she create symbolic overtones with these details?

3. Explain what Danticat means by "a year and a day," and how she weaves this motif into the structure of the essay.

4. What is the relationship between the introductory and concluding paragraphs, specifically in terms of Danticat's thesis?

5. Describe the persona that Danticat creates for herself, her family, and the Haitian people.

Responding in Writing

6. In an essay of analysis, explore the theme of migrating souls that Danticat weaves into her text. Do you believe that souls live on after death? Answer this question and others posed by the writer's theme.

7. Argue for or against the proposition that religion or faith can make a natural disaster more acceptable to the surviving victims.

8. Write an expository essay in which you explain what you have learned about the Haitian people from a careful critical analysis of Danticat's text.

Networking

9. With another student, analyze the mood that Danticat creates in her essay. Then write a collaborative or joint essay explaining the techniques Danticat uses to create a dominant impression of Haiti and the Haitian people.

10. Do a Google search for information on the Haitian earthquake of 2010. Using at least three sources, write a brief research paper on one aspect of the earthquake or its aftermath.

The Singer Solution to World Poverty

PETER SINGER

Peter Singer, the Ira W. DeCamp Professor of Bioethics at Princeton University's Center for Human Values, is one of the most influential—and assuredly the most controversial—philosophers of his generation. Born in Melbourne, Australia, in 1946 and educated at the University of Melbourne (B.A., 1967) and University College, Oxford (B.Phil., 1971), Singer has been a prolific writer and lecturer on such contentious social and ethical issues as infanticide, euthanasia, animal liberation, genetic engineering, and reproductive technologies. His books, which have been translated into almost two dozen languages, include *Practical Ethics* (1974, 1993), *Animal Liberation: A New Ethics for Our Treatment of Animals* (1975, 1990), *Rethinking Life and Death* (1995), *One World: The Ethics of Globalization* (2002), and *The Life You Can Save: Acting Now to End World Poverty* (2009). The following essay, which appeared in *The New York Times Magazine* in 1999 and was reprinted in *Best American Essays* (2000), has provoked the sort of criticism and debate that characterize Singer's provocative ideas.

Before Reading

Is it immoral to spend your money on luxuries when you could use this cash to help alleviate a starving child? Justify your response.

In the Brazilian film *Central Station*, Dora is a retired schoolteacher who makes ends meet by sitting at the station writing letters for illiterate people. Suddenly she has an opportunity to pocket $1,000. All she has to do is persuade a homeless 9-year-old boy to follow her to an address she has been given. (She is told he will be adopted by wealthy foreigners.) She delivers the boy, gets the money, spends some of it on a television set and settles down to enjoy her new acquisition. Her

1

neighbor spoils the fun, however, by telling her that the boy was too old to be adopted—he will be killed and his organs sold for transplantation. Perhaps Dora knew this all along, but after her neighbor's plain speaking, she spends a troubled night. In the morning Dora resolves to take the boy back.

Suppose Dora had told her neighbor that it is a tough world, other people have nice new TVs too, and if selling the kid is the only way she can get one, well, he was only a street kid. She would then have become, in the eyes of the audience, a monster. She redeems herself only by being prepared to bear considerable risks to save the boy.

At the end of the movie, in cinemas in the affluent nations of the world, people who would have been quick to condemn Dora if she had not rescued the boy go home to places far more comfortable than her apartment. In fact, the average family in the United States spends almost one-third of its income on things that are no more necessary to them than Dora's new TV was to her. Going out to nice restaurants, buying new clothes because the old ones are no longer stylish, vacationing at beach resorts—so much of our income is spent on things not essential to the preservation of our lives and health. Donated to one of a number of charitable agencies, that money could mean the difference between life and death for children in need.

All of which raises a question: In the end, what is the ethical distinction between a Brazilian who sells a homeless child to organ peddlers and an American who already has a TV and upgrades to a better one—knowing that the money could be donated to an organization that would use it to save the lives of kids in need?

Of course, there are several differences between the two situations that could support different moral judgments about them. For one thing, to be able to consign a child to death when he is standing right in front of you takes a chilling kind of heartlessness; it is much easier to ignore an appeal for money to help children you will never meet. Yet for a utilitarian philosopher like myself—that is, one who judges whether acts are right or wrong by their consequences—if the upshot of the American's failure to donate the money is that one more kid dies on the streets of a Brazilian city, then it is, in some sense, just as bad as selling the kid to the organ peddlers. But one doesn't need to embrace my utilitarian ethic to see that, at the very least, there is a troubling incongruity in being so quick to condemn Dora for taking the child to the organ peddlers while, at the same time, not regarding the American consumer's behavior as raising a serious moral issue.

In his 1996 book, *Living High and Letting Die*, the New York University philosopher Peter Unger presented an ingenious series of imaginary examples designed to probe our intuitions about whether it is wrong to live well without giving substantial amounts of money to help people who are hungry, malnourished or dying from easily treatable illnesses like diarrhea. Here's my paraphrase of one of these examples:

Bob is close to retirement. He has invested most of his savings in a   7 very rare and valuable old car, a Bugatti, which he has not been able to insure. The Bugatti is his pride and joy. In addition to the pleasure he gets from driving and caring for his car, Bob knows that its rising market value means that he will always be able to sell it and live comfortably after retirement. One day when Bob is out for a drive, he parks the Bugatti near the end of a railway siding and goes for a walk up the track. As he does so, he sees that a runaway train, with no one aboard, is running down the railway track. Looking farther down the track, he sees the small figure of a child very likely to be killed by the runaway train. He can't stop the train and the child is too far away to warn of the danger, but he can throw a switch that will divert the train down the siding where his Bugatti is parked. Then nobody will be killed—but the train will destroy his Bugatti. Thinking of his joy in owning the car and the financial security it represents, Bob decides not to throw the switch. The child is killed. For many years to come, Bob enjoys owning his Bugatti and the financial security it represents.

Bob's conduct, most of us will immediately respond, was gravely   8 wrong. Unger agrees. But then he reminds us that we, too, have opportunities to save the lives of children. We can give to organizations like UNICEF or Oxfam America. How much would we have to give one of these organizations to have a high probability of saving the life of a child threatened by easily preventable diseases? (I do not believe that children are more worth saving than adults, but since no one can argue that children have brought their poverty on themselves, focusing on them simplifies the issues.) Unger called up some experts and used the information they provided to offer some plausible estimates that include the cost of raising money, administrative expenses and the cost of delivering aid where it is most needed. By his calculation, $200 in donations would help a sickly 2-year-old transform into a healthy 6-year-old—offering safe passage through childhood's most dangerous years. To show how practical philosophical argument can be, Unger even tells his readers that they can easily donate funds by using their credit card and calling one of these toll-free numbers: (800) 367-5437 for UNICEF; (800) 693-2687 for Oxfam America.

Now you, too, have the information you need to save a child's life.   9 How should you judge yourself if you don't do it? Think again about

Bob and his Bugatti. Unlike Dora, Bob did not have to look into the eyes of the child he was sacrificing for his own material comfort. The child was a complete stranger to him and too far away to relate to in an intimate, personal way. Unlike Dora, too, he did not mislead the child or initiate the chain of events imperiling him. In all these respects, Bob's situation resembles that of people able but unwilling to donate to overseas aid and differs from Dora's situation.

If you still think that it was very wrong of Bob not to throw the 10 switch that would have diverted the train and saved the child's life, then it is hard to see how you could deny that it is also very wrong not to send money to one of the organizations listed above. Unless, that is, there is some morally important difference between the two situations that I have overlooked.

Is it the practical uncertainties about whether aid will really reach the 11 people who need it? Nobody who knows the world of overseas aid can doubt that such uncertainties exist. But Unger's figure of $200 to save a child's life was reached after he had made conservative assumptions about the proportion of the money donated that will actually reach its target.

One genuine difference between Bob and those who can afford to 12 donate to overseas aid organizations but don't is that only Bob can save the child on the tracks, whereas there are hundreds of millions of people who can give $200 to overseas aid organizations. The problem is that most of them aren't doing it. Does this mean that it is all right for you not to do it?

Suppose that there were more owners of priceless vintage cars—Carol, 13 Dave, Emma, Fred and so on, down to Ziggy—all in exactly the same situation as Bob, with their own siding and their own switch, all sacrificing the child in order to preserve their own cherished car. Would that make it all right for Bob to do the same? To answer this question affirmatively is to endorse follow-the-crowd ethics—the kind of ethics that led many Germans to look away when the Nazi atrocities were being committed. We do not excuse them because others were behaving no better.

We seem to lack a sound basis for drawing a clear moral line 14 between Bob's situation and that of any reader of this article with $200 to spare who does not donate it to an overseas aid agency. These readers seem to be acting at least as badly as Bob was acting when he chose to let the runaway train hurtle toward the unsuspecting child. In the light of this conclusion, I trust that many readers will reach for the phone and donate that $200. Perhaps you should do it before reading further.

Now that you have distinguished yourself morally from people who 15 put their vintage cars ahead of a child's life, how about treating yourself and your partner to dinner at your favorite restaurant? But wait. The money you will spend at the restaurant could also help save the lives of children overseas! True, you weren't planning to blow $200 tonight, but if you were to give up dining out just for one month, you would easily save that amount. And what is one month's dining out, compared to a child's life? There's the rub. Since there are a lot of desperately needy children in the world, there will always be another child whose life you could save for another $200. Are you therefore obliged to keep giving until you have nothing left? At what point can you stop?

Hypothetical examples can easily become farcical. Consider Bob. 16 How far past losing the Bugatti should he go? Imagine that Bob had got his foot stuck in the track of the siding, and if he diverted the train, then before it rammed the car it would also amputate his big toe. Should he still throw the switch? What if it would amputate his foot? His entire leg?

As absurd as the Bugatti scenario gets when pushed to extremes, the 17 point it raises is a serious one: only when the sacrifices become very significant indeed would most people be prepared to say that Bob does nothing wrong when he decides not to throw the switch. Of course, most people could be wrong; we can't decide moral issues by taking opinion polls. But consider for yourself the level of sacrifice that you would demand of Bob, and then think about how much money you would have to give away in order to make a sacrifice that is roughly equal to that. It's almost certainly much, much more than $200. For most middle-class Americans, it could easily be more like $200,000.

Isn't it counterproductive to ask people to do so much? Don't we run 18 the risk that many will shrug their shoulders and say that morality, so conceived, is fine for saints but not for them? I accept that we are unlikely to see, in the near or even medium-term future, a world in which it is normal for wealthy Americans to give the bulk of their wealth to strangers. When it comes to praising or blaming people for what they do, we tend to use a standard that is relative to some conception of normal behavior. Comfortably off Americans who give, say, 10 percent of their income to overseas aid organizations are so far ahead of most of their equally comfortable fellow citizens that I wouldn't go out of my way to chastise them for not doing more. Nevertheless, they should be doing much more, and they are in no position to criticize Bob for failing to make the much greater sacrifice of his Bugatti.

At this point various objections may crop up. Someone may say: "If 19 every citizen living in the affluent nations contributed his or her share I wouldn't have to make such a drastic sacrifice, because long before such levels were reached, the resources would have been there to save the lives of all those children dying from lack of food or medical care. So why should I give more than my fair share?" Another, related, objection is that the Government ought to increase its overseas aid allocations, since that would spread the burden more equitably across all taxpayers.

Yet the question of how much we ought to give is a matter to be   20
decided in the real world—and that, sadly, is a world in which we know that most people do not, and in the immediate future will not, give substantial amounts to overseas aid agencies. We know, too, that at least in the next year, the United States Government is not going to meet even the very modest United Nations–recommended target of 0.7 percent of gross national product; at the moment it lags far below that, at 0.09 percent, not even half of Japan's 0.22 percent or a tenth of Denmark's 0.97 percent. Thus, we know that the money we can give beyond that theoretical "fair share" is still going to save lives that would otherwise be lost. While the idea that no one need do more than his or her fair share is a powerful one, should it prevail if we know that others are not doing their fair share and that children will die preventable deaths unless we do more than our fair share? That would be taking fairness too far.

Thus, this ground for limiting how much we ought to give also fails.   21
In the world as it is now, I can see no escape from the conclusion that each one of us with wealth surplus to his or her essential needs should be giving most of it to help people suffering from poverty so dire as to be life-threatening. That's right: I'm saying that you shouldn't buy that new car, take that cruise, redecorate the house or get that pricey new suit. After all, a $1,000 suit could save five children's lives.

So how does my philosophy break down in dollars and cents? An   22
American household with an income of $50,000 spends around $30,000 annually on necessities, according to the Conference Board, a nonprofit economic research organization. Therefore, for a household bringing in $50,000 a year, donations to help the world's poor should be as close as possible to $20,000. The $30,000 required for necessities holds for higher incomes as well. So a household making $100,000 could cut a yearly check for $70,000. Again, the formula is simple: whatever money you're spending on luxuries, not necessities, should be given away.

Now, evolutionary psychologists tell us that human nature just isn't   23
sufficiently altruistic to make it plausible that many people will sacrifice so much for strangers. On the facts of human nature, they might be right, but they would be wrong to draw a moral conclusion from those facts. If it is the case that we ought to do things that, predictably, most of us won't do, then let's face that fact head-on. Then, if we value the life of a child more than going to fancy restaurants, the next time we

dine out we will know that we could have done something better with our money. If that makes living a morally decent life extremely arduous, well, then that is the way things are. If we don't do it, then we should at least know that we are failing to live a morally decent life—not because it is good to wallow in guilt but because knowing where we should be going is the first step toward heading in that direction.

When Bob first grasped the dilemma that faced him as he stood by 24 that railway switch, he must have thought how extraordinarily unlucky he was to be placed in a situation in which he must choose between the life of an innocent child and the sacrifice of most of his savings. But he was not unlucky at all. We are all in that situation.

Thinking about the Essay

1. Why does Singer begin his essay with an allusion to a Brazilian film that you probably have not seen? Do you find his introduction effective?

2. Where does Singer's claim appear? What evidence does he use, or does he rely on hypothetical examples and situations? Explain.

3. Singer calls himself "a utilitarian philosopher" (paragraph 5). What does he mean by this term, and how does the essay reflect his ethical approach to the problem of poverty?

4. How does Singer deal with potential objections to his argument?

5. Do you find Singer's "solution" to be convincing? Why or why not?

Responding in Writing

6. Write an argumentative essay in which you agree or disagree with Singer's solution to world poverty.

7. Write an explanatory essay in which you present your own viewpoint on making charitable contributions to help alleviate poverty or disease. Singer, for example, donates 20 percent of his income to Oxfam, a famine relief agency, and also some of his royalties to other charities. Would you do the same if you were in a position to do so?

8. What range of private acts aside from the one that Singer presents could help alleviate poverty and disease? Write an essay responding to this question.

Networking

9. With two other class members, have a discussion of the issues raised by Singer in his essay and your personal response to them. Share your opinions with the rest of the class.

10. Locate the UNICEF or Oxfam website and summarize its content.

Science vs. Hysteria

Norman E. Borlaug

> Norman E. Borlaug won the Nobel Peace Prize in 1970 for his efforts to reduce global hunger. He was born on a farm in Iowa in 1914 and studied genetics and plant biology at the University of Minnesota, where he received his B.S. (1937), M.S. (1939), and Ph.D. (1942). Borlaug earned an international reputation for his work in developing new strains of plants and cereals designed to alleviate world famine. As such he was a pioneer and for decades a central figure in the Green Revolution. From 1984 until the time of his death in 2009, Borlaug was a distinguished professor at Texas A&M University. In this 2003 essay, which appeared originally in *The Wall Street Journal*, Borlaug offers a balanced appraisal of the value of genetically engineered crops.

Before Reading

What is your opinion of genetically modified crops? Do you fear them or think they are safe for consumption? Explain.

Although there have always been those in society who resist change,   1
the intensity of the attacks against genetically modified (GM) crops from some quarters is unprecedented and, in certain cases, even surprising, given the potential environmental benefits that such technology can bring by reducing the use of pesticides. Genetic engineering of crops—plant breeding at the molecular level—is not some kind of witchcraft, but rather the progressive harnessing of the forces of nature to the benefit of feeding the human race. The idea that a new technology should be barred until proven conclusively that it can do no harm is unrealistic and unwise. Scientific advance always involves some risk of unintended outcomes. Indeed, "zero biological risk" is not even attainable.

Zambian President Levy Mwanawasa says he's been told by anti-bio-   2
technology groups that donated American corn is "poison" because it contains genetically modified kernels. Based on such misinformation, he is willing to risk thousands of additional starvation deaths rather than

distribute the same corn Americans have been eating for years with no ill effects.

Some other African leaders whose people also are facing hunger and 3 starvation say they're afraid to accept genetically modified corn because its pollen will "contaminate" local corn varieties with dire environmental consequences. Also, they say that they hope to export corn to Europe in the future and fear that their products would be rejected if genetically modified foods were allowed to enter their countries.

These concerns are unfounded. Temperate-zone corn (either GM or 4 normal) will not grow well in tropical African ecologies and, moreover, it has yellow grain while Africans prefer white grain. Thus, even if a curious farmer were to plant some GM grain received as food aid, its continued presence in the field is unlikely. Certainly in the case of Zambia, a land-locked country with poor transportation and low agricultural productivity, the prospects for exporting corn to Europe in the foreseeable future are almost zero.

If low-income, food-deficit nations—which desperately need access to 5 the benefits of science and technology—are being advised by governments and pressure groups in privileged nations to reject biotechnology, based on ideologically inspired pseudo-science, there is reason for serious concern. Of course, proper safeguards need to be put in place in Africa and elsewhere to regulate biotechnology research and the release of GM products. But to attempt to deny such benefits would be unconscionable.

Current GM crop varieties that help to control insects and weeds are 6 lowering production costs and increasing harvests—a great potential benefit to all Third World farmers. Future GM products are likely to carry traits that will improve nutrition and health. All of these technologies have more benefits to offer poor farmers and consumers than rich ones.

For example, Kenya is ready to field-test virus-resistant sweet pota- 7 toes that should yield 30% to 50% more of this important food staple. Virus-resistant bananas and potatoes have already been bred, but are being barred in African countries where people urgently need their higher yields. Indian researchers are developing a vaccine against the epidemic livestock disease, rinderpest, which can be genetically engineered into peanut plants. African farmers would be able to protect their draft animals simply by feeding them the peanut plants—again if biotech is allowed.

The needless confrontation of consumers against the use of transgenic 8 crop technology in Europe and elsewhere might have been avoided had more people received a better education in biological science. This educational gap —which has resulted in a growing and worrisome ignorance about the challenges and complexities of agricultural and food systems—needs to be addressed without delay. Privileged societies have the luxury of adopting a very low-risk position on the GM crops issue, even if this action later turns out to be unnecessary. But the vast majority of humankind does not have such a luxury, and certainly not the hungry victims of wars, natural disasters, and economic crises.

Thinking about the Essay

1. What is the purpose of Borlaug's introductory paragraph? How effective do you find this strategy? Justify your response with reference to the text.

2. Borlaug wrote this essay for a well-known and generally conservative daily publication. How does he address his audience? What elements of his argument would appeal to *The Wall Street Journal* readers?

3. Where does Borlaug state his claim? What are his key supporting points, and what types of evidence does he provide?

4. How does Borlaug employ the technique of refutation in this essay? What tone does he develop in dealing with those who might oppose his viewpoint?

5. How does Borlaug link his opening and concluding paragraphs? Why does he refer to "the human race" in the introduction and "humankind" at the conclusion?

Responding in Writing

6. Based on your critical reading of Borlaug's article, write a brief essay on what you perceive to be the benefits of genetically modified crops.

7. Write an argumentative essay supporting or opposing genetically modified crops.

8. Can genetically modified crops actually solve the problem of global famine? Answer this question in a persuasive essay.

Networking

9. Exchange your essay in response to Question 7 with another class member and offer a peer critique of your companion's paper. Focus on clarity of purpose, claim, and evidence.

10. Create a photo essay, complete with an introductory paragraph and captions, on the global use of genetically modified crops. Try to convey an opinion about the relationship between genetically modified crops and world hunger.

Technology Won't Feed the World's Hungry

ANURADHA MITTAL

Anuradha Mittal, a native of India, is founder and director of the Oakland Institute, a policy think tank that works to promote public participation and democratic debate on economic and social policy issues. Mittal is known internationally as an expert on trade, human rights, and agriculture issues. She has traveled widely as a public speaker and has appeared as guest and commentator on television and radio. Her articles on international public policy issues have appeared in *The New York Times* and in other journals worldwide. In the following article, which appeared in the July 12, 2001, issue of *Progressive Media Project*, Mittal argues that biotechnology cannot solve the problem of world hunger.

Before Reading

Do you see the debate over genetically engineered foods primarily in terms of your choice as a consumer or in terms of the way such technology would address world hunger?

Don't be misled. Genetically engineered food is not an answer to 1 world hunger.

The U.N. Development Program (UNDP) released a report last week 2 urging rich countries to put aside their fears of such food and help developing nations unlock the potential of biotechnology.

The report accuses opponents of ignoring the Third World's food 3 needs. It claims that Western consumers who do not face food shortages or nutritional deficiencies are more likely to focus on food safety and the loss of biodiversity, while farming communities in developing countries emphasize potentially higher yields and "greater nutritional value" of these crops.

But the UNDP has not done its homework. 4

In my country, India, for example, the debate pits mostly U.S.-trained 5 technocrats, seduced by technological fixes, against farmers and

Anuradha Mittal, "Technology Won't Feed the World's Hungry." This piece was originally written for the *Progressive Media Project*, 409 E. Main St., Madison, WI 53703. www.progressivemediaproject.org. Used by permission of *The Progressive*.

consumers who overwhelmingly say no to these crops. The people who are to use the modified seeds and eat the modified food often want nothing to do with them.

The report rehashes the old myth of feeding the hungry through miracle technology. As part of the 1960s Green Revolution, Western technology created pesticides and sent them to developing countries for agricultural use, which may have increased food production, but at the cost of poisoning our earth, air and water. 6

What's more, it failed to alleviate hunger. Of the 800 million hungry people in the world today, more than 200 million live in India alone. It's not that India does not produce enough food to meet the needs of its hungry. It's that organizations like the International Monetary Fund (IMF) have slashed public services and social-safety nets so that the food can't get to the needy. 7

More than 60 million tons of excess, unsold food grain rotted in India last year because the hungry were too poor to buy it. In desperation, some farmers burned the crops they could not market and resorted to selling their kidneys and other body parts, or committing suicide, to end the cycle of poverty. 8

A higher, genetically engineered crop yield would have done nothing for them. And if the poor in India are not able to buy two meals a day, how will they purchase nutritionally rich crops such as rice that is engineered to contain vitamin A? 9

The report compares efforts to ban genetically modified foods with the banning of the pesticide DDT, which was dangerous to humans but was effective in killing the mosquitoes that spread malaria. The Third World had to choose between death from DDT or malaria. It's appalling that even today the debate in developed countries offers the Third World the option of either dying from hunger or eating unsafe foods. 10

Malaria, like hunger, is a disease of poverty. When economic conditions improve, it disappears, just as it did in the United States and Europe. 11

The focus ought to be on the root causes of the problem, not the symptom. The hungry don't need a technological quick fix. They need basic social change. 12

In the Third World, the battle against genetically engineered food is a battle against the corporate concentration of our food system. Corporations are gaining control of our biodiversity and even our seeds. This is a potential stranglehold on our food supply. In response, developing countries are imposing moratoriums on genetically engineered crops. Sri 13

Lanka, Thailand, Brazil, Mexico and China, among others, have already done so.

The UNDP has been snookered about genetically engineered food. 14 The rest of us shouldn't be.

Thinking about the Essay

1. How does Mittal frame her paragraph-long **paraphrase** of the claims of the UNDP within the opening paragraphs of the essay?

2. Does Mittal's reference to India as "my country" have any effect on her argument? Would the argument be as strong without the personal element? Why or why not?

3. How does Mittal characterize the advocates of biotechnology who are the authors of the UNDP report?

4. According to Mittal, what is the role that corporations play in the promotion of biotechnology? How does this claim change her characterization of the motives for promoting such technology?

5. How effective is the colloquial language of the two-sentence concluding paragraph? Are there other examples of such language in the essay?

Responding in Writing

6. In a brief essay, connect Mittal's argument with other arguments presented in this chapter about economic infrastructure as the root cause of world health problems.

7. Argue for or against the use of biotechnology as a solution to world hunger by invoking an analogy of your own that you believe characterizes the reaction of opponents or supporters of such technology. Why is this analogy appropriate?

8. Do you think that adequate public services and social safety nets exist in the United States that prevent the kind of failure of resource distribution Mittal describes in India? Why do people go hungry in the United States today? Is this hunger the result of a systemic failure? Answer these questions in an argumentative essay.

Networking

9. In small groups, discuss your reservations (or enthusiasms) about genetically engineered food. Do you feel that you are reacting according to your limited interests as a Western consumer? Why or why not?

10. Go online and engage in a discussion group debate over genetically engineered food from a global, hunger-relief point of view.

A Development Nightmare

KENNETH ROGOFF

> Kenneth Rogoff was Charles and Marie Robertson Professor of International Affairs at Princeton University and is currently professor of economics and director of the Center for International Development at Harvard University. From 2001 to 2003, he served as chief economist and director of research at the International Monetary Fund. Rogoff has published extensively on government policy issues surrounding international finance, and he is also the coauthor (with Maurice Obstfeld) of the widely used graduate textbook *Foundations of International Macroeconomics* (1996). His most recent book is *This Time Is Different: Eight Centuries of Financial Folly* (2011). In the following article, which appeared in *Foreign Policy* magazine in January/February 2004, Rogoff examines the foreign aid policies of "rich" nations whose efforts to promote the economic development of other nations are mixed with fears about the distribution (and dilution) of the world's wealth.

Before Reading

Do you measure your own economic prosperity in relative terms? What are those terms?

Indulge in a dream scenario for a moment: Suppose the world awoke   1
tomorrow and, miraculously, every country suddenly enjoyed the same per capita income as the United States, or roughly $40,000 per year. Global annual income would soar to $300 trillion, or some 10 times what it is now. And while we're at it, suppose also that international education levels, infant mortality rates, and life expectancies all converged to the levels in rich countries. In short, what if foreign aid worked and economic development happened overnight instead of over centuries?

A heretical thought, perhaps. But I wonder sometimes what voters in   2
rich nations must be thinking when they reward their politicians for cutting already pathetic foreign-aid budgets. Is it possible that, deep down, the world's wealthy fear what will happen if the developing countries

Kenneth Rogoff, "A Development Nightmare," *Foreign Policy*, January/February 2004. *Foreign Policy* by Carnegie Endowment for International Peace; National Affairs, Inc Copyright 2004. Reproduced with permission of *Foreign Policy* in the format Textbook via Copyright Clearance Center.

really did catch up, and if the advantages their own children enjoy were shared by all? Would the dream become a nightmare?

Consider whether today's wealthy would materially suffer under such   3 a scenario. As things now stand, 290 million U.S. citizens already cause almost one-fourth of world carbon dioxide emissions. What if 1.3 billion Chinese and 1.1 billion Indians suddenly all had cars and began churning out automobile exhaust at prodigious U.S. rates? While the sun might not turn black and the ozone layer might not vaporize overnight, the environmental possibilities are frightening. And what of the price of oil, which is already notoriously sensitive to small imbalances in demand and supply? Absent huge new discoveries or brilliant new inventions, oil could easily reach $200 per barrel, as consumption and depletion rates accelerate. The mighty U.S. dollar would become a boutique currency and the euro experiment a sideshow. Investors would clamor for Chinese yuan and Indian rupees. The world's youth would grow up thinking that "Hollywood" must be a wordplay on "Bollywood," and McDonald's hamburgers would be viewed a minor ethnic cuisine. And a country such as Canada would suddenly have the economic heft of Luxembourg, with much of its population reduced to serving once poor, now rich, international tourists.

Let's face it: The rich countries would no longer feel rich. Humans   4 are social creatures; once we clear the hurdle of basic subsistence, wealth becomes a relative state of being. Even an optimist such as myself must concede that a world of equality between rich and poor nations would be shockingly different—and that is even disregarding the impact on global power politics. Still, such rapid economic development offers a clear upside for today's rich countries. Greater diversity and knowledge spillovers can breed much faster productivity growth, the ultimate source of wealth for everyone. Once properly educated, fed, and plugged in, inventive geniuses from South Asia and Africa might speed the development of clean and safe hydrogen power by two generations. And whereas commercial medical researchers might start spending more energy combating tropical diseases, now privileged citizens in temperate climates would still enjoy countless technological spin-offs. Indeed, such gains of rapid economic development could fully offset the losses to the rich.

By highlighting latent insecurities in rich countries, I certainly do not   5 mean to endorse or stoke them. But these underlying fears must be addressed. If globalization really works, then what is the endgame? What kind of political institutions are necessary to prepare—socially as well as psychologically—for success? It is easy for everyone to endorse the

United Nations Millennium Development Goals (MDG), which aim to satisfy basic human needs by 2015. (Unfortunately, the specific objectives are so limited that MDG ought to stand for the Minimum Development Goals.) But how far are rich nations willing to take development? How much are we prepared to give?

Of course, no one has developed a magic formula for how to make   6
countries grow, though economic researchers have identified a number of poisons. Corruption, overweening government intervention, and mountains of debt are contraindicated for countries attempting to develop (which is one reason most foreign aid should be recast as outright grants instead of loans). Though critics are correct to argue that foreign aid stymies growth by breeding corruption and stifling private enterprise, the empirical evidence suggests that aid can be productive when it supports good policies. Does trade help countries grow? Again, my read of the evidence says yes: If Europe and Japan gave up their outrageous farm protection and if the United States stopped competing with India for the title of anti-dumping champion of the world, poor countries would gain far more than if their aid inflows suddenly doubled. And, by the way, if poor countries gave up their own trade protectionism, their citizens would benefit by even more.

Even so, rich countries could easily afford to triple their aid budgets   7
without running the remotest risk of the "nightmare" scenario coming true. They could channel money into health in Africa, into education, and into infrastructure and other necessities with little danger of any rapid catch-up. (Though why the World Bank still lends to China, with more than $350 billion in hard currency reserves and a space program to boot, is difficult to explain.) Gallons of aid money, such as what Northern Italy has poured into Southern Italy for almost 60 years, help assuage development's growing pains, but progress rarely occurs quickly. Growth economics suggests that poor regions have a hard time closing the income gap on rich countries at a rate greater than 2 percent per year, even under the best of circumstances. Catch-up—when it happens at all—takes generations.

Rich countries need not be ambivalent or stingy. Certainly, if sudden   8
and rapid economic development were possible and actually materialized, many citizens in wealthy nations would feel jarred, even threatened. And some day, world income distribution will be radically different than it is today, but not anytime soon. Nightmare scenarios and fear of success need never stand in the way of sensible—and generous—development policies.

Thinking about the Essay

1. How does Rogoff undercut the utopian vision presented in the opening paragraph of the essay?

2. What motives does Rogoff attribute to members of "rich" nations? What evidence does he offer to support this attribution? Does Rogoff express any sympathy with these motives?

3. How would you characterize Rogoff's brand of irony in this essay? Highlight at least three different ironic passages and note some similarities and differences in tone between them.

4. What negative effects of economic progress does Rogoff acknowledge in the essay? Why does he wait to acknowledge these effects?

5. What policies does Rogoff endorse that would promote international economic development? What past and current policies does he attack? Why does he attack them? How are these inadequate policies connected with the interests and perceptions of "rich" nations?

Responding in Writing

6. In a brief essay, construct a "dream scenario" similar to Rogoff's, in which you envision the solution to a world health problem, and consider some additional negative side effects of the solution if this scenario were to be realized.

7. Do you fear the loss or erosion of your privileges as a member of a "rich" nation? Reflect on these fears in an essay blending narrative and expository elements.

8. Define what you see as the "endgame" of globalization. Is this a world you would like to live in? How do you see your children or grandchildren adapting to this world?

Networking

9. In groups of three or four, list some other cultural transformations that might occur under Rogoff's scenario. Do you fear the possibility of becoming culturally (or economically) marginalized? Why? Discuss those feelings within your group, and share the results of the discussion with the class.

10. Go online and research foreign aid statistics in the most recent U.S. federal budget. Do these numbers surprise you? Why or why not?

The Fate of the Earth: Can We Preserve the Global Environment?

I t is tempting to think that at one time—was it before 9/11, or before the explosion of the first atomic bomb, or before the Black Death?—the problems of the world were simpler and more manageable. But were they? After all, the Black Death of the thirteenth century liquidated more than a third of Europe's population. There have always been world conflicts and challenges that Earth's inhabitants have had to confront. So far, we have survived; we have not destroyed the planet. However, as the writers in this chapter attest, the fate of the Earth is uncertain, for humanity continues to be a flawed enterprise.

What is certain is that for the last several decades we have been moving into a new era in global history. This new era, as the writers in earlier chapters have revealed, is both like and unlike previous historical epochs. We do not have to accept the thesis of Francis Fukuyama that we have reached the "end" of history. At the same time, we do have to acknowledge that new challenges—scientific, ecological, economic, political, and cultural—await us in the new millennium. Numerous local and global problems need our sustained attention. Over the past decade, in particular, we have come to recognize that we have relationships and obligations to the planet and its inhabitants. A dust storm originating in Africa can sweep across the Atlantic, affecting ecologies in other continents. A nuclear accident in Russia can affect the milk of cows in Nebraska. Even the cars that we purchase and drive—as one author in this chapter asserts—can have an impact on the world's climate.

Clearly, then, in this new millennial era, we are part of a global environment. We have mutual obligations not to waste natural resources, to respect the environment, to harness science and technology to human and nonhuman benefit, and so much more. This new

Tourists visiting a Bedouin village in the Egyptian desert clearly affect the local ecosystem and indigenous community.

Thinking about the Image

1. How does the photographer frame this shot? Who is in the foreground, and who is in the background? What is the dominant impression?

2. Are you amused or surprised by the dress of the tourists? Why or why not?

3. What kind of story does this photograph tell about the impact of tourism on landscape and indigenous culture?

4. What do you think is the point of view of the photographer toward the people on the camels? How can you tell?

era is not necessarily more corrosive than previous epochs, but the stakes do seem to be higher. We now have to comprehend our reciprocal relationships at the numerous crossroads of nature and civilization. The *process* of civilization wherein we harness our physical, creative, scientific, political, intellectual, and spiritual resources is well advanced. However, the current condition of the global environment, as the writers in this last chapter testify, demands our attention.

By and large, the writers in this chapter, all of whom deal with subjects of consequence—global warming, biotechnology, environmental degradation, population growth, weapons of mass destruction—are not doomsday prophets. In fact, while offering cautionary statements about our shortsightedness and wastefulness, they tend to find hope for the world's environment. Whether finding once again a small spot in Eden in a remote Amazon jungle or contemplating the consequences of driving an SUV, these writers try to establish a moral basis for the continuation of the species—not just our human species but all varieties of life on Earth. We are not caught in an endless spiral that will end in mass extinction. But we do have to harness what Albert Schweitzer called "the devils of our own creation." Ultimately, we must find ways to coexist on Earth with nature and all living things.

The Obligation to Endure

RACHEL CARSON

Born in Pennsylvania in 1907, Rachel Carson became a leading figure in the world's emerging environmental movement. Abandoning an early interest in English literature, she concentrated instead on zoology, ultimately obtaining an advanced degree from the Graduate School of Johns Hopkins University. She was a marine biologist on the staff of the United States Fish and Wildlife Service for fifteen years, serving as editor in chief. Her first book was *Under the Sea Wind* (1941). With *The Sea Around Us* (1951), which sold millions of copies, was translated into dozens of languages, and won the National Book Award, Carson emerged as the best-known spokesperson for the preservation of the world's resources. In 1952, Carson resigned her government position to devote her time to writing. Her last book, *Silent Spring* (1962), from which the following essay is taken, aroused immediate controversy for its indictment of the use of pesticides. Carson died in 1964.

Before Reading

In the decades since *Silent Spring* was published, numerous pesticides have been banned—especially in the United States. Do you think that the problem no longer exists? Why or why not?

The history of life on earth has been a history of interaction between   1
living things and their surroundings. To a large extent, the physical
form and the habits of the earth's vegetation and its animal life have
been molded by the environment. Considering the whole span of earthly
time, the opposite effect, in which life actually modifies its surroundings,
has been relatively slight. Only within the moment of time represented
by the present century has one species—man—acquired significant power
to alter the nature of his world.

During the past quarter century this power has not only increased to   2
one of disturbing magnitude but it has changed in character. The most
alarming of all man's assaults upon the environment is the contamination
of air, earth, rivers, and sea with dangerous and even lethal materials.
This pollution is for the most part irrecoverable; the chain of evil it ini-
tiates not only in the world that must support life but in living tissues is
for the most part irreversible. In this now universal contamination of the
environment, chemicals are the sinister and little-recognized partners of
radiation in changing the very nature of the world—the very nature of its
life. Strontium 90, released through nuclear explosions into the air, comes
to earth in rain or drifts down as fallout, lodges in soil, enters into the
grass or corn or wheat grown there, and in time takes up its abode in the
bones of a human being, there to remain until his death. Similarly, chemicals sprayed on croplands or forests or gardens lie long in soil, entering
into living organisms, passing from one to another in a chain of poisoning
and death. Or they pass mysteriously by underground streams until they
emerge and, through the alchemy of air and sunlight, combine into new
forms that kill vegetation, sicken cattle, and work unknown harm on
those who drink from once pure wells. As Albert Schweitzer has said,
"Man can hardly even recognize the devils of his own creation."

It took hundreds of millions of years to produce the life that now   3
inhabits the earth—eons of time in which that developing and evolving
and diversifying life reached a state of adjustment and balance with its
surroundings. The environment, rigorously shaping and directing the life
it supported, contained elements that were hostile as well as supporting.
Certain rocks gave out dangerous radiation; even within the light of the
sun, from which all life draws its energy, there were shortwave radia-
tions with power to injure. Given time—time not in years but in
millennia—life adjusts, and a balance has been reached. For time is the
essential ingredient; but in the modern world there is no time.

The rapidity of change and the speed with which new situations are   4
created follow the impetuous and heedless pace of man rather than the

deliberate pace of nature. Radiation is no longer merely the background radiation of rocks, the bombardment of cosmic rays, the ultraviolet of the sun that have existed before there was any life on earth; radiation is now the un-natural creation of man's tampering with the atom. The chemicals to which life is asked to make its adjustment are no longer merely the calcium and silica and copper and all the rest of the minerals washed out of the rocks and carried in rivers to the sea; they are the synthetic creations of man's inventive mind, brewed in his laboratories, and having no counterparts in nature.

To adjust to these chemicals would require time on the scale that is   5
nature's; it would require not merely the years of a man's life but the life of generations. And even this, were it by some miracle possible, would be futile, for the new chemicals come from our laboratories in an endless stream; almost five hundred annually find their way into actual use in the United States alone. The figure is staggering and its implications are not easily grasped—500 new chemicals to which the bodies of men and animals are required somehow to adapt each year, chemicals totally outside the limits of biologic experience.

Among them are many that are used in man's war against nature.   6
Since the mid-1940s over 200 basic chemicals have been created for use in killing insects, weeds, rodents, and other organisms described in the modern vernacular as "pests"; and they are sold under several thousand different brand names.

These sprays, dusts, and aerosols are now applied almost universally   7
to farms, gardens, forests, and homes—nonselective chemicals that have the power to kill every insect, the "good" and the "bad," to still the song of birds and the leaping of fish in the streams, to coat the leaves with a deadly film, and to linger on in soil—all this though the intended target may be only a few weeds or insects. Can anyone believe it is possible to lay down such a barrage of poisons on the surface of the earth without making it unfit for all life? They should not be called "insecticides," but "biocides."

The whole process of spraying seems caught up in an endless spiral.   8
Since DDT was released for civilian use, a process of escalation has been going on in which ever more toxic materials must be found. This has happened because insects, in a triumphant vindication of Darwin's principle of the survival of the fittest, have evolved super races immune to the particular insecticide used, hence a deadlier one has always to be developed—and then a deadlier one than that. It has happened also because, for reasons to be described later, destructive insects often

undergo a "flareback," or resurgence, after spraying in numbers greater than before. Thus the chemical war is never won, and all life is caught in its violent crossfire.

Along with the possibility of the extinction of mankind by nuclear war, the central problem of our age has therefore become the contamination of man's total environment with such substances of incredible potential for harm—substances that accumulate in the tissues of plants and animals and even penetrate the germ cells to shatter or alter the very material of heredity upon which the shape of the future depends. 9

Some would-be architects of our future look toward a time when it will be possible to alter the human germ plasma by design. But we may easily be doing so now by inadvertence, for many chemicals, like radiation, bring about gene mutations. It is ironic to think that man might determine his own future by something so seemingly trivial as the choice of an insect spray. 10

All this has been risked—for what? Future historians may well be amazed by our distorted sense of proportion. How could intelligent beings seek to control a few unwanted species by a method that contaminated the entire environment and brought the threat of disease and death even to their own kind? Yet this is precisely what we have done. We have done it, moreover, for reasons that collapse the moment we examine them. We are told that the enormous and expanding use of pesticides is necessary to maintain farm production. Yet is our real problem not one of *over production*? Our farms, despite measures to remove acreages from production and to pay farmers not to produce, have yielded such a staggering excess of crops that the American taxpayer in 1962 is paying out more than one billion dollars a year as the total carrying cost of the surplus-food storage program. And is the situation helped when one branch of the Agriculture Department tries to reduce production while another states, as it did in 1958, "It is believed generally that reduction of crop acreages under provisions of the Soil Bank will stimulate interest in use of chemicals to obtain maximum production on the land retained in crops." 11

All this is not to say there is no insect problem and no need of control. I am saying, rather, that control must be geared to realities, not to mythical situations, and that the methods employed must be such that they do not destroy us along with the insects. 12

The problem whose attempted solution has brought such a train of disaster in its wake is an accompaniment of our modern way of life. Long before the age of man, insects inhabited the earth—a group of extraordinarily varied and adaptable beings. Over the course of time since man's 13 advent, a small percentage of the more than half a million species of insects have come into conflict with human welfare in two principal ways: as competitors for the food supply and as carriers of human disease.

Disease-carrying insects become important where human beings are 14 crowded together, especially under conditions where sanitation is poor, as in times of natural disaster or war or in situations of extreme poverty and deprivation. Then control of some sort becomes necessary. It is a sobering fact, however, as we shall presently see, that the method of massive chemical control has had only limited success, and also threatens to worsen the very conditions it is intended to curb.

Under primitive agricultural conditions the farmer had few insect 15 problems. These arose with the intensification of agriculture—the devotion of immense acreages to a single crop. Such a system set the stage for explosive increases in specific insect populations. Single-crop farming does not take advantage of the principles by which nature works; it is agriculture as an engineer might conceive it to be. Nature has introduced great variety into the landscape, but man has displayed a passion for simplifying it. Thus he undoes the built-in checks and balances by which nature holds the species within bounds. One important natural check is a limit on the amount of suitable habitat for each species. Obviously then, an insect that lives on wheat can build up its population to much higher levels on a farm devoted to wheat than on one in which wheat is intermingled with other crops to which the insect is not adapted.

The same thing happens in other situations. A generation or more 16 ago, the towns of large areas of the United States lined their streets with the noble elm tree. Now the beauty they hopefully created is threatened with complete destruction as disease sweeps through the elms, carried by a beetle that would have only limited chance to build up large populations and to spread from tree to tree if the elms were only occasional trees in a richly diversified planting.

Another factor in the modern insect problem is one that must be 17 viewed against a background of geologic and human history: the spreading of thousands of different kinds of organisms from their native homes to invade new territories. This worldwide migration has been studied and graphically described by the British ecologist Charles Elton in his recent book *The Ecology of Invasions*. During the Cretaceous Period, some hundred million years ago, flooding seas cut many land bridges between continents, and living things found themselves confined in what Elton calls "colossal separate nature reserves." There, isolated from others of their kind, they developed many new species. When some of the land masses were joined again, about 15 million years ago, these species began to move out into new territories—a movement that is not only still in progress but is now receiving considerable assistance from man.

The importation of plants is the primary agent in the modern spread 18 of species, for animals have almost invariably gone along with the plants, quarantine being a comparatively recent and not completely effective innovation. The United States Office of Plant Introduction alone has introduced almost 200,000 species and varieties of plants from all over the world. Nearly half of the 180 or so major insect enemies of plants in the United States are accidental imports from abroad, and most of them have come as hitchhikers on plants.

In new territory, out of reach of the restraining hand of the natural 19 enemies that kept down its numbers in its native land, an invading plant or animal is able to become enormously abundant. Thus it is no accident that our most troublesome insects are introduced species.

These invasions, both the naturally occurring and those dependent on 20 human assistance, are likely to continue indefinitely. Quarantine and massive chemical campaigns are only extremely expensive ways of buying time. We are faced, according to Dr. Elton, "with a life-and-death need not just to find new technological means of suppressing this plant or that animal"; instead we need the basic knowledge of animal populations and their relations to their surroundings that will "promote an even balance and damp down the explosive power of outbreaks and new invasions."

Much of the necessary knowledge is now available but we do not use 21 it. We train ecologists in our universities and even employ them in our governmental agencies but we seldom take their advice. We allow the chemical death rain to fall as though there were no alternative, whereas in fact there are many, and our ingenuity could soon discover many more if given opportunity.

Have we fallen into a mesmerized state that makes us accept as inevi- 22 table that which is inferior or detrimental, as though having lost the will or the vision to demand that which is good? Such thinking, in the words of the ecologist Paul Shepard, "idealizes life with only its head out of water, inches above the limits of toleration of the corruption of its own environment.... Why should we tolerate a diet of weak poisons, a home in insipid surroundings, a circle of acquaintances who are not quite our enemies, the noise of motors with just enough relief to prevent insanity? Who would want to live in a world which is just not quite fatal?"

Yet such a world is pressed upon us. The crusade to create a chemi- 23 cally sterile, insect-free world seems to have engendered a fanatic zeal on the part of many specialists and most of the so-called control agencies. On every hand there is evidence that those engaged in spraying operations exercise a ruthless power. "The regulatory entomologists ... function as prosecutor, judge and jury, tax assessor and collector and sheriff to enforce their own orders," said Connecticut entomologist Neely Turner. The most flagrant abuses go unchecked in both state and federal agencies.

It is not my contention that chemical insecticides must never be used. 24 I do contend that we have put poisonous and biologically potent chemicals indiscriminately into the hands of persons largely or wholly ignorant of their potentials for harm. We have subjected enormous numbers of people to contact with these poisons, without their consent and often without their knowledge. If the Bill of Rights contains no guarantee that a citizen shall be secure against lethal poisons distributed either by private individuals or by public officials, it is surely only because our forefathers, despite their considerable wisdom and foresight, could conceive of no such problem.

I contend, furthermore, that we have allowed these chemicals to be 25 used with little or no advance investigation of their effect on soil, water, wildlife, and man himself. Future generations are unlikely to condone our lack of prudent concern for the integrity of the natural world that supports all life.

There is still very limited awareness of the nature of the threat. This 26 is an era of specialists, each of whom sees his own problem and is unaware of or intolerant of the larger frame into which it fits. It is also an era dominated by industry, in which the right to make a dollar at whatever cost is seldom challenged. When the public protests, confronted with some obvious evidence of damaging results of pesticide applications, it is fed little tranquilizing pills of half truth. We urgently need an end to these false assurances, to the sugar coating of unpalatable facts. It is the public that is being asked to assume the risks that the insect controllers calculate. The public must decide whether it wishes to continue on the present road, and it can do so only when in full possession of the facts. In the words of Jean Roosted, "The obligation to endure gives us the right to know."

Thinking about the Essay

1. What is Carson's thesis or claim? Where does it appear, or is it implied? Justify your response.

2. Explain the tone of Carson's essay. How do such words as *dangerous, evil,* and *sinister* reinforce this tone?

3. Evaluate Carson's essay as a model of argumentation. What reasons does she provide to demonstrate the overpopulation of insects? How does she convince us of "the obligation to endure"? What remedies does she propose? What appeals does she make?

4. Identify all instances where Carson uses expert testimony. How effective is this testimony in reinforcing the writer's argument?

5. What is Carson's purpose in her final paragraph? How effective is it? Explain.

Responding in Writing

6. Write your own essay titled "The Obligation to Endure." You may focus on pesticides or any other topic—for example, genetically altered foods or global warming—to organize your paper.

7. In an essay, argue for or against the proposition that we spend too much time and money worrying about the state of the world environment.

8. Write a paper in which you present solutions to some of the problems that Carson raises in her essay.

Networking

9. Working in small groups, find out more about Rachel Carson and her involvement with environmental issues. In class discussion, evaluate her relevance to the environmental situation today.

10. Go online and find out more about pesticides commonly used today. Share your findings with the class. How safe are they? Would you use them as a homeowner, landscaper, farmer, or forestry official?

Talking Trash

ANDY ROONEY | Andrew A. Rooney, better known as "Andy" from his regular appearances on *60 Minutes* and his syndicated columns in more than 200 newspapers, was one of the nation's best-known curmudgeons, a writer and commentator who was frequently at odds with conventional wisdom on various issues. Born in Albany, New York, in 1919, he attended Colgate University before serving in the U.S. Army from 1942 to 1945 as a reporter for *Stars and Stripes*. Rooney wrote, produced, and narrated programs for some of the major shows in television history: He wrote material for Arthur Godfrey from 1949 to 1955, and for Sam Levenson, Herb

Shriner, Victor Borge, Gary Moore, and other celebrities who define many of the high points of early television comedy. Over the decades, Rooney also produced television essays, documentaries, and specials for ABC, CBS, and public television. A prolific writer, he was the author of more than a dozen books, including *My War* (1995), *Sincerely, Andy Rooney* (1999), *Common Nonsense* (2002), *Years of Minutes* (2003), and *60 Years of Wisdom and Wit* (2009). Known for his dry, unassuming, but acerbic wit (which from time to time got him in trouble with viewers and television studios), Rooney is at his best when convincing readers about simple truths. Andy Rooney died in 2011. In this essay, which appeared in 2002 in *Diversion*, he tells us the simple truth about our inability to moderate our wasteful ways.

Before Reading

Americans are perceived as being terribly wasteful. They discard food, appliances, clothing, and so much more that other peoples and societies would find useful. Do you agree or disagree with this profile of the wasteful American? And how do you fit into this picture?

L ast Saturday I filled the trunk of my car and the passenger seats 1 behind me with junk and headed for the dump. There were newspapers, empty cardboard boxes, bags of junk mail, advertising flyers, empty bottles, cans, and garbage. I enjoy the trip. Next to buying something new, throwing away something that is old is the most satisfying experience I know.

The garbage men come to my house twice a week, but they're very 2 fussy. If the garbage is not packaged the way they like it, they won't take it. That's why I make a trip to the dump every Saturday. It's two miles from our house, and I often think big thoughts about throwing things away while I'm driving there.

How much, I got to wondering last week, does the whole Earth 3 weigh? New York City alone throws away 24 million pounds of garbage a day. A day! How long will it take us to turn the whole planet Earth into garbage, throw it away, and leave us standing on nothing?

Oil, coal, and metal ore are the most obvious extractions, but any 4 place there's a valuable mineral, we dig beneath the surface, take it out,

"Talking Trash" by Andy Rooney. Reprinted by permission of The Estate of Andy Rooney and Essay Productions, LLC.

and make it into something else. We never put anything back. We disfigure one part of our land by digging something out and then move on to another spot after we've used up all its resources.

After my visit to the dump, I headed for the supermarket, where I 5 bought $34 worth of groceries. Everything was packed in something—a can, a box, a bottle, a carton, or a bag. When I got to the checkout counter, the cashier separated my cans, boxes, cartons, bottles, and bags and put three or four at a time into other bags, boxes, or cartons. Sometimes she put my paper bags into plastic bags. One bag never seemed to do. If something was in plastic, she put that into paper.

On the way home, I stopped at the dry cleaner. Five of my shirts, 6 which had been laundered, were in a cardboard box. There was a piece of cardboard in the front of each shirt and another cardboard cutout to fit the collar to keep it from getting wrinkled. The suit I had cleaned was on a throwaway hanger, in a plastic bag with a form-fitting piece of paper inside over the shoulders of my suit.

When I got home, I put the groceries where they belonged in various 7 places in the kitchen. With the wastebasket at hand, I threw out all the outer bags and wrappers. By the time I'd unwrapped and stored everything, I'd filled the kitchen wastebasket a second time.

It would be interesting to conduct a serious test to determine what 8 percentage of everything we discard. It must be more than 25%. I drank the contents of a bottle of Coke and threw the bottle away. The Coca-Cola Company must pay more for the bottle than for what they put in it. Dozens of things we eat come in containers that weigh more and cost the manufacturer more than what they put in them.

We've gone overboard on packaging, and part of the reason is that a 9 bag, a can, or a carton provides a place for the producer to display advertising. The average cereal box looks like a roadside billboard.

The Earth could end up as one huge, uninhabitable dump. 10

Thinking about the Essay

1. What is Rooney's claim? Where does he state it? What evidence does he provide to support his claim?

2. Does Rooney, writing about a serious problem, maintain a serious tone in this essay? What evidence in the essay leads you to your view?

3. How does Rooney structure his argument? Does he provide enough supporting points to back up his major claim or proposition? Why or why not?

4. Is Rooney merely making value judgments about himself, or does he have a broader purpose? How do you know?

5. Explain the style of this essay. Are Rooney's language and sentence structure accessible or difficult? How does his style facilitate your reading and appreciation of the essay?

Responding in Writing

6. Argue for or against the proposition that we are a wasteful society. As Rooney does, organize your essay around your own personal experience or your knowledge of family and friends.

7. Write an imaginative essay about the year 2050. Center the essay on Rooney's last sentence: "The Earth could end up as one huge, uninhabitable dump."

8. Write a letter to your local congressional representative outlining the need for your community to do more about controlling its waste flow. Offer specific remedies for improvement.

Networking

9. Divide into groups of three or four, and jot down some of the instances of waste you have encountered on your campus. Compare your list with other group members' lists. Which problems seem to be most common? Which are singular? Share and discuss your results with the rest of the class.

10. Utilizing one or more Web search engines, download information on waste management. What is the current status of this movement in the United States? Which cities or regions are doing the best job of managing their waste problems? Present your findings in class discussion.

We Can't Wish Away Climate Change

AL GORE

Al Gore (Albert Gore Jr.) is a former congressman, senator, and forty-fifth vice president of the United States. He was the Democratic candidate for the presidency in 2000, winning the popular vote but losing the electoral count when the Supreme Court on a 5-4 decision awarded Florida to George W. Bush. The son of a distinguished senator from Tennessee, Gore was born in 1948 and grew up in Washington, DC. He attended Harvard University (B.A., 1969) and served a tour of duty in Vietnam. A self-described "raging moderate," Gore became interested in environmental issues when he was in Congress, writing during that time the best-selling *Earth in the Balance: Ecology and the*

Human Spirit (1992). After his defeat in the 2000 presidential race, Gore became one of the world's most prominent advocates of environmental protection. His book *An Inconvenient Truth* (2006) and companion film, which won the Academy Award for best documentary, were highly successful, helping Gore to earn a Nobel Peace Prize in 2007. He is also the author of *The Assault on Reason* (2007) and *Our Choice: A Plan to Solve the Climate Crisis* (2010). As a businessman, he is an investor in alternative energy companies. In this essay, which was published in *The New York Times* in 2010, Gore warns about the dangers associated with global warming.

Before Reading

Do you think that global warming or climate change represents a danger to life on this planet? Why or why not?

It would be an enormous relief if the recent attacks on the science of 1 global warming actually indicated that we do not face an unimaginable calamity requiring large-scale, preventive measures to protect human civilization as we know it.

Of course, we would still need to deal with the national security risks 2 of our growing dependence on a global oil market dominated by dwindling reserves in the most unstable region of the world, and the economic risks of sending hundreds of billions of dollars a year overseas in return for that oil. And we would still trail China in the race to develop smart grids, fast trains, solar power, wind, geothermal and other renewable sources of energy—the most important sources of new jobs in the 21st century.

But what a burden would be lifted! We would no longer have to worry 3 that our grandchildren would one day look back on us as a criminal generation that had selfishly and blithely ignored clear warnings that their fate was in our hands. We could instead celebrate the naysayers who had doggedly persisted in proving that every major National Academy of Sciences report on climate change had simply made a huge mistake.

I, for one, genuinely wish that the climate crisis were an illusion. But 4 unfortunately, the reality of the danger we are courting has not been changed by the discovery of at least two mistakes in the thousands of pages of careful scientific work over the last 22 years by the Intergovernmental

Panel on Climate Change. In fact, the crisis is still growing because we are continuing to dump 90 million tons of global-warming pollution every 24 hours into the atmosphere—as if it were an open sewer.

It is true that the climate panel published a flawed overestimate of   5
the melting rate of debris-covered glaciers in the Himalayas, and used information about the Netherlands provided to it by the government, which was later found to be partly inaccurate. In addition, e-mail messages stolen from the University of East Anglia in Britain showed that scientists besieged by an onslaught of hostile, make-work demands from climate skeptics may not have adequately followed the requirements of the British freedom of information law.

But the scientific enterprise will never be completely free of mistakes.   6
What is important is that the overwhelming consensus on global warming remains unchanged. It is also worth noting that the panel's scientists—acting in good faith on the best information then available to them—probably underestimated the range of sea-level rise in this century, the speed with which the Arctic ice cap is disappearing and the speed with which some of the large glacial flows in Antarctica and Greenland are melting and racing to the sea.

Because these and other effects of global warming are distributed   7
globally, they are difficult to identify and interpret in any particular location. For example, January was seen as unusually cold in much of the United States. Yet from a global perspective, it was the second-hottest January since surface temperatures were first measured 130 years ago.

Similarly, even though climate deniers have speciously argued for sev-   8
eral years that there has been no warming in the last decade, scientists confirmed last month that the last 10 years were the hottest decade since modern records have been kept.

The heavy snowfalls this month have been used as fodder for ridicule   9
by those who argue that global warming is a myth, yet scientists have long pointed out that warmer global temperatures have been increasing the rate of evaporation from the oceans, putting significantly more moisture into the atmosphere—thus causing heavier downfalls of both rain and snow in particular regions, including the Northeastern United States. Just as it's important not to miss the forest for the trees, neither should we miss the climate for the snowstorm.

Here is what scientists have found is happening to our climate: man-   10
made global-warming pollution traps heat from the sun and increases atmospheric temperatures. These pollutants—especially carbon dioxide— have been increasing rapidly with the growth in the burning of coal, oil, natural gas and forests, and temperatures have increased over the same

period. Almost all of the ice-covered regions of the Earth are melting—and seas are rising. Hurricanes are predicted to grow stronger and more destructive, though their number is expected to decrease. Droughts are getting longer and deeper in many mid-continent regions, even as the severity of flooding increases. The seasonal predictability of rainfall and temperatures is being disrupted, posing serious threats to agriculture. The rate of species extinction is accelerating to dangerous levels.

Though there have been impressive efforts by many business leaders, 11 hundreds of millions of individuals and families throughout the world and many national, regional and local governments, our civilization is still failing miserably to slow the rate at which these emissions are increasing—much less reduce them.

And in spite of President Obama's efforts at the Copenhagen climate 12 summit meeting in December, global leaders failed to muster anything more than a decision to "take note" of an intention to act.

Because the world still relies on leadership from the United States, 13 the failure by the Senate to pass legislation intended to cap American emissions before the Copenhagen meeting guaranteed that the outcome would fall far short of even the minimum needed to build momentum toward a meaningful solution.

The political paralysis that is now so painfully evident in Washington 14 has thus far prevented action by the Senate—not only on climate and energy legislation, but also on health care reform, financial regulatory reform and a host of other pressing issues.

This comes with painful costs. China, now the world's largest and 15 fastest-growing source of global-warming pollution, had privately signaled early last year that if the United States passed meaningful legislation, it would join in serious efforts to produce an effective treaty. When the Senate failed to follow the lead of the House of Representatives, forcing the president to go to Copenhagen without a new law in hand, the Chinese balked. With the two largest polluters refusing to act, the world community was paralyzed.

Some analysts attribute the failure to an inherent flaw in the design 16 of the chosen solution—arguing that a cap-and-trade approach is too unwieldy and difficult to put in place. Moreover, these critics add, the financial crisis that began in 2008 shook the world's confidence in the use of any market-based solution.

But there are two big problems with this critique: First, there is no 17 readily apparent alternative that would be any easier politically. It is difficult to imagine a globally harmonized carbon tax or a coordinated multilateral regulatory effort. The flexibility of a global market-based policy—supplemented by regulation and revenue-neutral tax policies—is the option that has by far the best chance of success. The fact that it is extremely difficult does not mean that we should simply give up.

Second, we should have no illusions about the difficulty and the time 18 needed to convince the rest of the world to adopt a completely new approach. The lags in the global climate system, including the buildup of heat in the oceans from which it is slowly reintroduced into the atmosphere, means that we can create conditions that make large and destructive consequences inevitable long before their awful manifestations become apparent: the displacement of hundreds of millions of climate refugees, civil unrest, chaos and the collapse of governance in many developing countries, large-scale crop failures and the spread of deadly diseases.

It's important to point out that the United States is not alone in its 19 inaction. Global political paralysis has thus far stymied work not only on climate, but on trade and other pressing issues that require coordinated international action.

The reasons for this are primarily economic. The globalization of the 20 economy, coupled with the outsourcing of jobs from industrial countries, has simultaneously heightened fears of further job losses in the industrial world and encouraged rising expectations in emerging economies. The result? Heightened opposition, in both the industrial and developing worlds, to any constraints on the use of carbon-based fuels, which remain our principal source of energy.

The decisive victory of democratic capitalism over communism in the 21 1990s led to a period of philosophical dominance for market economics worldwide and the illusion of a unipolar world. It also led, in the United States, to a hubristic "bubble" of market fundamentalism that encouraged opponents of regulatory constraints to mount an aggressive effort to shift the internal boundary between the democracy sphere and the market sphere. Over time, markets would most efficiently solve most problems, they argued. Laws and regulations interfering with the operations of the market carried a faint odor of the discredited statist adversary we had just defeated.

This period of market triumphalism coincided with confirmation by 22 scientists that earlier fears about global warming had been grossly understated. But by then, the political context in which this debate took form was tilted heavily toward the views of market fundamentalists, who fought to weaken existing constraints and scoffed at the possibility that global constraints would be needed to halt the dangerous dumping of global-warming pollution into the atmosphere.

Over the years, as the science has become clearer and clearer, some 23
industries and companies whose business plans are dependent on unrestrained pollution of the atmospheric commons have become ever more
entrenched. They are ferociously fighting against the mildest regulation—
just as tobacco companies blocked constraints on the marketing of cigarettes for four decades after science confirmed the link of cigarettes to
diseases of the lung and the heart.

Simultaneously, changes in America's political system—including the 24
replacement of newspapers and magazines by television as the dominant
medium of communication—conferred powerful advantages on wealthy
advocates of unrestrained markets and weakened advocates of legal and
regulatory reforms. Some news media organizations now present showmen
masquerading as political thinkers who package hatred and divisiveness as
entertainment. And as in times past, that has proved to be a potent drug
in the veins of the body politic. Their most consistent theme is to label as
"socialist" any proposal to reform exploitive behavior in the marketplace.

From the standpoint of governance, what is at stake is our ability 25
to use the rule of law as an instrument of human redemption. After all
has been said and so little done, the truth about the climate crisis—
inconvenient as ever—must still be faced.

The pathway to success is still open, though it tracks the outer 26
boundary of what we are capable of doing. It begins with a choice by
the United States to pass a law establishing a cost for global warming
pollution. The House of Representatives has already passed legislation,
with some Republican support, to take the first halting steps for pricing
greenhouse gas emissions.

Later this week, Senators John Kerry, Lindsey Graham and Joe Lie- 27
berman are expected to present for consideration similar cap-and-trade
legislation.

I hope that it will place a true cap on carbon emissions and stimulate 28
the rapid development of low-carbon sources of energy.

We have overcome existential threats before. Winston Churchill is 29
widely quoted as having said, "Sometimes doing your best is not good
enough. Sometimes, you must do what is required." Now is that time.
Public officials must rise to this challenge by doing what is required; and
the public must demand that they do so—or must replace them.

Thinking about the Essay

1. How would you characterize Gore's tone in this essay? What is his purpose
   in using words like "unimaginable calamity" (paragraph 1), "naysayers"

(paragraph 3), and "open sewer" (paragraph 4)? What additional examples of this sort of diction can you locate?

2. Why does Gore allude to the National Academy of Sciences and the Copenhagen climate summit, as well as to several politicians including President Obama and Winston Churchill? What is his purpose here?

3. Explain the way that Gore constructs his argument. What is his claim and how does he reinforce it? What minor propositions does he establish? What is the nature of his evidence? Finally, how does he refute or deal with opposing viewpoints?

4. Where does Gore employ causal analysis and comparison and contrast? How do these strategies reinforce his argument?

5. According to Gore, the American political system must change. How persuasive is the writer's opinion, and why?

Responding in Writing

6. Argue for or against the proposition that climate change is a danger to humankind.

7. Analyze Gore's essay as a model of journalistic opinion writing. Discuss style, tone, paragraph organization, and such argumentative strategies as appeals to reason, emotion, and ethics.

8. Write an essay offering your plan to address and solve climate change.

Networking

9. Help to arrange a class viewing of Gore's documentary film *An Inconvenient Truth*. Afterward, discuss the film in relation to his essay.

10. Go online to find out more about the U.S. Congress and what it is doing (or not doing) to address the problem of climate change. Find out what your Congressional representative's position is on the issue, and then compose an e-mail to your representative expressing your own viewpoint.

Global Warming Delusions

Daniel B. Botkin

Daniel B. Botkin is a scientist who in his own words "studies life from a planetary perspective." With degrees in physics, biology, and literature, he offers broad interdisciplinary insights into the global ecosystem and the problems and dangers affecting it. A renowned figure in the forefront of the environmental sciences for decades, Botkin has developed computer models that are used worldwide to forecast global warming patterns. His many books include a widely used college textbook, *Environmental Sciences* (8th edition, 2010), as well as *Strange Encounters: Adventures of a Renegade Naturalist* (2003) and *Powering the Future* (2010). Botkin has taught at the University of California at Santa Barbara since 1979, where he is currently a professor emeritus. In this essay from the October 17, 2007, issue of *The Wall Street Journal*, Botkin offers a nuanced argument about global warming.

Before Reading

Why has global warming become such an issue in contemporary thought? Do you think that climate change is a major problem, given all the other political and environmental issues we confront? Why or why not?

Global warming doesn't matter except to the extent that it will affect 1 life—ours and that of all living things on Earth. And contrary to the latest news, the evidence that global warming will have serious effects on life is thin. Most evidence suggests the contrary.

Case in point: This year's United Nations report on climate change 2 and other documents say that 20%–30% of plant and animal species will be threatened with extinction in this century due to global warming—a truly terrifying thought. Yet, during the past 2.5 million years, a period that scientists now know experienced climatic changes as rapid and as warm as modern climatological models suggest will happen to us, almost none of the millions of species on Earth went extinct. The exceptions were about 20 species of large mammals (the famous megafauna of the last ice age—saber-tooth tigers, hairy mammoths and the like), which went extinct about 10,000 to 5,000 years ago at the end of the last ice age, and many dominant trees and shrubs of northwestern Europe. But elsewhere, including North America, few plant species went extinct, and few mammals.

We're also warned that tropical diseases are going to spread, and that 3 we can expect malaria and encephalitis epidemics. But scientific papers by Prof. Sarah Randolph of Oxford University show that temperature changes do not correlate well with changes in the distribution or frequency of these diseases; warming has not broadened their distribution and is highly unlikely to do so in the future, global warming or not.

The key point here is that living things respond to many factors in   4 addition to temperature and rainfall. In most cases, however, climate-modeling-based forecasts look primarily at temperature alone, or temperature and precipitation only. You might ask, "Isn't this enough to forecast changes in the distribution of species?" Ask a mockingbird. *The New York Times* recently published an answer to a query about why mockingbirds were becoming common in Manhattan. The expert answer was: food—an exotic plant species that mockingbirds like to eat had spread to New York City. It was this, not temperature or rainfall, the expert said, that caused the change in mockingbird geography.

You might think I must be one of those know-nothing naysayers   5 who believes global warming is a liberal plot. On the contrary, I am a biologist and ecologist who has worked on global warming, and been concerned about its effects, since 1968. I've developed the computer model of forest growth that has been used widely to forecast possible effects of global warming on life—I've used the model for that purpose myself, and to forecast likely effects on specific endangered species.

I'm not a naysayer. I'm a scientist who believes in the scientific method   6 and in what facts tell us. I have worked for 40 years to try to improve our environment and improve human life as well. I believe we can do this only from a basis in reality, and that is not what I see happening now. Instead, like fashions that took hold in the past and are eloquently analyzed in the classic 19th century book "Extraordinary Popular Delusions and the Madness of Crowds," the popular imagination today appears to have been captured by beliefs that have little scientific basis.

Some colleagues who share some of my doubts argue that the only   7 way to get our society to change is to frighten people with the possibility of a catastrophe, and that therefore it is all right and even necessary for scientists to exaggerate. They tell me that my belief in open and honest assessment is naïve. "Wolves deceive their prey, don't they?" one said to me recently. Therefore, biologically, he said, we are justified in exaggerating to get society to change.

The climate modelers who developed the computer programs that are   8 being used to forecast climate change used to readily admit that the models were crude and not very realistic, but were the best that could be done with available computers and programming methods. They said our options were to either believe those crude models or believe the opinions of experienced, data-focused scientists. Having done a great deal of computer modeling myself, I appreciated their acknowledgment of the limits of their methods. But I hear no such statements today.

Oddly, the forecasts of computer models have become our new reality, while facts such as the few extinctions of the past 2.5 million years are pushed aside, as if they were not our reality.

A recent article in the well-respected journal *American Scientist*   9 explained why the glacier on Mt. Kilimanjaro could not be melting from global warming. Simply from an intellectual point of view it was fascinating—especially the author's Sherlock Holmes approach to figuring out what was causing the glacier to melt. That it couldn't be global warming directly (i.e., the result of air around the glacier warming) was made clear by the fact that the air temperature at the altitude of the glacier is below freezing. This means that only direct radiant heat from sunlight could be warming and melting the glacier. The author also studied the shape of the glacier and deduced that its melting pattern was consistent with radiant heat but not air temperature. Although acknowledged by many scientists, the paper is scorned by the true believers in global warming.

We are told that the melting of the arctic ice will be a disaster. But   10 during the famous medieval warming period—A.D. 750 to 1230 or so— the Vikings found the warmer northern climate to their advantage. Emmanuel Le Roy Ladurie addressed this in his book "Times of Feast, Times of Famine: A History of Climate Since the Year 1000," perhaps the greatest book about climate change before the onset of modern concerns with global warming. He wrote that Erik the Red "took advantage of a sea relatively free of ice to sail due west from Iceland to reach Greenland.... Two and a half centuries later, at the height of the climatic and demographic fortunes of the northern settlers, a bishopric of Greenland was founded at Gardar in 1126."

Ladurie pointed out that "it is reasonable to think of the Vikings as   11 unconsciously taking advantage of this [referring to the warming of the Middle Ages] to colonize the most northern and inclement of their conquests, Iceland and Greenland." Good thing that Erik the Red didn't have Al Gore or his climatologists as his advisers.

Should we therefore dismiss global warming? Of course not. But we   12 should make a realistic assessment, as rationally as possible, about its cultural, economic and environmental effects. As Erik the Red might have told you, not everything due to a climatic warming is bad, nor is everything that is bad due to a climatic warming.

We should approach the problem the way we decide whether to buy   13 insurance and take precautions against other catastrophes—wildfires, hurricanes, earthquakes. And as I have written elsewhere, many of the actions we would take to reduce greenhouse-gas production and mitigate global-warming effects are beneficial anyway, most particularly a movement away from fossil fuels to alternative solar and wind energy.

My concern is that we may be moving away from an irrational lack 14 of concern about climate change to an equally irrational panic about it.

Many of my colleagues ask, "What's the problem? Hasn't it been a 15 good thing to raise public concern?" The problem is that in this panic we are going to spend our money unwisely, we will take actions that are counterproductive, and we will fail to do many of those things that will benefit the environment and ourselves.

For example, right now the clearest threat to many species is habitat 16 destruction. Take the orangutans, for instance, one of those charismatic species that people are often fascinated by and concerned about. They are endangered because of deforestation. In our fear of global warming, it would be sad if we fail to find funds to purchase those forests before they are destroyed, and thus let this species go extinct.

At the heart of the matter is how much faith we decide to put in 17 science—even how much faith scientists put in science. Our times have benefited from clear-thinking, science-based rationality. I hope this prevails as we try to deal with our changing climate.

Thinking about the Essay

1. How does Botkin undercut conventional approaches to the debate over global warming in his introductory paragraph and elsewhere in the essay?

2. Why does Botkin inject himself into this essay? What is his purpose? Do you find this strategy to be effective? Explain.

3. Does Botkin simply want to provide a pro/con argument, or does he want to argue a different approach or persuade readers to understand something else about global warming? Justify your response with reference to the text.

4. Does the writer make any value judgments, or is he strictly logical and objective in presenting his claim? Explain.

5. Explain the nature of the evidence that Botkin introduces to support his argument.

Responding in Writing

6. Write an essay in which you explain whether or not you found Botkin's essay to be convincing.

7. Compare and contrast the essays by Gore and Botkin.

8. Present your own views on global warming "delusions."

Networking

9. Form small groups and jot down all ideas that members have about global warming. Share your list in class discussion.

10. Conduct online research into computer modeling and its utility in predicting the impact of global warming on the world's ecologies. Write a summary of your findings.

To Save Chimps

JANE GOODALL | British naturalist Jane Goodall, born in London in 1934, has spent much of her adult life in the jungles of Tanzania engaged in the study of chimpanzees. Fascinated by animals since childhood, Goodall, after graduating from school, traveled to Kenya to work with the famed paleontologist Louis Leakey, serving as his assistant on fossil-gathering trips to the Olduvai Gorge region. In 1960, at Leakey's urging, Goodall started a new project studying wild chimpanzees in the Gombe Stream Chimpanzee Reserve in Tanzania. In 1965, Cambridge University awarded Goodall a Ph.D. degree based on her thesis growing out of five years of research in the Gombe Reserve; she was only the eighth person in the university's history to earn a doctorate without having earned an undergraduate degree. Goodall has received dozens of major international awards from conservation societies and environmental groups, including the Albert Schweitzer Award, two Franklin Burr Awards from the National Geographic Society, and numerous honorary doctorates from universities around the world. Among her many books are the widely read *In the Shadow of Man* (1971), *The Chimpanzees of Gombe: Patterns of Behavior* (1986), *Hope for the Animals of the World* (2009), and a two-volume autobiography in letters, *Africa in My Blood* (2000) and *Beyond Innocence* (2001). She also has written books for children and participated in media productions based on her work. This essay from the fall 2006 issue of *WorldView* reflects one of Goodall's core beliefs—that saving animals matters.

Jane Goodall "Save the Chimps" from *WorldView*; Fall 2006; 19, 3 Platinum Periodicals, pg. 27. *WorldView* by National Council of Returned Peace Corps Volunteers. Copyright 2006. Reproduced with permission of Carnegie Council on Ethics and International Affairs in the format Textbook via Copyright Clearance Center.

Before Reading

Goodall suggests that family planning can protect animals and the environment. Do you agree or disagree, and why?

When I arrived at Gombe National Park in western Tanzania to 1
study chimpanzees 47 years ago, lush forest stretched for miles along Lake Tanganyika's eastern shoreline and inland as far as I could see. Gradually, over the years, growing populations of local people and refugees struggling to survive in one of the world's poorest places have cut down the trees for firewood, to build homes and to clear the land for farming. By 1980, the trees outside the park had almost all gone. Much of the soil was exhausted. Looking for new land to clear, people have moved to the very steepest slopes of the escarpment, where heavy rains wash away the thin topsoil, cause terrible soil erosion and deadly mudslides. Women walk further and further from their villages in search of fuel wood, adding hours of labor to already difficult days.

This situation, of course, is not only grim for people but desperate 2
also for the chimpanzees of Gombe. The deforestation around the tiny 35-square-kilometer park prevents the chimpanzees from going beyond the park for food as they once did. And the availability of food is considerably reduced, particularly for the chimpanzee communities to the north and south. These two groups are frequently exposed to human disease as people press up to the park's boundaries. Moreover, when the northern and southern chimpanzee communities seek food in the central part of the park, they violate the territory of the central community. Brutal and often deadly violence breaks out. This is a present-day crisis. In the long term, the chimpanzees' future is even more grave; the genetic viability and overall health of these chimpanzees are likely to be compromised since they are unable to increase the gene pool by mating with chimps outside the park.

What can be done? It became clear that, to protect the chimpanzees 3
and their forest habitat, it would be necessary to help human populations around Gombe. Thus, in 1994 the Jane Goodall Institute created the Lake Tanganyika Catchment Reforestation and Education program. We call the program TACARE, or Take Care.

We realized it would be important to first gain the trust of the villag- 4
ers. Our team of Tanzanian staff began by asking the people what they needed. Not surprisingly, conservation was seldom listed on top: the villagers were concerned with growing more food, with health and with education. We started work with 12 villages and a grant from the

European Union. The program was so successful that we expanded it to 24 villages and have acquired some major funding from the U.S. Agency for International Development and several other donors. From the very first, TACARE was conceived as a holistic program and today has six areas of emphasis: community development, water and environmental sanitation, education, agriculture, forestry and health. We work with regional medical authorities to provide primary healthcare, basic information about hygiene and HIV-AIDS education.

Kigoma Region is one of the world's poorest regions. Largely due to   5 lack of education and inadequate health services, it has one of the highest fertility rates in the world, 4.8 percent, as well as high infant and maternal mortality. We launched our family planning activities in 1999 with a David and Lucile Packard Foundation grant to train local men and women as community-based distributors of family planning education and methods of birth control. Our long-term goal was to help the communities that surround Gombe improve the health of mothers and their babies, and to encourage spacing between births. We have 136 trained distributors who now serve in their villages by making house calls, speaking at family planning centers, and conducting private peer-counseling sessions. TACARE also raises awareness through village Family Planning Days, market speeches and public meetings. We use media and performance: plays and *ngoma*, or traditional singing and dancing, videos, calendars and T-shirts with project messages. We serve about 140,000, of which about half are women of child-bearing age.

To meet individual needs, TACARE provides a variety of family   6 planning methods and services to both men and women who request them. They include oral contraceptives and condoms, as well as referrals for clinical long-term and permanent methods such as intra-uterine devices, Depo-Provera, Norplant or voluntary sterilization for men and women.

The institute is the only NGO in rural Kigoma to provide family plan-   7 ning services at the grassroots level. Our trained educator-distributors offer our best chance of succeeding. Our program director at TACARE, Mary Mavanza, says, "Before we began our health services, family planning was almost unheard of in the Kigoma region. Using community-based peers is the best way to open doors and minds." They are critical sources of support and information for the park's neighbors.

Aisha, who has four children, was breastfeeding her three-month-old   8 baby girl when she became pregnant. Her tribe's custom and taboos told her that if she weaned her baby early, she and the baby would weaken and possibly die. She decided to perform an abortion. She took strong local herbs during the daytime and that night experienced severe abdominal pains and heavy bleeding. Her alarmed husband ran to his neighbor, TACARE's local educator-distributor, for advice. Relatives paid the boat fare to rush Aisha to the hospital, where she remained two days. When she returned home, our community-based distributor gave her nutritional advice and when she told him of her abortion, the distributor suggested birth control options. This mother of four children selected Depo-Provera injections.

"My children are doing fine," says Aisha now, "and I have enough   9 time to care for my family." She has started a small-scale business selling fish in the market. "I am happy by knowing that I won't conceive unless I plan for it."

We hear of many similar voices. Women who are able to control the   10 timing of childbirth can now pursue education or help support their families through small businesses. Their status rises within their families and communities. One mother of six, Nyamwiza, started oral contraceptives with the support of her husband, and found more time to sell fish in the market. She joined TACARE's micro-finance program, which gives small loans—mostly to women—for environmentally sustainable businesses. With her first loan, Nyamwiza expanded her fish business and sold cassava flour. Her husband helped her open a small shop to sell sugar, kerosene, oil, cigarettes and matches. The couple can now pay school fees and buy shoes, uniforms and books for their children. She wants her children to complete secondary school, an uncommon achievement in Kigoma Region.

TACARE places major emphasis on helping women because experi-   11 ence all over the world shows that as women's education levels rise, the family size lowers, so the ripple effects of family planning can be significant. We discovered that one of the reasons girls drop out of school when they reach puberty is the unhygienic latrines and a lack of privacy. So, we provide ventilated pit latrines to all schools.

Our family planning efforts still face significant challenges. The vil-   12 lagers of Kigoma Region have little exposure to the rest of the world and, therefore, tend to the traditional and the conservative. They prefer large families because more children mean more hands to help farm and fish, and the assurance of support in old age. Well-off families are traditionally large since it is considered a mark of prestige. Unfortunately, many are very poor families, which results in great hardship. A significant part or our job is taking our message about the educational and financial benefits of smaller families. A growing number of people understand the hardships posed by large families. Frequently they ask our community-based distributors why they did not come sooner.

While women instinctively appreciate having more control over their 13 fertility and childbirth, our distributors have to work harder to persuade men, who generally are reticent to even talk about family planning. So we seek them out on the fish landings and in the cafes.

Men's acceptance is sometimes hard-won. In Zashe village, one of 14 our distributors, Iddi Nanda, told me about a pregnant woman who came into the local dispensary with a sick one-year-old strapped on her back. She looked weak, too. When Iddi suggested family planning, she asked him to talk to her husband, who was a pastor.

When Iddi went to the woman's house the next day, the husband or- 15 dered Iddi to leave. After a few days, the wife went to Iddi and insisted he try again. This time the pastor threatened Iddi. One day months later the husband came to Iddi's door and begged to enter, promising he would not harm Iddi. The pastor's wife and children were all sick, he said, and he couldn't care for his family and attend to church matters. He also realized how much work his wife did each day. The pastor joined family planning services.

In just a few years, I can see how TACARE is benefiting the natural 16 environment. Woodlots have been established near the villages so women no longer need to search out and hack at stumps of trees on the steep slopes, stumps that could produce 20-foot trees in just five years. Forests are growing again outside Gombe park. This regeneration is crucial in protecting the watershed and preventing erosion. It also means the chimpanzees will soon be able to seek out other remnant populations, increasing the gene pool and providing hope for their long-term survival.

The program has won support from the Tanzanian government. 17 Recently, the Kigoma Regional Medical Office asked us to seek funding to extend the service to all of the villages in the district and to nearby Kasulu and Kibondo districts. We now receive significant support from government agencies, including USAID-Tanzania, which in 2005 asked us to co-host a workshop in Kigoma linking healthy families and healthy forests. More than 50 professionals took part, representing local and international NGOs working in the environment and development fields and local governments. And, USAID-Tanzania has asked us to use our approach in a pilot community-based program for people with AIDS in which our distributors would offer anti-retroviral therapy.

In 2004, I visited Kigoma and met with some TACARE participants.   18
A mother stood up in front of the group and told me she assumed she
would always struggle against poverty. With education in family planning, she decided to delay having another child, and started a small business. She began to realistically imagine a drastically different future.

"Thanks to TACARE, my children will be well-educated, they will be   19
well-fed, and they will be well-clothed," she said. "I want to thank
TACARE for giving me my life." In the end, that is our goal: changing
lives, one at a time, knowing that even in a generation or even a decade
our impact will have grown exponentially.

Thinking about the Essay

1. How do you interpret the author's title in light of your reading of this essay?
   Is Goodall's essay about saving chimpanzees, improving the lives of Africans, or a combination of purposes? Explain.

2. Analyze Goodall's introductory paragraph. How does it set the stage for the
   rest of the essay?

3. What connections does Goodall draw between the lives of Africans and
   chimpanzees? How does she organize her essay around these subjects?

4. What is Goodall's thesis? Does she state it in one sentence or a series of
   sentences, or does she imply it? Justify your response.

5. Goodall divides her essay into three sections. What is the essential topic of
   each section? Does she achieve unity and coherence among the parts?
   Why or why not?

Responding in Writing

6. Argue for or against the proposition that Goodall in this essay succeeds in
   linking the fates of chimpanzees and their local African population.

7. Write a personal essay in which you narrate and describe what you have
   learned from a family pet or from the natural world.

8. Reread Goodall's essay, and write a précis of her argument.

Networking

9. Divide into groups of three and four and list examples of the destruction of
   natural habitats in the United States and around the world. Present your list
   to the class along with other groups.

10. Go online with another classmate and find out about TACARE and/or the
    Jane Goodall Institute. Share your findings in class discussion.

A Place That Makes Sense

BILL MCKIBBEN | Bill McKibben was born in Palo Alto, California, in 1960 and studied at Harvard University (B.A., 1982). His writing focuses on the global ecosystem and the human impact on it. Frequently, he brings moral and religious ideas to bear on the ways in which our behavior—from consumerism to industrial shortsightedness—degrades the natural world. McKibben says that with respect to nature and Earth's ecosystem, he tries "to counter despair." In books like *The End of Nature* (1989), *Hope, Human and Wild: True Stories of Living Lightly on the Earth* (1995), *Long Distance: A Year of Living Strenuously* (2000), *Enough: Staying Human in an Engineered Age* (2003), and *Deep Economy: The Wealth of Communities and the Durable Future* (2007), McKibben balances a sense of alarm about our profligate waste of natural resources with a tempered optimism that we can revere and preserve our fragile planet. "What I have learned so far," McKibben observes, "is that what is sound and elegant and civilized and respectful of community is also environmentally benign." This essay by McKibben, which appeared in *The Christian Century* on September 23, 2008, poses a challenge: Are we living too large?

Before Reading

In his essay, McKibben asserts that "most places in the U.S. make so little sense" (paragraph 11). What do you think he means by this statement, especially as it relates to sustainable lifestyles and the environment?

Not far from Siena, in the Tuscan hill town of Montalcino, is the Abbey of Sant'Antimo. It was first built in—well, no one's certain. It was there by the ninth century. What you see now is a modern reconstruction, modern meaning 12th century. In other words, it's a part of the landscape.

And the landscape is a part of it. As I sat in the pews one afternoon earlier this summer, listening to the monks chant Nones in sonorous harmony, I kept looking past the altar to two windows behind. They framed prime views of the steeply raked farm fields in back of the sanctuary—one showed rows of dusty-leaved olive trees climbing a hill, the other rank upon rank of grapevines in their neat rows. With the crucifix in the middle they formed a kind of triptych, and it was easy to imagine not only the passion, but also one's cup running over with Chianti, one's head anointed with gleaming oil.

And easy enough, I think, to figure out why this Tuscan landscape is   3
so appealing to so many. Its charm lies in its comprehensibility—its scale makes intuitive, visceral sense. If you climb one of the bell towers in the hill towns of Tuscany, you look out on a compassable world—you can see where the food that you eat comes from, trace the course of the rivers. It seems sufficient unto itself, as indeed it largely was once upon a time. And in the ancient churches it's easy to construct a vision of the medieval man or woman who once sat in the same hard pew—a person who understood, as we never can, his or her place in the universe. That place was bounded by the distance one could travel physically—save for the Crusade years, it was probably easy to live a life without ever leaving the district. (Florentines speak of living an entire life in view of the Duomo.) And it was bounded just as powerfully by the shared and deep belief in the theology of the church. You knew your place.

Which is a phrase with several meanings. You would have been   4
deeply rooted in that world—it's hard to imagine there the identity crises that are routine in our world. You would have been considerably more rooted than we're comfortable with. You knew your place in the sense that you were born into it, and there was little hope of leaving if it didn't suit. Peasants were peasants and lords were lords, and never the two met. Inequality was baptized, questioning unlikely. The old medieval world made sense, but it was often an oppressive sense—hence the 500-year project to liberate ourselves in every possible way.

And though Tuscany still looks comprehensible—and is thus a suitable   5
backdrop for profitable tourism and powerful travel fantasy—it's now mostly sham. The farms remain, largely supported by farm subsidies from the European Union and the wine-buying habits of affluent foreigners. The villages are mostly emptied out, with only the old remaining—on weekends traffic swells as Florentines and Romans head to the country house. Even the churches are largely relics. Stop in for afternoon Mass and you're likely to find three or four old women listening to an African priest limp along in halting Italian—there aren't nearly the vocations necessary to fill these pulpits. Even the chanting monks at the Sant'Antimo abbey are imports—a French brotherhood that took over the church a decade ago.

Still, it's so alluring, this idea of rootedness. Especially for those of   6
us who live in places that make no sense at all. Where food travels

2,000 miles and arrives at a Wal-Mart. Where God lives at a mega-church without the tradition or culture to give worship much weight. How we thirst for places that make sense.

Which is why it was such a pleasure, a few days later, to find myself in a very different kind of church, this one compact, ultramodern, made of glass. Oh, and Lutheran. The ground floor, on this Thursday, was a day-care center filled with parents and kids; the second floor was all offices; and the third housed the sanctuary, a kind of window-girded nest. And when I looked out past the small cross, what I saw were the canals and sidewalks of Hammarby Sjostad—another place that makes sense. Real sense. 7

Hammarby Sjostad, a ten-minute ferry ride from the center of Stockholm, used to be an industrial brownfield, toxic and unpopulated. When Sweden bid to host the 2004 Olympics, it was slated to become the Olympic Village; the bid failed, but the momentum for a new neighborhood was enormous, and ground was broken seven or eight years ago. It was designed from the start to be an ecological gem, where the average person would live half again as lightly as the average Swede, who is already among the most ecologically minded citizens of the developed world. The whole place is a closed loop—food waste is turned into biogas, trash is burned for energy, water is recycled. None of it is outrageously high-tech; it's just all thought out. 8

And the fancy piping is actually only a small part of what makes the place work. The town requires an uncoerced but very real willingness to cooperate, to be part of a community. For instance: by the lobby of each 9

Waste tubes in Hammarby Sjostad require community cooperation to work properly.

apartment is a series of portholes built into the wall, each one connected to a pneumatic tube. You put food waste in one, paper trash in the next and so on—everything is sucked off to the right processing center. But if you put plastic in with banana peels, the system breaks down. So there's a little graph above the chutes showing how many times each building screwed up the month before. Building 7 (five stories high like most of the blocks in the development), three errant bags. Building 8, one. Building 9, none at all.

Or say you want to wash your clothes. There's no washing machine 10 in your flat—much energy is saved by having a wash house shared by a few buildings. You walk in and wave your key over a sensor, and up pops a digital display. You use it to book a time in the next few days to do your wash in the high-tech machines.

It's a reminder of why most places in the U.S. make so little sense. 11 Cheap energy has led Americans to sprawl endlessly out. We rattle around enormous houses and enormous suburbs, distant from each other in every sense of the word. (The average American eats meals with friends, family or neighbors half as often as he or she did 50 years ago.) Cheap fossil fuel has turned us into the first people in human history who have essentially no need of each other—a kind of hyperindividualism has replaced community.

So maybe Hammarby Sjostad's way of doing things would chafe a 12 little—the American cry has become "Don't tell me what to do," and it's hard to imagine us sharing washing machines with our neighbors. We don't even want to travel together—or at least we didn't until high gas prices began pulling us from our single-occupancy SUVs.

But the responsibilities come with deep pleasures. To stroll the streets 13 of this town is to realize that you've stumbled into a low-key paradise. On a fine day it seems as if all 25,000 residents are out and about, strolling the boardwalks and paths, oblivious to car traffic because it's almost nonexistent. (Parking is expensive, and who needs it—there's a fast ferry to town and a tram that comes by every few minutes.) The community was planned with bars every few blocks, with a community kayak dock, with playing fields and community centers, with shared barbecue pits. Swedes may not be gregarious, but there's the steady hum of community—clusters of moms pushing prams, for instance. (And if you want proof that this place works, the number of families with kids is higher than expected—they're having to build extra schools.) What I'm trying to say is, the place make sense.

The place makes sense in the world, as well. Here's the cost: the flats 14 are relatively small, between 600 and 1,000 square feet. That's two or three rooms plus a modest kitchen and a balcony. You can't have

There is very little automobile traffic in Hammarby Sjostad.

endless stuff because there's no room (everyone has storage space in the basement, and there's a special room for bikes). So there's way less space than we've come to consider normal—it's about like living in a trailer, maybe a double-wide.

But that's OK. When the community is an extended home recreation 15 center, you don't need a special warren in your dwelling. What it means is a resident of Hammarby Sjostad is able to live, more or less, at a level calculated to be sustainable for all of the world's 6 billion humans—as compared with the American lifestyle, which would require five additional earths if it were extended across all humanity. This is a place where people aren't drowning Bangladesh or spreading malarial mosquitoes or doing all the other things that come with living too large.

Which brings us back to the church. The state built it—Lutheranism is 16 the official religion in Sweden. And though I wasn't there on a Sunday, to judge by the number of chairs in the sanctuary, the congregation is a small percentage of the neighborhood. Still, there was a powerful sense that the gospel had been consulted in the construction of this town, if only instinctively. The rooted, practical gospel, the one that centers on loving your neighbor as yourself. I've never been in a place that made more sense.

Thinking about the Essay

1. McKibben published this essay in *The Christian Century*. What evidence do you find in the essay that suggests he writes for an audience interested in religious matters? What assumptions does he make about his intended audience? To what extent do you feel you are a member of that readership? Explain.

2. What exactly do the Abbey of Sant'Antimo and Hammarby Sjostad symbolize? How does McKibben develop these symbols? What comparative details emerge from his approach?

3. Why does McKibben present information on Tuscany in the first third of the essay, and then move to a town in Sweden? Is this strategy directly relevant to the subject he develops? Explain.

4. What is the author's argument? Where does he state his claim, and how effective is its placement? How does he employ personal experience, observation, and data to support his claim? Cite specific examples.

5. Explain the author's tone and how he achieves it. Is he optimistic or pessimistic about his subject? How do you know?

Responding in Writing

6. Write an essay explaining how you would design a town that offers an ecologically sustainable lifestyle.

7. Argue for or against the proposition that moral and religious considerations should override personal preferences when we make decisions that might affect our environment adversely.

8. Write an essay of extended definition in which you discuss the concept of "rootedness."

Networking

9. Divide into groups of three or four and discuss your views on "loving your neighbor as yourself" and how this concept might relate to environmental issues. Share your responses with the rest of the class. Also, mention whether your views were modified or changed during group discussion.

10. Go online and read messages of some of the professional newsgroups whose members are in the environmental movement. Select several messages regarding ecologically sustainable lifestyles, and write a report on your findings.

A Hole in the World

JONATHAN SCHELL

Jonathan Schell was born in New York City in 1943. Following graduate study in Far Eastern history at Harvard University and additional study in Tokyo, Schell accompanied an American forces operation in South Vietnam in the winter and spring of 1967 that resulted

in the evacuation of an entire village after "pacifica-
tion" failed. He wrote a graphic description of the
destruction of Vietnamese villages in *The Village of
Ben Suc* (1967) and *The Military Half: An Account of
Destruction in Quang Ngai and Quang Tin* (1968).
Just as his first two books excoriated the American
presence in Vietnam, Schell in his third book, *The Time
of Illusion* (1976), offered a critique of the Nixon
administration and the Watergate scandal. Schell's next
book, *The Fate of the Earth* (1982), still one of the
most persuasive treatments of the dangers of nuclear
war, became a best seller. Schell returned to the subject
of nuclear proliferation in *The Gift of Time: The Case
for Abolishing Nuclear Weapons* (1998) and *The Seventh Decade: The New Shape of Nuclear Danger*
(2007). He currently is the peace and disarmament correspondent for *The Nation* and Harold Willens Peace
Fellow at the Nation Institute. In the following essay,
published in *The Nation* on October 1, 2001, Schell
uses the events of 9/11 to raise the even more
frightening specter of nuclear destruction.

Before Reading

How has 9/11 made you more aware of the dangers posed by weapons of
mass destruction? Do you carry this awareness with you, or does the prospect
of an attack with a weapon of mass destruction seem remote and unthreaten-
ing? Explain your response.

On Tuesday morning, a piece was torn out of our world. A patch of   1
blue sky that should not have been there opened up in the New
York skyline. In my neighborhood—I live eight blocks from the World
Trade Center—the heavens were raining human beings. Our city was
changed forever. Our country was changed forever. Our world was
changed forever.

It will take months merely to know what happened, far longer to   2
feel so much grief, longer still to understand its meaning. It's already
clear, however, that one aspect of the catastrophe is of supreme importance for the future: the danger of the use of weapons of mass destruction, and especially the use of nuclear weapons. This danger includes
their use by a terrorist group but is by no means restricted to it. It is

Jonathan Schell, "A Hole in the World." Reprinted with permission from the October 1, 2001
issue of *The Nation*. For subscription information, call 1-800-333-8536. Portions of each
week's *Nation* magazine can be accessed at http://www.thenation.com.

part of a larger danger that has been for the most part ignored since the end of the cold war.

Among the small number who have been concerned with nuclear arms in recent years—they have pretty much all known one another by their first names—it was commonly heard that the world would not return its attention to this subject until a nuclear weapon was again set off somewhere in the world. Then, the tiny club said to itself, the world would awaken to its danger. Many of the ingredients of the catastrophe were obvious. The repeated suicide-homicides of the bombers in Israel made it obvious that there were people so possessed by their cause that, in an exaltation of hatred, they would do anything in its name. Many reports—most recently an article in the The New York Times on the very morning of the attack—reminded the public that the world was awash in nuclear materials and the wherewithal for other weapons of mass destruction. Russia is bursting at the seams with these materials. The suicide bombers and the market in nuclear materials was that two-plus-two that points toward the proverbial necessary four. But history is a trickster. The fates came up with a horror that was unforeseen. No one had identified the civilian airliner as a weapon of mass destruction, but it occurred to the diabolical imagination of those who conceived Tuesday's attack that it could be one. The invention illumined the nature of terrorism in modern times. These terrorists carried no bombs—only knives, if initial reports are to be believed. In short, they turned the tremendous forces inherent in modern technical society—in this case, Boeing 767s brimming with jet fuel—against itself. 3

So it is also with the more commonly recognized weapons of mass destruction. Their materials can be built the hard way, from scratch, as Iraq came within an ace of doing until stopped by the Gulf War and as Pakistan and India have done, or they can be diverted from Russian, or for that matter American or English or French or Chinese, stockpiles. In the one case, it is nuclear know-how that is turned against its inventors, in the other it is their hardware. Either way, it is "blowback"—the use of a technical capacity against its creator—and, as such, represents the pronounced suicidal tendencies of modern society. 4

This suicidal bent—nicely captured in the name of the still current nuclear policy "mutual assured destruction"—of course exists in forms even more devastating than possible terrorist attacks. India and Pakistan, which both possess nuclear weapons and have recently engaged in one of their many hot wars, are the likeliest candidates. Most important—and 5 most forgotten—are the some 30,000 nuclear weapons that remain in the arsenals of Russia and the United States. The Bush Administration has announced its intention of breaking out of the antiballistic missile treaty of 1972, which bans antinuclear defenses, and the Russians have answered that if this treaty is abandoned the whole framework of nuclear arms control built up over thirty years may collapse. There is no quarrel between the United States and Russia that suggests a nuclear exchange between them, but accidents are another matter, and, as Tuesday's attack has shown, the mood and even the structure of the international order can change overnight.

What should be done? Should the terrorists who carried out Tuesday's attacks be brought to justice and punished, as the President wants to do? Of course. Who should be punished if not people who would hurl a cargo of innocent human beings against a fixed target of other innocent human beings? (When weighing the efficiency—as distinct from the satisfaction—of punishment, however, it is well to remember that the immediate attackers have administered the supposed supreme punishment of death to themselves.) Should further steps be taken to protect the country and the world from terrorism, including nuclear terrorism? They should. And yet even as we do these things, we must hold, as if to life itself, to a fundamental truth that has been known to all thoughtful people since the destruction of Hiroshima: There is no technical solution to the vulnerability of modern populations to weapons of mass destruction. After the attack, Secretary of Defense Rumsfeld placed U.S. forces on the highest state of alert and ordered destroyers and aircraft carriers to take up positions up and down the coasts of the United States. But none of these measures can repeal the vulnerability of modern society to its own inventions, revealed by that heart-breaking gap in the New York skyline. This, obviously, holds equally true for that other Maginot line, the proposed system of national missile defense. Thirty billion dollars is being spent on intelligence annually. We can assume that some portion of that was devoted to protecting the World Trade Center after it was first bombed in 1993. There may have been mistakes—maybe we'll find out—but the truth is that no one on earth can demonstrate that the expenditure of even ten times that amount can prevent a terrorist attack on the United States or any other country. The combination of the extraordinary power of modern technology, the universal and instantaneous spread of information in the information age and the mobility inherent in a globalized economy prevents it.

6

Man, however, is not merely a technical animal. Aristotle pointed   7
out that we are also a political animal, and it is to politics that we
must return for the solutions that hold promise. That means returning
to the treaties that the United States has recently been discarding like
so much old newspaper—the one dealing, for example, with an International Criminal Court (useful for tracking down terrorists and bringing them to justice), with global warming and, above all, of course,
with nuclear arms and the other weapons of mass destruction, biological and chemical. The United States and seven other countries now
rely for their national security on the retaliatory execution of destruction a million fold greater than the Tuesday attacks. The exit from
this folly, by which we endanger ourselves as much as others, must be
found. Rediscovering ourselves as political animals also means understanding the sources of the hatred that the United States has incurred
in a decade of neglect and, worse, neglect of international affairs—a
task that is highly unwelcome to many in current circumstances but
nevertheless is indispensable to the future safety of the United States
and the world.

It would be disrespectful of the dead to in any way minimize the ca-   8
tastrophe that has overtaken New York. Yet at the same time we must
keep room in our minds for the fact that it could have been worse. To
lose two huge buildings and the people in them is one thing; to lose all
of Manhattan—or much, much more—is another. The emptiness in the
sky can spread. We have been warned.

Thinking about the Essay

1. This essay appeared less than a month after the 9/11 disaster. Do you
   think that the writer exploited the catastrophe, or is his purpose valid?
   Explain your response.

2. Schell's credentials as a specialist on nuclear proliferation are impressive.
   Is this essay geared to a highly intelligent audience or a more general one?
   Cite internal evidence to support your response.

3. How is the essay organized? Where does the introduction begin and end?
   What paragraphs constitute the body? Where is the conclusion? What
   markers assisted you in establishing these stages of essay development?

4. Reduce the logical structure of Schell's argument to a set of major and
   minor propositions. Is his conclusion valid in light of the underlying reasons? Explain.

5. What assertion in the essay do you most agree with, and why? Which assertion do you find dubious or unsupported, and why?

Responding in Writing

6. Write an essay in which you agree or disagree with Schell's statement that the danger of the use of weapons of mass destruction is "of supreme importance for the future" (paragraph 2).

7. Schell asserts that the United States has neglected its role in international affairs, including its abandonment of international treaties, thereby endangering the nation's security. Argue for or against his claim.

8. Write an analysis of Schell's style in this essay. Begin with the title itself and how it resonates throughout the essay. Discuss the impact of such graphic uses of language as "the heavens were raining human beings" (paragraph 1). Identify those stylistic techniques the author uses to persuade us to accept the logic of his position.

Networking

9. Divide into groups of between three and five, and create a simulation game whereby a specific city is threatened by a weapon of mass destruction. Imagine the steps taken to thwart the attack, and determine if these steps would be successful or not. Present your scenario to the class.

10. Using an Internet search engine, locate information on nuclear disarmament. Using the information retrieved, write a report on what various groups, agencies, and governments are doing to reduce and prevent the spread of nuclear weapons.

Conducting Research
in the Global Era

Introduction

The *doing* of research is as important a process as the *writing* of a research paper. When scholars, professors, scientists, journalists, and students *do* research, they ask questions, solve problems, follow leads, and track down sources. The process of research as well as the writing of the research paper has changed radically over the last ten years, as the Internet now makes a whole world of resources instantly available to anyone. Skillfully navigating your way through this wealth of resources, evaluating and synthesizing information as you solve problems and answer questions, enhances your critical thinking and writing abilities and develops the tools you will need for professional success.

A research paper incorporates the ideas, discoveries, and observations of other writers. The information provided by these scholars, thinkers, and observers helps to support your own original thesis or claim about a topic. Learning how to evaluate, adapt, synthesize, and correctly acknowledge these sources in your research protects you from charges of plagiarism (discussed later). More importantly, it demonstrates to you how knowledge is expanded and created. Research and research writing are the cornerstone not only of the university but of our global information society.

The research paper is the final product of a process of inquiry and discovery. The topics and readings in this book bring together voices from all over the world, discussing and debating issues of universal importance. As you develop a topic, work toward a thesis, and discover sources and evidence, you will use the Internet to bring international perspectives to your writing. More immediately, your teacher will probably ask you to work in peer groups as you refine your topics, suggest resources to each other, and evaluate preliminary drafts of your final research paper. Although the primary—and ultimate—audience for your research paper is your teacher, thinking of your work as a process of discovery and a contribution to a larger global conversation will keep your perspective fresh and your interest engaged.

The Research Process

A research paper is the final result of a series of tasks, some small and others quite time consuming. Be sure to allow yourself plenty of time for each stage of the research process, working with your teacher or a peer group to develop a schedule that breaks down specific tasks.

The four broad stages of the research process are

1. Choosing a topic
2. Establishing a thesis
3. Finding, evaluating, and organizing evidence
4. Writing your paper

Stage One: Choosing a Topic

Reading and discussing the often urgent issues addressed in this book may have already given you an idea about a topic you would like to explore further. Your attention may also have been engaged by a television news report, an international website that presented an unexpected viewpoint, or a speaker who visited your campus. Even if your teacher assigns a specific topic area to you, finding—and nurturing—a genuine curiosity and concern about that topic will make the research process much more involving and satisfying. Some topics are too broad, too controversial (or not controversial enough), too current, or too obscure for an effective research paper.

Determining an Appropriate Research Topic

Ask yourself the following questions about possible topics for your research paper:

- Am I genuinely curious about this topic? Will I want to live with it for the next few weeks?
- What do I already know about this topic? What more do I want to find out?
- Does the topic fit the general guidelines my teacher has suggested?
- Can I readily locate the sources I will need for further research on this topic?

Exercise: Freewriting

Review your work as your class progresses, taking note of any readings in the text that particularly appealed to you or any writing assignments that you especially enjoyed. Open a new folder on your computer, labeling it "Research Paper." Open a new document and title it "Freewriting." Then write, without stopping, everything that intrigued you originally about that reading or that assignment. Use the questions on page 404 to prompt your thinking.

Browsing

Having identified a general topic area of interest, begin exploring that area by *browsing*. When you browse, you take a broad and casual survey of the existing information and resources about your topic. There are many resources to consult as you begin to dig deeper into your topic, nearly all of which can be found at your campus library. Begin at the reference desk by asking for a guide to the library's reference collection.

- *General Reference Texts.* These include encyclopedias, almanacs, specialized dictionaries, and statistical information.
- *Periodical Index.* Both in-print and online versions of periodical indices now exist (the electronic versions are often subscription-only and available only through academic and some public libraries). A periodical index lists subjects, authors, and titles of articles in newspapers, journals, and magazines. Some electronic versions include both abstracts (brief summaries) and full-text versions of the articles.
- *Library Catalog.* Your library's catalog probably exists both online and as a "card catalog"—an alphabetized record organized by author, title, and subject—in which each book has its own card in a file. Begin your catalog browsing with a subject or keyword search. Identify the *call number* that appears most frequently for the books you are most likely to use—that number will point you to the library shelves where you'll find the most useful books for your topic.

Making a Global Connection

Unless you read another language, the information you find in books is not likely to be as international or immediate in perspective as that which you will find in periodicals and online. The information you find through the card catalog will direct you toward books that provide in-depth background information and context, but for the most up-to-date information as well as a perspective from the nation or countries involved in your topic, your online and periodical research will probably be most useful.

- *Search Engines.* For the most current and broadest overview of a research topic, a search engine such as Google, Windows Live, or Yahoo! can provide you with an ever-changing—and dauntingly vast—range of perspectives. Many search engines, including these three, have international sites (allowing you to search in specific regions or countries) as well as basic translation services. At the browsing stage, spending time online can both stimulate your interest and help you to focus your topic. Because websites change so quickly, however, be sure to print out a page from any site you think might be useful in the later stages of your research—that way, you'll have a hard copy of the site's URL (uniform resource locator, or Web address). (If you're working on your own computer, create a new folder under "favorites" or "bookmarks" entitled "Research Project," and file bookmarks for interesting sites there.)

Stage Two: Establishing a Thesis

Moving from a general area of interest to a specific *thesis*—a claim you wish to make, an area of information you wish to explore, a question you intend to answer, or a solution to a problem you want to propose—requires thinking critically about your topic. You have already begun to focus on what *specifically* interests you about this topic in the freewriting exercise on page 404. The next step in refining your topic and establishing a thesis is to determine your audience and purpose for writing.

Determining Your Audience and Purpose

- Where have you found, through your browsing, the most interesting or compelling information about your topic? Who was the audience for that information? Do you consider yourself to be a part of that audience? Define the characteristics of that audience (e.g., concerned about the environment, interested in global economics, experienced at traveling abroad).
- *Why* are you most interested in this topic? Do you want to encourage someone (a friend, a politician) to take a specific course of action? Do you want to shed some light on an issue or event that not many people are familiar with?
- Try a little imaginative role playing. Imagine yourself researching this topic as a professional in a specific field. For example, if your topic is environmental preservation, imagine yourself as a pharmaceuticals researcher. What would your compelling interest in the topic be? What if you were an adventure traveler seeking new destinations—how would your approach to the topic of environmental preservation change?
- If you could have the undivided attention of anyone, other than your teacher, with whom you could share your knowledge about this topic, who would that person be and why?

Moving from a Topic to a Thesis Statement

Although choosing a topic is the beginning of the research *process*, it is not the beginning of your research *paper*. The course that your research will take and the shape that your final paper will assume are based on your *thesis statement.* A thesis statement is the answer to whatever question originally prompted your research. To narrow your topic and arrive at a thesis statement, ask yourself specific questions about the topic.

Using Questions to Create a Thesis Statement

General Topic	More Specific Topic	Question	Thesis Statement
Preserving the global environment	Preserving the rain forest	What is a creative way in which people could try to preserve the rain forest?	Ecotourism, when properly managed, can help the rain forest by creating economic incentives for the people who live there.
Economic security for women in the developing world	Creating economic opportunities for women in the developing world	What approaches could help women in the developing world establish economic security for themselves and their communities?	Microloans are a creative and empowering way of redistributing wealth that allows individual women to develop their own economic security.
AIDS in Africa	The incidence of AIDS in African women	How are international organizations working to stop the spread of AIDS among African women?	Improving literacy and educational opportunities for African girls and women will help to stem the spread of AIDS.
Dating and courtship between people of different religions	Dating behavior among second-generation American Hindu or Muslim teenagers	How are kids from conservative cultural or religious backgrounds negotiating between their family's beliefs and the pressures of American popular culture?	Encouraging multicultural events helps teenagers learn about each others' cultures and beliefs.

Stage Three: Finding, Evaluating, and Organizing Evidence

Developing a Working Bibliography

A working bibliography is a record of every source you consult as you conduct your research. Although not every source you use may end up cited in your paper, having a consolidated and organized record of *everything* you looked at will make drafting the paper as well as preparing the Works Cited page much easier. Some people use their computers for keeping a Works Cited list (especially if you do much of your research using online databases, which automatically create citations). But for most people—even if many of your sources are online—index cards are much more portable and efficient. Index cards allow you to easily rearrange the order of your sources (according to priority, for example, or sources that you need to double-check). The cards let you jot down notes or summaries, and they slip into your bookbag for a quick trip to the library.

Whether your working bibliography is on a computer or on index cards, always record the same information for each source you consult. Note that current Modern Language Association (MLA) guidelines now stipulate italics in place of underlining. If you are preparing your working bibliography on a computer, use italics for book titles, magazine titles, etc.; use underlining on handwritten index cards.

Checklists for Working Bibliographies

Information for a book:

- ❑ Author name(s), first and last
- ❑ Book title
- ❑ Place of publication
- ❑ Publisher's name
- ❑ Date of publication
- ❑ Library call number
- ❑ Page numbers (for specific information or quotes you'll want to consult later)

Information for an article in a journal or magazine:

- ❑ Author name(s), first and last
- ❑ Article title
- ❑ Magazine or journal title
- ❑ Volume and issue number (when issue number is available)
- ❑ Date of publication
- ❑ Page numbers
- ❑ Library call number

Information for online sources:

❑ Author (if there is one)
❑ Title of an article or graphic on the Web page
❑ Title of website, if different from the above
❑ Version or edition
❑ Publisher or sponsor of the site (if any)
❑ Date of publication (if available)
❑ Date of your online access
❑ URL (website address; not usually included in your Works Cited list unless it would be unlikely your reader could find the correct source or if your instructor requires one)
❑ *Some sites include information on how they prefer to be cited. You'll notice this information at the bottom of a main or "splash" page of a site, or you'll see a link to a "citation" page.*

Sample working bibliography note: Article

Honey, Martha. "Protecting the Environment: Setting Green Standards for the Tourism Industry." *Environment* 45.1 (2003): 8–12.

Sample working bibliography note: Online source

World Tourism Association. "Global Code of Ethics for Tourism." <http:www.// world-tourism.org/projects/ethics/principles.html>.

Consulting Experts and Professionals

In the course of your research you may discover someone whose work is so timely, or opinions so relevant, that a personal interview would provide even more (and unique) information for your paper. Look beyond the university faculty for such experts—for example, if your topic is ecotourism, a local travel agent who specializes in ecotourism might be able to give you firsthand accounts of such locales and voyages. If your topic is second-generation teenagers balancing conservative backgrounds with American popular culture, hanging out with a group of such kids and talking with them about their lives will give you the kind of first-person anecdote that makes research writing genuinely fresh and original. Think of "expertise" as being about *experience*—not just a title or a degree.

Checklist for Arranging and Conducting Interviews

❑ Be certain that the person you wish to speak to will offer a completely unique, even undocumented, perspective on your topic. Interviewing someone who has already published widely on your topic is not the best use of your research time, as you can just as easily consult that person's published work.

❏ E-mail, telephone (at a business number, if possible), or write to your subject well in advance of your paper deadline. Explain clearly that you are a student writing a research paper, the topic of your paper, and the specific subject(s) you wish to discuss.

❏ An interview can be conducted via e-mail or over the telephone as well as in person. Instant messaging, because it can't be easily documented and doesn't lend itself to longer responses, is not a good choice.

❏ Write out your questions in advance!

Conducting Field Research

Field research involves traveling to a specific place to observe and document a specific occurrence or phenomenon. For example, if you were writing about the challenges and opportunities of a highly diverse immigrant community (such as Elmhurst, Queens), you might arrange to spend a day at a local school, park, or coffee shop. Bring a notebook, a digital camera, a tape recorder—anything that will help you capture and record observations. Although your task as a field researcher is to be *unbiased*—to objectively observe what is happening, keeping an open mind as well as open eyes—you'll want to always keep your working thesis in mind, too. For example, if your thesis is

> Allowing students in highly diverse American communities to create events that celebrate and respect their own cultural traditions within the general American popular culture helps to create understanding between teenagers and their immigrant parents

your field research might take you to a high school in an immigrant community to observe the interactions among teenagers. You'll want to record everything—both positive and negative, both expected and surprising—that you observe and overhear, but you won't want to get distracted by a teacher's mentioning the difficulties of coping with many different languages in the classroom. That's fascinating, but it's another topic altogether.

Checklist for Arranging and Conducting Field Research

❏ If your field research involves crossing a private boundary or property line—a school, church, hospital, restaurant, etc.—be sure to contact the institution first to confirm that it's appropriate for you to visit. As with the guidelines for conducting a personal interview, inform the person with whom you arrange the visit that you are a student conducting field research and that your research is for a classroom paper.

❏ Respect personal boundaries. Some people might not want to be photographed, and others might be uneasy if they think you are taking notes on their conversation or behavior. If you sense that your presence is making someone uncomfortable, apologize and explain what you are doing. If they are still uncomfortable, back off.

❏ When you use examples and observations from your field research in your research paper, do not use the first person as part of the citation. Simply describe what was observed and under what circumstances.

Not recommended: When I visited the dog park to see how the personalities of dogs reflect those of their owners, I was especially attracted to the owner of a bulldog named Max. When I introduced myself to Max's owner, George T., and explained my project to him, George agreed with my thesis and pointed out that the owners of large, athletic dogs like Rottweilers tended to be young men, and the owners of more sedentary dogs (like Max) seemed to be a little mellower.

Recommended: A visit to a local dog park revealed the ways in which the personalities of dogs reflect those of their owners. George T., the owner of a bulldog named Max, pointed out that the younger men at the park were accompanied by large, athletic dogs like Rottweilers, while more sedentary people (like George) tended to have mellower breeds such as bulldogs.

Assessing the Credibility of Sources

After browsing, searching, observing, and conversing, you will by now have collected a mass of sources and data. The next step is to evaluate those sources critically, using your working bibliography as a road map back to all the sources you have consulted to date. This critical evaluation will help you to determine which sources have the relevance, credibility, and authority expected of academic research.

Checklist for Assessing Source Credibility

❏ Do the table of contents and index of a book include keywords and subjects relevant to your topic? Does the abstract of a journal article include keywords relevant to your topic and thesis? Does a website indicate through a menu (or from your using the "search" command) that it contains content relevant to your topic and thesis?

❏ How current is the source? Check the date of the magazine or journal and the copyright date of the book (the original copyright date, not the dates of reprints). Has the website been updated recently, and are its links current and functioning?

❏ How authoritative is the source? Is the author credentialed in his or her field? Do other authors refer to this writer (or website) in their work?

❏ Who sponsors a website? Is it the site of a major media group, a government agency, a political think tank, or a special-interest group? If you are unsure, print out the home page of the site and ask your teacher or a reference librarian.

Taking Notes

Now that you have determined which sources are most relevant and useful, you can begin to read them with greater attention to detail. This is *active reading*—annotating, responding to, and taking notes on what you are reading. Taking careful notes will help you to build the structure of your paper and will ensure accurate documentation later. As with the working bibliography, you can take notes either on your computer or on index cards. For online sources, you can cut and paste blocks of text into a separate word-processing document on your computer; just be certain to include the original URL and to indicate that what you have cut and pasted is a *direct quote* (which you might later paraphrase or summarize). Some researchers cut and paste material in a font or color that is completely different from their own writing, just to remind them of where specific words and concepts came from (and as protection against inadvertent plagiarism).

There are three kinds of notes you will take as you explore your resources:

- Summaries give you the broad overview of a source's perspective or information and serve as reminders of a source's content should you wish to revisit later for more specific information or direct quotes.
- Paraphrases express a source's ideas and information in your own language.
- Direct *quotations* are best for when an author or subject expresses a thought or concept in language that is so striking, important, or original that to paraphrase it would be to lose some of its importance. Direct quotations are *exact* copies of an author's own words and are always enclosed in quotation marks.

Checklist for Taking Notes

❑ Take just one note (paraphrase, summary, or analysis) on each index card. Be sure to note the complete source information for the quote on the card (see the Checklists for Working Bibliographies on page 408 for what information is required).

❑ Cross-check your note-taking cards against your working bibliography. Be sure that every source on which you take notes has a corresponding entry in the working bibliography.

❑ Write a subtopic on top of each card, preferably in a brightly colored ink. Keep a running list of all of your subtopics. This will enable you to group together related pieces of information and determine the structure of your outline.

Sample note: Summary

Subtopic	Indigenous peoples and ecotourism
Author/title	Mastny, "Ecotourist trap"
Page numbers	94
Summary	The Kainamaro people of Guyana are actively involved with the development of ecotourism in their lands, ensuring that their cultural integrity takes precedence over financial gain.

Sample note: Paraphrase

Subtopic	Indigenous peoples and ecotourism
Author/title	Mastny, "Ecotourist trap"
Page numbers	94
Paraphrase	Actively involving indigenous peoples in ecotourism arrangements is important. A representative for the Kainamaro people of Guyana, Claudette Fleming, says that although this community first worried about maintaining their cultural integrity, they came to see that ecotourism would be a more beneficial way to increase their income and at the same time control their lands and culture than other industries such as logging.

Sample note: Direct quotation

Subtopic	Indigenous peoples and ecotourism
Author/title	Mastny, "Ecotourist trap"
Page numbers	94
Direct quotation	"The Kainamaro are content to share their culture and creativity with outsiders—as long as they remain in control of their futures and the pace of cultural change."

Understanding Plagiarism, Intellectual Property, and Academic Ethics

• *Plagiarism.* Plagiarism is passing off someone else's words, ideas, images, or concepts as your own. Plagiarism can be as subtle and accidental as forgetting to add an in-text citation or as blatant as "borrowing" a friend's paper or handing in something from a website with your own name on it. Most schools and colleges have explicit, detailed policies about what constitutes plagiarism, and the consequences of being caught are not pretty—you may risk anything from failure on a particular assignment to expulsion from the institution. There are two basic ways to avoid plagiarism: (1) Don't wait until the last minute to write your paper (which will tempt you to take shortcuts); and (2) give an in-text citation (see page 418) for absolutely everything you include in your research paper that didn't come out of your own head. It's better to be safe and overcite

than to be accused of plagiarism. For a straightforward discussion of plagiarism, go to http://www.georgetown.edu/honor/plagiarism.html.

- *Intellectual Property.* If you've ever considered wiping your hard disk
  clean of free downloaded music files out of the fear of being arrested or
  fined, then you've wrestled with the issue of intellectual property. Intellectual property includes works of art, music, animation, and literature—as
  well as research concepts, computer programs, and even fashion. Intellectual property rights for visual, musical, and verbal works are protected by
  copyright law. When you download, for free, a music track from the
  Internet, you are violating copyright law—the artist who created that
  work receives no credit or royalties for your enjoyment and use of his or
  her work. When you cut and paste blocks of a website into your own
  research paper without giving credit, you are also violating copyright law.
  To respect the intellectual property rights of anyone (or anything) you cite
  in your research paper, you carefully *cite* the source of the information.
  Using quotes from another writer, or images from another artist, in your
  own academic paper is legally defined as "fair use"—*if* you make it clear
  where the original material comes from.

- *Ethics and the Academic Researcher.* As you enter an academic conversation about your research topic, your audience—even if it's only your
  teacher—expects you to conduct yourself in an ethical fashion. Your
  ethos, literally, means "where you stand"—what you believe, how you
  express those beliefs, and how thoughtfully and considerately you relate
  to the "stances" of others in your academic community. In the professional academy, researchers in fields from medieval poetry through cell
  biology are expected to adhere to a code of ethics about their research.
  Working with the ideas and discoveries of others in their academic communities, they are careful to always acknowledge the work of their peers
  and the contributions that work has made to their own research. You
  should do the same. When you leave school, these basic ethical tenets
  remain the same. You wouldn't hand in another rep's marketing report as
  your own, you wouldn't claim credit for the successful recovery of another
  doctor's patient, and you wouldn't put your name on top of another
  reporter's story. To violate professional ethics is to break the trust that
  holds an academic or professional community together.

Stage Four: Organizing and Outlining Your Information

Now that you have gathered and evaluated a mass of information, the
next step is to begin giving some shape and order to what you have discovered. Writing an outline helps you to think through and organize your
evidence, determine the strengths and weaknesses of your argument, and
visualize the shape of your final paper. Some instructors will require you
to hand in an outline along with your research paper. Even if an outline

isn't formally required, it is such a useful and valuable step toward moving from a pile of index cards to a logical, coherent draft that you should plan to create one.

Checklist for Organizing Your Information

❏ Gather up all of your note cards and print out any notes you have taken on your computer. Double-check all of your notes to make sure that they include accurate citation information.

❏ Using your list of subtopics, group your notes according to those subtopics. Are some piles of cards enormous, while other topics have only a card or two? See if subtopics can be combined—or if any subtopics could be further refined and made more specific.

❏ Set aside any note cards that don't seem to "fit" in any particular pile.

❏ Find your thesis statement and copy it out on a blank index card. Go through the cards in each subtopic. Can you immediately see a connection between each note card and your thesis statement? (If not, set that note card aside for now.)

❏ Do not throw away any of the note cards, even if they don't seem to "fit" into your current research plan. You probably won't use every single note card in your paper, but it's good to have a continuing record of your work.

Basic Outlining

Many word-processing programs include an "outline" function, and your instructor may ask you to follow a specific format for your outline. An outline is a kind of road map for your thought processes, a list of the pieces of information you are going to discuss in your paper and how you are going to connect those pieces of information to each other as well as back to your original thesis. You can begin the outlining process by using the note cards you have divided into subtopics:

    I. Most compelling, important subtopic
      A. Supporting fact, quote, or illustration
      B. Another interesting piece of evidence that supports or illustrates the subtopic
        1. A direct quotation that further illustrates point B
        2. Another supporting point
          a. Minor, but still relevant, points

Another useful outlining strategy is to assign each subtopic a working "topic sentence" or "main idea." As you move into the drafting process, you can return to those topic sentences/main ideas to begin each paragraph.

The Writing Process

A research paper is more than a collection of strung-together facts. No matter how interesting and relevant each individual piece of information may be, your reader is not responsible for seeing how the parts make up a whole. Connecting the evidence, demonstrating the relationships between concepts and ideas, and proving how all of it supports your thesis are entirely up to you.

Drafting

The shape of your outline and your subdivided piles of index cards provide the framework for your rough draft. As you begin to write your essay, think about "connecting the dots" between each piece of evidence, gradually filling in the shape of your argument. Expect your arrangement of individual note cards or whole subtopics to change as you draft.

Remember that you are not drafting a final paper, and certainly not a perfect paper. The goal of drafting is to *organize* your evidence, to get a sense of your argument's strengths and weaknesses, and to test the accuracy of your thesis and revise it if necessary. Drafting is as much a thinking process as it is a writing process.

If you get "stuck" as you draft, abandon whatever subtopic you are working on and begin with another. Working at the paragraph level first—using the evidence on a subtopic's note card to support and illustrate the topic sentence or main idea of the subtopic—is a much less intimidating way to approach drafting a research paper.

Finally, as you draft, be sure that you include either an in-text citation (see page 418) or some other indication of *precisely* where each piece of information came from. This will save you time when you begin revising and preparing the final draft as well as the Works Cited list.

Incorporating Sources

As you draft, you will build connections between different pieces of evidence, different perspectives, and different authors. Learning how to smoothly integrate all those different sources into your own work, without breaking the flow of your own argument and voice, takes some practice. The most important thing to remember is to accurately indicate the source of every piece of information as soon as you cite it.

One way to smoothly integrate sources into your paper is through paraphrase. For example:

> The educational benefits of ecotourism can help future generations to respect the environment. "Helping people learn to love the earth is a high calling and one that can be carried out through ecotourism.

Ecotourism avoids much of the counterproductive baggage that often accompanies standard education" (Kimmel 41).

In revision, this writer used paraphrase to move more gracefully from her main point to the perspective provided by her source:

> Teachers like James R. Kimmel have called the ecotourism experience a "nirvana" for educating their students. "Helping people learn to love the earth is a high calling and one that can be carried out through ecotourism," he observes, noting that the "counterproductive baggage" such as testing and grading are left behind (Kimmel 41).

This system of indicating where exactly an idea, quote, or paraphrase comes from is called *parenthetical citation.* In MLA and APA style, which are required by most academic disciplines (see pages 418–420), these in-text citations take the place of footnotes or endnotes.

Using Transition Verbs Between Your Writing and a Source

Using conversation verbs as transitions between your own writing and a direct quote can enliven the style of your paper. In the previous example, the writer uses the verb "observes" rather than just "states" or "writes." Other useful transitions include:

Arundhati Roy argues that ...

Amy Tan remembers that ...

Barbara Ehrenreich and Annette Fuentes compare the results of ...

Al Gore admits that ...

Naomi Shihab Nye insists that ...

Hisham Matar vividly describes ...

Revising and Polishing

The drafting process clarified your ideas and gave structure to your argument. In the revision process, you rewrite and rethink your paper, strengthening the connections between your main points, your evidence, and your thesis. Sharing your essay draft with a classmate, with your instructor, or with a tutor at your campus writing center will give you an invaluable objective perspective on your paper's strengths and weaknesses.

Checklist for Your Final Draft

❏ Have I provided parenthetical citations for every source I used?

❏ Do all of those parenthetical citations correspond to an item in my Works Cited list?

❏ Does my essay's title clearly and specifically state my topic?

❏ Is my thesis statement identifiable, clear, and interesting?

❏ Does each body paragraph include a topic sentence that clearly connects to my thesis?

❏ Do I make graceful transitions between my own writing and the sources I incorporate?

❏ When I shared my paper with another reader, was I able to answer any questions about my evidence or my argument using sources already at hand? Or do I need to go back to the library or online to "fill in" any questionable areas in my research?

❏ Does my conclusion clearly echo and support my thesis statement and concisely sum up how all of my evidence supports that thesis?

❏ Have I proofread for clarity, grammar, accuracy, and style?

❏ Is my paper formatted according to my instructor's guidelines? Do I have a backup copy on disk and more than one printed copy?

Documentation

From the beginning of your research, when you were browsing in the library and online, you have been documenting your sources. To document a source simply means to make a clear, accurate record of where exactly a piece of information, a quote, an idea, or a concept comes from, so that future readers of your paper can go back to that original source and learn more. As we have seen, careful attention to documentation is the best way to protect yourself against inadvertent plagiarism. There are two ways you document your sources in your paper: within the text itself (*in-text* or *parenthetical* citation) and in the Works Cited list at the end of your paper.

What Do I Need to Document?

• Anything I didn't know before I began my research
• Direct quotations
• Paraphrases
• Summaries
• Specific numerical data, such as charts and graphs
• Any image, text, or animation from a website
• Any audio or video
• Any information gathered during a personal interview

Parenthetical (In-Text) Citation

MLA style for documentation is most commonly used in the humanities and is the format discussed here. Keep in mind that different academic disciplines have their own documentation guidelines and styles, as do some organizations (many newspapers, for example, have their own "style guides"). An in-text citation identifies the source of a piece of information as part of your own sentence or within parentheses. In MLA style, the parenthetical information includes the author's name and the page number (if appropriate) on which the information can be found in the original source. If your readers want to know more, they can then turn to your Works Cited page to find the author's name and the full bibliographic information for that source. Always place the in-text or parenthetical citation as close to the incorporated source material as possible—preferably within the same sentence.

Guidelines for Parenthetical (In-Text) Citation
Page numbers for a book

The end of the Second World War began Samuel Beckett's greatest period of creativity, which he referred to as "the siege in the room" (Bair 346).

Bair describes the period immediately after the Second World War as a time of great creativity for Samuel Beckett (346).

In the first parenthetical citation, the author is not named within the student writer's text, so the parentheses include both the source author's name and the page number on which the information can be found. In the second example, the source author (Bair) is mentioned by name, so there is no need to repeat that name within the parentheses—only the page number is needed.

Page numbers for an article in a magazine or journal

Wheatley argues that "America has embraced values that cannot create a sustainable society and world" (25).

Page numbers for a newspaper article

Cite both the section letter (or description of the section) and the page.

Camera phones are leading to new questions about the invasion of privacy (Harmon sec. 4:3).

A spokesperson for the National Institutes of Health has described obesity as the greatest potential danger to the average American's health (Watts B3).

Website

Arts and Letters Daily includes links to opinions and essays on current events from English-language media worldwide.

Article 2 of the proposed Global Code of Ethics for Tourism describes tourism
"as a vehicle for individual and collective fulfillment" (*world-tourism*).

When an online source does not give specific "page," screen, or paragraph
numbers, your parenthetical citation must include the name of the site.

Works Cited List

Gather your working bibliography cards, and be sure that every source you
cite in your paper has a corresponding card. To construct the Works Cited
list, you simply arrange these cards in alphabetical order, by author. The
Works Cited page is a separate, double-spaced page at the end of your
paper.

Formatting Your Works Cited List

- Center the title, Works Cited, at the top of a new page. Do not underline it, italicize it, or place it in quotation marks.
- Alphabetize according to the author's name, or according to the title
(for works, such as websites, that do not have an author). Ignore words
such as *the*, *and*, and *a* when alphabetizing.
- Begin each entry at the left margin. After the first line, indent all other
lines of the entry by five spaces (one stroke of the "tab" key).
- Double-space every line.
- Place a period after the author, the title, the publishing information,
and the medium of publication (Print, Web, CD-ROM, etc.).
- Italicize book and Web page titles. Titles of articles, stories, poems, and
parts of entire works in other media are placed in quotation marks.

Guidelines for Works Cited List

Book by one author

Ruiz, Teofilo F. *The Terror of History*. Princeton, NJ: Princeton UP: 2011. Print.

Multiple books by the same author

List the author's name for the first entry. For each entry that follows, replace the
author's name with three hyphens.

Holzer, Harold. *Lincoln at Cooper Union*. New York: Simon and Shuster, 2004.
Print.

___. *Lincoln: President-Elect*. New York: Simon and Shuster, 2008. Print.

Book with two or three authors/editors

Goodbody, Axel, and Kate Rigby, eds. *Ecocritical Theory*. Charlottesville: UP
   Virginia, 2011. Print.

Book with more than three authors/editors

Freeman, Arthur, James Pretzer, Barbara Fleming, and Karen M. Simon. *Clinical
   Applications of Cognitive Therapy*. 2nd ed. New York: Springer, 2004. Print.

Alternatively, in this case, you can use the first name only and add *et al.* ("and
   others.")

Book or publication with group or organization as author

Modern Language Association. *MLA Handbook for Writers of Research Papers*.
   7th ed. New York: MLA, 2009. Print.

Book or publication without an author

Chase's Calendar of Events 2012. New York: McGraw, 2012. Print.

Work in an anthology of pieces all by the same author

Thomas, Lewis. "The Youngest and Brightest Thing Around." *The Medusa and
   the Snail: More Notes of a Biology Watcher*. New York: Viking, 1979. Print.

Work in an anthology of different authors

Chase, Katie. "Man and Wife." *The Best American Short Stories 2008*. Ed.
   Salman Rushdie. Boston: Houghton, 2008. Print.

Work translated from another language

Eco, Umberto. *The Prague Cemetery*. Trans. Richard Dixon. New York: Houghton
   Mifflin Harcourt, 2012. Print.

Entry from a reference volume

For dictionaries and encyclopedias, simply note the edition and its date. No page
   numbers are necessary for references organized alphabetically, such as encyclopedias (and, obviously, dictionaries).

Merriam-Webster's Medical Desk Dictionary. Rev. ed. Boston: Cengage, 2006. Print.

"Carriera, Rosalba." *The Oxford Companion to Western Art*. Ed. Hugh Brigstoke.

Oxford: Oxford UP, 2001. Print.

Article from a journal

Note that current MLA guidelines no longer make a distinction between journals that are numbered continuously (e.g., Vol. 1 ends on page 208, Vol. 2 starts on page 209) or numbered separately (i.e., each volume starts on page 1). No matter how the journal is paginated, all of them must contain volume *and* issue numbers. (To indicate the issue number, place a period and the number after the volume number.) One exception is journals with issue numbers only; simply cite the issue numbers alone as though they are volume numbers.

Blair, Kristen L. "New Media Affordances and the Connected Life." *CCC* 63.2

(Dec. 2011): 314–27. Print.

Enoch, Jessica. "Resisting the Script of Indian Education: Zitkala-Sa and the

Carlisle Indian School." *College English* 65.1 (2002): 117–41. Print.

Article from a weekly or biweekly periodical

Denby, David. "War Horse." *New Yorker* 2 Jan. 2012: 78. Print.

Article from a monthly or bimonthly periodical

Perlin, John. "Solar Power: The Slow Revolution." *Invention and Technology*

Summer 2002: 20–25. Print.

Article from a daily newspaper

Sciolino, Elaine. "The French, the Veil, and the Look." *The New York Times* 17

Apr. 2011: 4. Print.

If the newspaper article goes on for more than one page, add a sign to the first

page number.

Newspaper or periodical article with no author

"Groups Lose Sole Authority on Chaplains for Muslims." *The New York Times*

14 Oct. 2003: A15. Print.

Unsigned editorial in a newspaper or periodical

"Monitoring Syria." Editorial. *The Washington Post* 29 Dec. 2011: sec. A:16. Print.

Letter to the editor of a newspaper or periodical

Post, Diana. Letter. "U.S. Should Stand Against Rape." *Ms.* Fall 2011: 7. Print.

Film, video, DVD

If you are writing about a specific actor's performance or a specific director, use that person's name as the beginning of the citation. Otherwise, begin with the title of the work. Specify the media of the recording (film, video, DVD, etc.).

Princess Mononoke. Dir. Hayao Miyazaki. Prod. Studio Ghibli, 1999. Miramax, 2001. Videocassette.

Eames, Charles and Ray. *The Films of Charles and Ray Eames, Volume 1: Powers of Ten*. 1978. Pyramid Home Video, 1984. Videocassette.

Television or radio broadcast

"Alone on the Ice." *The American Experience*. PBS. KRMA, Denver, 8 Feb. 1999. Television.

Arnold, Elizabeth. "The Birds of the Boreal." *National Geographic Radio Expeditions*. NPR. WNYC, New York, 14 Oct. 2003. Radio.

A sound recording

Bukkene Bruse. "Wedding March from Osterdalen." *Nordic Roots 2*. Northside, 2000. CD.

Personal interview

Give the name of the person you interviewed, how the interview was conducted (phone, e-mail, etc.), and the date of the interview.

Jackson, Janet. Telephone interview. 12 Sept. 2011.

Clinton, Hillary. E-mail interview. 8 Aug. 2012.

Online sources

MLA no longer recommends the inclusion of URLs (Web addresses) in the Works Cited entries. However, you should include URLs when the reader probably cannot find the source without them or if your instructor requires them.

Web page/Internet site

Give the site title, the name of the site's author or editor (if there is one), electronic publication information, medium of publication (Web), your own date of access, and the site's URL, if needed. (If some of this information is not available, just cite what you can.)

Arts & Letters Daily. Ed. Denis Dutton. 2003. Web. 2 Sept. 2003.

Document or article from an Internet site

Include the author's name, document title, information about a print version (if applicable), information about the electronic version, medium of publication (Web), date of access, and URL (if needed).

Brooks, David. "The Organization Kid." *The Atlantic Monthly* April 2001: 40–54.
   Web. 25 Aug. 2003.

Book available online

The citation is similar to the format for a print book, but include as much information as you can about the website as well as the date of your access to it.

Einstein, Albert. *Relativity: The Special and General Theory.* Trans. Robert W.
   Lawson. New York: Henry Holt, 1920. *Bartleby.com: Great Books Online.*
   2003. Ed. Steven van Leeuwen. Web. 6 Sept. 2003.

Wheatley, Phillis. *Poems on Various Subjects, Religious and Moral. Project*
   Gutenberg. 2003. Ed. Michael S. Hart. Web. 6 Sept. 2003.

Database available online

Bartleby Library. 2003. Ed. Steven van Leeuwen. Web. 28 Sept. 2003.

Source from a library subscription database

Academic and most public libraries offer to their members access to subscription-only databases that provide electronic access to publications not otherwise available on free-access websites. According to current MLA guidelines, the name of the subscription service and the institution that provided the access need not be included in the Works Cited entry.

Mastny, Lisa. "Ecotourist Trap." *Foreign Policy* Nov.–Dec. 2002: 94. *Questia.*
   Web. 10 Oct. 2003.

Rossant, John. "The Real War Is France vs. France." *Business Week* 6 Oct. 2003:
   68. *MasterFile Premier.* Web. 13 Oct. 2003.

Newspaper article online

Zernike, Kate. "Fight Against Fat Shifts to the Workplace." *The New York Times.*
The New York Times, 12 Oct. 2003. Web. 12 Oct. 2003.

Journal article online

Salkeld, Duncan. "Making Sense of Differences: Postmodern History, Philosophy
and Shakespeare's Prostitutes." *Chronicon: An Electronic History Journal* 3.1
(1999). Web. 5 Apr. 2003.

E-mail

Give the writer's name, the subject line (if any) enclosed in quotation
marks, the date of the message, and the medium of transmission (e-mail).

Stanford, Myles. "Johnson manuscripts online." Message to the author. 12 July
2003. E-mail.

Electronic posting to an online forum

Many online media sources conduct forums in which readers can respond
to breaking news or ongoing issues. Citing from such forums is difficult
because many people prefer to post anonymously; if the author's user-
name is too silly or inappropriate, use the title of the post or the title of
the forum to begin your citation and determine its place in the alphabetical order of your Works Cited list.

Berman, Piotr. 6 Oct. 2003. "Is Middle East Peace Impossible?" Web. 13 Oct.
2003. <http://tabletalk.salon.com/webx?13@@.596c5554>.

Sample Professional Essay (MLA Style)

Leaking All over the Page

LAURA KIPNIS

"We were warned to expect 'dirty tricks,'" he tweeted. "Now we have the first one." He'd been set up, he told reporters. His lawyer attributed the allegations to "dark forces," part of a "greater plan" to discredit him (Harnden). The "we" (and "he") in question was Julian Assange, a thirty-nine-year-old Australian and founder of guerrilla media organization WikiLeaks, which dedicates itself to embarrassing governments and corporations through strategic leaks of classified and secret documents to the media. Assange has yet to be formally charged with anything, although he's currently under house arrest at the English country estate of one of his supporters and facing extradition to Sweden after allegedly sexually assaulting two women there. The women, both WikiLeaks supporters, did consent to have sex with him, but apparently not the kind of sex he had in mind. As one of them put it, "Not only was it the worst screw of my life, it was also violent" (qtd. in Davies).

The details of the police reports have, in turn, been strategically leaked to the media, generating a worldwide outbreak of commentary, argumentation, and conspiracy theories, as well as a $1.5 million book deal with American and British publishers for Assange's memoirs. Little known until recently, Assange, a digital age international scofflaw, is now an international celebrity. The quantity of information in circulation about him increases exponentially

The writer hooks the reader at the outset with an intriguing quote.

Citations in parentheses signal MLA style.

The writer provides background.

with each passing day: details on everything from his complexion (ghostly) to his relationship with his mother (complicated) to his personality (egomaniacal, self-aggrandizing, charming one moment and autocratic the next—he himself says he's "somewhere on the autistic spectrum" [qtd. in Hosenbail]). Thanks to the assault allegations, now we even have play-by-play accounts of his sexual style: caddish or criminal, depending on whom you ask.

One problem in writing about contemporary scandal, I've found, having recently completed a book on the subject I started a decade ago, is the unending barrage of new material coupled with the rapid exhaustion rate of the example pool. "Are you going to include this new scandal or that one?" everyone you know queries so helpfully every time another ingenue self-implodes or the latest billion-dollar Ponzi scheme is exposed, until the prospective manuscript starts resembling one of those Jorge Luis Borges stories about the infinite book with an indefinite number of pages containing every known instance and scrap of information relating to its ostensible subject, driving writers, readers, and librarians to despair.

Given the shelf-life issue, no doubt Assange will be superseded by a hundred new scandals long before these remarks hit print. But at the moment he's impossible to ignore, which is the sine qua non of a good scandal: somehow you can't look away. This one also happens to put conventional political affiliations and divisions up for grabs: it's not just feminists against leftists; it's leftists against First Amendment advocates and Pentagon Papers–era First Amendment advocates against WikiLeaks-era First Amendment advocates and feminists accusing other feminists of being rape apologists. No less a public-sphere feminist than Naomi Wolf has ridiculed the rape accusations against Assange as motivated by "hurt feelings" at best ("Julian Assange"), despite having created a miniscandal a few years

The writer establishes her authority and her thesis.

The writer begins an extended definition and analysis of celebrity scandal.

The writer refers to experts for support.

back herself by accusing Harold Bloom of groping her thigh some twenty years earlier, when she'd been his student ("Sex"). Has she somehow forgotten this? Among the reasons high-profile scandal cases are magnets for so much social commentary is the infinitely useful opportunities for disavowal and disidentification they create.

As a self-appointed scandal theorist, and one not tethered to any particular academic discipline (my long-ago formal education was in art), I must start, when confronted with such a superb trove of material, by asking, *Now* what? One of the attractions of scandal as a subject is how little of theoretical interest has been written on it to date: it's pretty much virgin terrain, despite the vast amount of social real estate it occupies. You're forced to make your methodology up as you go along, feeling your way through pitch-black sewers on hands and knees, grasping at glimmers of insight. There's no recipe; each case necessarily generates its own techniques. The method, such as it is, emerges from the contours and particulars of the scandals themselves.

A concern about such procedures, obviously, is that the transgressions and embarrassments of the particular scandal might seep into the writing of the case or color the analysis. Still, transforming scandalizers into characters in a narrative does demand some level of authorial identification, some imagined proximity to their particular logic or illogic. (Perhaps this approach borrows more from novelists than social critics.) Another concern is not knowing exactly where you'll end up—you can lose your bearings or your overview of the situation, as have the protagonists themselves, of course, which is what got them into such a mess in the first place. You may discover alien dimensions in your own thinking that aren't what you intended to stand for; your instincts may lead you astray. You may not even subscribe to your own conclusions in the end. Occasionally, practical decisions must be made: am I really willing to say "X" or "Y" in print?

The writer establishes a breezy, self-effacing tone.

The writer provides a basic thesis concerning scandal theory.

The writer explores issues and problems in developing a theory of celebrity scandal.

It's not that there isn't *any* critical distance but that critical proximity can be more useful. I'd go so far as to say that drawing on your worst impulses is the only way to understand contemporary scandals and the instant celebrities they create. Speaking of worst impulses, I confess that my interest in the Assange case probably had less to do with its sociopolitical dimensions than its parabolic ones: the pleasant shapeliness of a moral fable peeking through the tawdry details. Assange used exposé for what he sees as political purpose, only to have exposé turned against him for feminist purposes. Note the satisfying formal symmetry, the chiastic structure, the O. Henry twist: he who exposes the secrets of the powerful shall have his own powerful secrets similarly exposed.

The writer makes a strong emotional claim about her interest in scandal.

Please don't think that I'm in favor of governmental payback or dirty tricks, should those turn out to have been in play. (Assange's lawyer did initially suggest the whole thing had been a "honey trap," though Assange himself later poo-pooed the idea [Davies].) Whatever it is that draws me to the biographical and psychological excesses being paraded through the public square, I fear it has as much to do with the tropes, puns, homologies, and literary resonances in these narratives as the sociological ones, which could be a form of excess in its own right.

I suspect, however, that this surplus is exactly what's so captivating about scandal. You're going around, minding your own business, and these split-off fragments of other people's repressions and wishes come hurtling at you from the social ether like messages in a bottle, one bedeviled psyche flagging down another, scattering coded clues and demanding to be deciphered. There's this intersubjective gravitational pull. But *then* what, methodologically speaking? Conventional modes of sociopolitical analysis yield banalities, yet following the path of fascination propels you into the murk of the unknown. For writers, there's always a certain queasy thrill in projecting fascinations and attractions you don't entirely understand

The writer analyzes the reasons why we are attracted to scandal.

into the public arena, though if your subject matter is other people's dirty secrets and public self-immolations and your method is following errant interpretative instincts and seeing where they lead, what dirty secrets are you yourself exposing in the process? No doubt more of them than you care to know.

The cases I've found myself compelled by haven't tended to be the highest-profile or glitziest ones; they've been closer to home, episodes in which someone relatively ordinary, though perhaps professionally accomplished, is thrust into celebrity or notoriety by following some desire or obsession or grudge where it leads while remaining curiously indifferent to potential social consequences. Through some brew of inadvertency or compulsion or recklessness, the blunder is brought to light (as such things generally are), frequently wrecking the scandalizer's life in the process.

But scandals are also public performances: they're about people enacting their tangled, furtive longings and grudges on a national and sometimes international scale, scattering unconsciousness around in public for everyone else to trip over, violating norms and taboos with imagined impunity as though superegos didn't exist. Often there's a theatrical whiff about these psychodramas: the curtain opens a bizarre private world of chaos and misjudgment, and the rest of us are thrust into the role of audience. It's a role we play to the hilt: commenting on the action like a Greek chorus, dissecting motives like amateur psychoanalysts, maybe nervously pondering our own susceptibility to life-wrecking inchoateness. Every scandal reproduces this complicatedly codependent relationship between a scandal protagonist and a scandal public, precisely because scandal requires an audience: if no one paid attention, scandal would cease to exist. In short, we all have crucial roles to play in scandal formation: scandalizers screw things up in showy, provocative ways while the rest of us luxuriate in the warm glow of imaginary

> The writer develops the proposition that scandal is public performance and self-deception.

imperviousness that other people's life-destroying stupidities invariably provide, castigating transgressors for their moral failings while disavowing any similar propensities of our own.

Of course, disavowing such propensities is how scandalizers come to find themselves in the midst of a scandal in the first place. The uniting feature in most scandal cases is some major blind spot, some form of splitting. How else can a socialized being so completely suspend awareness of social punishment, be so incapable of thinking a couple of steps ahead? This element of self-obliviousness, and what it implies about the willingness of otherwise rational people to volunteer for public pillorying, is not exactly reassuring. But are we in the audience so much more self-knowledgeable? One suspects not. I'm pretty sure that my own capacity for self-knowledge is nothing to gloat about.

But how would I know? As the psychologist Herbert Fingarette points out in his rather alarming 1969 study *Self-Deception*, it's not just that "spelling things out" (38) to oneself is an acquired skill (like driving a car, as he puts it [41]) but that there can be overriding reasons to avoid doing it and to avoid becoming conscious that you're avoiding doing it. Self-examination isn't a very reliable talent, as it turns out; the available techniques are spotty at best. As the novelist-critic J. M. Coetzee frets in his essay "Confession and Double Thoughts," it's impossible to know whether the "truth" you discover in your occasional feeble attempts at self-examination is anything close to truth and not just some self-serving fiction, since the "unexamined, unexaminable principle" governing your conclusions "may not be a desire for the truth but a desire to *be a particular way*" (221)—to seem rational and coherent to yourself, for instance. In other words, all the self-examination in the world isn't going to help you if you're bent on self-deception or if one part of you is bent on deceiving another part, which is no doubt true of any of us at least some of the time. That's what having an unconscious means, and thanks for nothing.

As we know, scandal in the Internet age offers an embarrassment of riches when it comes to proving this point. The Internet and scandal are Siamese twins joined at the forehead, with the most excruciatingly private details about other people's inner lives and desires and failures of self-management archived online forever, to do with what you will. And the details are so weirdly gripping! Roland Barthes, writing about the odd biographical details that particularly pierced him in old photographs (the *punctum*, in his often cited term), refers to them as "part-objects," which "flatter a certain fetishism of mine." They nourish his "amorous preference" for certain kinds of knowledge, providing him—at least some facet of him—with delight (30).

The writer mentions the impact of the Internet on scandal.

As usual, Barthes had the courage of his fetishes, though as fetishes go, let's just say his tended to be fairly dignified ones. For my part, such delights are also tinged with discomfiture. They're rabbit holes, plummeting you into the muckiness of someone else's interiority, where you paddle around frantically trying to get your bearings.

The writer offers a self-referential comment.

Take the details in the leaked police reports on Assange. The allegation is that during a ten-day stay in Stockholm, Assange had sexual encounters with two women, both WikiLeaks supporters, that started as consensual but became coercive to the point of rape. One of the women, identified as Miss A, had arranged Assange's trip to Sweden and let him stay in her apartment. She charges that he pulled off her clothes and snapped her necklace, and though she more or less went along with all this, she protested when she realized Assange was trying to have unprotected sex with her. When she tried to put a condom on him, he stopped her by pinning her arms. He finally agreed to use the condom but then deliberately ripped it, she accuses, and ejaculated without withdrawing. Assange denies all this, countering that

The writer develops case studies relating to the Assange scandal.

he continued to sleep in her flat with her permission for the following week; if he'd assaulted her, why would she allow him to stay? Miss A concurs that he stayed but says that they'd stopped having sex because he'd exceeded the limits of what she could accept. However, he approached her one day at her apartment, naked from the waist down, and rubbed against her. Nevertheless, after this encounter, Miss A still threw a party for Assange at her flat (Davies).

Then Assange met a second woman, Miss W, at a seminar arranged by Miss A. When the two of them began having sex at her flat, Assange also refused to wear a condom; like Miss A, Miss W refused to have sex without one. Assange gave up and fell asleep, but during the night they woke up and had sex after he reluctantly agreed to use a condom. In the morning Miss W woke up to find Assange again having sex with her, and when she asked if he was wearing a condom, he said no. Miss W had never had unprotected sex before, she said, and the leaks from a police interview with her former boyfriend confirm this. According to the ex, it would have been unthinkable for her. Despite these conflicts, both women allegedly continued to see Assange during the remainder of his stay (Burns and Somaiya).

When the two women eventually learned of their similar experiences with Assange and that he'd been seeing both of them at the same time, they went to the police to see if they could compel him to take an HIV test, which he'd already refused to do, saying he didn't have the time. The police said they couldn't force him to take a test and that the women's statements would have to be passed on to a prosecutor for further action to be taken. (In Sweden "unlawful coercion" is prosecutable under rape statutes.) That night the story was leaked to Swedish papers. When journalists asked Assange for his reaction, his response was that the sex had been consensual. When asked if he was promiscuous, he replied, "I'm not promiscuous. I just really like women" (qtd. in Mostrous).

some reason these slightly perturbing details
ρ playing though my mind like an annoying song.
ιhen we have the homology between Assange's
alleged aversion to condoms and his political commitment to leaks. As it happens, leakiness was one of
the themes in my scandal book, *How to Become a
Scandal*, spurred on by Freud: "No mortal can keep
a secret. If his lips are silent, he chatters with his fin-
gertips; betrayal oozes out of him at every pore"
(77–78). Notice how *viscous* Freud makes the whole
thing sound—betrayal doesn't trickle or drip or
bleed; it *oozes*, mucouslike (or worse). The point
seems to be that human beings can't help spilling
clues all over the place about the mess of embarrassing conflicts and metaphysical anguishes lodged
within. The viscosity of the substance in question
should interest anyone who's ever struggled to quash
some delinquent libidinal urge; presumably this
would be everyone.

The leaky-vessel problem struck me as a useful
starting point for a book on scandals, and certain
people's proclivities for getting into them. Why? All I
can tell you is that leakiness kept *seeking me out*. It
even turned out (as I realized only after the book
went to press) that diapers figured in *two* of the scandal cases I wrote about, speaking of leakiness. In one
an astronaut drove cross-country to attack a romantic rival, supposedly wearing adult diapers along the
way to avoid making rest stops (25–67); in another a
renowned judge threatened his ex-lover while imper-
sonating a fat, diabetic, diaper-wearing detective
from Texas (68–109). Scandal cases often do seem to
contain these strangely antic elements, as though an
invisible screenwriter with a penchant for bad puns
were working behind the scenes. What's a diaper, after all, but the perfect symbol for incontinent feelings, for being out of control? Consider the usual
idioms for falling afoul of social codes: getting yourself in "deep shit," winding up with your life "in the
toilet." These scandal protagonists couldn't have

The writer develops the extended metaphor of scandal theory as a narrative of "leakiness."

found a better symbol if they'd tried. (Or had they? The unconscious has a particular sense of humor, not to mention a potty mouth, or so it's been said; Freud wrote a classically unfunny book on the subject.) The diaper motif rather brilliantly distills the scandalizer's situation down to its essence, since what's an adult in diapers but someone whose self-management skills have critically failed?

This isn't very dignified territory, to say the least. Also, you start wondering what unknown elements are leaking through *your* prose onto the page. It struck me numerous times in the course of writing on scandal how many alarming similarities there are between writing and scandal, poised as writers so often are between the murky chasms of unknowingness and whatever thin protections against it form or style provide (so you hope). If the terrain of scandal is especially riddled with compulsion, neurosis, and a thousand other unflattering propensities, so is writing about it. Writing on scandal means writing about unconsciousness, along with every variety of ugly feeling, compulsion, self-destruction, and failed self-knowledge. But the only method really adequate to the subject is letting your mind veer where it wants to and risking some embarrassing leakage yourself. This isn't a tidy procedure. But as Fingarette laments, regarding the waywardness of his own investigations into self-deception, "As in characteristic when paradox lies at the heart of things, there is a particular slipperiness about this object of investigation" (13). Slipperiness, leakiness—clearly we're into some damp terrain.

As celebrity studies emerges as an academic discipline, the question of what to do with all the embarrassing scandal effluvia will have to be addressed. A certain amount of dampness is inevitable for anyone who embarks on such a path. Yielding to the logic—or illogic—of these leaky narratives, favoring a poetics of proximity over critical distance, transports investigators to unexpected and possibly alarming places. Of course, the usual methods of academic

come with their own risks: banality, general-
overfamiliarity—in other word, dryness.

Which brings me back to the Assange case. After
Assange left Sweden, the police issued an international arrest warrant compelling him to return to
Sweden for hearings. Whether the allegations will
hold up or whose version of these events is true
doesn't really matter for the purposes of scandal:
scandal details don't have to be true to be scandalous. The substrata of meanings and associations that
accrue around the narratives give them their social
resonance, not their factuality. Yet by what method
are these substrata to be excavated?

The historian Sean Wilentz has impugned Assange
for being offended by any actions that are cloaked,
which Wilentz regards as simpleminded (qtd. in Italie).
Condoms, cloaks … something in the scandal theorist
perks to attention. Assange is accused of ripping a
condom? Obviously—isn't he committed to penetrat-
ing every security protocol he can? Aha! There's that
punster-symbologist, working behind the scenes again.
The language of scandal is especially plastic, stretching
this way and that and sullying everything in its path,
transforming anything it encounters into material.
Although Barthes doesn't mention it in *Camera
Lucida*, another definition of the word *punctum*,
according to *Wiktionary*, is "the sharp tip of any part
of the anatomy." It can also be a tiny orifice, as
defined in *Oxford Dictionaries*, like the small opening
that allows tears to drain from eyes. Reading this, the
scandal theorist's antenna again perks up: more leakiness. Let Barthes's remark that the punctum isn't necessarily in good taste stand as a warning to others
who might venture down this road.

The writer prepares for her conclusion.

In her conclusion, the writer offers a reflection on scandal theory and the language of scandal.

Works Cited

The writer presents her citations in MLA format.

Barthes, Roland. *Camera Lucida: Reflections on Photogra-
    phy*. Trans. Richard Howard. New York: Hill, 1982. Print.
Burns, John F., and Ravi Somaiya. "Confidential Swedish
    Police Report Details Allegations against WikiLeaks

Founder." *The New York Times*. New York Times, 18 Dec. 2010. Web. 24 Dec. 2010.

Coetzee, J. M. "Confession and Double Thoughts: Tolstoy, Rousseau, Dostoevsky." *Comparative Literature* 37.3 (1985): 193–232. Print.

Davies, Nick. "10 Days in Sweden: The Full Allegations against Julian Assange." *Guardian*. Guardian News and Media, 17 Dec. 2010. Web. 28 Dec. 2010.

Fingarette, Herbert. *Self-Deception*. 1969. Berkeley: U of California P, 2000. Print.

Freud, Sigmund. "Fragment of an Analysis of a Case of Hysteria." 1905. *Standard Edition*. Vol. 7. London: Hogarth, 1961. 64–94. Print.

Harnden, Toby. "Julian Assange's Arrest Warrant: A Diversion from the Truth?" *Telegraph*. Telegraph Media Group, 22 Aug. 2010. Web. 28 Dec. 2010.

Hosenbail, Mark. "Special Report: Julian Assange versus the World." *Reuters*. Reuters, 13 Dec. 2010. Web. 28 Dec. 2010.

Italie, Hillel. "Authors, Historians Debate Leaks of WikiLeaks." *Pantagraph.com*. Pantagraph, 4 Dec. 2010. Web. 9 June 2011.

Kipnis, Laura. *How to Become a Scandal: Adventures in Bad Behavior*. New York: Metropolitan, 2010. Print.

Mostrous, Alexi. "People Power Will Come to My Rescue, WikiLeaks Founder Predicts." *Times*. News Intl. Trading, 21 Dec. 2010. Web. 28 Dec. 2010.

"Punctum." *Oxford Dictionaries Online*. Oxford UP, n.d. Web. 1 July 2011.

"Punctum." *Wiktionary*. Wikimedia, n.d. Web. 1 July 2011.

Wolf, Naomi. "Julian Assange Captured by World's Dating Police." *Huffington Post*. TheHuffingtonPost, 7 Dec. 2010. Web. 28 Dec. 2010.

___. "Sex and Silence at Yale." *New York Magazine*. New York Media, 1 Mar. 2004. Web. 28 Dec. 2010.

Glossary of Rhetorical Terms

allusion A reference to a familiar concept, person, or thing.

analytical essay An essay that defines and describes an issue by breaking it down into separate components and carefully considering each component.

annotation Marking up a text as you read by writing comments, questions, and ideas in the margins.

argument A *rhetorical strategy* that involves using *persuasion* to gain a reader's support for the writer's position.

assertion A statement that a writer claims is true without necessarily providing objective support for the *claim*.

audience The assumed readers of a text.

brainstorming An idea-generation strategy. Write your topic, a keyword, or *thesis* at the top of a blank piece of paper or computer screen, and for ten or fifteen minutes just write down everything you associate with, think of, or know about that topic.

cause and effect/causal analysis A *rhetorical strategy* that examines the relationships between events or conditions and their consequences.

claim In *argument*, a statement that the author intends to support through the use of *reasons*, *evidence*, and appeals.

classification A *rhetorical strategy* that divides a subject into categories and then analyzes the characteristics of each category. See also *division*.

cognitive styles Different and individual approaches to thinking and understanding, especially in regard to how we process language and text.

coherence A characteristic of effective writing, achieved through careful organization of ideas and the skillful use of *transitions*.

colloquial language Informal language not usually found in an academic essay but appropriate in some cases for purposes of *illustration*.

comparison and contrast Two strategies that are often used to complement one another in the same essay. Comparison examines the similarities between two or more like subjects; contrast examines the differences between those subjects.

process The work of writing, moving from notes and ideas through
    multiple *drafts* to a "final" essay. All writers develop their own composing
    process as they become more comfortable with writing.
conflict A struggle between two opposing forces that creates suspense, tension,
    and interest in a *narrative*.
conventions The expectations general readers have of specific kinds of writing.

deduction An *argument* that begins with a clearly stated *claim*, and then uses
    selected evidence to support that claim. See also *induction*.
definition/extended definition A writing strategy that describes the nature of an
    abstract or concrete subject. Extended definition is a kind of essay based on
    that definition, expanding its scope by considering larger issues related to the
    subject (for example, the different ways in which different groups of people
    might define a term like *freedom*).
description A kind of writing based on sensory observations (sight, hearing,
    smell, touch) that allows readers to imaginatively re-create an experience.
diction The "style" of language, either written or spoken, from which inferences
    about the speaker's education, background, and origins can be made. Your
    choice of diction in a piece of writing depends on your intended *audience* and
    your *purpose*.
discourse Dialogue or conversation. In the study of rhetoric, *discourse* refers to
    the ways a specific group of people, organization, or institution speaks to and
    about itself.
division A *rhetorical strategy* that breaks a subject down into smaller parts and
    analyzes their relationship to the overall subject.
drafting Moving from notes and an outline to the general shape and form of a
    "final" essay. Writers often go through multiple "drafts" of an essay, moving
    ideas around, tinkering with the language, and double-checking facts.

editorialize An "editorial" in a newspaper offers the collective opinion of the
    newspaper's management on a *topical* issue. Writers "editorialize" when
    they offer opinions on a subject of topical interest. Unlike the approach of
    an *argument*, editorializing writers do not always consider the viewpoints
    of their opponents.
evidence In an *argument*, the facts and expert opinions used to support a *claim*.
exemplification See *illustration*.
expository essay An essay that seeks to explain something by combining different
    rhetorical strategies, such as *classification* and *description*.
extended definition See *definition*.

figurative language Imaginative language that compares one thing to another in
    ways that are not necessarily logical but that are nevertheless striking, origi-
    nal, and "true." Examples of figurative language are *metaphor, simile*, and
    allusion.

illustration Also called *exemplification*. The use of examples to support an essay's main idea. A successful illustrative essay uses several compelling examples to support its *thesis*.

imagery Descriptive writing that draws on vivid sensory descriptions and *figurative language* to re-create an experience for a reader.

induction In *argument*, a strategy that uses compelling evidence to lead an *audience* to an inevitable conclusion. See also *deduction*.

invective Angry or hostile language directed at a specific person (or persons).

irony A *rhetorical strategy* that uses language to suggest the opposite of what is actually being stated. Irony is used frequently in works of *satire* and works of humor.

major proposition See *claim*.

metaphor The comparison of two unlike things to one another for *figurative* effect.

minor proposition In *argument*, the position a writer goes on to defend through *reasons* and *evidence*. See also *claim*.

motif A simple theme (often a phrase or an image) that is repeated throughout a *narrative* to give it a deeper sense of *unity* and to underscore its basic idea.

narration/narrative A type of writing that tells a story. In an essay, narration is often used to describe what happened to a person or place over a certain period of time.

op-ed style Named for the "opinion and editorial" pages of newspapers, "op-ed style" describes brief *arguments* written for a general *audience* that are supported by *evidence* commonly accepted as "true" or "expert."

paraphrase Stating another author's opinions, ideas, or observations in your own words. When you paraphrase, you still give full credit (through in-text citation) to the original author.

persona The voice of the author of an essay or story, even if that voice never uses the first person or gives any further details about its "self." Your persona, in an academic essay, might be that of a concerned citizen, a sociological researcher, or a literary critic.

personal essay An essay written in the first person (the "I" point of view) that uses personal experience to illustrate a larger point.

persuasion A *rhetorical strategy*, often used in *argument*, that seeks to move readers to take a course of action or to change their minds about an issue.

point of view The perspective and attitude of a writer or narrator toward the subject.

précis A *summary* of the relevant facts, statements, and *evidence* offered by an essay, especially an *argument*.

ₒ Any idea-generation strategy that gets you "warmed up" for drafting essay.

ᴄess analysis A kind of essay that describes, in chronological order, each step or stage of the performing of an action (a "how-to" essay).

prologue A brief statement or introduction to a longer work (originally, the introduction to a play spoken by one of the actors).

proposition A *thesis* statement, or *claim*, that suggests a specific action to take and seeks the support of readers to take that action. A proposition is supported by *evidence* demonstrating why this course of action is the best to take. See also *major proposition* and *minor proposition*.

purpose The reason a writer takes on a subject as well as the goal the writer hopes to achieve.

reader response theory Loosely defined, the idea that every reader brings an individual approach and background of knowledge to a text and responds to a text in a unique way.

reasons In *argument*, *evidence* you offer that your reader will accept as legitimate support for your *claim*. See also *minor proposition*.

rebuttal In *argument*, a considered response to an opposing point of view.

reflective essay An essay in which you examine and evaluate your own actions or beliefs, learning more about yourself in the process.

refutation In *argument*, proof that someone (usually the opposition) is incorrect.

revision The stage in the writing process in which you revisit your draft, reading and rewriting for clarity and *purpose*, adding or subtracting relevant *evidence*, and perhaps sharing your essay with additional readers for comment.

rhetoric The deliberate and formal use of language, usually in writing, to illustrate an idea or demonstrate a truth. The writer of rhetoric always has in mind an *audience* and a *purpose*.

rhetorical strategies Key patterns that writers employ to organize and clarify their ideas and opinions in an essay.

satire Writing that uses humor, often mocking, to call attention to stupidity or injustice and inspire social change. Satirists call attention to the foibles of groups, institutions, and bureaucracies rather than of individual people.

sensory detail Details based on the five senses (touch, sight, smell, taste, sound) that enhance descriptive writing.

simile A style of *figurative language* that compares two unlike things using *like* or *as*. See also *metaphor*.

stipulative definition Creating, based on your own experience and opinions, a definition of a term (generally an abstract term, such as *globalization*) for the purposes of your own *argument*.

style A writer's own unique sense for, and use of, language, *imagery*, and *rhetoric*. Some writers are immediately recognizable by their style; other times, a writer needs to consider *audience* and *purpose* when developing an appropriate style for a particular rhetorical task.

summary As a critical reading strategy, the brief restating (in your own words) of an essay's *thesis*, main points, and *evidence*. Summarizing can help you better understand the logic of a writer's argument and the way an essay is organized. See also *p̃récis*.

symbol Something that stands for, or represents, something else. All numbers and letters are symbols, in that they stand for concepts and sounds.

thesis In an essay, a brief statement that concisely states the writer's subject and opinion on that subject.

tone The writer's "voice" in an essay that, through the use of *diction* and *figurative language*, as well as other *rhetorical strategies*, conveys the writer's feelings about the subject.

topical Relating to an issue or subject drawn from current events or that is of immediate interest to the *audience*.

topic sentence The sentence encapsulating the focus, or main idea, of each paragraph of an essay.

transition The language used to connect one idea to the next in an essay. Skillful use of transitions helps to give an essay *coherence*, allowing the reader to smoothly follow the writer's train of thoughts as well as to clearly see the connections between those thoughts and supporting *evidence*.

unity A quality of good writing that goes beyond *coherence* to an overall sense of completion. A writer achieves unity when the reader feels that not a word needs to be added to (or taken away from) the essay.

usage In rhetorical studies, the ways in which language is commonly used in speaking and writing.

visual texts Anything that conveys an idea without necessarily using language (photographs, advertisements, cartoons, graffiti, etc.).

voice See *tone*.

warrant In *argument*, a plausible *assertion* that a reader must agree with in order to accept the *claim*.

Glossary of Globalization Terms

acculturation The adoption by one *culture* of features from another, often as a result of conquest or colonialization—for example, the use of French as a primary language in many former French colonies in Africa.

anarchy The absence of any authority; total individual freedom.

assimilation The adoption of a society's *culture* and customs by immigrants to that society. At both an individual and a group level, the process is gradual and often reciprocal.

balkanization (From the breakup of the countries of the Balkan Peninsula, in Europe, into hostile and frequently warring nations after World War I.) To break apart into smaller, hostile nations or entities, as in the division of the former Yugoslavia and the breakup of the former Soviet Union.

bilingualism/multilingualism Functional literacy in two or more languages; policies that promote the acquisition of more than one language.

biotechnology The application of science, especially genetic engineering, to living organisms in order to effect beneficial changes.

borderless economy Through alliances such as *NAFTA* and the European Union, the movement toward the *free trade* of goods and services across national borders.

capital The resources (money, land, raw material, labor, etc.) used to produce goods and services for the open market.

capitalism Economic system based on the ownership and exchange of goods and services by private individuals, and through which individual accumulation of resources is relatively unchecked by governmental regulations.

caste An ancient Indian system of social hierarchy, now much in decline, that held that social status was inherited and could not be changed. The term is more broadly used to indicate a class of people who cannot move up the social hierarchy.

centrist Politically inclined toward moderation and compromise.

civil liberties Guarantees of certain rights, such as freedom of speech and right of assembly. In the United States, these rights are upheld by the

Constitution (although they are also frequently challenged in society as well as in the courts).

Cold War From 1945 to 1991, a period of tensions and hostilities between the Soviet Union and its Warsaw Pact allies and the United States and its *NATO* allies. The era was marked by massive arms proliferation and mutual paranoia and distrust.

collectivity The sharing of resources and responsibilities among a community or social group, rather than dividing and accumulating individually.

colonialism/postcolonial From the sixteenth through the mid-twentieth century, the conquest and ruling of peoples in Asia, Africa, and South America by European nations.

commercialization The transformation of a concept or idea into something that can be marketed, bought, and sold.

communism Political *ideology* based on the public ownership of resources and centralized planning of the economy. Based on the philosophy of Karl Marx (1818–1883), who sought alternatives to what he saw as the exploitation of the working classes by the rise of *industrialization.*

conservative In the United States, referring to a political *ideology* that supports individual liberties and minimal governmental involvement in the economy. Also, a social inclination toward traditional morals and values and a resistance to change.

consumerism Until recently, policies and practices meant to protect consumers from bad business practices. Has come to mean a lifestyle focused on the accumulation of material goods at the expense of other values.

Creole Refers to both languages and peoples, with different specific implications depending on the geographical region discussed. Generally, refers to a people or language that is the result of a mingling of *cultures, races*, and *ethnicities*, often due to colonization.

culture The shared customs, traditions, and beliefs of a group of people. These shared values are learned by members of the group from each other, and members of a specific culture share, create, contribute to, and preserve their culture for future generations.

democracy A political system through which *enfranchised* citizens (people who are acknowledged by the state as citizens and have been granted the right to vote) determine governmental courses of action through elections.

developing world Nations, especially those formerly colonized or under *imperialist* domination, now moving toward *industrialization* and economic and political stability.

diaspora Originally applied to Jewish people living outside of Israel; now applied to groups of people "dispersed" or widely scattered from their original homelands.

disarmament Originally a *Cold War* term used to describe ongoing negotiations between the *superpowers* to limit and eventually dismantle weapons systems; now describes the diplomatic work of convincing nations to stop or reverse the production of weapons (especially nuclear).

disenfranchised See *enfranchisement.*

ecosystem The fragile web of relationships between living beings and their environment.

emigration Leaving one country for another. See also *immigration*.

enfranchisement The granting of the right to vote to an individual or a group. To be "disenfranchised" is to have no vote, and by extension no voice in determining your own or your community's governance.

ethnic/ethnicity Referring to a shared sense of common religion, *race*, national, and/or *cultural* identity.

ethnic cleansing An organized effort to force or coerce an *ethnic* group from a region. In recent history, efforts at ethnic cleansing in places like Rwanda and Serbia have led to *genocide*.

ethnocentrism The belief that one's own *culture* or *ethnic* identification is superior to that of others.

ethnology The anthropological study of *cultures*.

Eurocentric/Eurocentrism A worldview that believes European or Western values to be superior.

expatriate Someone who lives in a country where he or she is not a citizen.

fascism An extremely repressive political *ideology* that exercises complete control over individual and *civil liberties* through the use of force.

feminism The theory that women should have the same political, economic, and social rights as men.

free-market economy An economic system in which individuals, acting in their own self-interest, make decisions about their finances, employment, and consumption of goods and services. In a free-market economy, the government provides and regulates common services such as defense, education, and transportation.

free trade Unrestricted trade of goods and services between countries, free from tariffs (which artificially inflate the prices of imported goods) and quotas (which limit the importation of certain goods in order to protect a country's own industries).

fundamentalism Reactionary movement to establish traditional religious values and texts as the primary and/or governing *ideology* in a society.

genocide The organized destruction of a group of people because of their *race*, religion, or *ethnicity*.

global village Term coined in the 1960s by media critic Marshall McLuhan to describe the ability of new communications technologies to bring peoples together.

global warming A gradual increase in global temperature and resulting changes in global climate, caused by the accumulation of "greenhouse gases" from the burning of fossil fuels and the deterioration of the ozone layer (which shields the earth from ultraviolet rays).

globalization The consolidation of societies around the world due to international trade, economic interdependence, the reach of *information technologies*, and the possible resulting loss of local traditions, languages, values, and resources.

GMO (genetically modified organism) A living entity (plant, animal, or microbe) that has been altered in some way through the intervention of genetic engineering.

hegemony The domination of one state, entity, or social group over another.

homogenous Referring to a society or *culture* of very limited diversity whose citizens share very similar racial and/or *ethnic* backgrounds.

human rights The Universal Declaration of Human Rights ratified by the United Nations in 1948 seeks to guarantee that all human beings have a fundamental dignity and basic rights of self-determination.

ideology A belief system that determines and guides the structure of a government and its relation to its citizens.

immigration The movement of people from their homeland to a new nation. See also *emigration*.

imperialism/empire The economic and cultural influence, and occasionally domination, of nations or peoples by stronger nations. The motives of "imperialist" nations are usually economic (the seeking of raw resources, the opening of new markets for trade) and/or *ideological* (e.g., in the nineteenth century, the British imperialist idea that England had a "duty" to bring "civilization" to other parts of the globe).

indigenous Referring to peoples understood to be "natives" or original inhabitants of lands now threatened by *urbanization* or other factors. Opponents of *globalization* argue that the *cultures* of indigenous peoples are under particular threat from the forces of *globalization*.

industrialization The transformation of an economy from agricultural to industrial, often followed by *urbanization*.

information age Term coined by media scholar Marshall McLuhan in 1964 to discuss the rapidly expanding reach (at the time, through television, radio, and print) of technologies that spread information.

information technology Any electronic technology that enhances the production and dissemination of textual, visual, and auditory content, such as computers and cellular telephones.

liberal Implying a political and social tolerance of different views and lifestyles. In the United States, applies to a political preference for increased governmental involvement, especially in matters of social welfare.

Luddite From an early nineteenth century anti-*industrialization* movement in England; now describes a person who is opposed to technological progress because of its possible dehumanizing effects.

marginalization The effects of social and governmental policies that leave some members of a society *disenfranchised*, unable to seek or participate in common resources (such as education and health care), and/or unable to freely express themselves and their views.

Marxism A philosophy based on the work of political economist Karl Marx (1818–1883) and from which *socialism* and *communism* are derived. Marxist political thought focuses on the relationships between economic resources, power, and *ideology*, with the goal of redistributing resources equitably.

mestizo A Hispanic American of mixed European and *indigenous* ancestry.

monocultural Referring to a *culture* that is *homogenous* and resists diversification.

multiculturalism The belief that all *cultures* have intrinsic worth and that the diversity of *cultures* within a society is to be encouraged and celebrated.

multilateralism Cooperation between two or more nations on international issues.

NAFTA (North American Free Trade Agreement) An agreement between the United States, Canada, and Mexico that reduces governmental intervention in trade and investment between these countries.

nationalism Personal and communal feelings of loyalty to a nation; patriotism.

NATO (North Atlantic Treaty Organization) Defense alliance originally created in 1949 to counter the potential threat of the Soviet Union and its Warsaw Pact allies; now includes some of those former enemies in its membership.

naturalization The granting of citizenship, with its rights and privileges, to an immigrant.

NGO (nongovernmental organization) Organizations such as the International Red Cross, Doctors Without Borders, and the International Olympic Committee that provide aid or promote international cooperation without the specific involvement or oversight of governments.

patriarchy A society or worldview that subordinates women.

pluralism Encouragement by a society of competing and divergent political viewpoints.

political asylum Protection guaranteed by a government to refugees fleeing persecution in their own country because of their political beliefs or activism.

polygamy In some *cultures*, the practice of marrying more than one wife.

polyglot A person who speaks several languages, or referring to a community or *culture* in which several languages are spoken.

pop culture Values, traditions, and shared customs and references generated by the mass media, as opposed to values based on religion or *ideology*.

privatization The sale and transfer of formerly government-owned assets (such as utilities) to private corporations.

progressive Referring to a political inclination toward active reform, especially in *social justice*.

protectionism A government's efforts to protect its own agricultural and manufacturing industries from international competition. See also *free trade*.

race A group of people who have ancestry, physical characteristics, and *cultural* traditions in common. There is no genetic or "scientific" basis for the defining or classifying of an individual's "race."

rogue state A controversial term coined by the United States to describe states that act irrationally and that pose particular dangers to the United States and its allies. During the Clinton administration, the term was briefly replaced with "state of concern." Some opponents of *globalization* describe the United States itself as a "rogue state" for taking military, economic, and environmental actions without the participation or consideration of other states.

social justice A popular movement to redistribute wealth, resources, and political power more equitably among the members of a society.

socialism A political *ideology* based on considerable governmental involvement in the economy and other social institutions.

sovereignty The power of a state to govern itself and to defend its own interests.

Stalinism Referring to the methods of Joseph Stalin, general secretary of the Communist Party of the USSR and ruler of the Soviet Union from 1922 to 1953. A brutal dictator, his economic policies of forcing rapid *industrialization* and collectivization of agriculture resulted in massive suffering.

superpower During the *Cold War*, term used to describe both the United States and the Soviet Union.

terrorism The use of random violence, especially against civilian targets, by ideologically motivated groups or individuals in an attempt to create social upheaval and to achieve recognition of their agenda.

Third World Term generally applied to nations moving toward *industrialization* and economic stabilization; the term *developing world* is now more commonly used.

totalitarianism An extremely repressive political system that attempts to completely control every aspect of a society through the use of force.

transnational A corporation or entity that conducts business and policy across national borders and has interests in several different nations.

urbanization The massive shift of a nation's peoples from rural, agrarian communities to large urban areas, usually as a result of *industrialization*.

utopia An idealized, speculative nation or system of government.

welfare state A nation that assumes primary governmental responsibility for the health, education, and social security of its citizens, often in exchange for heavy individual tax burdens.

Index